Hands Across Borders

A Multicultural Reader for Writers

Elizabeth Rodriguez Kessler
California State University, Northridge

Roberta Orona-Cordova, Consultant
Santa Monica College

Stephanie Packer, Consultant
Miami-Dade Community College

Anne Perrin, Consultant
University of Houston

Longman

New York   San Francisco   Boston
London   Toronto   Sydney   Tokyo   Singapore   Madrid
Mexico City   Munich   Paris   Cape Town   Hong Kong   Montreal

Vice President/Editor-in-Chief: Joe Terry
Senior Acquisitions Editor: Steven Rigolosi
Development Editor: Barbara Santaro
Senior Marketing Manager: Melanie Craig
Production Manager: Charles Annis
Project Coordination, Text Design, and Electronic Page Makeup: Shepherd, Inc.
Cover Design Manager: Wendy Fredericks
Cover Designer: Joe dePinho
Cover Photo: © Ghislain & Marie deLossy/Getty Images Image Bank
Print Buyer: Roy Pickering
Printer and Binder: Hamilton Printing Co.
Cover Printer: Coral Graphic Services

For permission to use copyrighted material, grateful acknowledgment is made to the copyright holders on pp. 367–369, which are hereby made part of this copyright page.

Library of Congress Cataloging-in-Publication Data

Rodriguez Kessler, Elizabeth.
    Hands across borders : a multicultural reader for writers / Elizabeth
    Rodriguez Kessler.
        p. cm.
    Includes bibliographical references and index.
    ISBN 0-321-09573-1—ISBN 0-321-09574-X
        1. Readers—Social sciences. 2. Pluralism (Social sciences)—Problems,
    exercises, etc. 3. English language—Rhetoric—Problems, exercises, etc.
    4. Report writing—Problems, exercises, etc. 5. Culture—Problems,
    exercises, etc. 6. College readers. I. Title.

PE1127.S6 R63 2002
808'.0427—dc21   2002016065

Please visit our website at http://www.ablongman.com

ISBN 0-321-09573-1

2 3 4 5 6 7 8 9 10—HT—05 04 03

To Anne and Maria

Contents

PART TWO: Multicultural Readings

PART THREE: Expanding Your Reading and Writing Skills

Preface

As an individual who enjoys writing and one who also knows that students frequently do not, I began this text with a desire to help students recognize that writing does not have to be painful and that their experiences and backgrounds are important not only in constructing their identities but also in supplying them with numerous ideas from which to develop their writing assignments. Thus, by relying on the conditions, values, beliefs, and so forth that differentiate us from one another, I braved the controversy that rages among academics today: the debate over whether we should teach multiculturalism. Many academics shy away from it for many reasons; however, one reason frequently given is that it tends to segregate the cultures. *Hands Across Borders: A Multicultural Reader for Writers* refuses to do that. Set up with a thematic organization, *Hands Across Borders* attempts to unite rather than divide. By selecting topics that students are concerned with regardless of ethnicity, I have attempted to create microcosmic communities within each chapter, populated by a variety of voices that offer insights into aspects that are important in our lives. Because not only our campuses but our cities and neighborhoods are reflecting a diverse cultural population, students need to be more informed about what members of those ethnically different cultures think, believe, and feel, as well as how they act. Thus, the following article by Susan Straight in the *Los Angeles Times* appeared at an appropriate time, and I include it in the Preface rather than in a chapter, as it sets the tone of this text.

Ground Zero of the New California

Susan Straight

1   My three daughters became obsessed with my high school yearbook last month. They spent hours studying the pictures and laughing at the hairstyles of their father and me and our friends. Their father had a big Afro, as did most of the African-American kids, and I had Farrah Fawcett-style wings, though mine weren't as impressive as those of the other blond girls. They made fun of the

long hair of one guy who still lives nearby. His mother is Salvadoran and his father Polish, and the kids took that picture out to show another neighbor who is working on our house; his father is from Hermosillo, Mexico, and his Anglo mother is from Tucson, Arizona.

2   The high school is one my daughters will likely attend, and, like our neighborhood, it is just as ethnically mixed today as it was back then. Our children are part of the 4 percent of Californians who checked more than one box in last year's census, whose just-released figures show that more and more Californians are multiracial, young, and living in the inland areas of the state.

3   But out here in Riverside, we've been reflecting these statistics for decades. I find it funny, and affirming, that everyone else is finally catching up.

4   The yearbook was unearthed during my mother's recent move into a brand-new house in a master-planned community on the edge of Riverside, between the established city and the burgeoning community of Moreno Valley, which is where many black and Latino families have settled after moving from too-pricey or crime-ridden areas of Los Angeles. My mother's house has fresh carpet, that smell of new drywall. When we step outside, yearbook in hand, we see acres of raw, decomposed granite being molded into banks and flattened for driveways, another reality of the new California reflected in the census.

5   The girls and I agree that we wouldn't trade our home in an old neighborhood in Riverside for all this newness. We live three blocks from the hospital where two of my girls were born. I was born there, too, in 1960, and their father in 1959. Even back then, we were a multiracial community, largely because of nearby March Air Force Base, whose planes still cruise over the new tracts that have added thousands of residents to Riverside.

6   In the living room of my 1910 Craftsman house, originally surrounded by orange groves, but now by other small bungalows, my girls and I page through the yearbook. They see the senior portrait of Virgie Saucedo, now Burroughs, who lives on the next block. She is Chicano, married to an Anglo man, and their three kids played on a trampoline we admired for several seasons. They see a goofy freshman photo of my brother's best friend Mark, who just painted our house. His mother is Filipino and father Anglo. They see my childhood neighbor Ed, whose mom is Japanese and dad Filipino.

7   When we get to the basketball team photo, all those young men standing in a semicircle on the court, it's a perfect photo opportunity for multiracial California: Richard, German mother and African-American father; George, Japanese mother, African-American father; John, Mexican-born mother, white father, and a host of others—Irish-American, Mississippi-born black, Jewish and Alaskan Indian, and every mix you could imagine.

8   At forward stands their father, whose ancestors are Creek and Cherokee, Irish and African. In the game shots, I am at the scorekeeper's table, just behind him. My father is American of French descent, my stepfather was born in Canada, and my mother is from Switzerland. She used to sit in the

bleachers during these basketball games and knit, while my husband's father, Oklahoma-born, sat near her and yelled, "Fall, ball!" We were already connected as a couple, as a family, in 1978, and when I moved to Los Angeles to attend USC, I was astonished that so many people questioned our relationship.

9   "In our neighborhood, everybody's mixed already," I found myself saying over and over, discovering that the rest of California wasn't like Riverside. It seemed so puzzling why they hadn't figured out how to live together.

10   Throughout the last century, people of all races and ethnicities came to Riverside, to the Inland Empire, for the climate and abundance—of land, of jobs. And when they came, they married each other.

11   At the turn of the century, the citrus industry employed Japanese, Chinese, Italian, black, and Mexican workers, many of whom settled here and intermarried and had children whose children I grew up with. At Sav-On the other day, I stood in line behind two elderly Mexican-born women whom I recognized from my childhood. While we waited endlessly for prescriptions, I listened to them talk about working for the Blue Banner packing house, where they sorted oranges for decades.

12   Our basketball team looked like that because so many men who'd been stationed at March Air Force Base decided never to return to Louisiana or Mississippi or Florida, where life was so harsh for African-Americans in the 1960s. They stayed in Riverside, and their children married the children of European and Mexican immigrants.

13   We all have our own kids now, and many of us live in old neighborhoods like mine. I see friends from high school every day, like Jaimie and her husband Bobby, white and black, whose kids are shades of gold and brown. My neighbor Arleen, whose parents are Chicano, born in California of Mexican descent, married Darryl, who was black and Indian. Her three daughters are slightly older than mine, slightly darker-skinned than mine, and already talking to boys when we see them walking home from school.

14   My girls are all in elementary school, and they play frequently on a street two blocks over with their best friends. Three of those friends have Mexican-American fathers and white mothers. The other friend is the father whose photo is in the yearbook; his daughter reflects his wife's blond fairness and his own Salvadoran mother's expressive dark eyes.

15   I cannot catalogue the racial mixtures of all their friends, but I can tell of their supreme indifference to the entire discussion. They play baseball and Barbies, and they eat foods from every continent. They are oblivious to categories and hues.

16   The smell of lumpia and barbecue and hamburgers drifts over our faded asphalt street, and on the sidewalks all the kids ride bikes and scooters, shouting at each other, oblivious to what they look like or what city they live in, I'm sure. They just know the carob trees and pepper trees, planted by the city fathers who moved here from New England and the Midwest at the turn of the last century, are dropping brown pods and red fragrant berries whose scent rises under their wheels.

* * *

Although the article fails to take into consideration a rising new culture—children of gay parents who live with their mother and her female partner or their father and his male partner, as well as the increasing number of self-disclosed gays and lesbians in the communities—*Hands Across Borders* recognizes it in an effort to insure that their voices, just as the voices of other identified cultures, are heard. This issue, in fact, was featured on Friday, August 3, 2001, when Barbara Walters interviewed children of gay and lesbian parents on *20/20.* "Ground Zero of the New California," on the other hand, does reference the number of multiracial families in one community and how the residents of the community are so accustomed to this phenomenon that they do not see the problems others see. This article, in conjunction with the other selections, exposes students not only to the diversity among us but to contemporary issues they must face.

AN OVERVIEW

Hands Across Borders is divided into three major sections: Part One—Reading and Writing Skills, Part Two—Multicultural Readings, and Part Three—Expanding Your Reading and Writing Skills. Before students begin writing formal essays, they have an opportunity to begin improving their skills through building their reading, learning, and vocabulary skills, as well as by writing informal assignments and formal letters. In **Part One—Reading and Writing Skills,** students learn the basics by reading about and writing paragraphs in the different modes. They then learn the structure of the informative and argumentative essays, and they have an opportunity to construct essays incorporating the different modes.

In **Part Two—Multicultural Readings,** students have an opportunity to read selections organized thematically and written primarily as personal narratives but also as informative, argumentative, and persuasive essays, poetry, and short stories. Beginning with creation myths and legends, and moving through various stages and concerns most people encounter as they grow up, the section ends with Confrontations, a chapter that presents six arguments that discuss three topics from opposing positions and one essay without an opposing side. Some instructors prefer not to discuss the topic of religion in the classroom; therefore, because each of these chapters is a relatively independent thematic unit, instructors should not feel that they must teach every selection in every chapter, every chapter, or even teach them in the order they are presented. Although the students will not be able to read all fifty-seven selections, the students and instructors have a variety of choices based on rhetorical strategy, length, and difficulty.

In **Part Three—Expanding Your Reading and Writing Skills,** students have an opportunity to develop the skills they have learned and apply them to analysis of creative prose literature, poetry and argumentative/persuasive writings. Part Three also provides a short section on how to complete research, a section on MLA documentation with a sample paper, and finally, a glossary of terms.

PEDAGOGY

Hands Across Borders is founded on several premises. The first is that writing is a skill; therefore, the instructional material begins with the construction of the basic elements of composition, provides models, gives students opportunities to practice each element, and progresses to increasingly more complex assignments. The current philosophy concerning composition is to move away from teaching students to write in particular modes/patterns (descriptive, comparison-and-contrast, and so forth) because "real" writing incorporates the different modes rather than requires a single approach. I totally agree; however, this text is constructed on the premise that students must be familiar with modes such as description, comparison, contrast, and so forth or they will not know how to write them or that they may incorporate these techniques into their writing. Furthermore, the student might not even know that some of these modes exist. By first bringing the modes and their particular qualities into the student's conscious awareness, the instructor will help the student writer begin to practice using a variety of patterns in a paper. With a little direction, the student writers will also become cognizant of how the modes work in published writings. In fact, if you turn to my directions on how to write a descriptive paragraph, you will see that I explain that the use of comparison and/or contrast and exemplification can be used instead of "rely[ing] solely on listing adjective after adjective" (39). The text encourages students to experiment as they write—for example, in the Introduction to Chapter 10, Confrontations—but always to follow their instructor's directions.

I also borrow my approach from an individual who some might not consider a teacher, but who, in fact, knew how to motivate his "students" and help them improve, and who watched them become great in their field: Coach Vince Lombardi. Lombardi's method takes professional athletes, men at the top of their profession, and makes them begin training with the basics. He required drill and practice of the essential elements and moved them along until they could analyze the plays, apply their knowledge to the game, and ultimately evaluate their own performance. In essence, Lombardi adopted Bloom's Taxonomy of Learning, beginning at the knowledge level and building on it, then moving to the higher-level thinking skills. The approach *Hands Across Borders* takes is similar: students learn the basics, practice them, analyze how others use them in their works, incorporate them into their own writings, and determine their success through peer evaluations. Through revision, students continue to practice until they have mastered a particular weakness. As I point out to the students, learning a skill is behavior modification, and to indicate that they have learned, they must improve the way they write.

A second premise this text assumes is that in learning to write, students should learn a formalized structure and write the thesis-driven essay. This is another traditional concept that some instructors reject, believing that we are placing "artificial" impositions upon a student's writing. This text leans definitely toward a traditional construction in formal writing that is usually required in exit writing proficiency exams, administered in some institutions before a student can move from a developmental course into an academic one and before a student can graduate. To offset the feeling of being stifled by structure, students are given various opportunities for prewriting activities that encourage them to generate ideas and reader response entries, which are generally written informally unless the instructor specifies otherwise. There are various questions and writing assignments following each selection, each chapter, and many sections in Part One that require formal and informal writing.

A final premise that this text assumes is that good writers are good readers; therefore, the strategies for reading move from relatively straightforward selections to those that are increasingly challenging. Furthermore, each selection in Part Two is followed by questions that first reflect reading comprehension and move to progressively more difficult and lengthier assignments. After each selection, readers will discover three sets of exercises. The first uses knowledge-based questions about the passage. The second requires short paragraphs, short essays, or journal writings. The third involves higher-level thinking skills, extended writing, group/collaborative assignments, and assignments that are generated from the passage but are frequently in modes different from the passage they read. At the end of each chapter, the students are offered further writing suggestions for specific rhetorical strategies and writing projects. Rhetorically speaking, the vast majority of the selections are personal narratives. However, just as students incorporate various modes of writing into any assignment, so, too, do the authors whose works the students will read.

The appendices address the concerns of expanding the students' reading and writing skills by including instructional material on how to write about nonfiction, how to complete research, and how to handle MLA formatting. The Glossary of Literary and Composition Terms provides definitions that are similar to explanations within the instructional material but can be more easily located. Instead of providing a glossary for the unfamiliar words in the selections, I have required that students look up certain words that are key to helping them understand the reading preceding the selection, but I have also provided definitions in the margin for other terms.

The instructional material is user-friendly; however, there could be a concern about pronoun usage. Several points need to be made here. When I am writing generally about student problems or giving general explanation, I use third person. However, when I am giving directions or instructions, I address the students directly in second person. As for sexist language, I try to escape the cumbersome "he or she" and the vague "they/them" by alternating between the masculine and feminine pronouns.

Another attempt to make the reading student-friendly is the incorporation of boxes that summarize lengthy material in a point-by-point system. This system works in conjunction with the opening section on learning styles. Although students use a variety of cognitive strategies and styles, I have described one of the more popular and easier ways to determine how students learn so that users of this book might acquire some insight into their strengths and weaknesses. Although there are not many, I have included maps, pictures, and a cartoon at the beginnings of the chapters to introduce the student visually to at least one of the issues to be discussed. I also include frequent short writing exercises, giving students an opportunity to practice a particular element in an isolated context before having to write a longer piece.

THE TEACHING AND LEARNING PACKAGE

A complete **instructor's manual** is available to accompany *Hands Across Borders*. Prepared by the author, the instructor's manual includes a comprehension quiz for each reading in the text, as well as teaching tips and suggestions. To order a copy, please contact your Longman sales representative. 0-321-09575-8

In addition, a series of other skills-based supplements is available for both instructors and students. All of these supplements are available either free or at greatly reduced prices.

For Additional Reading and Reference

The Dictionary Deal

Two dictionaries can be shrinkwrapped with *Hands Across Borders* at a nominal fee. *The New American Webster Handy College Dictionary* is a paperback reference text with more than 100,000 entries. *Merriam Webster's Collegiate Dictionary*, 10th edition, is a hardback reference with a citation file of more than 14.5 million examples of English words drawn from actual use. For more information on how to shrinkwrap a dictionary with your text, please contact your Longman sales representative.

Penguin Quality Paperback Titles

A series of Penguin paperbacks is available at a significant discount when shrinkwrapped with this text. Some titles available are Toni Morrison's *Beloved*, Julia Alvarez's *How the Garcia Girls Lost Their Accents*, Mark Twain's *Huckleberry Finn, Narrative of the Life of Frederick Douglass*, Harriet Beecher Stowe's *Uncle Tom's Cabin*, Dr. Martin Luther King, Jr.' s *Why We Can't Wait*, and plays by Shakespeare, Miller, and Albee. For a complete list of titles or more information, please contact your Longman sales consultant.

100 Things to Write About

This 100-page book contains 100 individual assignments for writing on a variety of topics and in a wide range of formats, from expressive to analytical. Ask your Longman sales representative for a sample copy. 0-673-98239-4

Newsweek Alliance

Instructors may choose to shrinkwrap a 12-week subscription to *Newsweek* with any Longman text. The price of the subscription is 57 cents per issue (a total of $6.84 for the subscription). Available with the subscription is a free "Interactive Guide to *Newsweek*"—a workbook for students who are using the text. In addition, Newsweek provides a wide variety of instructor supplements free to teachers, including maps, Skills Builders, and weekly quizzes. For more information on the Newsweek program, please contact your Longman sales representative.

Electronic and Online Offerings

[NEW] The Longman Writer's Warehouse

The innovative and exciting online supplement is the perfect accompaniment to any developmental writing course. Developed by developmental English instructors specially for developing writers, The Writer's Warehouse covers every part of the writing process. Also included are journaling capabilities, multimedia activities, diagnostic tests, an interactive handbook, and a complete instructor's manual. The Writer's Warehouse requires no space on your school's server; rather, students complete and store their work on the Longman server, and are able to access it, revise it, and continue working at any time. For more details about how to shrinkwrap a free subscription to The Writer's Warehouse with this text, please consult your Longman sales representative. For a free guided tour of the site, visit *http://longmanwriterswarehouse.com*.

The Writer's ToolKit Plus

This CD-ROM offers a wealth of tutorial, exercise, and reference material for writers. It is compatible with either a PC or Macintosh platform, and is flexible enough to be used either occasionally for practice or regularly in class lab sessions. For information on how to bundle this CD-ROM FREE with your text, please contact your Longman sales representative.

The Longman English Pages Web Site

Both students and instructors can visit our free content-rich Web site for additional reading selections and writing exercises. From the Longman English pages, visitors can conduct a simulated Web search, learn how to write a resume and cover letter, or try their hand at poetry writing. Stop by and visit us at *http://www.ablongman.com/englishpages*.

The Longman Electronic Newsletter

Twice a month during the spring and fall, instructors who have subscribed receive a free copy of the Longman Developmental English Newsletter in their e-mailbox. Written by experienced classroom instructors, the newsletter offers teaching tips, classroom activities, book reviews, and more. To subscribe, visit the Longman Developmental English Web site at *http://www.ablongman.com/basicskills*, or send an e-mail to *Basic Skills@ablongman.com*.

For Instructors

[NEW] Electronic Test Bank for Writing

This electronic test bank features more than 5,000 questions in all areas of writing, from grammar to paragraphing, through essay writing, research, and documentation. With this easy-to-use CD-ROM, instructors simply choose questions from the electronic test bank, then print out the completed test for distribution. CD-ROM: 0-321-08117-X Print version: 0-321-08486-1

[NEW] The Longman Guide to Classroom Management

is the first in a series of monographs for developmental educators. Written by Joannis Flatley of St. Philip's College, it focuses on issues of classroom etiquette, providing guidance on dealing with unruly, unengaged, disruptive, or uncooperative students. 0-321-09246-5

[NEW] The Longman Instructor Planner

is an all-in-one resource for instructors. It includes monthly and weekly planning sheets, to-do lists, student contact forms, attendance rosters, a gradebook, an address/phone book, and a mini almanac. It is free upon request. 0-321-09247-3

Competency Profile Test Bank, Second Edition

This series of 60 objective tests covers ten general areas of English competency, including fragments, comma splices and run-ons, pronouns, commas, and capitalization. Each test is available in remedial, standard, and advanced versions. Available as reproducible sheets or in computerized versions. Free to instructors. Paper version: 0-321-02224-6 Computerized IBM: 0-321-02633-0 Computerized Mac: 0-321-02632-2

Diagnostic and Editing Tests, Third Edition

This collection of diagnostic tests helps instructors assess students' competence in Standard Written English for purpose of placement or to gauge progress. Available as reproducible sheets or in computerized versions, and free to instructors. Paper: 0-321-08382-2 CD-ROM: 0-321-08782-8

ESL Worksheets, Third Edition

These reproducible worksheets provide ESL students with extra practice in areas they find the most troublesome. A diagnostic test and post-test are provided, along with answer keys and suggested topics for writing. Free to adopters. 0-321-07765-2

Longman Editing Exercises

Fifty-four pages of paragraph editing exercises give students extra practice using grammar skills in the context of longer passages. Free when packaged with any Longman title. 0-205-31792-8

80 Practices

A collection of reproducible, ten-item exercises that provide additional practices for specific grammatical usage problems, such as comma splices, capitalization, and pronouns. Includes an answer key, and free to adopters. 0-673-53422-7

CLAST Test Package, Fourth Edition

These two 40-item objective tests evaluate students' readiness for the CLAST exams. Strategies for teaching CLAST preparedness are included. Free with any

Longman English title. Reproducible sheets: 0-321-01950-4 Computerized IBM version: 0-321-01982-2 Computerized Mac version: 0-321-01983-0

TASP Test Package, Third Edition

These 12 practice pre-tests and post-tests assess the same reading and writing skills covered in the TASP examination. Free with any Longman English title. Reproducible sheets: 0-321-01959-8 Computerized IBM version: 0-321-01985-7 Computerized Mac version: 0-321-01984-9

Teaching Online: Internet Research, Conversation, and Composition, Second Edition

Ideal for instructors who have never surfed the Net, this easy-to-follow guide offers basic definitions, numerous examples, and step-by-step information about finding and using Internet sources. Free to adopters. 0-321-01957-1

Teaching Writing to the Non-Native Speaker

This booklet examines the issues that arise when non-native speakers enter the developmental classroom. Free to instructors, it includes profiles of international and permanent ESL students, factors influencing second-language acquisition, and tips on managing a multicultural classroom. 0-673-97452-9

For Students

[NEW] The Longman Writer's Journal

This journal for writers, free with *Hands Across Borders*, offers students a place to think, write, and react. For an examination copy, contact your Longman sales consultant. 0-321-08639-2

[NEW] The Longman Researcher's Journal

This journal for writers and researchers, free with this text, helps students plan, schedule, write, and revise their research project. An all-in-one resource for first-time researchers, the journal guides students gently through the research process. 0-321-09530-8

Researching Online, Fifth Edition

A perfect companion for a new age, this indispensable new supplement helps students navigate the Internet. Adapted from *Teaching Online*, the instructor's Internet guide, *Researching Online* speaks directly to students, giving them detailed, step-by-step instructions for performing electronic searches. Available free when shrinkwrapped with this text. 0-321-09277-5

Learning Together: An Introduction to Collaborative Theory

This brief guide to the fundamentals of collaborative learning teaches students how to work effectively in groups, how to revise with peer response, and how to coauthor a paper or report. Shrinkwrapped free with any Longman Basic Skills text. 0-673-46848-8

A Guide for Peer Response, Second Edition

This guide offers students forms for peer critiques, including general guidelines and specific forms for different stages in the writing process. Also appropriate for freshman-level course. Free to adopters. 0-321-01948-2

Thinking Through the Test, by D. J. Henry

This special workbook, prepared specially for students in Florida, offers ample skill and practice exercises to help student prep for the Florida State Exit Exam. To shrinkwrap this workbook free with your textbook, please contact your Longman sales representative. Available in two versions: with and without answers. Also available: Two laminated grids (one for reading, one for writing) that can serve as handy references for students preparing for the Florida State Exit Exam.

Acknowledgements

The birth of a book, just like any conception and birth, does not occur in isolation. This conception and birth are no different. There are many individuals who will go unnamed and others will go into categories because there is no possible way to credit all my composition students who have sat in my classes, cried in my various offices, celebrated when they won essay contests, and generally watched their own progress from halting scribblers to young men and women with voices of their own. I thank you for your invaluable contribution to my growth as a composition teacher. And then there are my own professors and colleagues who taught me to strive for improvement and to revise, revise, revise.

The next set of individuals who must be mentioned are those professors who believed in me at University of Houston, especially Dr. James Kastely, without whom this text would never have been written. To Dr. Terrell Dixon, I offer enormous thanks for trusting me as a research assistant with his texts, for preparing me for all the adventures I have had creating my text, for teaching me so much in his classes, and ultimately, for allowing me to become his friend and colleague.

Of course my family comes next. My mother, Margaret Listenberger, has always been there for me and has provided invaluable assistance when I have needed it. Jim Kessler and our son, David, have listened, encouraged, and offered constructive suggestions, love, patience, and a critical eye.

To my circle of friends and colleagues at Houston Community College and California State University, I offer undying gratitude: Carlos Villacis, Iris Rozencwajg, Sharon Klander, Randy Watson, Linda Koffel, Syble Simon, Linda Daigle, Alan Ainsworth, and Vickie Frazer; Roberta Orona-Cordova, Linda Overman, Irene Clark, Pam Bourgeois, Pat Murray, Ranita Chatterjee, Donald Hall, and Fortuna Ippoliti. You were with me from the beginning and are still my friends. Thank you.

Additionally, I want to thank Dr. Maria González for being the first to field-test the text and especially her students who used it and offered suggestions and comments. Others who participated in field-testing included Syble Simon at Houston Community College; Linda Overman and Dr. Mary Pardo at California State University at Northridge; and Roberta Orona-Cordova at Santa Monica College. Thank you for all the work it took to field test and to offer comments about your findings.

Three individuals, Roberta Orona-Cordova, Stephanie Packer, and Iris Rozencwajg, were also instrumental as consultants at the beginning of the process, helping me select the most appropriate readings for the text. Thank you.

I also want to thank Steve Rigolosi at Longman for his patience and guidance and Liza Rudneva for getting me started in the right direction. And, of course, I owe a great deal of gratitude to the authors who shared their work and allowed me to use it in this text.

There are, however, two friends without whom I could never have met my deadline. Maria González took time away from her annual visit home to work aggressively on acquiring permissions, to research names and dates, and to do much of the legwork I was too busy to do. Anne Perrin took time away from studying for her comprehensive exams, found replacement articles, wrote an article for me when I desperately needed one to complete a chapter, researched MLA, worked on permissions, and generally kept us fed and organized. You were both at my side through every step of the conception, labor, and delivery and deserve to be *las madrinas* to this child. You remain my dearest companions. Thank you.

I would also like to thank all those who reviewed the proposal and manuscript at various stages in its development:

Poonam Arora, University of Michigan, Dearborn; Barbara Arthur, University of Houston; Bonny Bryan, Santa Barbara City College; Michael Darcher, Pierce College; Darlynn R. Fink, Clarion University of Pennsylvania; Jerald L. Ross, Southwestern Illinois College; Iris Rozencwajg, Houston Community College–Central; Melita Schaum, University of Michigan–Dearborn; Linda S. Weeks, Dyersburg Sate Community College; and Daniel Zimmerman, Middlesex County College.

My hope is that *Hands Across Borders: A Multicultural Reader for Writers* takes some of the mystery out of writing and out of many of the world's cultures for our students. It is written with the student in mind primarily and with the instructor as a partner in the teaching of writing. I am open to constructive criticism, so if you have any suggestions, recommendations for new or other works, or any general comments to make, please feel free to write to me or e-mail me, and I will respond, for I, too, love to write. To modify an old cliché, break a pencil.

Elizabeth Rodriguez Kessler
Northridge, California
elizabeth.kessler@csun.edu

PART ONE

Reading and Writing Skills

Introduction to the Student Reader

The title of this textbook, *Hands Across Borders: A Multicultural Reader,* is an invitation to you, the reader and student writer, to investigate the various cultures that compose the United States. Stories, personal narratives, essays, and poetry are included here, by authors who may represent your cultural heritage. Although not all ethnicities could be included, this anthology attempts to incorporate as wide a variety of cultures as possible.

One definition of the term *border* is a political and geographical line or space that separates one country from another, but this anthology broadens that definition. Borders exist not only between countries but between ourselves and the people who surround us. We construct borders that prevent us from associating with others because of differences in beliefs about religion, education, gender, sexual orientation, death, and other privately held philosophies. These readings will introduce students in any culture to beliefs, traditions, religions, rituals, and conflicts different from their own. In other words, this textbook should help you reach across those imaginary dividing lines to other people from different backgrounds. While the line will probably always remain, because individuals will continue to hold personal beliefs that they are not willing to change, this text gives readers an opportunity to learn what people beyond their borders believe. This, in turn, should help readers understand why others act, react, or respond the ways they do. Readers may come away from the works still reluctant to accept new beliefs, but they also leave more informed than they were prior to reading the pieces.

Another purpose for the readings is to offer student writers a variety of models to use as they construct their own writing assignments. For example, a number of personal narratives are offered; however, the purposes and constructions vary. And, in addition to traditiionally structured models of argumentative essays, developed from a clearly stated thesis and structured in a way that uses rhetorical techniques to convince their readers, Chapter 10, Confrontations, includes two final essays that depart from the traditional structure. They are no less argumentative than formal essays, but they are written from a personal perspective. Although student writers must follow the guidelines set by instructors and departments, this text offers alternative ideas and modes with which to experiment.

In addition to the readings in Part II are two other sections. Part I offers instructional information about how to improve the student writers' skills in reading, vocabulary, and composition. Part III moves the writers beyond the basics and expands skills in reading and writing about literature as well as in the use of the Internet and the World Wide Web. Research techniques and MLA format for formal writing are also included. Thus, the border that has separated student writers from successful completion of their writing assignments and expansion of their skills is also about to be crossed.

This is a text constructed with your needs in mind. We hope you will discover that you have talents and knowledge that need refining and strengthening. On the other hand, you will find you are learning material that is brand-new and intended to help you grow as a writer and as a better informed person. Learning is defined as behavior modification, and keeping that in mind will help you realize that when you write a thesis sentence according to your instructor's directions or construct an essay that incorporates the required elements consistently, you are changing your behavior. The trick is to improve the skills you have acquired and become more proficient. This text is designed to help you become a more successful student writer.

IMPROVING YOUR READING SKILLS

This chapter begins with the assumption that you want to improve your reading and writing skills. Regardless of what level you read and write at, that level can always be improved, even when you are reading academically advanced texts and writing at advanced levels. For example, let's say your best friend is in his third year of higher education. That status presupposes that he has been reading and writing quite well for years. However, have you heard your friend complain about struggling with a philosophy class or a physics class because he simply does not understand the reading assignments? What is happening to your friend is basically what is happening to you. You have both found a weakness in a skill that each of you has been practicing since elementary school with varying degrees of success. You have obviously been successful because you are still reading. Stop now for a moment and answer the following questions based on this paragraph:

1. To whom have I just been compared?
2. What does the author assume in this chapter?

These are simple enough questions to answer if you have been concentrating on the passage. On the other hand, if you allow your mind to wander to other concerns—the bills, the test on Tuesday, the family problems—then you discover that reading is not always the issue. Concentration is. That's why it's always a good idea to stop reading—or looking over the words—occasionally and ask yourself what you have just read. An even better exercise is to write in one or two sentences a summary of the main idea expressed in the assignment. If you can't answer the question or write the summary, then you should reread what your eyes glanced over. Yes, it takes more time, but if you can't do it now, you probably won't be able to answer the questions your instructor asks you in class the next day either. The reply, "I really read it, but I don't remember that part," will be only partially true. Your eyes glanced over the words, but you neither comprehended nor retained the message.

Many people discover that they learn best by combining learning styles: visual, oral, auditory, and kinesthetic. Thus reading in conjunction with writing—summarizing, paraphrasing, taking notes, writing questions about the passage that you did not understand—helps many students learn more easily than if they simply read the passage.

You might want to stop here and think about how you learn best.

- Do you learn best by listening to your instructor lecture? (Auditory learner)
- Do you learn best by repeating what you have read? (Visual, oral, and auditory learner)
- Do you learn better if you listen to the instructor and take notes while he is explaining a lesson? (Auditory and kinesthetic learner)
- Do you learn better by listening and reading the points the instructor puts on the board or overhead transparency as she is lecturing? (Visual and oral learner)
- Does taking notes as you listen and read the board increase your understanding of the material? (Visual, auditory, and kinesthetic learner)
- When you are studying, does underlining or highlighting specific information help you remember it better? (Visual and kinesthetic learner)

These questions as well as others address the way individuals learn. Have you figured out how you learn best?

Reading and writing are skills, and as with any skill you want to become proficient in—swimming, piano playing, painting, football—you must practice. A dedicated pianist does not give up when he finds a difficult piece. Furthermore, the performer does not settle for continuing to play pieces of equal difficulty. He must challenge himself to improve. Just as a high school athlete cannot settle for high school-level training when she is competing for a place on a college team, neither can you settle with being able to read and write at a level that does not advance your skills.

Therefore, just as this text is about crossing cultural boundaries, it is also about surpassing the boundaries that serve as obstacles for personal and academic growth. Through practice, determination, patience, and concentration, you will steadily grow beyond the abilities you have today.

➤ Follow-Up Questions

1. What are the four different kinds of learning styles discussed in the passage? What does each involve to learn?
2. How are reading skills similar to playing the piano or football?

➤ Short Writing Assignments

1. Write a journal entry that describes your feelings about reading. Think about what you like and dislike to read. What about the material you dislike makes it difficult to read? Include a few sentences that explain the process you use to become an active reader.
2. Consider your learning style and the classes you have been successful in. Why were you successful in those classes? What learning style(s) did you use to learn what was required in your class? Write a journal entry describing the process you used to learn the material in your most successful class. Which learning styles did the process include?

VOCABULARY BUILDING FOR BETTER READING AND WRITING

First, let's look at vocabulary learning skills that have not worked. Do you remember being in classes where you had to memorize lists of vocabulary words for a weekly test? This happened in classes like biology, foreign language, health, and so forth. What happened? How many words do you still remember today—much less use? Most of us memorized the lists, took the tests, and promptly forgot the words after the tests. Why? We didn't continue to use the words. They did not become part of our personal vocabulary. The experience fulfills the adage, "Use it or lose it." Once we know what doesn't work, we know it will be futile to continue to repeat a process that fails.

If you look at the selections in Part II of this text, you will find lists of vocabulary words before each work that could pose a problem to you or that will give you an idea about the piece. The generally recommended ways to approach vocabulary building include the following:

- try to determine the meaning contextually;
- look up the word in the dictionary;
- keep a set of note cards on which you write the word, its definition(s), and the sentence the word was in when you found it in the reading selection;
- complete an exercise that requires you to use the word in an original sentence;
- complete matching, fill-in-the-blank, and other related exercises using the new words;
- take a quiz on the meanings of the words; and
- use the words as part of your own spoken and written language when appropriate.

Even though each of these suggestions works, none works every time for every person. Looking up words can be tedious and time consuming, especially if you find many words that are difficult to understand in context. However, if you do not get an accurate definition, you will lose some of the meaning of the selection. And sometimes when you think you know the definition, the word still does not make sense in the sentence. To complicate matters further, the author may even be speaking metaphorically, comparing one idea to something different; in such a case, understanding the meanings of the words may not allow you to understand the message.

For example, in Zitkala-Sa's personal narrative, "The School Days of an Indian Girl," there are three words/phrases preceding the passage: *brave, iron horse,* and *pale faces*. In everyday reading and speaking, most people understand the definition of *brave* as "courageous" or "without fear." *Iron* is usually defined as a strong, hard metal, and *horse* is an animal. The same approach applies to *pale*: "colorless or whitish," and *face*: "from the forehead to the chin." However, in the context of Sa's narrative, a *brave* is a warrior, especially among North American Indians; an *iron horse* is the name North American Indians use for the train; and a *pale face* is a term used by some North American Indians which means a white person.

Fortunately, all words and their meanings are not that complex; however, you will find that working your way through the dictionary yields rewards. Now, whether you write the definition and the sentence on a note card is your decision, but if the words are important enough to you and you think you won't remember them, you might choose to use that procedure. The best way to build your vocabulary, however, is to use the words appropriately once you have learned the meanings. It might sound awkward at first, but as you continue to add new words to your spoken and written vocabulary, you will begin to see and hear a difference. You will understand more when you are reading, and your writing will sound better. A word of warning: When you incorporate new words into your writing, they must sound natural rather than stand out like a synonym you found in a thesaurus. Improving your vocabulary is then a cumulative process: one that builds on what you have learned previously. Before you know it, your speaking and writing vocabulary will increase and you will find yourself writing with a language that is more formal, varied, and interesting.

➤ Follow-Up Questions

1. List three ways to improve your vocabulary.
2. Explain how Zitkala-Sa's personal narrative could pose problems even for readers who know what individual words mean.
3. What are some advantages to improving your vocabulary?

➤ Short Writing Assignments

1. To see how using big words from a thesaurus can be inappropriate, take the title of one or two of your favorite songs, look up each important word in a thesaurus, and substitute the new word for the one in the song. Write a comparison-and-contrast paragraph explaining why one title, the original or the newly created one, is better than the other.

2. Find a paragraph you wrote in your journal. Go to your thesaurus and substitute all important words (nouns, pronouns, adjectives, adverbs, and verbs) with one of the synonyms listed for each in the thesaurus. Analyze the new paragraph to determine if it means exactly what you wanted to say in the original. Write a comparison-and-contrast paragraph explaining which paragraph is better and why.

THE READING PROCESS

Since this is a writing text, you might be asking yourself why the author is spending so much time talking about reading. Good reading is the key to becoming a good writer. The articles, short stories, and poems that writers read influence them in their own approach to writing. Professional writers, too, have increased their vocabulary by reading and by following steps to improve their store of words. Just as vocabulary building incorporates the element of writing to facilitate learning, so, too, does writing help in the reading process. Good writers aren't born that way. They, like all of us, had to learn to read and write.

Before you begin, ask yourself this question: What does "facilitate" mean? Did you know its meaning when you read it? Did you stop to look it up or figure it out from context clues before you continued reading? Can you write a paraphrase of the sentence that has "facilitate" in it? Do you remember reading about learning styles in the preceding section? The three learning styles can be combined to "[help] many students learn more easily than if they simply read the passage." Writing is a kinesthetic learning style, one that requires movement. Therefore, from these context clues, you should be able to understand that "facilitate" means "to help" in this context. If you went through the process above, you are showing evidence of not only working at building your vocabulary but also of becoming an effective, active reader.

To become an effective and active reader, you must follow steps that other successful readers follow. If what you have done in the past has not worked, then it's time to try a new strategy, one that will feel comfortable and that you will continue to use in all your reading assignments.

Pre-Reading

1. Know what the assignment is. Even the most earnest student sometimes goes to class unprepared because he read the wrong selection. Check your syllabus or notes to make sure you're reading the correct work.

2. Set aside time for your reading. This means knowing when it is best for you to read. Some students read better early in the morning; others prefer late evening. Snatching time between classes does not usually work for serious, sustained reading. Therefore, develop a routine that fits your needs and will help you be successful.

3. Be prepared. Make sure you have paper, pen, a highlighter, proper lighting, your dictionary, and any snacks you will need to complete the reading assignment. Make sure the environment is conducive for reading and that as many distractions as possible have been eliminated. This is your time.

4. Check the length of the article. If it is long, will you have to read it in more than one session? Do you have time to read it in the time you set aside? Should you leave it for another time and complete your other assignments first?

5. Look carefully at the title. Does it indicate what the piece will be about? Do you have any background in the area or will you be reading about something totally new to you? Even if the assignment is short, if you are unfamiliar with the information presented, it might take a long time to read.

6. Look at the vocabulary list if one is present. Familiarize yourself with any term you do not know. (See the discussion on vocabulary building in the preceding pages.)

7. Look for bold headings. They should give you an indication about what is important in the reading. Also look for bold or italicized words. The author is trying to send a message that this is important.

8. Check for questions at the end of the passage. There is no rule that says you can't begin by reading the questions first. Doing so will help you get an idea of what you should be reading for. This is also good practice for taking entrance exams that give reading passages and questions to answer about them.

9. Determine what kind of selection you will be reading. Some students approach each reading assignment in the same manner; that strategy sometimes prevents them from being successful. Is it a short story? An essay? A personal narrative? A poem? Each kind of writing has different characteristics. If you are not familiar with the types of nonfiction, look at Appendix 1: Reading and Writing about Nonfiction for an explanation about what you should be reading for.

10. Look at the pre-reading sections that precede the selection. These pre-reading guides should help you focus your thoughts about the selection. Some guides will give you insight into the author and/or ask questions that provoke responses to the work.

11. Make pre-reading notes, journal entries, or questions. By completing step 10, you will be able to think about possible writing topics, questions you might want to jot down before you read, or journal entries you might want to make about the topic before you read. This last step will help you clarify in your mind how you feel about controversial issues before you expose yourself to someone else's beliefs. You should begin to see that becoming a good writer works together with becoming a good reader.

This is the beginning. It may sound as if it will take a lot of time; however, once you make it a practice to complete these steps, they will become second nature, and you will find that you can do them quickly. They can become part of your reading and writing routine, and you will be prepared to read the selection with an informed mind.

STEPS FOR PRE-READING

1. Know the correct assignment.
2. Set aside time for your reading by establishing a routine.
3. Be prepared with all the essentials you need.
4. Check the length of the article to see if you can complete it in one session or have to break it into two or more.
5. Look carefully at the title.
6. Look at the vocabulary list.
7. Look for bold headings and bold words.
8. Check the questions at the end of the passage.
9. Determine what kind of reading selection it is and modify your reading method for it.
10. Review the pre-reading material that precedes the selection.
11. Make pre-reading notes, questions, and journal entries about the assignment.

Reading

Now that you have completed the basic "warm-up exercises," it's time to read the selection. Keep in mind the purpose for reading this particular assignment. In other words, is it part of a unit you are studying in class? Does your instructor want you to read it for style? Why are you reading this? If you don't know or don't remember, take a moment to review your notes and the directions your instructor gave you.

1. Read the entire selection quickly. This way you will get the overall idea, tone, and direction of the article.

2. Review the follow-up questions again to see if you can answer any after your quick reading. If you can't, you will at least begin the next step with the questions fresh in your mind. If you can, answer them quickly by jotting down notes. You can come back after the second reading and expand the answers so you will be prepared for class.

3. Begin reading slowly and thoroughly.

4. Keep your pen or highlighter in hand. You will want to mark important details, names of people/characters, dates, and other pertinent information you should remember. You will also want to write questions in the margins beside paragraphs you find confusing.

5. Read each selection correctly. If this is a **persuasive essay,** identify the **thesis** and find the points the author uses to try to persuade you. If this is a short story, follow the pattern of development for the **plot,** identify the **charac-**

ters, and notice the **style.** If this is an **informative essay,** look for all the **details** that describe or explain the subject. If this is a poem, look for **figurative language, style, stanzas,** and feelings. Read it aloud and listen to the way it sounds. As you can see, no two selections will be read in the same way if they are different kinds of writing.

6. If you find your mind wandering, stop immediately. Think about the last part you remember reading and begin from there. Write a brief **summary** to help you remember what you read. List the points that the author made. If you need to take a break, do so, but return ready to concentrate.

7. If there are breaks in the reading, places where new sections begin, stop after each and review what you have read. Ask yourself questions such as: What was the main idea of the section? Were there words I did not understand that kept me from understanding the passage? Were there complex sentences that I did not understand? If you had difficulty with any of these areas, review the section you read again. Since what follows is probably dependent upon the part you did not understand, re-rereading the confusing passage slowly and thoroughly will help you prepare for the next section. Be sure to write questions in the margin if you still find any passage confusing.

8. Review the marks you have made in the reading, noticing their importance.

STEPS FOR SUCCESSFUL READING

1. Read the entire selection quickly.
2. Review the questions at the end.
3. Begin reading slowly and thoroughly.
4. Keep your pen or highlighter in hand.
5. Read each selection correctly.
6. If you find your mind wandering, stop immediately.
7. If there are breaks in the reading, stop after each and review what you have read.
8. Review the marks you have made in the reading, noticing their importance.

Follow-Up Strategies

Completing the reading is not the final step. To be an active reader, you must be sure you comprehend what you have read. Finish the assignment by completing the following steps.

1. Answer the questions at the end. Sometimes they are based on a literal reading, which means that they are asking if you remember the details of the selection. Some questions, however, will be more thought-provoking. These in-depth questions will not have answers you can find in the reading. Instead, they will require that you look at the ideas presented from different perspectives or apply your previous knowledge and experience to the reading. They may even ask you to evaluate the reading selection based on a given criterion. These questions are important for developing higher-level thinking skills. Now is the time to practice writing the full answers. This will help you practice paragraph development and fluency in your writing skills. Instead of answering questions with a simple *yes* or *no*, set up a **topic sentence** that states your position and write a paragraph of four or five additional sentences that support that position. This will not only help you prepare for your class, it will also help you in responding to short-answer questions that your instructor might ask you in a quiz about the reading. You will also be able to use these responses as you participate in class discussion.

2. Take notes for class discussion. Do this first by reviewing the marked parts of the reading. If you marked parts of the reading, you might want to use them to take notes for class discussion. If you have questions, jot them down in the margin of the selection next to the paragraph that caused you difficulty. This way you will be prepared to ask specific questions in class about what you read. You will be able to direct the instructor and the class to the exact page and paragraph without having to thumb through the pages and look unprepared.

3. Write a reader response journal entry about this selection. Be sure to follow your instructor's directions. Your instructor might ask you to write a summary of the reading passage, or to respond. Remember that responding is different from summarizing. When you respond, you explain any of the following points:

- if you agreed or disagreed with the article and why;
- if you liked or disliked the article and why;
- if you can associate with the events in the article and how;
- if you can identify with any of the characters/people in the article and how;
- if you learned anything from the article;
- if you would recommend this article to a friend and why; and
- what your response to the author might be if you had a chance to talk to him or her.

There are, of course, other ways you might respond, but these are a few of the most frequently used responses.

4. Review mentally how you felt about the reading. Go back to the points mentioned above and review them in your mind. Answer two of the following questions: Did you agree or disagree with the author? Why? Did the selection answer the questions you had about the topic, or do you have further questions for the author? Did the story end the way you wanted it to end? How do you feel about the characters? Even though you are not required to do so, you might want to make notes for class discussion.

FOLLOW-UP STRATEGIES

1. Answer the questions at the end.
2. Take notes for class discussion.
3. Write a Reader Response entry or a summary.
4. Review mentally how you felt about the reading.

Successful reading and writing take time and dedication. If you have had difficulties in the past, don't be discouraged. You are beginning a new self-improvement plan, and as with any other, it will be slow at first, but the rewards will come if you are consistent in your practices. When you encounter problems, your instructor will be there ready to help you move forward. And as with all improvement plans, you must want to change because you see a need. If you follow a routine that fits your needs, not only will you begin to improve your reading and writing skills, you may find that reading gives you a new way to relax and enjoy yourself and that writing provides an outlet for your ideas, feelings, and creativity that you had not realized before.

➤ Follow-Up Questions

1. List the three major steps in approaching a reading assignment.
2. Each major step has smaller steps or directions for successful reading. List two small directions from each major step and explain why you think each is important.
3. Explain what it means to "read each selection correctly." Give an example of at least two different kinds of writing and how each should be read.

➤ Short Writing Assignments

1. Write a reader response journal entry about this section, "The Reading Process," discussing the following points. Do not just answer the questions. Create a well-developed paragraph that responds to this section by addressing these and other issues you can think of.
   • What did you think about the directions?
   • Will you try to use any of the suggestions? Why?
   • Which directions do you already use that are successful?
   • Which new directions do you think could help you most?
2. Find a younger person, possibly a sibling, a friend, or your child, who is learning how to read or who is having trouble reading. Practice these directions with the young reader for several days in short time periods. Watch the reader's progress. Talk to the reader after she has come home from school and practiced the method on an assignment. Did the reader express satisfaction with her work in class that day? Write a short paper describing the reader, the reading assignment, the process you used to help the reader, and the feelings expressed by the reader after the assignment was due. Evaluate the results of the process after using it several times with the same reader.

IMPROVING YOUR WRITING SKILLS

While the main purpose of the preceding section was to help you improve your reading skills, it also emphasized the role that being a good reader plays in becoming a good writer. Steps to improve your reading skills that also incorporate writing to help you remember are **listing, summary,** and **paraphrase.** To help you analyze and understand, you should write questions about the material in the margins and answer the questions at the end of the selections—first in brief form and then in fully elaborated paragraphs. Finally, you should keep a journal to express your feelings, jot down questions, respond to the reading, or write creative pieces. At the end of the section, as well as at the end of the preceding sections, you were asked to begin practicing your writing skills. This chapter will build on these skills, with the guidance of your instructor, help you polish your skills in writing various assignments and teach you how to write some types of assignments you may never have written before.

Purpose of Writing

Before you begin writing, it's important to know the purpose of writing. Why do you write? Some students respond by saying that the only reason they write is because they have to complete assignments that their instructors have given them. Other students acknowledge that they write **letters,** e-mail messages, notes to friends, or private poems and short stories. And employers say they write memos to their employees, business letters, and letters of reference or recommendation. Even though the reason for writing any particular piece varies, the purpose remains the same: to communicate with someone who is not able to speak with you directly. If a student turns in a paper, the student is trying to communicate to his instructor the extent that he has understood the assignment or acquired the knowledge or information the instructor assigned. Whether it is through a paper, a memo, or a letter, the writer always has the responsibility of being clear and precise so that the message will be delivered accurately. For example, read the following response to a birthday party invitation. The writer is responding for herself and for her friends:

> Dear Shamika,
>
> Thanks for the birthday invitation. I talked to Mary Jane Peggy Sue and Alicia. We will all be there.
>
> Sincerely,
>
> Cindy

Unless Shamika knows everyone who has been invited, she will have difficulty knowing if four (Mary Jane, Peggy Sue, Alicia, and Cindy), five (Mary, Jane,

Peggy Sue, Alicia, and Cindy) or six (Mary, Jane, Peggy, Sue, Alicia, and Cindy) people are attending. If Shamika were speaking to Cindy, the inflection in Cindy's voice would clarify the number; however, verbal as well as non verbal communication is missing when we write. Facial expressions, hand gestures, nods, winks, and other physical indications we make to punctuate what we say and indicate if we're serious, teasing, or being ironic or sarcastic are missing from the written page.

Some writers, however, feel free to insert : -) or : -(in informal correspondence to help the reader get a clearer message. Those signs, however, do not replace correct punctuation or precise word choice. For example, **synonyms** do not always convey the same connotations even though they may be close in meaning. Charles Dickens would not have made the following potential mistake.

CHOOSE THE CORRECT WORD

(Petite or Tiny) Tim had no Christmas presents because of his family's poverty.

Although *petite* and *tiny* have the same denotation, *small*, petite is usually an adjective that refers to women; therefore the two cannot always be substituted for each other.

Furthermore, structure sometimes creates confusion. In the following box, which is correct?

Running across the street, the car hit the dog.
or
Running across the street, the dog was hit by the car.

The key is who or what was running? The dog was. The phrase that opens the sentence describes the subject. Therefore, the first sentence is wrong, because the car could not have been "running across the street."

ACCURATE COMMUNICATION REQUIRES THE WRITER TO

- be clear,
- be precise,
- use correct punctuation,
- use correct structure.

Audience

Since the purpose of writing is communication, you must also remember your audience. You do not speak to everyone using the same language, so naturally you will not write to everyone using the same language, either. Although the following is an extreme example, it makes the point. Imagine yourself enrolled during the fall semester in a multicultural studies class. Your instructor assigns a research project over the different traditions practiced in the United States at Christmas, and you decide to write about the origins of Santa Claus and how the practice evolved. Then you go to your writing class, and your writing instructor is teaching the importance of audience. Your instructor has just collaborated with a second-grade teacher at a local elementary school to work on the issue of audience also. The children will write letters to Santa Claus, telling him what they want for Christmas. In turn, your class will receive the letters and answer each one personally, pretending to be Santa Claus. Although this might sound like an "elementary" exercise, it is a good one to teach both the children and the college students the importance of audience.

Brainstorm for a few moments about the changes you and your classmates will have to make in your writing styles and approaches to communicate with the second graders. As you can see by the list you have made, there are many differences you will have to take into account because of your audience. Different issues must be addressed and different levels of vocabulary must be used. The issue of whether to use a computer or to handwrite the project is a concern. Even the problem of what kind of paper to use when writing to the children becomes an issue. Do you use plain white typing paper? You know you can't use college rule paper. Of course these kinds of considerations will not appear in your multicultural studies class because you will be writing in a way that is traditional for the college student. You have established your audience to be of a certain nature and education. Consequently, you are relatively comfortable writing for your instructor. The problem comes when you forget that not everyone reads at the same level or for the same purpose. It is then that you must remember to consider your audience.

In case you haven't noticed, if you are a student applying for a job, some of these same problems arise. Should you use a different vocabulary if you are applying for a job in medicine as opposed to a job as a computer specialist? Should you use a certain kind of style when you type your résumé? Should you use the expensive paper to print your cover letter on, or should you use personal stationery? What topics do you include in your cover letter?

Therefore, not only what you write but to whom you write makes a big difference. Even though the example of writing letters to second graders might be somewhat extreme, it has a great deal in common with the choices you must make when writing to a prospective employer.

Literature as Communication

If we consider communication to be the key to good writing, we must now understand why we can still read great literature that was written centuries ago.

The ideas that Homer, Cervantes, Shakespeare, Milton, Camus, and others who rank among the classics wrote are still being read today. Why? They were able to find enduring topics and were able to communicate not only with their generation but with generations who have followed them. William Faulkner, an American southern writer who was awarded the Nobel Prize for Literature explained writing and the writer this way:

> [The writer must leave] no room in his workshop for anything but the old verities and truths of the heart, the old universal truths lacking which any story is ephemeral° and doomed—love and honor and pity and pride and compassion and sacrifice. . . . The poet's, the writer's, duty is to write about these things. It is his privilege to help man endure by lifting his heart, by reminding him of the courage and honor and hope and pride and compassion and pity and sacrifice which have been the glory of the past.

ephemeral:
short-lived

To communicate is to write clearly and precisely, in order to speak to those to whom you are writing without confusion. While you and your peers might not achieve the stature of Faulkner or Shakespeare, you are beginning where they began in their writing careers.

Thus you will continue to cross borders, have new experiences, and interact with others who may have more or less experience than you in certain writing situations. You might find yourself the leader in group work that involves writing in a particular mode or about a particular topic with which you are familiar. At other times, you might be a participant who follows, receiving help and instruction rather than providing guidance. If you are in a peer-editing situation with another student, you will have to depend on what you have learned to help your peer prepare to revise a paper. Regardless of your role, you play an important part in your own success as well as in the success of your group and your class. By working independently as well as collectively with others, you will find yourself growing in ways you never imagined—and your writing will also improve.

➤ Follow-Up Questions

1. What four qualities does accurate writing need?
2. Why should writers consider their audience before they begin writing?
3. Why can we understand the writings of Homer, Shakespeare, and Faulkner today?

➤ Short Writing Assignment

Pretend you want to take a one-week vacation from work and you have vacation time coming. Your company requires a letter notifying your employer of any time off you will take that extends beyond two business days. Write a letter to your employer explaining what and when you will take your vacation. In addition to work, you also have to let your child's school know you will be taking her out of school for a week for a family vacation.

However, you know that this violates the attendance policy at your daughter's school. Will the letter you write to your employer be copied and sent to your daughter's school or will you have to change the content? Write a letter to each audience and be ready to discuss each in class.

THE PARAGRAPH

Prewriting

The fundamental stepping stone to good writing begins with the word. A writer then places it in combination with others to make sense and create thoughts by writing phrases and sentences. The diagram below gives some examples:

The Word	The Phrase	The Sentence
cat	the unusual cat	The unusual cat had a loud cry.

As the thought grows and expands, the sentences multiply, creating the paragraph, a group of sentences that develops one idea. If you take the above example to the next stage, you will discover that you can write a variety of paragraphs that are identified by their pattern: descriptive, personal narrative, and comparison-and-contrast. Although there are more patterns, we will explore these first.

Let's say your writing instructor assigned the class a topic: Write a paragraph about your pet. Rather than give directions immediately, your instructor lets you and the class determine the kind of approach you want to take. You are one of the students who owns a pet, and you know that you have a lot that you can say about it. Your first step is to narrow down the topic not only from pet, to your own pet, but to how you want to approach the topic. To do so, you must first complete a prewriting step. This may be done in one or more of the following ways: freewriting, focused freewriting, brainstorming, collaborative brainstorming, clustering, or answering journalistic questions.

In **freewriting** you are completing an activity that is comparable to warm-up exercises that you might do before you go jogging or running. Let your mind wander and then begin writing about whatever comes to mind. Since you are trying to discover a topic to write your essay about, you will move from total freedom to the topic that you have in mind—something dealing with your assignment. Write quickly for a time that you have set, say five minutes, and do not worry about spelling, punctuation, grammar or anything else. The goal of freewriting and focused freewriting is to get your mind actively engaged in discovering a topic for this paper. When you are finished, review what you have written, highlighting any idea that is relevant. You can add the details later.

Since you already have a pet and you know what you want to write about it, you can complete **focused freewriting** instead of allowing yourself to write whatever comes to your mind about any pet. You will probably find that you have anecdotes about times you have shared with your pet. You might write about when and how you and your pet first met. You might write about interesting characteristics about your pet. As you see in the word-phrase-sentence example above, the animal being discussed is an unusual cat that has a loud cry. In focused freewriting, you allow your mind to move from one idea to the next without censoring yourself about what should or should not come next. This exercise is meant to generate ideas that can later be developed.

Another prewriting strategy is **brainstorming** (or **collaborative brainstorming**). To brainstorm, determine the topic that you have to write about and then quickly jot down ideas, questions, phrases, words, or comments that might be related to the topic. For example, if you were writing about pets, you might have a piece of paper with the following brainstorming notes.

Focused Brainstorming

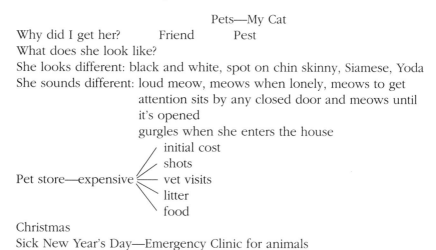

Pets—My Cat

Why did I get her?   Friend   Pest

What does she look like?

She looks different: black and white, spot on chin skinny, Siamese, Yoda

She sounds different: loud meow, meows when lonely, meows to get
                          attention sits by any closed door and meows until
                          it's opened
                          gurgles when she enters the house

Pet store—expensive
- initial cost
- shots
- vet visits
- litter
- food

Christmas

Sick New Year's Day—Emergency Clinic for animals

As you can see from this example, **focused brainstorming** moves in different directions, questioning and associating freely based on the narrowed topic that is given. When you participate in collaborative brainstorming, you have the opportunity to brainstorm with a small group in class or with the class as a whole. In that kind of exercise, even more ideas can be raised because of the number of people participating.

Since you already know you will write about your pet, you do not necessarily need to participate in collaborative brainstorming unless you think other students' suggestions or questions might help you add to your own ideas. Other pet owners might have had experiences similar to yours and you might want to jot them down. Or you might want to talk to someone who has the same kind of pet as yours to see if your pet's eating behavior is similar to his or hers. This will give you material for writing a comparison-and-contrast paper.

If you decide to use the **prewriting** strategy called **clustering,** you will make free associations with the topic of your choice, allowing yourself to add more to each point that you associate. (See the example on the next page.)

You will sometimes find that as you complete the clustering (or **webbing or mapping,** as this strategy is sometimes called), you will have a disproportionate diagram as well as extensive information you will have to narrow down for a single-paragraph assignment. You will also find that some associations will be unequal in number.

Clustering

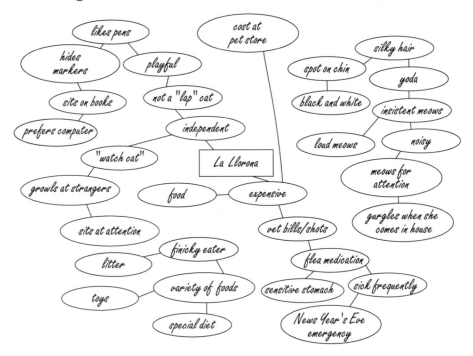

When you use **journalistic questions,** you ask the following:

Who?	When?	How?
What?	Where?	Why?

These questions allow you to explore the **plot** of the story or paragraph to get ideas to develop your topic.

PREWRITING STRATEGIES:

1. **Freewriting and focused freewriting**—exercises that depend on free association in writing as quickly as possible about as many ideas as you can generate in a set time, either about the topic or without restrictions.
2. **Brainstorming and collaborative brainstorming**—exercises that list as many points as possible in single words, phrases, sentences, questions,

and so forth that are associated with your topic. Collaborative brainstorming is completed with a group.

3. **Clustering, webbing, or mapping**—an exercise similar to brainstorming but with the added component of associating not only with the key topic but with the topics that are spinning off the main idea.

4. **Journalistic questions**—an exercise in which you answer the questions who? what? when? where? why? and how? about the topic you are writing about.

➤ Prewriting Exercise I

Now that you have read the section on prewriting, you are prepared to practice prewriting exercises on your own. Below is a list of general topics that can be used with any of the prewriting strategies discussed above. If your instructor does not assign this, you might take a little time on your own to freewrite, brainstorm, cluster, or create journalistic questions to help you feel at ease with these techniques.

1. holidays	4. vacation spots	7. languages
2. cars	5. sports	8. cultures
3. summer jobs	6. music	9. traditions

➤ Prewriting Exercise II

Now complete a prewriting exercise on the topic that your instructor has given you for your paragraph. Remember that you do not have to use all four strategies. Choose the one that feels most comfortable for you and that will give you the most supporting information to choose from.

Taking Control

If you look back at the brainstorming and clustering strategies one student completed, you will see that since there are so many ideas present, he has to take control of the direction his paragraph will follow. This means narrowing his topic. Looking at the clustering example, you will find that the writer can write a descriptive paragraph about *La Llorona* or he can write a personal narrative. If he talked to others who own cats and discovered characteristics that *La Llorona* had in common with other cats, he can also write a comparison-and-contrast paper. He might choose, however, to focus on only one of the modes: comparison or contrast.

The Descriptive Paragraph

A **descriptive** paragraph appeals to as many of the senses—sight, smell, taste, hearing, and touch—as applicable. *La Llorona's* owner, Julian, is going to write a descriptive paragraph about her. He will have to convey to his readers how she looks, sounds, smells, and feels. In other words, he cannot simply depend on his visual impression of the cat. And since her name and many of her characteristics indicate that she is a vocal cat, he will want to focus on those traits. Since she is a sickly cat, she might have an offensive odor occasionally, or her food might create a penetrating odor in his house. He might or might not want to include those ideas. However, it is his choice, since he has quite a number of details. The cluster also includes a reference to Yoda. That might make an interesting detail—a comparison that many science fiction moviegoers will be able to identify with. You might notice that her color and the silkiness of her fur are additional details that appear in the cluster. Beyond her physical descriptions, you might notice that she has a definite personality: not a "lap cat," plays with pens, hides markers, prefers computers, and is a "watch cat." Even though *La Llorona* is not your cat, you, too, as a writer have enough information in the cluster to write a lengthy one-paragraph descriptive paper about her.

But neither you nor Julian is ready to begin writing. Even though he has the pattern for his paragraph, he has not decided on the controlling sentence: his topic sentence. Depending on his instructor, he may place the topic sentence as the first sentence of the paragraph, thus announcing immediately what the paragraph will be about. With this placement, he tells his readers what to expect. Or, he may include it in the middle of the paragraph. With this approach, he would use introductory or explanatory material that leads up to his main idea and follow it with supporting information. Or, he may include the topic sentence at the end of the paragraph. Usually a writer who uses a topic sentence at the end is writing about a controversial topic. In such a case, if the writer were to begin with the **claim** that she is presenting, she would be in danger of losing the audience. Consequently, the writer builds the case gradually and states the topic sentence as the concluding sentence, thereby keeping the attention of the reader to the end. A writer must control not only the direction of the paragraph but also the reader's attention. The topic sentence will help you do that.

A topic sentence also helps you provide unity in your paragraph, ensuring that you remain on topic. If you refer frequently to your topic sentence as you are writing, you should be able to maintain your focus on your subject and on the pattern of development. Remember: The purpose of all sentences that you write in a paragraph is to develop or support the topic sentence. In Julian's case, any sentence that wanders from the description of *La Llorona* will be off topic and will distract his readers from his main purpose.

CHARACTERISTICS OF THE TOPIC SENTENCE

1. It controls the direction and the main idea of the paragraph.
2. It can be located
   - at the beginning of the paragraph, to announce the topic to the reader;
   - in the middle of the paragraph, to allow introductory or explanatory material to come first; or
   - at the end, for controversial topics, so as not to lose the reader.
3. It provides unity, ensuring that the writer remains on topic.

To write a topic sentence for a paragraph on your pet, you must first move from general to specific. The topic "pet" is general. If you move from "pet" to "cat," you have narrowed your topic, but you will not be writing about all the cats in the world. Therefore, you must narrow "cat" even further to your own cat, just as Julian did with *La Llorona*.

DESCRIPTIVE TOPIC SENTENCE

La Llorona's loud meowing at three o'clock in the morning at my closed bedroom door is only one of her qualities that make her dear to me.

As you can see, Julian has indicated that his pet is a cat without mentioning the word. Furthermore, he has indicated that this will be a descriptive paragraph about her by mentioning "her qualities." He has established control and direction, and he is now ready to proceed to the next point.

Organization

To help writers stay on topic, some individuals use a simple outline that will organize the details into a coherent order. You have probably heard your instructor refer to unity and coherence in writing. Be sure not to confuse one term for the other. **Unity** refers to remaining on topic. **Coherence** means that your ideas or details are arranged in a logical order, moving smoothly and logically from one point to the next. If you are writing a descriptive paragraph, you might arrange the details spatially, beginning at one point and proceeding to another: front to back, top to bottom, near to far. You might begin with concrete details—those that you can feel and see—and move to those you must perceive through other senses: smell, hear, and taste. Or you might move in the reverse direction.

Using the topic sentence above and the characteristics from the clustering example, you will see how Julian created an outline for a descriptive paragraph.

First, he stated his topic sentence.

La Llorona's **loud meowing at three o'clock in the morning at my closed bedroom door is only one of her qualities that make her dear to me.**

Second, he reviewed the characteristics in the clustering example and divided them into categories. For example,

   I.   Physical characteristics
  II.   Personality characteristics

Third, he found the words or phrases that fit the categories and placed them under the appropriate division. For example,

   I.   Physical characteristics
      A. Black and white
      B. Spot on her chin

      C. Silky fur

      D. Noisy

      E. Loud meows

  II. Personality characteristics

      A. Playful

      B. Not a "lap cat"

      C. Likes to play with pens

      D. Hides markers

      E. "Watch cat"

Although there are other characteristics, Julian has taken control of the paragraph by indicating that these are the qualities he will write about. Notice that this is just a working outline and that the paragraph might be arranged in an order different from the way the characteristics are arranged. Do you see where a change can be made in the first division? Notice that how *La Llorona* sounds comes after what she looks like, but the topic sentence indicates that she is a noisy pet. For coherence, the writer should continue the description of *La Llorona* as a cat that meows loudly rather than move immediately into what she looks like and back to what she sounds like.

    Notice also that in the prewriting Julian mentions only one characteristic, of *La Llorona* being a "watch cat." Unless the writer elaborates by using other qualities to support that thought, the paragraph will be underdeveloped in that section. He might drop the characteristic, add more points to expand the idea, or change to another one. Because this is an **informal outline,** the writer may change points as he goes along. The writer may even add points not considered during the **prewriting** or outlining processes, as long as the new ideas remain on topic and flow smoothly.

The First Draft

Let's look at the first draft of the paragraph describing *La Llorona.*

> [1]La Llorona's loud meowing at three o'clock in the morning at my closed bedroom door is only one of her qualities that make her dear to me. [2]She made so much noise, I had to ask the salesperson to pick her out of the case and let me hold her. [3]It was then that I noticed that she looked like she had been put in a clothes drier to fluff dry. [4]When she looked up at me with her big, blue eyes and I saw that spot on her chin, I knew that I could not leave without taking her with me. [5]Llorona grew to look like Yoda from *Star Wars* movies with her big ears and pointed nose. [6]Where Yoda is reverentially quiet, Llorona screams her demands to be allowed into any room that has a closed door. [7]Once she is inside, she looks around and walks out, satisfied that nothing needs her attention. [8]If she does not get the attention she wants, she will either meow at the nearest person or stand beside her chosen human until he or she bends down to rub her tummy.

If you read the paragraph, you see that although it looks complete, there are spots where information appears to be missing. Look at the beginning of sentence 2. There seems to be a gap between when the cat cries in the morning and when she was crying at the pet store. As you continue reading, you discover in sentence 4 that she has "big blue eyes" and a "spot on her chin," as well as "big ears and pointed nose" in sentence 5 (comparing her to Yoda), but you still don't know what color she is, even though the outline clearly indicates that she is black and white. In fact, those are the only sentences that attempt to describe her physically. The writer then reverts to her meows and begins to discuss her personality. Notice that sentence 6 is a comparison-and-contrast sentence, contrasting the cat's noisy quality with Yoda's quiet nature. Although the paragraph stops, it does not conclude. The author does not use a **concluding sentence,** one that pulls the ideas together to make this paragraph sound complete. The **peer editor** of the writer of this paragraph should tell the student to add more details and a concluding sentence when he revises it.

Revision

Now let's look at the revised version. The highlighted words and sentences have been added to the original.

> ^{1}La Llorona's loud meowing at three o'clock in the morning at my closed bedroom door is only one of her qualities that make her dear to me. ^{2}**In fact, her meows were what called my attention to her among the other kittens in the showcase of the pet store.** ^{3}**She was screaming so loudly that her cries could be heard by everyone standing around looking at the kittens.** ^{4}She made so much noise, I had to ask the salesperson to pick her out of the case and let me hold her. ^{5}It was then that I noticed that she looked like she had been put in a clothes drier **on the fluff cycle.** ^{6}**She was almost weightless beneath all that soft black and white fur.** ^{7}When she looked up at me with her big, blue eyes and I saw that **black** spot on her chin, I knew that I could not leave without taking her with me. ^{8}**Even though she continued to meow loudly as the salesperson sold me accessories and completed the transaction, I was reassured that she simply missed her mother and that she would eventually grow out of her vocalizations.** ^{9}**How wrong that statement was!** ^{10}As she grew older, the only thing that changed was her fluffy fur. ^{11}It is now silky and smooth instead of standing out, making her look like a ball of fluff. ^{12}Llorona **only** grew to look like Yoda from *Star Wars* movies with her big ears and pointed nose. ^{13}Where Yoda is reverentially quiet, Llorona screams her demands to be allowed into any room that has a closed door. ^{14}Once she is inside, she looks around and walks out, satisfied that nothing needs her attention. ^{15}**If she has been outside for a while, she sits on the window sill that looks into the den and demands entrance.** ^{16}When she saunters in, she gurgles her thanks at being allowed to enter or her irritation at being made to wait so long. ^{17}She then throws herself onto the

kitchen floor where everyone has to step over her or move her out of the way. [18]If she does not get the attention she wants, she will either meow at the nearest person or stand beside her chosen human until he or she bends down to rub her tummy. [19]**Even though I left the Spanish word for cat,** *gata* **off her name, La Llorona, it is understood, and she certainly fulfills its translation: The Hollering Kitty.**

Even though a writer lengthens a piece, that does not always mean that it has been improved. In this case, however, you should see that the new, high-lighted material includes more details, both those that were on the outline and from the clustering. It also relies on the use of contrast again in sentences 8–11. Furthermore, in writing the concluding sentence, Julian pulls you back to the name he gave the cat and explains not only that it is Spanish but its significance to his pet. If you do not know the Mexican myth of *La Llorona*, you might ask your classmates about her to see if the name, in fact, does fit the pet.

As you can see, Julian has chosen to complete the instructor's assignment to write a paragraph about his pet in a descriptive mode. When you read the paragraph, you should be able to visualize *La Llorona* in your mind's eye and possibly hear her loud crying in your imagination. You are receiving both visual and auditory images of the cat, and if you know the myth of the Hollering Woman, you can even see her in your mind moving from place to place, calling for her children. You can also see that the author has inserted emotional language into the paragraph, creating a **subjective** description, one that moves beyond a simple presentation of the subject to create a personal tone that enhances the message. If this paragraph were simply about the cat's loud cries, demands, and personality and did not include some indication of how the author felt about the pet, the paragraph would be an **objective** description, one that describes the subject clearly but remains outside the emotional world.

Only the writer can determine what **tone** she wants to set when writing the piece. As a beginning writer, this should be important to you; you should also be aware that even major authors are concerned about this element in their writing. For example, Edgar Allan Poe, Anne Rice, Stephen King, and others use tone to achieve a certain effect: horror, fear, curiosity. They may build the tension in a scene to scare the reader by referring to the unknown, to darkness, or to the emotions of a character. Although you are not necessarily writing to entertain, you want to create a certain effect in your reader by using tone.

A DESCRIPTIVE PARAGRAPH

1. conveys to the render how the subject of the paper looks, sounds, smells, tastes, and feels through specific details, both **concrete** and **abstract;**
2. uses a topic sentence that indicates the paragraph will be descriptive;
3. may be organized spatially: from top to bottom, near to far, front to back, and so forth;

4. may be written as **subjective description** (including emotions);
5. may be written as **objective description** (omitting references to emotions); and
6. may be concerned with tone.

It is also important to remember that just because a writer chooses to use a certain **mode** of writing, primarily, in this case, description, there are no rules that say other modes cannot also be incorporated to aid in description. By describing *La Llorona* as a kitten and later as an adult cat, the writer uses contrast. He uses comparison and contrast to show how even though *La Llorona* looks like Yoda, she does not sound like him. This mode of comparison also incorporates exemplification, or the use of an example that the writer believes the readers should be familiar with. As you can see, description does not rely solely on listing adjective after adjective but can use other modes of writing as well.

Remember also that once you finish revising your paragraph you must take time to edit it for spelling, punctuation, syntax, and sentence structure.

For descriptive writing by a published author, look at the last paragraph of Anne Perrin's essay, "Kids," in Chapter 2: Youth.

➤ Short Writing Assignment

Look at the prewriting exercise you completed earlier. Using the points you wrote in your prewriting exercise, construct your topic sentence so that you will control your paragraph. Choose the points you want to use from your prewriting exercise based on your topic sentence. Now that you are finished prewriting, write your first draft. It is best to let the draft sit on your desk or in your computer for a few days before returning to it, but if you don't have time, take it to a reader who can spot problems and be honest. You don't want a reader who will simply praise it when you know it probably needs improvement. After you have had someone read it, make the corrections in your second draft. Make sure you have included the following points:

- a topic sentence;
- descriptive words, phrases, examples, and so forth;
- use of one or two senses beyond the visual;
- some emotional description;
- a clear organizational pattern; and
- a concluding sentence.

The Personal Narrative

Although the preceding paragraph on *La Llorona* was written in a descriptive mode, if you review the clustering and the brainstorming strategies again, you will find that the paragraph could have been written from a different perspective. The owner of the cat could have discussed his experiences with the pet. You already know that the writer bought *La Llorona* as a kitten from a pet store, that the owner has watched *La Llorona* grow up, and that he, among other members of his house-hold, has to step around the cat in the kitchen and open doors for her. These details were worked into a descriptive paragraph that not only describes the pet but also gives a little insight into what it is like to live with the animal. Elements of personal narrative have been included but are not the primary focus of the paragraph. Now you will have an opportunity to watch the author construct a paragraph about *La Llorona* telling you a story, a **personal narrative,** about an incident with the cat.

As with the descriptive paragraph, you must take control of the direction of the paragraph by constructing a topic sentence that indicates that this will be a personal narrative. In this case, since the incident happened to you and to the animal, the topic sentence needs to indicate the main participants in the **narrative.** Since the paragraph is also going to tell a story, the topic sentence should also briefly identify the incident.

TOPIC SENTENCE FOR THE PERSONAL NARRATIVE

I woke up New Year's Day concerned because my cat, La Llorona, was not crying loudly at my door to be let in.

Looking at this sentence, you should see that the participants are intro-duced, but the actual incident is not. Questions arise in the reader's mind: Did the cat get out? Was the cat caught in another room? Was she in trouble and un-able to meow? This topic sentence hints that something was wrong and creates curiosity in the reader, causing her to want to discover the change in the cat's behavior. You may want to use this as a topic sentence for a practice paragraph. Look at the next sentence that Julian wrote.

TOPIC SENTENCE FOR A PERSONAL NARRATIVE

On New Year's Day, only six weeks after I bought La Llorona from the local pet store, I woke up to find her lying listlessly in the den next to a small mound of regurgitated food.

This example is clearly much more specific about the direction of the para-graph. The reader has no doubt that the kitten is sick, and there is a weak sug-gestion that the local pet store might be involved.

If you look at the clustering and brainstorming strategies, you will be able to find details that point to the creation of this narrative. But because this will be a story, not just a description, you may want to answer the **journalistic ques-tions** instead of making an outline. Just as a reporter tries to discover all the facts before she writes the news article, an essay writer wants to know all the el-ements of the story, also.

Therefore, using the details in the two prewriting strategies he used, Julian fills in the answers to the journalistic questions:

JOURNALISTIC QUESTIONS

Who? La Llorona, her owner, the vet

What? La Llorona is sick.

When? New Year's Day morning

Where? At home

Why? Question for the vet to answer

How? Question for the vet to answer

In writing a narrative, there are several elements that you must take into consideration. First, just as in the descriptive paragraph, you must consider the order by which the paragraph will be organized. Because a personal narrative is a story, you may want to organize it **chronologically,** according to time sequence. You will need to use **transitions:** words, phrases, or sentences that move the story smoothly from one point to the next; and you will need to use appropriate verb tense. Because this happened to you, you will usually tell the story in the past tense. Look at the sample topic sentences above. Julian begins in the past tense, using the following verbs: *woke* and *was* [not] *crying* in the first sentence, and *bought* and *woke* in the second. Another element that should be included in the narrative is **description.** Just as the descriptive paragraph included narration, so, too, will the narrative include descriptive details to give the reader a full sense of what happened. Yet another consideration is approach: if this were written by a reporter, he or she might rely on an objective approach; however, because it is a personal narrative, the subjective approach will probably work more effectively. Therefore, the writer will describe emotions he experienced. You might also use **personification,** or the attributing of human characteristics to a nonhuman subject.

The First Draft
Let's look at the first draft of the paragraph.

> [1]I woke up New Year's Day concerned because my cat, La Llorona, was not crying loudly at my door. [2]Worried, I jumped out of the warmth and comfort of my bed and into the chilly room. [3]Walking into the den, I spotted what looked like a black and white rug lying beside an unidentifiable mound. [4]I rushed for the telephone book, looked under veterinarians, and miraculously found

a local 24-hour emergency clinic. [5]Talking to her to reassure her, as well as myself, that she would be ok, I ran to the bedroom to change and clean up. [6]I then hauled out the hated animal carrier, and I placed a soft towel in it to soften the bumps in the road. [7]We were the only patients at the vet's office, so La Llorona was seen immediately. [8]The vet took the kitten's temperature and blood samples, examined her thoroughly, and prescribed two kinds of medication. [9]The vet finally took a stool sample and gave me directions about caring for La Llorona during the next few days. [10]The most humorous yet hear-wrenching image I will carry forever with me is of La Llorona weakly walking—tail dragging, head down—into her carrier as we prepare to leave the vet's office, sick but on the road to recovery.

Again, the writer has left out a lot of information; therefore, the paragraph should raise questions in your mind. For example, why didn't the owner check the kitten before getting the phone book? Why was the animal carrier a "hated" object? How far was the emergency clinic from home? Did the vet offer any explanation for *La Llorona's* condition? Although there is a tone of concern for the sick kitten, the writer sounds more worried about getting to the vet than about the condition of the pet.

Revision

With these points in mind, let's look at the new draft. Remember, the highlighted parts are new words and sentences that have been added. The author also edited the work by changing "hear-wrenching" to "heart-wrenching."

[1]I woke up New Year's Day concerned because my cat, La Llorona, was not crying loudly at my door. **[2]Accustomed to early morning wake-up calls for food and attention, much like an infant who has recently come home from the hospital, I checked my clock and discovered that I had slept past nine o'clock.** [3]Worried, I jumped out of the warmth and comfort of my bed and into the chilly room. **[4]I opened the door—no kitty waiting to rush past me and climb up the covers to find a spot among the blanket and sheet.** [5]Walking into the den, I spotted what looked like a black and white rug lying beside an unidentifiable mound. **[6]La Llorona opened her eyes as she heard me approach, and I could see the effort it took for her to lift her head. [7]She opened her mouth, but the noisy meow remained silent. [8]Unconcerned with the regurgitated food on the carpet, I picked her up, and she felt even lighter than when I first held the squirming active kitty four weeks before. [9]Questions raced through my mind: What vet would be open today? [10]What made her sick? [11]Was it my fault? [12]Will she live? [13]Putting her down gently in her favorite spot,** I rushed for the telephone book, looked under veterinarians, and miraculously found a local 24-hour emergency clinic. [14]Talking to her to reassure her, as well as myself, that she

would be ok, I ran to the bedroom to change and clean up. [15]I then hauled out the hated animal carrier, and **as** I placed a soft towel in it to soften the bumps in the road, **I had visions of a different kitty: one who hated being confined and fought vigorously at being enclosed.** [16]**On New Year's Day, it was almost as if she had made a resolution to be a better kitty and not fight.** [17]**I wanted my old kitty back.** [18]**I raced to the vet, grateful that no radar units were on patrol that day.** [19]**Even though the clinic was not too far from the house, we arrived in record time since few cars were on the road so early.** [20]We were the only patients at the vet's office, so Llorona was seen immediately. [21]The vet took the kitten's temperature and blood samples, examined her thoroughly, and prescribed two kinds of medication, **explaining that because of the cramped conditions at pet stores, animals sometimes become infected with bacteria and even parasites that incubate for several weeks before making the pet ill.** [22]The vet finally took a stool sample and gave me directions about caring for La Llorona during the next few days. [23]The most humorous yet heart-wrenching image I will carry forever with me is of La Llorona weakly walking **without protest**—tail dragging, head down—into her carrier as we prepared to leave the vet's office, sick but on the road to recovery.

Again, Julian has expanded the paragraph, adding more detail, both emotional and physical, to give the reader a clearer sense of his experience with his pet. Look at the journalistic questions and see if all of the questions have been answered to your satisfaction. Because this is a story, you should feel tension mounting. Do you? Do you feel a movement that indicates a beginning, a middle, and an end? Do you feel satisfied with the concluding sentence? Do you have any questions that have not been answered in your mind? Although the narrative includes another person, the vet, you do not hear the doctor speaking directly. Instead, you read a paraphrased version of the doctor's explanation of the cat's condition. Do you think dialogue would have enhanced the paragraph or do you like the way it is written without the dialogue? Explain your answer.

THE PERSONAL NARRATIVE

1. tells a story about an event that happened to the author;
2. includes descriptive detail;
3. is usually subjective rather than objective;
4. is usually organized chronologically
5. uses transitions to move the action smoothly from one point to the next;
6. has a defined beginning, middle, and end;

continued

THE PERSONAL NARRATIVE CONTINUED

7. sometimes builds emotional tension;
8. may be written from the first-person point of view;
9. usually includes other individuals;
10. may but does not have to include dialogue;
11. provides a conclusion that indicates that the experience is over and any problems have been resolved or no longer exist;
12. is usually written in past tense; and
13. may or may not include a lesson and that was learned from the - experience.

To see how a published author wrote an extended descriptive personal narrative, you might want to read "The Struggle to Be an All-American Girl" by Elizabeth Wong in Chapter 6: Language.

Comparison-and-Contrast Paragraph

As you have seen in the sample paragraphs about the pet, *La Llorona*, the author has incorporated elements of comparison and contrast to add to the details of the pieces. By now you should be discovering that most writing is not completed in a single **mode.** Instead, a writer may incorporate different modes to convey the idea that he or she is trying to present. If, however, your instructor wants you to write in a specifically **comparison-and-contrast** mode, you can do so.

Many students confuse the terms *comparison* and *contrast*, thinking they mean the same thing. To **compare** means to point out the similarities between two objects, people, animals, concepts, or other entities. You want to find as many characteristics as possible that they have in common. For example, if you have siblings who have gone to the same school you attended, you might have heard former teachers tell you, "You are just like your sister." They are making comparisons between two people. Sometimes history instructors want you to find comparable points between the causes of two wars or two strategies used to fight a war. A biology teacher might want you to find the similarities between an ant colony and a beehive. An English instructor might want you to compare two poems or two characters in a novel. An art instructor might want you to compare two styles of painting. What they are asking you to do is to look at objects, concepts, writings, fictional characters, and behaviors to find their similarities. These assignments require higher-level thinking skills because you have to **analyze** the objects and so forth for particular qualities and look at them individually to see which characteristics they share.

The same is true of **contrast;** however, when you perform a contrast exercise, you are finding the differences between two given elements. For example, your former teachers may have told you, "You are so different from your brother." Or the instructors mentioned in the above paragraph may make the assignment changing the words "compare" and "find their similarities" to "contrast" and "find their differences."

Let's look at which points Julian used for *La Llorona*. Julian used the clustering exercise and compared *La Llorona* with Yoda; and he finds that he also has points to contrast: her appearance and her personality.

By writing comparison-and-contrast paragraphs about *La Llorona* and another cat, the writer will be writing to inform his or her readers. However, as the above hypothetical assignments by instructors in different classes demonstrate, there might be another purpose for writing in a comparison-and-contrast mode. The history instructor might want the students to compare and contrast strategies to determine which one is better, thus using this mode as a form of **persuasion.** The art instructor might ask the student to compare and contrast styles to encourage the student to make an **evaluation** of the styles from his or her own appreciation of art. This kind of comparison and contrast is frequently done when shoppers are trying to determine which brand to buy, which sofa would look better in their living room, which bank account would yield better service and interest, and so forth. Although you may be writing one of your first comparison-and-contrast papers, you will find that you perform this kind of analysis in your daily life. You are simply formalizing a process that you have been working with for years.

Writing both a comparison paragraph and a contrast paragraph using *La Llorona* might take some more prewriting. The three prewriting strategies discussed so far have focused on the cat and her owner, with no references to any other cat. The writer could compare and/or contrast the young *La Llorona* with the adult cat and use the material provided. However, if Julian is interested in seeing how *La Llorona* acts, eats, or becomes ill in comparison to other cats, he will have to take more notes, interview other cat owners, or rely on memories of cats that he owned in the past. In this case, Julian also has another female cat, bought at approximately the same time and at the same place as *La Llorona*. They are almost the same age, and except for a few days, they have grown up together. Therefore, he will rely on observed behavior rather than on gathering information from others about their cats.

To determine the direction the paragraph will go, Julian must decide whether to combine the similarities and differences within one paragraph or separate them into two. The controlling device for the paragraph will continue to be the topic sentence (see next page).

Notice that there is a difference between the first example and the last two. In the first example, the writer maintains a general view of the cats by saying that they "share many qualities" in the first part of the sentence and then focuses on a specific area of contrast; "their personalities differ enormously." The last two examples, however, list three distinct areas *La Llorona*'s owner will use to compare her with or distinguish her from the other cat. Each topic sentence controls the paragraph, but the last two announce specific points to the reader, and the writer must stay within the limits he has set. If he wanders to other areas in his first draft, he may correct the content to follow the topic sentence or he may correct the topic sentence to follow the content. Remember, revision allows for changing the first draft.

TOPIC SENTENCE FOR COMPARISON-AND-CONTRAST PARAGRAPH

My cat, La Llorona, shares many qualities with my other cat, Gabby, but their personalities differ enormously.

TOPIC SENTENCE FOR A COMPARISON PARAGRAPH

My cat, La Llorona, shares many qualities with my other cat, Gabby, in the areas of predatory behavior, finicky eating habits, and age.

TOPIC SENTENCE FOR A CONTRAST PARAGRAPH

My cat, La Llorona, is quite different from my other cat, Gabby, in the areas of personality, size, and health.

The First Draft

For the **first draft** of the comparison-and-contrast paragraph, Julian has chosen to focus on the characteristics that show the differences between her and Gabby. The writer has developed a prewriting cluster, similar to the one he created for *La Llorona*, and has selected differing characteristics to focus on. He chose the last topic sentence to organize the paragraph.

[1]My cat, La Llorona, is quite different from my other cat, Gabby, in the areas of personality, size, and health. [2]Both cats were purchased at the same time; however, Llorona is a few weeks older than Gabby. [3]Despite the fact that Llorona is the "senior" cat, Gabby is much bigger. [4]This comes from their heritage. [5]Gabby is bigger because she is a tabby that has bigger bones and puts on weight more easily. [6]Llorona, on the other hand, is part Siamese even though she does not display the color typical of a Siamese. [7]Siamese cats are more nervous and active than tabbies which accounts for their difference in size. [8]Llorona is quite slender even though she eats almost as much as Gabby. [9]Being from different cat families could also explain the difference in their personalities. [10]While Gabby likes to find a quiet spot or a comfortable lap for a nap after she eats, Llorona races around the house, chasing real or imaginary flying bugs. [11]As a kitten, Llorona always chased her tail, but Gabby couldn't be bothered with such activity. [12]Today Llorona continues to tail chase while all Gabby catches are dreams. [13]When they go outside, their personalities develop even further in different directions. [14]Although they are both in generally good health from eating and sleeping, if one is

going to get sick, it will be Llorona. [15]Her Siamese nervousness frequently affects her stomach, making her have diarrhea.
[16]Gabby, on the other hand, goes through life comfortable and
without Llorona's misery.

Analysis

Even though you cannot talk with Julian, you can read his paragraph with a critical eye, especially since you have seen two previous assignments move from
first draft to second. You will now complete a **peer analysis** in which you analyze this paragraph based on criteria for writing a comparison-and-contrast paper.

PEER ANALYSIS EXERCISE

First, read the paragraph completely without marking it. Then, answer each
question by making a checkmark beneath the work *Yes, No*, or *Almost*.

Criteria   Yes   No   Almost

1. Does the writer provide a topic sentence? _____

2. Does the topic sentence indicate a
comparison-and-contrast mode or one
of the two? _____

3. Do you know the subjects the writer will
compare and/or contrast? _____

4. Do you know the qualities the author will will
use to compare and/or contrast? _____

5. Is each quality fully explained in the
paragraph? _____

6. Is each quality discussed in the order given
in the topic sentence? _____

7. Did the writer focus only on the qualities
announced in his topic sentence? _____

8. Does the writer provide a good
concluding sentence? _____

9. What questions would you want to ask the writer about his first draft?

10. What suggestions would you give the author to correct any criterion that
was not marked *Yes*? Address each individually.

The answers to the criteria questions are on the last page of this section, and the answers to the short-answer questions will vary. As a peer editor, you should be as careful and objective as possible, to help the writer improve the quality of and meet the requirements for his paper. You should not give the writer false information if, in fact, you see problems. As a writer, you want a peer editor to be honest in editing your paper. It would be nice if all the marks fell under *Yes,* but that doesn't always happen. You need an honest and good reader who will tell you the truth about your writing so you can improve it.

Revision

We can assume that Julian had a good peer editor. Read the second draft below and determine if he fixed the problems in the first draft.

Second Draft

[1]My cat, La Llorona, is quite different from my other cat, Gabby, in the areas of size, personality, and health. [2]Both cats were purchased at the same time; however, Gabby is much bigger even though Llorona is the "senior" cat. [3]This comes from their heritage. [4]Gabby is a tabby that has bigger bones and puts on weight more easily. [5]Llorona, on the other hand, is part Siamese even though she does not display the color typical of a Siamese. [6]Siamese cats are more nervous and active than tabbies which accounts for their difference in size. [7]Llorona is quite slender even though she eats almost as much as Gabby. [8]Being from different cat families could also explain the difference in their personalities. [9]While Gabby likes to find a quiet spot or a comfortable lap for a nap after she eats, Llorona races around the house, chasing real or imaginary flying bugs. [10]As a kitten, Llorona always chased her tail, but Gabby couldn't be bothered with such activity. [11]Today Llorona continues to tail chase while all Gabby catches are dreams. [12]When they go outside, their personalities develop even further in different directions. [13]Llorona crouches in tall grass, attempting to catch birds, squirrels, or other trespassers in her yard. [14]Her nervous impatience, however, warns her prey when they see the grass shaking. [15]Gabby, on the other hand, finds activity tiresome and prefers to sit in the sun and preen in preparation for another long nap. [16]Although they are both in generally good health from eating and sleeping, if one is going to get sick, it will be Llorona. [17]Her Siamese nervousness frequently affects her stomach, making her have diarrhea. [18]Gabby, on the other hand, goes through life comfortable and without Llorona's misery. [19]Even though they are different, they are good companions and provide quite a bit of entertainment to me and my family.

If we practice comparison-and-contrast analysis now, we should see the following similarities and differences:

- The topic sentence is the same but it has been reorganized.
- Rather than omit sentence 2, it has been reorganized to show that age, a frequent indicator of size, is not a cause of the difference in cat size in *La Llorona* and Gabby.
- Sentences 3 through 7 remain because they provide the causes of the cats' sizes. This is a development of the point.
- Sentences 13 through 15 were added to develop sentence 12.
- Sentence 19 is the newly added concluding sentence.

In looking at this contrast model, you as a student writer should remember that this is not the only way to write a contrastive paragraph. For more information about comparison and contrast, you can turn to the section "Writing the Essay." Although we will return to *La Llorona* in essay writing, for the moment we will allow her to chase her visions without us as we move on to different topics and to different modes of writing.

➤ Short Writing Assignments

1. Based on the topic you used to create a prewriting exercise, think of a similar topic that you can compare or contrast with your original topic. Follow a prewriting exercise and then write a comparison or contrast paragraph.
2. Using a first and second draft of a paper you have already written, write a comparison-and-contrast analysis similar to the one that followed the second draft contrasting *La Llorona* with Gabby.

Cause and Effect

The purpose of writing a cause and effect paragraph is to show why events occur and the outcome. Frequently, history instructors ask students to analyze a battle strategy to see how the plans contributed to the success or failure of the battle. They also want students to consider other factors that contributed to the outcome, for example, weather, soldiers' fatigue, or diet. When this analysis is completed, the student writes a paper that discusses or explains the causes for the outcome of that particular battle.

If you return to the contrastive paragraph, which explains the differences between *La Llorona's* and Gabby's eating habits, you will discover that in addition to being written as contrastive, it also fits the criterion for a causal paragraph. Because of each cat's eating habits and activity, they are different sizes. Julian explains that each cat eats almost the same amount but that their activity differs. While there are other factors, he has chosen to focus on those two.

If Julian were to investigate the effects of their eating habits and activity, he might discover that difference in size is only one of the effects. For example, if Gabby is eating more and sleeping or resting after her meals, she could be gaining extra weight, increasing her cholesterol, and losing her ability to preen properly or adequately defend herself in a threatening situation. *La Llorona*, on the other hand, might be more fit physically, have a more playful personality, be a more successful predator of birds and squirrels, and be better able to defend herself than Gabby.

➤ Short Writing Assignment

1. Using the above information, construct a paragraph that begins with an appropriate topic sentence about the effects of the cats' eating habits and activity patterns. Then develop the points mentioned, and end with a good concluding sentence.
2. Write a cause or effect paragraph based on one of the following topics:

    AIDS   Overeating
    Energy depletion   Changing graduation requirements
    Unemployment   Annual forest fires
    Space junk   Reducing the protection of national parks
    Divorce   "Drive-through" weddings

Exemplification

To create an **exemplification** paragraph, writers use specific illustrations or examples to support or develop an **assertion.** Many speakers and teachers use this technique to clarify their message. If you watched the 2000 presidential debates and speeches when Al Gore and George W. Bush were running against each other, you would have heard Gore discuss HMOs as a general concept and then create a concrete context, by referring to specific families with specific medical problems. To help the general public understand a complex issue, Gore used exemplification, incorporating everyday illustrations everyone could identify with. Read the following paragraph and see if you can find examples of clichés the author is encouraging his students to remove from their writing.

> Teaching students to recognize and rid their writing of clichés has been an uphill battle. Teachers fight tooth and nail to convince their writers to reduce the number of clichés because readers can spot them a mile away. Therefore, instead of producing original writing, students use "trite, stereotype expressions" that they think will work well for them but that only leave them sadder but wiser when they get their grade back. However, regardless of the many times teachers get on their soapbox, students dig their heels in and refuse to tow the mark. Sometimes teachers think they have put the cart before the horse by telling students what not to do before teaching them vocabulary skills. In fact, some teachers are afraid of throwing the baby out with the bath water by stifling the students' creativity. Needless to say, it's a never-ending battle that almost requires the heart of a lion to jump into the fray and try to succeed despite all odds, knowing it's in their students' best interest that they give it the All-American try and help them win one, if not for themselves then, for the Gipper.

THE PARAGRAPH • 39

Hopefully, you will not only recognize the number of examples the writer has used to make her point, you will also see the humor in the piece. By using exaggeration and repetition, teachers convey their ideas to their students, but they do not necessarily bore their students or antagonize them. The use of examples and illustrations provides an excellent way to clarify information.

➤ Short Writing Assignment

Write an exemplification paragraph over one of the following topics:

Pets	Vacation spots
Wars	Boring activities
Comfort food	Your ideas of success
Swim wear	Lines men give women/women give men
Parents' rules	Television talk shows

Definition

A definition paragraph provides the meaning of a concept or object in various ways. Definitions themselves come in two forms: denotative and connotative. A denotative definition is one that comes directly from a dictionary; a connotative definition suggests emotional or personal secondary meanings attached to certain terms. For example, although a home is considered a residence, to think of home in terms of family, love and warmth is to attach a connotative or secondary meaning to the word *home*. To write definition paragraphs, a student may use other patterns or modes of development: narration, exemplification or process. If you analyze the following exemplification paragraph, you will find that the author his incorporated a denotative definition and numerous examples to define the term **cliché** even further. Read the following example and decide which pattern(s) are being used.

> Mother's Day is the one day set aside to honor the woman who gave birth to us or who raised us as her children. When we think of our mothers, we frequently recall incidents such as the time she left work early to be present at a recital or when we were sick, and she stayed up all night at our bedside. The qualities of love, dedication, sacrifice, concern, and nurturing appear instantly in those incidents, and we have an image in our minds of a woman who is forever young and always there when we need her. Today's mom, however, has changed somewhat from the saccharine depiction Hallmark displays. The contemporary mom in many cases has replaced the apron (she probably doesn't even own one) with a briefcase and her time embroidering with chauffeuring children to different activities. Homemade cookies are now baked from the rolls of dough found in the refrigerated section in the grocery store, and pizza delivery is now a routine way to have dinner. Mothers may have changed in their activities, but we know that their love and care haven't.

➤ Short Writing Assignments

1. Analyze the above paragraph for the different patterns that are used or suggested. You will find that writers incorporate a variety of modes regardless of the primary pattern they use. As you write more notice how your style is changing. List the different patterns, give a specific example, and explain how it can be used to help write a definition paragraph.
2. Refer to the assignment following the "exemplification" section. Choose one topic and incorporate definition, denotative and connotative, into the paragraph that you write.

Division and Classification

Division and classification paragraphs are different from each other. A division paragraph breaks a single item into many components. For example, if you look at the title of this section of your text, you will see it is called "The Paragraph." To create an orderly approach to instruction, the section is divided into smaller units: "Description," "Personal Narrative," "Comparison-and-Contrast," and so forth. Another example is a house. A house is normally not composed of one large room, and even when it is, for example a loft in a converted building, the residents use dividers to create spaces with certain purposes and separated from the other spaces: living room, kitchen, bedroom, and so forth. Consider the following paragraph about an assisted living facility.

> Because my mother is still an active, vital woman who needs the companionship, activities, and care I cannot provide, she moved into an assisted living facility, The Towers. This was a perfect choice for her because her apartment is quite large, accommodating much of her furniture and giving her a sense of living at "home." Many of the other facilities we visited offered a large single room that was frequently shared by a roommate. The Towers has several floors on which individuals with different needs live. My mother has the companionship of others who are in similar health condition, active, and relatively independent. The friends she has made in the building are mainly her neighbors who enjoy many of the same activities offered by the staff: gardening, bridge, and weekly trips to the mall and grocery store. Another component of The Towers is the care they provide. My mother is on a floor that has a registered nurse to dispense medication three times a day for residents who need it. The nurse also offers daily blood pressure screening, nutrition advice for residents with special dietary needs, exercise classes, and office hours for personal consultation. The living conditions, residents, and care are components that answer the needs of many looking for an assisted living facility.

As you read the paragraph, you should note that the author breaks down even the component of his mother's facility into smaller elements. He also uses contrast to describe how his mother's living quarters are different from those offered by other senior citizen homes.

The following paragraph is an example of classification. Instead of taking an item and breaking it down, it takes a number of separate items and categorizes them based on shared characteristics. The key to good classification is to make sure that there are at least three categories, and that they do not overlap. Think about the food in a grocery store or the merchandise in a department store. The items have been categorized for the shoppers' convenience in locating each item. Read the following paragraph that classifies movies.

> Today's parents have enough worries to concern them without having to worry about the movies their children go see; therefore, many parents limit their children's viewing by relying on the rating systems used to classify each film. If their children are eighteen years old or younger, parents may allow them to choose from movies labeled G for a general audience of any age or PG, a category that recommends parental guidance because of language, some crude humor, and material unsuitable for children. PG13 is another category that recommends parental guidance with parents being strongly cautioned to give guidance to children younger than thirteen because the movie may contain some objectionable thematic references, language, adventure action, violence, or sensuality that some children are not ready for. On the other hand, movies rated R are restricted for viewers eighteen or older or for individuals seventeen or younger with a parent or adult companion because of scenes of nudity, strong language, intense violence, and mature themes; and NC17 admits no one seventeen or younger. This system, while only as good as the ticket salespeople, is better than no system at all for concerned parents.

➤ Short Writing Assignments

1. Look at one multipurpose room in your house and divide it into components. Write a division paragraph that describes each component using at least one other pattern for writing in this section.
2. Go to your local grocery store and analyze their method of categorization. Remember you need more than two classes, so refrigerated and non-refrigerated foods are categories that are still too broad. Write a paper that classifies the food in your grocery store and use several **patterns** of writing discussed in this section.

Process

Sometimes known as a *how-to* paragraph, a **process analysis** can be written for one of two reasons: to show how something works, such as the digestive system, a jet motor, an ant colony, or a factory, to name a few; or to give step-by-step instructions that someone can follow, such as how to bake a German chocolate cake, how to build a model airplane, how to program a VCR, or how to install software onto your computer. With the number of self-help books on the market that instructs readers how to lose weight, gain self-esteem, reduce the risk of heart attacks, cancer, or other controllable conditions, become a millionaire before you are thirty, and so on, this must be a relatively easy pattern to follow. Describing a process requires the writer to know the system being explained while giving instructions involves being able to give clear, sequential steps so someone can follow the directions. Try teaching a child how to tie her shoelaces. Or, remember the last time you had to follow written directions to hook up your printer to your computer or assemble a child's toy. For an example, read the following **informative** paragraph that describes the system used to run a doctor's office.

> Most people who have had to wait to be seen in a doctor's office think that it is uncaring to those who are sick and inefficiently run; however, there is usually a system in progress that attempts to ensure that all patients are seen in a timely manner. Dr. Zepeda's office was no different from others. At 9.00 clock, Ms. Morales and her assistant receptionist would open the office, check the office systems, and begin answering the phones, making last-minute appointments. By 9:30, the first appointments would begin arriving, fully knowing that the doctor would not be there until 10:00 because he was completing rounds at the hospital or performing surgery. At 9:30 the nurse's aide would arrive and begin preparing rooms, restocking empty jars with tongue depressors, cotton balls, and other required items. She would also begin the pre-examination phase at 9:45, just as the nurse would arrive. The nurse's aide would take the patient's weight, height, temperature and blood pressure, listen to and record their symptoms and tell them how to undress in preparation for the doctor. When the nurse arrived, she would socialize with others, ensure that all was ready, review the patients' charts, and make sure all the rooms were filled so Dr. Zepeda could begin seeing patients after he reviewed the charts at 10:00. By 10:10, Dr. Z had spoken to the staff, put on his white coat, and begun seeing patients. Although patients would be scheduled every ten minutes, some obviously took longer than others. After they were seen, patients would pay their bill, make another appointment if necessary, and leave. By 11:30 everyone would be ready for a fifteen minute break followed by a continuation of the assembly line process that would continue until 3:00 when everyone would break for a thirty-minute lunch. In between patients, the nurse's aide also cleaned rooms and instruments, refilled jars, and put new patients into rooms. Meanwhile the office staff would make appointments, check insurance forms, keep track of billing and payments, and refile charts. At 5:00 the office doors would close, but Dr. Zepeda and his nurse would continue to see late or waiting patients. The assistant receptionist and nurse's aide would leave at that time. At 5:45, Dr. Z would stop seeing patients to reconcile the day's activities and fee collection with Ms. Morales. By 6:00 she would leave and the nurse would assume office staff and nurse's aide's duties until they finished seeing patients. By 7:00 Dr. Zepeda and his nurse would leave the office. Although some patients would have to wait to see Dr. Z after the appointed time, he would see everyone and give each patient his undivided, concerned care that was always reflected in a well-run office.

The above passage was definitely written by someone who knows first-hand the workings of that particular doctor's office. Notice that the tone is objective, not allowing for personal feelings to slip in. The purpose of this kind of process paper is to convey information so that the reader will understand it. An elaborate description of each section is not needed.

The next paragraph gives directions for beginning the process of making a counted cross-stitch work.

I have completed many pieces of embroidery and crewel, but no one can imagine my shock when I opened the package of a beautiful picture entitled Lady Mime and discovered that there was no pattern to follow printed on the fabric. Where do I begin? If you have ever considered completing a counted cross stitch piece, let me offer some directions the package does not give. First, separate the threads into colors using the guide on the package as your number guide. Many people who work with numerous colors of thread use a piece of plastic or cardboard with several small, numbered slits along one edge. Each thread is matched with the number and inserted into the appropriate slit to separate it from the others. If you have only five or six colors of thread, that's fine; but if you have ten, fifteen, or twenty, you run the risk of tangling the thread as each color intertwines with its neighbors. Buy zip-lock baggies instead that are held together with a round key ring. You can use as many as the ring will hold, the thread stays clean, and it doesn't tangle with others. If you have beads, get holders that seal tightly and are easy to dip a needle into. Divide the beads into their properly marked containers and put them aside because they won't be used until the stitching is complete. Next, unfold and iron the fabric. You must find the center point on the fabric, but because it's been folded for packaging, it is not going to be done with precision. Iron out the wrinkles. Then before you fold, either baste the raw edges or use masking tape folded around the edges of the fabric to prevent raveling. Now fold the fabric in half and then in a quarter. The corner that does not open (three corners open and one does not) is the center of your fabric. Mark it by creasing the fabric lightly there or by marking it with a straight pin. Open the fabric, keeping the center marked. That is where you will begin stitching. The rest of the directions are clearly explained on the enclosed directions sheet. Regardless of whether you are a novice counted cross stitcher or an old timer, read the directions completely to avoid surprises. With concentration and perseverance, you should produce an heirloom.

This paragraph was also written by someone who has experience with the process. The importance of her directions is that she provides "trade secrets" newcomers don't know and have no way of knowing without experiencing trial and error first. When the author gets the readers to the point where the directions provided by the manufacturers give adequate instruction, she stops and sends the readers on their way.

➤ Short Writing Assignments

1. Go back to the opening sections of Part I and reread the explanations of learning styles. Write a process paragraph that explains how to determine what kind of a learner your audience is. You might need to complete a little research that explains the characteristics more fully.

2. Everyone is good at doing something. Some people are good at putting in their contact lenses, others are good at baking cookies, while others are good at training dogs. Think of a skill you have that you are very good at. Write a step-by-step set of directions for completing the activity. When you finish writing, follow the directions precisely as they were written, making revisions when needed. Once they say what you want them to say, give them to a friend to follow. Listen to your friend's suggestions,

complaints, or compliments, and revise accordingly. Finally, prepare a copy of the directions for your instructor and present the directions orally to the class, bringing all equipment needed to complete the activity.

Answers to peer analysis of Julian's paper:

1. Yes	5. Almost
2. Yes	6. Almost
3. Yes	7. No
4. Yes	8. No

JOURNALS

The preceding section explained the rules and techniques of writing formal essays. Yet there are other ways to approach writing, and you have been doing them for years. In this section, we will take a more relaxed approach—which does not mean that it is not as important. It means that it does not have the strict rules and formality that were discussed previously. To help you benefit from informal writing, instructors frequently assign personal journals, reader response journals, or letters. Each has a different purpose and approach and usually taps into your more personal and emotional sides.

In a **journal,** writers spend time expressing their feelings, thoughts, and ideas. The writers may be budding poets, short story writers, or essayists, and so they keep the beginnings of new works or ideas that they may not have had time to develop completely in a writer's notebook or journal. By preserving these preliminary ideas in one place, the writers can return to them later, develop the ideas, and produce a finished manuscript. A personal journal may mean different things to different people, but one of the main notions about a journal is that it is usually a private place where the writer can express anything without fear of criticism or embarrassment. So when an instructor indicates that he or she wants you to write a journal entry to be submitted later, it may feel like someone is intruding into your personal, private life. That is a normal feeling but one that you, as a writer, will have to overcome by taking a different perspective on the definition of a journal.

When writing journals for class, you will still be asked to reflect on your feelings about certain topics, but this will be an academic exercise that will help you stretch your understanding of ideas and concepts before or after you have read information about the topic. In some cases, you may have strong feelings about a topic—let's say, your own childhood—and by writing about the topic, you will be able to clarify those feelings. In another assignment, you may be asked to determine where you stand on controversial issues, for example gay rights, before you have been exposed to others' ideas that may make you feel differently. Although you are looking deeply into yourself to determine where you stand and how you feel, you will still have to share this assignment with your instructor and possibly with the members of your class. If a topic is highly emotional to you some instructors may ask you to complete the assignment but will refrain from reading the entry and from calling on you to read it in class. The instructor may ask you to share some of your thoughts, but you will be able to choose those parts that you can discuss without feeling that your privacy has been invaded. Regardless of the issue, it is best to write about the topic, especially if it is highly personal. That way you will know why the selections you read make you angry or make you feel in total agreement. You may discover areas of sensitivity that you did not know you had before. In any case, journal writing helps clarify thoughts, feelings, and ideas. It will help you generate ideas and develop fluency in writing. And it will help you understand the general direction of the reading selections either before or after you read them.

Journal writing, unlike essay writing, may be done in a variety of ways. First, there is generally no formal structure to it. It may or may not be written in paragraph form or even in complete sentences. It may incorporate questions that may remain unanswered until a later date. It may include personal experiences that help explain why you feel a certain way. It may be emotionally expressive and highly critical of a point that bothers you. Or it could be used to analyze your position on daily topics, such as politics, religion, ethics, war, family, and others that you might not want to discuss with anyone else yet because you are still uncertain about where you stand. But the most important point is that journal writing is yours.

JOURNAL ENTRIES CAN BE

- written informally;
- emotionally expressive;
- used to explore your feelings about controversial issues;
- used to record questions that you will answer at a later time;
- a place for private thought that you do not have to share with others;
- a collection of undeveloped ideas for future short stories, essays, poetry, or personal narratives;
- a way to generate writing and become more fluid in expression; and
- a record of special events that you can return to and explore more fully.

➤ Short Writing Assignments

1. Begin keeping a journal in which you will make at least one entry weekly. Allow yourself to reflect over the issues that might have created unhappiness, anger, joy, curiosity, or any other feelings during the week. How did you handle the issues? Could you have acted differently? Record as many of your thoughts and feelings as possible and what they meant to you.

2. Go to your institution's library and find a copy of a writer's journal that has been published. Read it and write an informative report discussing the major topics covered in

the journal, the tone the writer used, and any special features you found as you read. In your conclusion, evaluate the journal for the points listed in the box, giving specific examples of how the journal followed the points.

READER RESPONSE JOURNALS

Similar to personal journals are reader response journals. Instructors frequently assign **reader response journals** to determine that the student is completing the reading assignment and also to see whether the student understands it. This is an excellent way for you to prepare for class discussion, because you can jot down questions you might have, passages you do not understand, or ideas you want to expand. There are several ways to write reader responses, and all can be informal and personal.

The first response may be done as a **paraphrasing** or restatement of the reading assignment. This will help you clarify what you think the work says, help your instructor determine what you find most important, and help you focus on patterns or ideas you might have missed, misunderstood, or misread. Through class discussion about the reading selection, you will be able to share your thoughts as recorded. You will also be able to listen to the responses of your classmates, who have interpretations different from yours. What you may discover about your response, as well as about those of other people's, is that the responses may be coming from a perspective that is based on gender. For example, women may respond quite differently from men to a narrative like "Ain't I a Woman?" (in Chapter 7, Living with Others). Some men do not understand the need women have to declare their identity publicly. Many women, on the other hand, understand and admire Sojourner Truth's courage to stand up and speak at a time when being a slave and/or a woman were reasons for depriving her of her voice and identity.

Another response you might make involves your feelings. In addition to explaining what you read, you may also explain how you feel about what happens in the work. For example, you might identify with a particular character in a story. You might understand, agree, or disagree with the actions performed by certain characters in a story, and you might put yourself in the same position as the character. For example, the short story "What Sally Said" (Chapter 7: Living with Others) may elicit strong feelings from both male and female readers. Male readers may feel angry when they read about the narrator's abuse by her father. Female readers, on the other hand, might feel empathy with Sally and possibly identify with her. Your response can be simple or complex, immediate or in-depth. Regardless of the extent of the response, you are getting involved with the work, which is how you will better understand it.

If you have begun to respond with your feelings, you can move naturally into the third level of response: personal associations with the actions or characters in the work. This response goes beyond sharing a feeling, in that it reflects a sense of your experience and relationship with the work. You might have experienced the same kind of activity that you read about, and you can anticipate the outcome or be surprised at a strange twist. You might also discover that, in addition to responding from a perspective of gender, you might be able to respond from a cultural perspective. For example, in "The Color Yellow" (Chapter 5, Education), the narrator experiences sexist behavior from a female member of her own family. This kind of oppressive treatment of women by older women in one's own culture is not unusual, as the elders are practicing what they have been taught and see no problems involved in such behavior. By writing about your experience, you may be able to clarify in your own mind your feelings about these kinds of experiences, whether you are the one who felt the pain or the one who inflicted it.

One of the things you must remember about reader response journals is that these three types of responses are not mutually exclusive. In other words, you may combine summarizing the work, expressing your feelings, and associating with the characters. You may also ask questions and state opinions. Usually you will not include research unless your instructor directs you to do so. Sometimes, your instructor may give you specific directions or questions to answer about a work. The purpose of the reader response journal is to make sure that you have the opportunity to express your opinions and your understanding about a story, even if you are not prone to speaking up in class.

READER RESPONSE JOURNALS CAN BE

- written informally;
- a way for an instructor to check that you have completed your reading assignment;
- a place where you respond to a reading selection;
- a place to record questions to be asked in class next time you meet;
- a directed assignment that requires that you respond to certain questions the instructor wants you to pursue;
- interpretation of a reading selection;
- expressions of feelings about a reading selection;
- a way to discover the thoughts and feelings of others who have read the same selection; and
- a way to read actively.

➤ Short Writing Assignment

Read any selection from Part II and write a reader response journal entry after you finish. Which of the methods did you use to respond to the work? Could you have used others?

CORRESPONDENCE

E-mail

In this age of speed and technology, the art of letter writing has become almost obsolete. We can make a phone call and connect with the other person, even if the individual we want to talk with is not at home. Cellular phones have made people more accessible at just about any time or in any place.

On the other hand, computers still require that we compose messages to friends in writing. Some writers rely on e-mail instead of the U.S. Postal Service, because of the e-mail's convenience and speed. Electronic mail, or e-mail, retains the semblance of the old-fashioned letter, but it allows for less formality in many cases. Yet, there are some points that writers must keep in mind when writing either formal or informal e-mail messages.

- It is best to avoid slang and imprecise wording. After all, you still have to remember your audience and the fact that the message is being read without your presence.
- In e-mail, it is best to write your ideas briefly and clearly. Most people do not have time to read lengthy e-mail messages, so they want the messages to be concise. Some people cannot print out their e-mail, so they may skim the messages rather than devote the amount of time that you would want them to dedicate to such reading.
- If you write an e-mail message at your place of employment, the message does not belong to you. It is the property of your employer, and he or she has access to it. Do not be surprised at the lack of security surrounding your e-mail. What you may think is private correspondence may not be.
- Be sure to include your mailing address, in case the individual receiving your e-mail message prefers to reply via the U.S. Postal Service. Also include the standard salutation and closing.

POINTS ABOUT E-MAIL MESSAGES

- avoid slang and imprecise wording;
- write your ideas briefly and clearly;
- remember that e-mail messages you write and receive at work do not belong to you;
- include your mailing address so that your correspondent may reply to you by U.S. Postal Service if necessary.

Letters

On the other hand, if you continue to depend on the mail, you will be using the standard letter format that you learned before. You may be required to write formal **letters**, as in Chapter 3: Home and Family, where one of the questions in the "Suggested Chapter Projects" asks you to write a letter to a state representative. You may or may not mail it, but it needs to follow the appropriate business letter format. Thanks to the easy access to Internet and the great number of search engines available, you might be able to find addresses—whether e-mail or business—for individuals such as authors, business people, musicians, and others, who would have been difficult or impossible to access before the advance in technology. In other cases, you will be asked to write informal letters to individuals such as friends, far-flung relatives, parents, or others. Here, too, the standard letter format is appropriate, but the content may be written with more informality.

FORMAL LETTERS ARE

- written to business people, instructors, employers, agencies, and so forth—usually but not always to people you do not know personally;
- written with formal language; and
- sometimes used to request information, submit résumés, make a complaint, recommend individuals for positions or awards, and so forth.

INFORMAL LETTERS ARE

- written to friends, relatives, parents, fellow employees, and other people you usually know on a friendly basis;
- written with informal language; and
- sometimes used to express feelings, emotions, personal disclosures, or responses to other informal letters.

Refer to the formal letter below, which was written to request an interview.

return address
```
17642 Summer Place
Spring, Texas 77090
14 May 2001
```

inside address
```
Professor Rudolfo Anaya
Department of English
University of New Mexico
Albuquerque, NM
```

Dear Professor Anaya:] salutation

body paragraphs
```
I am a graduate student completing work toward my
doctorate and specializing in Mexican-American
literature. I recently read your novel, Bless Me,
Ultima, and I have some questions I would like to
ask you about it.

I will be in Albuquerque on the weekend of July 13.
If it is a convenient time for you, could I set an
appointment on Friday or Saturday to meet with you?
You can reply to my home address or to my e-mail
address, cynthiaallende@earthlink.net, or you may
call me at (281) 222-0111.

Thank you for your help in this matter.
```

Sincerely,   ] closing

Cynthia Allende   ] written signature

Cynthia Allende] typed signature

Analysis

Look at the components of this letter marked on the letter itself. The writer did not use official university or personalized stationary; she used white, unlined 8 1/2" by 11" paper. She typed the letter single-spaced, double-spacing between the elements: return address, inside address, salutation, paragraphs in the body, and closing. Between the closing and the typed name, she quadruple-spaced, leaving three blank lines of type where she signed her name. Notice also that each paragraph begins at the margin rather than being indented.

ELEMENTS OF THE FORMAL LETTER

Return Address does not include your name. It may be omitted if you use official stationary. In that case, type the date in the center of the first line of type below the letterhead.

Inside Address (of the person receiving the letter) should contain the complete address.

Salutation or **greeting** should be followed by a colon in a formal letter. If you do not know the name of the person to whom you are writing, you may begin with "Dear Committee Members" or other appropriate title. If you do not know the title of a woman you are writing to, you may use the abbreviation "Ms."

The Body of the letter contains the substance. It is divided into paragraphs indicated by a double space between each rather than by indenting each.

The Closing may be either formal or informal. "Sincerely," "Respectfully," and so forth are formal closures, while "Regards" or "Best Wishes" are informal.

The Signature should appear as you sign other documents.

The Typed Signature comes below your written signature.

The abbreviation of "Enc.," indicating that you are including something for the reader, should be typed double-spaced after the signature. If you are sending a copy of the letter to another person, type "cc: additional recipient's name" double-spaced below the signature, to alert the reader.

Another common formal letter is one written to apply for a job. Look at the following example. Notice that it is written on personalized stationary.

Andrew J. Huang, Ph. D.
50612 North Avenue
Santa Monica, CA 90404
(310) 876-21254
andrewhuang@cssm.edu

7 October 2000

Dr. Jonathan Marks
Director of Composition
Department of English
California State University
18111 Nordhoff Street
Northridge, CA 91330-8248

Dear Dr. Marks:

I am responding to the job posting you submitted to the Career Center at California State University at Northridge. I am applying for the position of adjunct instructor to teach your Freshman Composition courses.

I graduated from Ohio State University in 1999 with my Ph. D. in English with a specialization in Asian-American Literature. During my studies, I worked as a teaching assistant and teaching fellow. I was given my own Freshman Composition classes to teach and I was responsible for creating a syllabus, choosing the text, creating the assignments and grading. I have taught at several community colleges in Ohio and California, including Santa Monica College and California State University at San Bernardino.

Enclosed are my curriculum vita, writing samples of my latest articles on pedagogy in the composition classroom, and sample syllabi I have used.

I am available for an interview, and I look forward to hearing from you.

Sincerely,

Andrew J. Huang, Ph. D.

Enc.

As you can see, this letter contains elements that are different from the first model.

A COVER LETTER FOR A JOB APPLICATION

highlights, interprets, and reshapes the information on the writer's résumé or curriculum vita to draw attention to specific qualities, activities, or other related jobs the applicant has held; it does not simply repeat the vita;

announces in the first paragraph the job the writer is applying for and where she or he found the announcement;

mentions any special reason for applying for this position, such as fitting into the writer's career goals;

lets the prospective employer know that the applicant is available for an interview or notifies the employer about the time when the applicant can be reached to set up an appointment.

➤ Short Writing Assignment

Visit the Career Center at your institution and look for possible positions that you might be interested in and that you are qualified for. Get a copy of the job description and the information about whom to write to and where to send the letter. Practice writing a cover letter for a job you might want based on the job description you found.

WRITING THE ESSAY

The Informative Essay

The thought of writing a paper that is longer than a paragraph and that sustains an idea through multiple paragraphs can be a frightening thought, especially if a student writer lacks self-confidence in her writing skills. However, if the student writer has read this textbook's discussion on how to write different kinds of paragraphs and has successfully completed some of the assignments, she has acquired the tools needed to begin writing the essay. Another point that should help relieve anxiety is to remember that the primary purpose of writing is communication. We communicate daily in sustained and even lengthy conversations and arguments. The key to doing it on paper is to find the appropriate topic. Few writers can sound convincing and interesting if they are not involved with their topic.

Writing as Communication

Look at the following tree diagram. If you are a visual learner, you will enjoy a diagram that explains the details of a lesson in a brief outline form. There is, however, accompanying narrative for those who have difficulty with diagrams that lack explanation.

First, accept the assertion that the purpose of writing is communication. If you do, then you must ask, what is the purpose of communication? The answer is, as shown in the second level of the diagram: to entertain, to reflect, to inform, and to persuade. Finally, the third level of the diagram indicates the patterns of writing that can be employed to achieve the purposes.

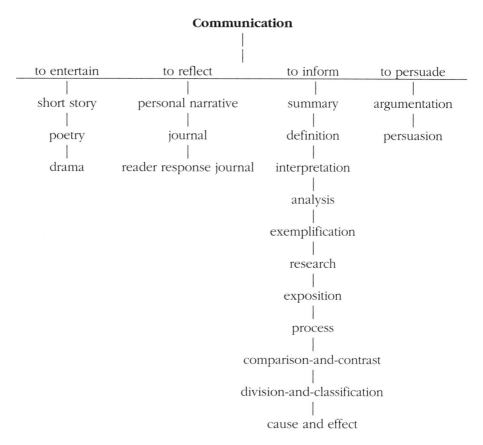

Communication

to entertain	to reflect	to inform	to persuade
short story	personal narrative	summary	argumentation
poetry	journal	definition	persuasion
drama	reader response journal	interpretation	
		analysis	
		exemplification	
		research	
		exposition	
		process	
		comparison-and-contrast	
		division-and-classification	
		cause and effect	

To Entertain

This text incorporates short stories and poetry in addition to the other forms of writing. However, because the primary purpose of this course is to help you build and improve your informative and persuasive writing skills, you will probably not spend much time writing to entertain. On the other hand, you might be required to write an analysis of a short story or poem or to use a short story or poem as a stimulus for reflective writing in your journal or for a possible topic to expand later in your reader response journal.

To Reflect

Reflective writing is best done in personal narratives, journals and reader response journal entries. To write reflectively means to examine an issue, an activity, a time in your life, a person, a relationship, or other personal events that you have experienced or known and after thinking or "reflecting" about the particular point, arrive at a conclusion about how the incident, time period, or person affected or changed you. The majority of the selections in this text are written as personal narratives. In the essay, "Shame" (Chapter 2, Youth), Dick Gregory does not simply remember having a strong attraction for a little girl in his class; he reflects on how and why he behaved the way he did. If "Shame" were simply about a memory of the girl and the specific incident, a reader might come away from it saying, "Okay, that was a nice story. So what?" The "So what?" is answered by the reflection describing what he learned from his experience with her. Gregory also reflects in his **narration** about the homeless man who had no money to pay for his meal. Because he explains the lesson he learned, the reader is not left asking, "So what?" The difference between personal narrative writing and a journal or reader response writing is that the narrative is a sustained writing assignment, which can be used as a fully developed piece or as part of a longer work. Refer to the sample essay about *La Llorona* that follows to see how personal narrative is used as only one paragraph of a longer work.

To Inform

Writing intended to **inform** can make use of many patterns. Any one of the **patterns** can be used to develop a sustained writing assignment; however, each can also be used to add variety to an essay that informs. For example, look at Carol Tarvis's essay "How Friendship Was 'Feminized'" (in Chapter 6, Language). The title indicates analysis in that the reader will see that friendship has undergone change: It has been "feminized." If the reader begins with the opening paragraph, she will see that Tarvis uses exemplification to give the reader illustrations of male friendships. The opening sentence of the second paragraph is clearly contrastive, showing a difference between male and female friendships, and it is repeated in paragraph 7. In paragraph 3, Tarvis incorporates **research** to develop the concept of "male bonding." She uses research again in paragraph 8 as well as **definition,** exemplification, and **evaluation.** By paragraph 10, Tarvis has incorporated a personal narrative. Her next two paragraphs revert to research, and her conclusion offers suggestions. In a twelve-paragraph essay, Tarvis sustains and develops her analysis of friendship through the use of process, exemplification, contrast, research or exposition/explanation, definition, evaluation, and personal narrative modes. Tarvis's ability to blend the patterns into a cohesive and unified essay displays a skill that comes only with practice.

To Persuade

The other major purpose of communication is to persuade. Although many people use the terms argument and persuasion interchangeably, the words are not synonymous. To argue or to write an **argument** means to use logic and facts to support and convince an opposing person of the writer's **position.** The writer is trying to change a reader's mind. To do so, she or he must use subtlety and negotiation, rather than move unflinchingly into a situation where no concession is possible. To do the latter would be frustrating to both opponent and writer. How many times have we heard someone say, "He [or she] just won't listen"? Writers don't want that to be said about them or about the way they present their information. If that happens, the writer loses because the reader will stop reading.

Persuasion, on the other hand, attempts to change readers' minds but also requires that the readers act. It takes argumentation one step further by asking the readers to become active participants. For example, a persuasive essay might convince the readers to support a particular candidate, but it also requires that the readers get out and vote. This happens frequently in newspaper editorials, when an editor endorses certain candidates, positions in bond elections, propositions, and so forth. It is not enough to sway the minds of the readers; an editor must also convince them to vote for or against a particular issue.

In Chapter 10: Confrontations, you will find paired articles in which the authors use argumentation skills to try to convince their readers of opposing positions. Although Chapter 10 is devoted exclusively to argument, other essays in Part II are examples of argument, also. And, as with informative writing, argument also employs different patterns of composition even though the basic development requires specific rhetorical devices.

➤ Follow-Up Questions

1. What is the primary purpose of writing?
2. Why is "How Friendship Was 'Feminized'" used as an example to discuss **informative** writing?
3. Explain the difference between argumentation and persuasion.

Getting Started—The Informative Essay
This is frequently the hardest part for student writers. However, in practicing the prewriting strategies introduced in "The Paragraph" section, most student writers find they have some ideas to begin with. Review those procedures as steps of the writing process, and you will find your ideas beginning to flow.

PRE-WRITING STRATEGIES

- **Freewriting/Focused Freewriting**: Write for a set time about anything. Write for a set time about anything concerning your topic. (See pp. 18–19.)
- **Brainstorming**: Select your topic and write notes, questions, words, and incidents in brief phrases that refer to your topic. (See p. 19.)
- **Clustering/Mapping/Webbing**: Begin with your topic and through free association, cluster ideas that arise from your main topic. You may continue to free associate with the resulting ideas. (See pp. 19–20.)
- **Journalistic Questions**: Who? What? When? Where? Why? How? Answer each question about your topic briefly. (See p. 20.)

Another element that might be needed to complete a longer work is additional information. You might need to do some form of research before you begin writing. For example, you might want to interview a friend or relative about an incident in a personal narrative. Another interviewing strategy for an informative paper is to talk to someone who was involved in the incident that you are discussing. For example, for a paper on an aspect of World War II, you might talk to a veteran to learn firsthand experience. If you choose to conduct an interview with someone, keep the following points in mind.

- **Set up a place and time to meet, and be on time (or better, a few minutes early).** If you interview a stranger, choose a public place and let someone know where you will be and approximately how long the interview is to last. It is best not to go to a stranger's home or to a place where you feel uncomfortable. If you feel ill at ease, try to reschedule the appointment or cancel it. No paper is worth putting yourself in jeopardy.
- **Be prepared.** Have a list of open-ended questions. Questions that can be answered with a *Yes* or *No* will not help you develop your essay.
- **Introduce yourself and explain the purpose of your project** as soon as you meet the individual you will interview. Describe the project and its purpose and ask the person if she or he has any questions about the interview before you begin.
- **Be prepared.** You will need to take written notes, so have pen and paper ready. If you want to tape the interview, request permission first. Don't be surprised if the individual declines. If your interviewee agrees, expect the interview to be somewhat stilted at first. If you tape the interview, have the recorder, tape, batteries, and microphone in working order. Even if you tape the session, take written notes of important remarks. Even the best equipment is known to break down at the most annoying times.
- **Allow the interviewee to ask questions or add information**. Sometimes the person you interview might have interesting or valuable information that did not fit your questions. Ask him if he would like to ask any questions or add any information you did not cover.
- **Thank the individual** for her time and help.
- **Remain professional.** If you do not know the person, do not offer your phone number or address. If your subject wants to see a final copy of the interview, offer to mail it to his or her address.

POINTS FOR CONDUCTING AN INTERVIEW

- Set up a place and time to meet, and be on time or early.
- Be prepared with questions.
- Introduce yourself and explain the purpose of your project immediately.
- Be prepared to take notes or to record the interview.
- Allow the interviewee to ask questions or add information.
- Thank the person.
- Remain professional.

Another way to gather information is to do research. Appendix 2 provides detailed directions about conducting research; here, we will discuss preliminary strategies.

- **Definitions.** If you need to write a **definition** of your topic, find an appropriate dictionary. While the standard desk dictionaries are usually adequate, you might need a specialized dictionary that defines medical, legal or other terms.
- **Background information.** In an **informative** essay, you might need to provide background information such as dates, locations, directions, statistics, and so forth. Gather these data before you begin writing or you will have to break your concentration and your writing schedule to find them.
- **World Wide Web.** If you use the World Wide Web for information as well as the library, be sure your sources are reliable and that you document your sources appropriately. (See Appendix 3: MLA Documentation and Sample Paper.)

➤ Short Writing Assignments

1. Pretend you are a reporter for your school's newspaper and you have been given the assignment to interview a student from a country other than the United States. Create some questions that you might use. Consider your audience to be the student body, which is composed of people with diverse backgrounds, and include anything that you think your audience would be interested in reading about.
2. Determine the appropriate dictionary to find the definitions for the following words:

   Heart disease   Carburetor   *Habeas corpus*   Existentialism

   Now, look them up and write the definition or a summary for each. Provide documentation for the source (refer to Appendix 3: MLA Documentation and Sample Paper).

Choosing Your Topic

The first thing to remember about successful writing is that you should write about a topic you are familiar with or interested in. When William Faulkner began writing, his first three novels were failures. When he spoke with Sherwood Anderson, another American novelist, Anderson told him to write about things, events, and people he knew. Faulkner listened to him; left New Orleans; returned to Oxford, Mississippi; and began writing the successful novels that were based on his family and his childhood experiences in a fictional county resembling the one he grew up in. Not only was he successful, he also won a Nobel Prize for his work.

If your instructor gives a list of suggested topics, choose one you like and know something about. If you must invent a topic, pick one that you will enjoy spending time with. Even if you don't like writing, you will be working with a topic you enjoy.

Narrowing Your Topic

A mistake student writers frequently make is to choose a topic that is too broad for the assignment. If you are asked to write about a historical event, "World War II" is not an appropriate topic. Ask yourself the following questions:

- **Purpose:** What is the purpose of the assignment? Is it to entertain? To reflect? To inform? Or to persuade?
- **Length:** What is the length requirement: a single paragraph, an essay of 500 to 700 words, or a 5-page research paper?
- **Time:** How much time have I been given to complete this assignment? How much time do I have to complete this assignment? How much time do I need to complete this assignment? How much time am I willing to devote to this assignment? What is the due date?
- **Topics:** What topics has my instructor provided? Do I like any of them or know anything about them? Would I prefer writing about something else that fits the requirements of length and purpose?
- **Location of writing:** Is the paper to be written in class or out of class?

Once you have clarified these points, especially purpose and length, you can choose your topic. Look at the chart below.

General Topics	Possible Writing Patterns	Narrowed Topic
Write a paper about pets.	personal narrative, descriptive, comparison-and-contrast, exemplification, definition, division and classification	My cats, La Llorona and Gabby
Write a paper about rock music.	division and classification, comparison-and-contrast, definition, description, exemplification, evaluation	Elvis Presley's early music
Analyze the kinds of talk shows on television.	division and classification, comparison-and-contrast, description, exemplification, evaluation, cause and effect	news magazines and their extended viewing nights
Explain the impact of urban renewal in major downtown areas.	cause and effect, descriptive, comparison-and-contrast	Enron Field
Describe shopping at a local mall.	descriptive, comparison-and-contrast, process, division and classification	Galleria shopping

Collaboration

Sometimes working in groups to get started generating ideas on similar topics helps student writers begin writing. Once considered cheating, collaborative efforts have been found to increase the number of ideas produced, improve the quality of material created, and encourage community building within a class or organization. Individuals who once had to work alone, isolated from others and dependent solely on their own abilities, are now being asked to share ideas, combine written material with follow writers into one document, and offer constructive criticism to improve the product. In some cases, all group members' names are cited, and in other cases, the group as a whole is given credit. If you work in a collaborative group, you might or might not be held responsible for the creation of an entire essay. Your instructor will give directions as to what is expected and required.

Structure of the Essay—Overview

Now that you have gathered your thoughts and expanded your ideas, you can begin to consider the structure of the essay. The main idea of your paper will be stated in the **thesis,** which, depending on your instructor, may be one or two sentences and stated as an **assertion;** or it may be an assertion plus the points you will use in your body paragraphs, to indicate the direction you are going in your paper. Place your thesis in your introduction, and it will tell your readers what to expect as they read the essay. Each body paragraph will begin with a **topic sentence** that is generated from the thesis. In other words, you will not be rewriting your thesis for every paragraph; rather, your topic sentence will be an element that supports and develops the thesis. Because this sentence indicates what the paper will be about, students sometimes feel the need to begin the thesis with clauses such as "In this paper, I will show," "This paper will be about," or "This paper will demonstrate." Such an opening tends to distract the reader from the important part of the thesis—that which follows those words. Therefore, you should begin with whatever idea would follow that opening.

Let's say you are going to write about the first topic in the preceding chart, "Write a paper about pets." To facilitate our discussion, we are going to return to *La Llorona*, Gabby, and their owner. Their owner, Julian, has already written three paragraphs about the cats, and he has kept the papers in his journal, or writer's notebook. Now he can create a thesis, write an introduction, revise the paragraphs to reflect an appropriate topic sentence for each paragraph, and write a conclusion. If you have kept any of your paragraph assignments, you could recycle them into an essay that you might want to write.

The conclusion of your essay will include a restated thesis, now without the points you might have listed. You may **summarize** the paper by taking each point and talking about it in one or two sentences and ending with a good concluding sentence; or you may choose to elaborate on the kinds of pets people have, ending generally. Whatever you do, be sure to check with your instructor to find out her preference.

Building Block: The Thesis

The **thesis** is the most important part of your essay. It is the controlling or main idea that your essay supports, defends, and develops. Many published authors prefer to use an *implied thesis,* one that can be arrived at by reading the essay, instead of a *stated thesis,* which clearly announces the main idea of the piece. However, student writers are encouraged to include a statement of the main idea in their informative essays. This usually appears in the introduction. Your instructor will tell you whether you should place it at the beginning of the introduction or at the end. To be effective, your thesis should be clearly stated and specific. Begin with the main idea. Because we will use *La Llorona* and her friends to construct the sample essay, the remainder of this section will discuss the material already written in the section "The Paragraph," but in greater depth.

The assignment given to the student writer is to write about a pet or pets. *La Llorona's* owner, Julian, has already completed prewriting, drafting, and revision stages of three different kinds of paragraph patterns, and he will use these to construct his essay. He kept his work in a portfolio, a folder that contains writings a student wants to showcase and which will be reviewed at the end of the semester by the instructor or by a composition committee. Students can return to the works in the portfolio to revise or to use them in different ways. Julian has decided to pull the paragraphs that are already good as independent paragraphs and to revise them into paragraphs that will demonstrate cohesion and unity in the essay. The first thing he has to consider is his thesis, the main idea of the entire essay.

As you can see, Julian will write his thesis after he has already begun his essay. Some students are able to do that; in fact, it is easier for some student writers to get some of their ideas on paper before they determine their thesis. This strategy allows them to get started writing without feeling restricted or limited. The danger is that without a controlling central or main idea, the work may wander to non-unified, incoherent paragraphs that don't create a tightly woven work. If what you have done in the past feels comfortable to you and helps you write essays successfully, you should check with your instructor to see if she agrees. If she does not, use the following directions to try a new approach.

Because the assignment is to write an informative essay, Julian and his classmates know they can incorporate a variety of **patterns** into their essays. Julian has already written descriptive, personal narrative, and comparison-and-contrast paragraphs with the addition of cause and effect in the comparison-contrast paragraph. If he were starting this essay without the benefit of prewritten paragraphs, he could have decided to write an essay that is primarily descriptive, using the various patterns to describe and inform his readers about *La Llorona*. The next step is the construction of the thesis, or the main idea of the essay. Here are the drafts Julian wrote until he was satisfied.

General Topic: Write a paper about pets.

Specific Topic: My pet, La Llorona, my cat

Thesis: My cat, La Llorona is small and unusual.

My pet cat, La Llorona, captured my attention by her size and noisiness and continued to

> La Llorona's size and noisiness first captured my attention, but her personality and the immediate
>
> Noisy, tiny, and fluffy, the black and white kitten at the pet shop captured my attention, but I didn't know the extent of her personality until she lived with me and my family and my other cat, Gabby.

As you can see, Julian, even with the benefit of having three paragraphs already written, did not have an easy time writing his thesis. The first attempts focused only on her description; however, when he realized that description was only part of the assignment, he revised his approach. He included description (noisy, tiny, fluffy, black and white kitten), personal narrative (lived with me and my family), and a suggestion of comparison-and-contrast (other cat, Gabby). Because cause and effect is a pattern embedded within the comparison-and-contrast paragraph, the writer does not have to include it in his thesis.

➤ Short Writing Assignment

Using the general topics listed below,
- narrow each one to a specific topic that you can write about in a short paragraph;
- decide and list which patterns of development you can use to write the paragraph;
- write a working thesis for each topic.

Tools	Cars	Relatives	Universities	Part-time jobs

Building Block: The Introduction
Many student writers have difficulty writing the introduction because it does not get to the topic immediately. Even though it is the first paragraph of the essay, it does not necessarily have to be the first paragraph the student writer begins with. Julian has three paragraphs already written and now must write the introduction. Students who are just beginning the assignment might have only a blank page. If they completed the prewriting strategies, they might look at what they wrote about pets. Because *La Llorona* is the specific topic of the following essay, Julian did not want to write about her immediately. In fact, he chose to follow the points about writing introductions listed below.

AN INTRODUCTION

- arouses your readers' interest in the topic;
- avoids announcing the topic immediately;
- leads gradually from the general idea to the specific;
- maintains a consistent purpose, style, and tone with the rest of the essay; and
- includes your thesis.

A writer wants to arouse readers' interest to keep them reading. If the writer announces the specific topic immediately, readers would perhaps lose interest once they read the opening sentence. On the other hand, some instructors prefer that student writers begin with the main idea. Follow your instructor's directions. If we look at the introduction as a picture, we can see it in one of two shapes: the inverted triangle or the rectangle.

The triangle represents an introduction that starts generally and comes to the specific point: the thesis.

The rectangle represents an introduction that starts out specifically and develops the idea. Ask your instructor where he wants you to place the thesis.

In the inverted triangle, Julian begins with the general topic—in this case, pets—and narrows down to the specific topic, *La Llorona*, in the thesis. In the rectangle, the writer, Cindy, begins with her specific topic, Hercules; develops the idea, and ends with a thesis. In both cases the authors use definition to explain the concept assigned. Julian defines *pet* while Hercules' owner, Cindy, defines *Chihuahua*. Read each introduction and decide which one you prefer.

The Inverted Triangle

Animals have historically been wild, but in time many species were domesticated, leading to the creation of pets. No longer having to live exclusively outside and to be dependent on their own hunting skills for survival, these animals have been tamed with the primary purpose of being "kept as a companion" (<u>Random House</u> 1009). Once the pet lives with its owner for years, it becomes part of the family, is loved, and is cared for almost as if it were human. My pet, a cat I named La Llorona, became part of my family immediately after I brought her home from the pet store. Noisy, tiny, and fluffy, the black and white kitten at the pet shop captured my attention, but I didn't know the extent of her personality until she lived with me and my family and my other cat, Gabby

The Rectangle

As a dog owner, I have found my pet, Hercules, a Chihuahua, brings me hours of pleasure. The definition, "one of a Mexican breed of very small dogs with a rounded head, prominent eyes, and large ears" (<u>Random House</u> 235) does not begin to explain what

Hercules is to me. This miniature warrior displays an enormous personality and shares my apartment, keeping me from being lonely. I had no idea that the gift of a tiny companion could bring me such pleasure because of his size and attitude.

➤ Short Writing Assignment

Using one of the topics from page 61 create two introductory paragraphs: one in the triangle pattern and one in the rectangle pattern. Which one do you prefer?

Building Block: The Body Paragraphs

If the introduction looks like an inverted triangle or a rectangle, what should the body paragraphs look like? Because the body paragraphs are presenting informative material of equal specificity, each paragraph will be represented by rectangles.

Body Paragraphs Represented as Rectangle

> **Body Paragraph #1**
> **develops the first idea in the thesis**

> **Body Paragraph #2**
> **develops the second idea in the thesis**

> **Body Paragraph #3**
> **develops the third idea in the thesis**p

Since the thesis is the last sentence of the introduction, it acts as a natural transition into the first point Julian or Cindy will discuss in their first body paragraph. Julian returns to the descriptive paragraph, because it is the first point he makes about *La Llorona*. The first question Julian has to answer is whether or not his present topic sentences, the sentences that control the development of the paragraphs, are generated from the thesis, the controlling idea of the essay. To do so, he wrote the thesis first and then each of the topic sentences below the thesis.

Thesis: Noisy, tiny, and fluffy, the black and white kitten at the pet shop captured my attention, but I did not know the extent of her personality until she came to live with me and my family and my other cat, Gabby.

Topic Sentence #1: La Llorona's loud meowing at 3 o'clock in the morning at my closed bedroom door is only one of her qualities that makes her dear to me.

Topic Sentence #2: I woke up New Year's Day concerned because my cat, La Llorona was not crying loudly at my door.

Topic Sentence #3: My cat, La Llorona, is quite different from my other cat, Gabby, in the areas of size, personality and health.

Each topic sentence appears to have been generated from the thesis, so Julian decided to keep them and continue with his conclusion.

Building Block: The Conclusion

Once the writer has finished supporting and developing the assertion in the thesis, she must write her conclusion. The conclusion should be a fully developed paragraph that brings a sense of closure to the reader. The writer can summarize the main points from the essay by making it an inversion of the introduction, (represented by a normal triangle), beginning with the thesis and gradually becoming general. Or, she can state the thesis, draw conclusions from the material presented, provide a discussion of what she has learned, and finish with a good concluding sentence. This kind of conclusion is represented by a rectangle, similar to the body paragraphs as everything is equally developed.

A CONCLUSION

- begins with a restated thesis,
- either draws conclusions or summarizes the main points stated in the essay,
- does not introduce any new information,
- ends with a good concluding sentence, and
- brings a sense of closure to the main idea.

Julian decided to conclude his essay by following the triangle pattern. Notice that he begins with a restated rather than a repeated thesis.

> Although La Llorona is no longer the fluffy, little kitten I bought several years ago, her personality will continue to entertain us and make her an important part of our family. She is truly an example of a kitty that makes a good companion even if she is not a lap cat. Her vet has promised that her frenzied excursions around the house will slow down, but I don't think she will ever achieve the docile nature of Gabby. However, neither I nor the rest of the family would want that. La Llorona is a special cat that will truly live everyday to its fullest and tolerate her human family sharing her house with her.

Julian began with a restated thesis, summarized ideas that were developed in the body paragraphs, and ended with an excellent concluding sentence. Here is the first draft of his essay complete with a catchy title that provides humor and a double meaning.

The Cat's Meow

Animals have historically been wild, but in time many species were domesticated, leading to the creation of pets. No longer having to live exclusively outside and to be dependent on their own hunting skills for survival, these animals have been tamed with the primary purpose of being "kept as a companion" (Random House 1009). Once the pet lives with its owner for years, it becomes part of the family, is loved, and is cared for almost as if it were human. My pet, a cat I named La Llorona, became part of my family immediately after I brought her home from the pet store. Noisy, tiny, and fluffy, the black and white kitten at the pet shop captured my attention, but I didn't know the extent of her personality until she lived with me and my family and my other cat, Gabby.

La Llorona's loud meowing at three o'clock in the morning at my closed bedroom door is only one of her qualities that makes her dear to me. In fact, her meows were what called my attention to her among the other kittens in the showcase of the pet store. She was screaming so loudly that her cries could be heard by everyone standing around looking at the kittens. She made so much noise, I had to ask the sales person to pick her out of the case and let me hold her. It was then that I noticed that she looked like she had been put in a close drier on the fluff cycle. She was almost weightless beneath all that soft black and white fur. When she looked up at me with her big, blue eyes and I saw that black spot on her chin, I knew that I could not leave without taking her with me. Even though she continued to meow loudly as the sales person sold me accessories and completed the transaction, I was reassured that she simply missed her mother and that she would eventually grow out of her vocalizations. How wrong that statement was! As she grew older, the only thing that changed was her fluffy fur. It is now silky and smooth instead of standing out, making her look like a ball of fluff. Llorona only grew to look like Yoda from Star Wars movies with her big ears and pointed nose. Where Yoda is reverentially quiet, Llorona screams her demands to be allowed into any room that has a closed door. Once she is inside, she looks around and walks out, satisfied that nothing needs her attention. If she has been outside for a while, she sits on the window sill that looks into the den and demands entrance. When she saunters in, she gurgles her thanks at being allowed to enter or her irritation at being made to wait so long. She then throws herself onto the kitchen floor where everyone has to step over her or move her out of the way. If she does not get the attention she wants, she will either meow at the nearest person or stand beside her chosen human until he or she bends down to rub her tummy. Even though I left the Spanish word for cat, gata off her name, La Llorona, it is understood, and she certainly fulfills its translation: The Hollering Kitty.

I woke up New Year's Day concerned because my cat, La Llorona, was not crying loudly at my door. Accustomed to early morning wake-up calls for food and attention, much like an infant who has recently come home from the hospital, I checked my clock and discovered that I had slept past nine o'clock. Worried, I jumped out of the warmth and comfort of my bed and into the chilly room. I opened the door—no kitty waiting to rush past me and climb up the covers to find a spot among the blanket and sheet. Walking into the den, I spotted what looked like a black and white rug lying beside an unidentifiable mound. Llorona opened her eyes as she heard me approach, and I could see the effort it took for her to lift her head. She opened her mouth, but the noisy meow remained silent. Unconcerned with the regurgitated food on the carpet, I picked her up, and she felt even lighter than when I first held the squirming active kitty four weeks before. Questions raced through my mind: What vet would be open today? What made her sick? Was it my fault? Will she live? Putting her down gently in her favorite spot, I rushed for the telephone book, looked under veterinarians, and miraculously found a local 24-hour emergency clinic. Talking to her to reassure her, as well as myself, that she would be ok, I ran to the bedroom to change and clean up. I then hauled out the hated animal carrier, and as I placed a soft towel in it to soften the bumps in the road, I had visions of a different kitty: one who hated being confined and fought vigorously at being enclosed. On New Year's Day, it was almost as if she had made a resolution to be a better kitty and not fight. I wanted my old kitty back. I raced to the vet, grateful that no radar units were on patrol that day. Even though the clinic was not too far from the house, we arrived in record time since few cars were on the road this early. We were the only patients at the vet's office, so Llorona was seen immediately. The vet took the kitten's temperature and blood samples, examined her thoroughly, and prescribed two kinds of medication, explaining that because of the cramped conditions at pet stores, animals sometimes become infected with bacteria and even parasites that incubate for several weeks before making the pet ill. The vet finally took a stool sample and gave me directions about caring for Llorona dur-

Gabby

La Llorona
Photographer: Elizabeth Rodriguez Kessler (both photos)

ing the next few days. The most humorous yet heart-wrenching image I will carry forever with me is of Llorona weakly walking without protest—tail dragging, head down—into her carrier as we prepared to leave the vet's office, sick but on the road to recovery.

My cat, La Llorona, is quite different from my other cat, Gabby, in the areas of size, personality, and health. Both cats were purchased at the same time; however, Gabby is much bigger even though Llorona is the "senior" cat. This comes from their heritage. Gabby is a tabby that has bigger bones and puts on weight more easily. Llorona, on the other hand, is part Siamese even though she does not display the color typical of a Siamese. Siamese cats are more nervous and active than tabbies which accounts for their difference in size. Llorona is quite slender even though she eats almost as much as Gabby. Being from different cat families could also explain the difference in their personalities. While Gabby likes to find a quiet spot or a comfortable lap for a nap after she eats, Llorona races around the house, chasing real or imaginary flying bugs. As a kitten, Llorona always chased her tail, but Gabby couldn't be bothered with such activity. Today Llorona continues to tail chase while all Gabby catches are dreams. When they go outside, their personalities develop even further in different directions. Llorona crouches in tall grass, attempting to catch birds, squirrels, or other trespassers in her yard. Her nervous impatience, however, warns her prey when they see the grass shaking. Gabby, on the other hand, finds activity tiresome and prefers to sit in the sun and preen in preparation for another long nap. Although they are both in generally good health from eating and sleeping, if one is going to get sick, it will be Llorona. Her Siamese nervousness frequently affects her stomach, making her have diarrhea. Gabby, on the other hand, goes through life comfortable and without Llorona's misery. Even though they are different, they are good companions and provide quite a bit of entertainment to me and my family.

Although Llorona is no longer the fluffy, little kitten I bought several years ago, her personality will continue to entertain us and make her an important part of our family. She is truly an example of a kitty that makes a good companion even if she is not a lap cat. Her vet has promised that her frenzied excursions around the house will slow down, but I don't think she will ever achieve the docile nature of Gabby. However, neither I nor the rest of the family would want that. La Llorona is a special cat that will truly live everyday to its fullest and tolerate her human family sharing her house with her.

➤ Extended Writing Assignment

Now you are ready to write the first draft of your informative essay. If you have paragraphs that you have written that have the same topic, you may recycle them into the essay, if your instructor allows you to do so. If not, you should begin with a new topic and follow the step-by-step process that we have just discussed.

Building Block: Revision

Even though Julian's essay looks good and appears to be complete, he still has to complete the revision stage. Each of his paragraphs was revised independently to ensure that they met the criteria required for an introduction, for descriptive, personal narrative, and comparison paragraphs, and for a conclusion. Refer to the block of information that follows each the section, below, to use as a checklist as you write and complete your paragraphs.

Julian's next step in the revision process is to look at the paper as a whole to ensure that it flows and gives the impression of a single piece rather than of independent paragraphs. This is achieved through the use of **transitions,** words, phrases, or sentences that appear between sentences or paragraphs to create a bridge between ideas.

When Julian was constructing his thesis, he took time to list his topic sentences to see if they were generated from it. They were, so he continued. Now, however, he must see if each topic sentence flows smoothly from the last sentence of the preceding paragraph. Julian reread the last sentence of each paragraph and discovered that small revisions need to be made in one topic sentence and a major change is needed in another.

Last Sentence of Introduction (Thesis): Noisy, tiny, and fluffy, the black and white kitten at the pet shop captured my attention, but I did not know the extent of her personality until she came to live with me and my family and my other cat, Gabby.

Topic Sentence #1: La Llorona's loud meowing at 3 o'clock in the morning at my closed bedroom door is only one of her qualities that makes her dear to me.

Explanation: Julian decided that the topic sentence for Body Paragraph 1 works well and chose to use it since he mentioned "her qualities" in addition to her meowing. That general word opened the paragraph to a discussion not only of how she sounds, but also of her appearance and her personality.

....

Last Sentence of Body Paragraph #1: Even though I left the Spanish word for cat, <u>gata</u> off her name, La Llorona, it is understood, and she certainly fulfills its translation: The Hollering Kitty.

Topic Sentence #2: I woke up New Year's Day concerned because my cat, La Llorona was not crying loudly at my door.

Explanation: In this sentence, the ideas move well from one paragraph to the next; however, the wording is repetitive. The audience already knows that *La Llorona* is Julian's cat, so he decided to leave out the words, "my cat." He also decided to rearrange the order of the opening clause so that it could be read in the following way: "On New Year's Day, I woke up. . . ." This sentence now flows more smoothly from the preceding paragraph: "On New Year's Day, I woke up concerned because La Llorona was not crying loudly at my door."

....

Last Sentence of Body Paragraph #2: The most humorous yet heart-wrenching image I will carry forever with me is of Llorona weakly walking without protest—tail dragging, head down—into her carrier as we prepared to leave the vet's office, sick but on the road to recovery.

Topic Sentence #3: My cat, La Llorona, is quite different from my other cat, Gabby, in the areas of size, personality and health.

Explanation: Julian recognized immediately that there is no transition or connection between the paragraphs even though the third idea is introduced in the thesis. He changed the topic sentence to "Even before Llorona became ill, she started showing through her size, personality, and health that she was quite different from Gabby, my other cat."

....

Last Sentence of Body Paragraph #3: Even though they are different, they are good companions and provide quite a bit of entertainment to me and my family.

First Sentence of Conclusion (Restated Thesis): Although Llorona is no longer the fluffy, little kitten I bought several years ago, her personality will continue to entertain us and make her an important part of our family.

Explanation: The transition between the third body paragraph and the conclusion comes naturally as the conclusion begins with a restated thesis.

A question usually arises in student writers' minds about where the **transition** should be placed. It can come as the last sentence of a paragraph or as the topic sentence of the next. The danger in putting the transition at the end of a paragraph is that if a new topic is introduced, it might sound disruptive and off-topic from the idea in the topic sentence. Many writers prefer to use the topic sentence as a transition.

Another major point involves the construction of transitions. They may be created by using individual words, such as *furthermore, however, additionally,* and others. They may also be formed from phrases, such as *on the other hand, as a result, of course,* and others. To achieve coherence in an essay, writers are aware not only of the need for transitions but also of the fact that they serve different functions. For example, if you are writing a contrastive paragraph or essay, words and phrases such as *but, however, yet, nevertheless, even though,* and *in contrast* are appropriate. To compare ideas, you might consider *similarly, likewise, in the same manner.* When you write a personal narrative, you want to show a sequence of actions, and rather than repeating *next* or *and then,* you could vary your transitions with *furthermore, second* (not secondly), *again, later, afterward, before, since,* and other words. Personal narratives also tend to describe place, so transitions could include *above, below, beyond, on the other side, adjacent to,* and other directional words and phrases. If you want to show cause and effect, the most popular words are *consequently, thus,* and *therefore.* There are, however, others, such as *because, as a result, otherwise,* and *hence.* Finally (another transition), if you are concluding or summarizing a point or your essay, you might use *finally, in conclusion, therefore, that is, in other words,* or other words that you believe bring closure.

In addition to using such transition words and phrases, the way you construct your sentences also contributes to smooth transitions. For example, Julian's Topic Sentence #2, uses no transition words or phrases from the list. Instead, Julian repeated the idea of "Hollering Kitty" from the preceding sentence and indicated that *Llorona* "was not crying loudly." The use of repetition works as a transition as long as it is not done too frequently. The same caution applies to using transition words and phrases: Do not overuse them.

Another element of revision is to make sure the sentences read smoothly. Return to Julian's Topic Sentence #2: "I woke up New Year's Day concerned because my cat, La Llorona, was not crying loudly at my door." He did not like the way it sounded originally, so he rewrote it to begin with a prepositional phrase, "On New Year's Day. . . ." In Topic Sentence #1, Julian did not like the repetition

WRITING THE ESSAY • 71

of "her" so he changed the first "her" to "the." Later he changed his mind and returned "the" to "her" despite the repetition.

In Body Paragraph #1, Julian changed "in the showcase of the pet store" to "in the pet store showcase," eliminating a prepositional phrase and wordiness: "In fact, her meows were what called my attention to her among the other kittens in the pet store showcase." He also changed "that soft black" to "her soft black," and "that black spot" to "a black spot": "She was almost weightless beneath her soft black and white fur. When she looked up at me with her big, blue eyes and I saw a black spot on her chin. . . ." He also added a sentence following "ball of fluff" as a transition: "Her growth pattern, like that of many children, resulted in disproportionate features and some friends began calling Llorona Yoda."

In Body Paragraph #2, Julian changed[1] "infant that" to "infant who,"[2] "spot among" to "spot between,"[3] "this early" to "so early," and[4] "weakly walking" to "walking weakly": "[1]Accustomed to early morning wake-up calls for food and attention, much like an infant who has recently come home from the hospital. . . . [2]no kitty waiting to rush past me and climb up the covers to find a spot between the blanket and sheet. [3]We arrived in record time since few cars were on the road so early. [4]The most humorous yet heart-wrenching image I will carry forever with me is of Llorona walking weakly without protest. . . ."

In Body Paragraph #3, he changed "to me and my family" to "my family and me": "They are good companions and provide quite a bit of entertainment to my family and me."

In the Conclusion, Julian changed "everyday" to "every day": "La Llorona is a cat that will truly live every day to its fullest. . . ."

While some of these revisions were cosmetic, others were needed, especially the additional sentence in Body Paragraph #1.

Cindy's essay developed the same patterns as Julian's; however, her use of comparison-and-contrast differed somewhat from her classmate's. Julian constructed his paragraph in what is known as *point-to-point,* where each point is countered immediately within the same paragraph. Very little development is made in a point-to-point pattern. The other method that can be used is subject-to-subject. In this pattern, an idea is more fully developed and can be countered within the same paragraph, moving into an opposite or similar idea with the help of a transition, or it can be developed in the next paragraph with an equal amount of development. Cindy's contrasting paragraph is as follows:

```
    Hercules is certainly different from the first dog I found
when I was still living at home with my parents. Hercules was a
gift from a dear friend. She had wrapped him up in a warm towel
and brought him to me. He was the tiniest dog I had ever seen,
and since he was almost hairless, he was shivering inside his
makeshift nest. Since it was Christmas, the weather was freez-
ing, and no amount of warmth seemed to be enough for him. I
took him to my fireplace and put him snuggly inside one of my
warm house slippers. After a short time, he stopped shivering
```

and looked at us, too tired to lap the warm milk my friend had
heated while I watched him carefully. While we tried to warm
him some more, I told Edie about my other dog, Reindeer whom I
found on a different Christmas morning sniffing through the
discarded wrapping. Reindeer was a beautiful, large golden re-
triever. He had obviously been taken care of, but his owners
were no where to be found. Friendly and eager to please, Reindeer came up to me, tongue hanging out and eyes bright. I
brought him in the house, and he seemed to be respectful of the
tree and furniture. My mother was not pleased, but my brothers
and father fell in love with him almost as quickly as I did. We
decided to keep him until we could find his owners, but no one
ever answered the ads. After three weeks of trying, Reindeer
became my dog, but I gladly shared him with my family.

As you can see, the paragraph develops in a contrasting manner, beginning
with the tiny, helpless Hercules and moving to the strong and independent Reindeer. Whereas Julian's paragraph moves back and forth between *La Llorona* and
Gabby, Cindy's develops her discussion of Hercules and then contrasts him with
the bigger animal. Each is a form of comparison-and-contrast development; your
decision to use the patterns should be based on how much information you
have or how important the details are.

Building Block: Editing

Modern technology has come to the aid not only of students but of anyone who
uses a computer. Word processing software provides tools such as Spell-Check and
Grammar-Check that alert the user to problems. Student writers should use these
tools. On the other hand, using the tools does not eliminate the need for good
proofreading skills. For example, even though Julian wrote the descriptive paragraph at least twice before he used it in the essay, submitted it for grading, incorporated it in the essay, exposed it to Spell-Check at least three times, and read it numerous times before the first essay draft, it wasn't until he was completing the
revision step for the essay that he noticed the error in Body Paragraph #1. The
clause that he wrote, "she had been put in a *close* drier on the fluff cycle" has a
homonym, a word that sounds like another word but is spelled differently and has a
different meaning. Julian used "close" instead of "clothes." The Spell-Check did not
catch it because "close" is spelled correctly, and his readers did not catch the error
because the sound registered as "clothes" when they read it quickly. Thus, even
though Spell-Check and Grammar-Check are good tools, they are not fail-safe.

Another problem that Julian did not catch was his typing of *La Llorona*.
Whenever a writer uses a language other than English they must italicize or underline the word. Julian underlined <u>gata</u> in Body Paragraph #1, but he failed to
underline or italicize the cat's name, possibly because it had become such a
common term to him. Now by using the tool, "Find and Replace," Julian can
change the typeface for the Spanish name. Finally, in Body Paragraph #3, Julian
used a comma and a period where he should have used only a period. By using
his delete key, he can take care of that problem.

POINTS FOR EDITING

- If you use a computer, use Spell-Check and Grammar-Check faithfully.
- Correct the errors the tools highlight.
- If you don't have Spell-Check or Grammar-Check, use a dictionary, have a friend peer edit your work, visit your campus Writing Lab, or ask your instructor for help.
- Always proofread carefully.

Building Block: Format

Julian isn't quite finished. To produce a finished product, Julian must format it according to his instructor's directions. Format decisions include whether to use a title page, where to put the page numbers, how to document quotations, how wide the margins should be, and how to write the Works Cited page. All of this information can be found in Appendix 3: MLA Documentation and Sample Paper. Below is how the first part of Julian's first page looks, now that he has formatted his essay and is ready to submit it for a grade.

```
                                                   Torres 1

Julian Torres
Dr. Lynn Baker
English 1301
26 November 2001


                       The Cat's Meow

   Animals have historically been wild, but in time many
species were domesticated, leading to the creation of pets.
No longer having to live exclusively outside and to be de-
pendent on their own hunting skills for survival, these ani-
mals have been tamed with the primary purpose of being "kept
as a companion" (Random House 1009). Once the pet lives with
its owner for years, it becomes part of the family.
```

THE ARGUMENTATIVE ESSAY

Consider the following essay prompts:

Unborn Victim's Rights

A husband and his pregnant wife are driving home one evening. The wife is due to deliver her baby daughter, also known as the fetus, in two weeks. Suddenly the couple's car is hit by a drunk driver. When the mother arrives at the hospital, she delivers the baby who is brain dead. The infant is placed on life support long enough for her father to see her and make the decision to remove the infant from the life support system.

The drunk driver has been arrested for violating the law. Should he be charged with vehicular manslaughter for killing the unborn fetus?

According to federal law, the fetus is not a human being and, therefore, has no rights. To charge the drunk driver with vehicular manslaughter would be unconstitutional because *Roe v. Wade* created the law that allows unborn fetuses to be aborted because they are not defined as human beings until they can live independent of their mother's body. To be able to charge the drunk driver or any other individual who causes death to a fetus would mean that a law would have to be written giving constitutional rights to the unborn, including charging anyone who killed the unborn human being with murder, and therefore reversing *Roe v. Wade*.

According to the parents of the dead infant, their fetus was a human being approximately two weeks from being born. They contend that had the baby been born naturally, she would have survived outside her mother's womb. Because the fetus had had a measurable heartbeat, brain activity, and normal movement, it was a living human being and was murdered by the drunk driver.

Directions: Decide whether or not the drunk driver should be held responsible for the death of the unborn fetus. Take a position and, using the above points, defend and support your claim.

Frozen Fertilized Human Embryos

Many couples who have had difficulty conceiving a child decide to harvest the woman's eggs, fertilize them with her partner's sperm, and allow them to grow into embryos. Once the embryos have reached a certain stage, they are frozen for future use by the couple. These embryos are considered by some to be human life and by others to be "potential" life.

Many of these couples have decided for various reasons not to have more children, but they have not decided what to do with the frozen embryos. They have several options: destroy them, introduce them into the mother to see if she becomes pregnant, sell or give them to an infertile couple, or harvest them scientifically for their organs or stem cells.

Directions: Choose one of the options and write a paper that supports your position and argues against the opposing points and position.

Cleaning Up Air Pollution

Take a position on the following topic and write a persuasive essay about it: cleaning up air pollution.

These above prompts are examples of topics you could be asked to write an argumentative or persuasive essay about. Each requires that the writer convince the readers to change their minds, but the prompts ask the writer to approach a given issue in three different ways. Before you begin writing argument, however, you need to understand the difference between argumentation and persuasion.

To Argue or to Persuade?

Argumentation means to convince an individual who holds an opposing position to change her or his mind about the topic. *Persuasion,* however, not only indicates that the writer will try to influence readers and change their minds, but will also attempt to convince the readers to act.

Structure

The structure of an argumentative persuasive essay is similar to the structure of an informative essay. It begins with an introduction, which usually sets forth the thesis. In persuasive writing, the thesis may also be referred to as the *proposition* or the **claim.** There are two styles used in writing argument: argument with the thesis stated in the introduction, and argument where the thesis is delayed until all the points and counterpoints have been made and discussed. At that point, the author takes a stand and makes an assertion based on the strongest arguments.

Choosing a Topic: Fact or Opinion

To begin an argumentative or a persuasive essay, you must select a debatable topic. Since facts are not debatable, the assertion or thesis should be created from an opinion that can be supported with fact. A belief that is purely subjective in nature cannot be argued on the basis of facts. For example, when an assertion such as "I find Beethoven's *Fifth Symphony* to be the most beautiful work of music ever composed" is made, it cannot be argued on a basis of fact because beauty is **subjective.** If the person who favors Beethoven's *Fifth Symphony* were arguing its merit on style, construction, or any other point that can be judged by using set criteria, though, the point would be debatable. On the other hand, a statement such as "Our local grocery store manager recently hired a sushi chef for the deli department, and he provides sushi for customers daily" is also not arguable. That the manager hired a chef is indisputable, and that the chef makes sushi daily is also a fact. Customers might argue the freshness, the quality, or the variety available but not the points listed in the original sentence.

➤ Short Writing Assignment

Determine if the following statements are fact or opinion.
- Cell phones cause brain tumors.
- The Houston Rockets won the NBA Championship when Robert Horry was on the team.
- Losing Robert Horry to the Los Angeles Lakers cost the Houston rockets an NBA Championship.
- Consistent exercise prevents heart attacks.
- The death penalty prevents criminals from committing serious crimes.

Kinds of Logical Thinking

When writers prepare to convince their audience, their evidence must be clear, accurate, relevant, adequate, and reasonable. The thesis or claim must have come from a thoughtful consideration of the points the writers present to their readers. Thus, these are not random ideas writers use to build their argument. Rather, they are the most convincing points the writers know.

The method by which a writer develops an argument can be done through deductive or inductive reasoning. The triangle pattern, which we discussed earlier in terms of introduction patterning, also represents deductive reasoning. **Deductive reasoning** begins with a general assertion, or major premise, that is believed to be true, moves to a more specific assertion, or minor premise, that gives an example of the major premise, and finally to the thesis or conclusion which should follow logically and thus is valid. Valid does not mean the same thing as true; it only means that the conclusion follows the premise. Look at the following example of a syllogism:

Major Premise (general assertion): All mothers are female.

Minor Premise (specific example): Queen Elizabeth is a mother.

Conclusion (thesis): Therefore, Queen Elizabeth is a female.

This is valid because its conclusion follows from the premises. It is true because it makes an accurate claim (the information is consistent with the facts), and it is sound because the syllogism is both valid and true.

Inductive reasoning, on the other hand, draws conclusions from facts and observations in evidence. Consider the final arguments made by a district attorney who is attempting to convict a defendant for murder. Even though the jury has listened to all the evidence presented by the witnesses, the district attorney reviews the points in evidence that he believes will lead to a verdict (conclusion) of guilty.

CLOSING ARGUMENTS (INDUCTIVE REASONING)
DISTRICT ATTORNEY

The defendant owned the gun that the bullet came from that killed the victim.

The defendant had had a serious argument with the victim hours before the victim was found dead.

The defendant's fingerprints were found at the crime scene on a glass that had been used around the time of the victim's death.

The defendant had the blood of the murdered victim on his clothes.

From these facts, you can only conclude that the defendant is guilty.

The defendant testified that the gun had been reported stolen five years prior to the murder.

The defendant had had an argument with the victim but had sent the victim flowers before the murder in an attempt to reconcile.

The defendant's mother testified that she was with the victim during the time of the shooting.

Therefore, based on the defendant's testimony and his mother's, you have enough evidence to create reasonable doubt and find the defendant not guilty.

Although inductive reasoning can present pieces of evidence in clear, distinct form, inductive reasoning can never lead to conclusions that are certain. Once all the points are gathered and examined, the readers (or, in this case, the jury) must make an inductive leap to a conclusion. This is also known as an **inference,** a conclusion about the unknown based on the known. Thus, to make as accurate a conclusion as possible, we must have as much evidence as possible.

Evidence

To convince a jury, the lawyers for both sides must gather information through research. They must explore all possible sources, revisiting some and dropping others. The lawyers look for the most reliable sources that are believable and that can provide testimony to support their claim: the defendant is guilty or not guilty.

To convince your readers, you, too, should have reliable evidence. Consider the following comment as a support for the defense: "Oh, I know he's innocent because I love him" or "I've known him since high school, and he couldn't have murdered anyone." Just as neither of these assertions provides factual evidence, neither does an assertion in a paper based purely on emotion or personal opinion. Thus, they weaken the argument and your credibility for knowing how to select reliable sources. The length and kind of argument you need to produce will determine how much evidence you will have to gather through research.

Presenting Evidence

When you write an argumentative essay, you must be careful to avoid using flawed arguments, those which seem reasonable but are not. Sometimes writers use these flawed arguments or **fallacies** unknowingly or accidentally, and some writers use them intentionally because they sound logical. The following are a few of the most common fallacies.

Generalizations

- **Hasty generalizations** arrive at conclusions without sufficient evidence. For example, to conclude that your significant other is unfaithful to you because someone saw him at a restaurant with a woman other than you is to jump to conclusions without enough evidence. The other woman could have been his sister, a business colleague, a classmate, or an old friend. You don't have enough information; therefore, the conclusion is a hasty generalization.
- **Sweeping generalizations** occur when a writer makes an absolute statement about a group for which there are no exceptions. High school students frequently use this fallacy to convince their parents to let them go somewhere or do something they want to do: "Everyone is going to the party Saturday night."
- **Stereotypes** are sweeping generalizations that make assumptions about all members of a group. See Chapter 8: Misconceptions, for examples of stereotypes. Making comments that are stereotypes or sweeping generalizations reduces a speaker's credibility (when a single example is cited that is an exception): "Proponents of capital punishment support it as a legal form of revenge."

The Either/Or Fallacy, or the False Dilemma This fallacy offers a complex situation as having only two sides. "To survive a heart attack, a patient must reduce stress or increase the amount of exercise she gets."

The False Analogy An analogy compares two unlike things. A **false analogy** assumes that because an issue, a concept, a person, or so forth is similar to another issue, concept, or person in some ways, they are similar in others. "Leaving the *Titanic* and other sunken vessels at the bottom of the sea is like dumping garbage into our oceans, another form of pollution."

The Red Herring A **red herring fallacy** is one that shifts the focus of the reader away from the main argument. "The newest makeup on the market is being banned by environmentalists, but the manufacturer is a big contributor to the March of Dimes."

The Bandwagon Fallacy **The bandwagon fallacy** invites readers literally to "jump on the bandwagon," a cliché that indicates that the reader should believe something because so many other people already believe it. If the reader does not endorse the idea, he will be left behind. "The teachers' union supports the new candidate for school board because she will reduce the dropout rate among many student populations."

Appeal to Emotion An **appeal to emotion** is an attempt to divert the reader from the facts of an argument by relying primarily on emotions rather than on logic. Usually fear and pity are the two most common emotions unethical writers rely on when they run out of reasons or know they have an issue that can affect many people through the use of emotions:

In a recent court case involving road rage, a woman tearfully described a man who jumped out of his car, yelled at her, grabbed her six-year-old dog from her car, and threw it into the busy freeway traffic where it was killed before her eyes.

➤ Short Writing Assignment

On your way home or while running an errand, look at the advertisements on billboards or look through newspapers at the advertisements. Notice what fallacies the advertisers use. Select two different examples of fallacies used in ads and identify the fallacy, explain what the advertiser wanted to achieve by using it, and whether or not you think it works on the general public.

Writing the Argumentative Essay

Just as in writing the informative essay, writing the **argumentative essay** requires preparation. Knowing the stumbling blocks discussed in the preceding pages should alert writers to possible problems: valid vs. invalid deductive reasoning, uncertain conclusions drawn from inductive reasoning, and commonly used fallacies and appeals to emotion. The next step is to consider the audience.

Audience

The question of whom the writer is trying to convince is crucial. If a writer were attempting to justify the actions of Vietnam War "draft dodgers" to a Veterans of Foreign Wars group or to members of the American legion, that writer would probably be unsuccessful. If a writer were attempting to convince a group of environmentalists to support President George W. Bush's desire to drill for oil in the national park in Alaska, that writer also would be wasting time. Therefore, student writers should target members of the undecided group in the middle rather than staunch opponents of a proposition or the firmly supportive group that already backs the proposition. Those individuals in the middle who are wavering need well-developed, thoughtful arguments that provide fresh new evidence or a fresh approach that raises their interest. The writer should always assume that the audience will be skeptical and possibly hostile if the issue is highly controversial. In these cases, the writer must build sound, strong arguments.

Prewriting

Prewriting is also crucial to writing a successful argumentative essay. After you have chosen a topic, you need to make two lists. One list states reasons supporting the topic you have chosen and a second list states reasons opposing the topic. This does not mean that you have chosen your position yet; it only means that you have found points that support and oppose your topic. Many students have difficulty understanding why they need to know the opposition's points. Keep in mind that if you don't know what the opposition thinks, you are at a disadvantage. Knowing the opposition's points provides the writer with an opportunity to present a rebuttal or refutation. To refute a point is to show how it is in error or wrong; to rebut is basically the same process, to oppose with proof to the contrary. Thus, not to know your opposition's beliefs is to leave yourself open to a surprise attack for which you have no defense, refutation, or rebuttal. It reduces your credibility, and it makes you appear narrow-minded in your awareness of only the points that support your position. It indicates that you cannot concede or acknowledge any constructive aspects of the opposition's argument and that you have made no provisions to accommodate or compromise.

Cleaning Up Air Pollution

Points in Favor	Points Opposed
1. It decreases health problems such as lung cancer, heart attacks, and emphysema.	1. It requires trained inspectors to test the amount of pollution in the air.
2. It cuts down on the problem of global warming.	2. It requires people to identify companies that are violating the law.
3. It provides visually pleasing views.	3. It requires regular and costly monitoring systems to be implemented to measure pollution being released into the environment.
4. Air pollution damages seals around windows.	4. It is too costly to install air pollution filtering devises in equipment already in place.
5. Air pollution destroys the older architecture and statues.	5. It would require a change in driving laws, reducing the speed limits from 70 miles per hour to 55 miles per hour.
6. Air pollution clogs up air filters in cars and air conditioners.	

Look at the three sample prompts cited on pages 73–74. When student writers are assigned a topic to write about outside of class, they are more likely to receive a prompt that is worded more like the third example. For such an assignment, the student writer must discover through research points that argue for or against the topic. Once she has gathered the points, she needs to list the positive points and the negative points about her topic. Below is an example of points for both sides of the air pollution topic.

Now that she can see the points made by opposing sides, she is prepared to determine her position, select the points that will defend her position, select the counter-arguments, and write her thesis.

➤ Short Writing Assignment

From the list below, select one topic and write points that support the issue and points that oppose it. You might have to complete some research to supply points. Be sure that your sources are current and reliable.

- The use of HMOs
- Government-subsidized child care for working women
- Affirmative action
- Free college education for any graduate in the top 10% of his/her graduating class
- Reducing the highway speeds from 70 miles per hour to 55 miles per hour

Building Block: The Introduction

In the informative essay, Julian and Cindy included a definition of their topics. In an argumentative or persuasive essay, the writer should provide background information prior to starting the argument.

BACKGROUND INFORMATION

- helps establish the writer's credibility;
- provides information that the reader might not know;
- supplies information that might be needed as the writer develops the argument but which does not fit into the present paragraph;
- provides a historical, social, medical, legal or other context for the argument;
- uses a neutral rather than a defensive tone to begin the essay; and
- can provide a summary of other people's opinions.

The structure of the introduction can look like the informative essay's introduction, with the writer adopting the triangle or the rectangle pattern. A difference, however, arises in the placement of the proposal/claim/thesis. It can be included in the introduction so that the reader immediately understands the writer's position, or the writer can present the issue in an unbiased manner, leaning in neither direction. At the end of the essay, after considering the claims and counterclaims, the writer can inductively arrive at a conclusion, which in this case is the thesis. Most instructors prefer to see a stated thesis in the introduction, though, so check with your instructor for her requirements.

➤ Short Writing Assignments

1. Using one of the first two prompts presented on pages 73–74 write an introduction that presents background information about the topic and uses the last sentence as the thesis/claim.
2. Using one of the first two prompts, write an introduction that does not provide a proposal/claim/thesis.

Building Block: The Body Paragraphs

Once the writer has chosen a position and written a thesis that clearly states the position, or once the writer has chosen the points to be used to build the proposition or claim, she can begin writing the body paragraphs. To do so, the writer will normally begin with her weakest argument and progress to her strongest. She must also summarize and refute the opposition's points. Structurally, the essay may develop the opposing points in individual paragraphs and then move to the supports, to refute the opposition. The opposing points may be discussed briefly at the beginning of two or more paragraphs, with a transition leading to the refutation after the opposing point in each paragraph. Look at the following example. Although there is no introduction provided, there is a thesis or claim.

Cleaning Up Air Pollution

Claim: Tightening the federal regulation on industrial air emissions should be delayed because of insufficient data to determine effects on health, the financial burden of such added regulations, and limited number of personnel qualified to regulate such controls.

One of the main concerns proponents of air pollution clean-up use to foster their argument for stronger regulation of industrial air is the issue of health. Problems related to circulation, such as heart and lung diseases, and to skin irritations are among the pro-regulators' main arsenal of weapons aimed at the industrial sector's perceived abuse of the country's air quality. However, what such proponents fail to provide is a direct one-to-one correlation between a particular factory's emissions and the health issues of the community. Nor do such groups possess any community-wide data or study which shows any type of chemical interaction between the various types of waste air generated by the community's industrial companies. Instead of looking to the industrial sector, which is already heavily regulated and monitored by state and federal agencies, the proponents of industrial clean-up should consider not only the fumes created by the automobiles they drive but also the household chemicals used directly within their own home, chemicals which often carry poison warnings on them and which are in constant and close proximity to the individual family members.

As you can see, the topic sentence is generated from the thesis and develops into a point that is held by the opposition. After discussing the opposition's point sufficiently to display a knowledge of the argument, the writer provides a transition that moves into her refutation: "However, what such proponents fail to provide . . . ." If the student had a better understanding of her opponent's position, she could have developed the point more fully into a complete paragraph, used the transition, and devoted the next paragraph to a full rebuttal of the opposition's point. The essay that follows uses this kind of construction. Regardless of which construction student writers choose, they should remember to leave their strongest argument until the end.

If the essay is to be written as an outside class project, student writers should try to go to the library or visit the World Wide Web to gather information about the topic. One of the best library references to use to find sources is the *Readers' Guide to Periodical Literature,* which provides monthly supplements that are divided into topics, arranged alphabetically, and displayed in bibliographic format. It is usually kept on the reference desk for easy access. A student may also check with a librarian about other indices for various professional fields. If the student needs material other than periodicals, she can go to the computer catalogue, type in the term to be researched and receive book titles, call numbers, and locations of books that might provide further information. When researching, the student writer should try to find current information, statistics, examples, and facts provided by experts in the field, to help establish her credibility. For further discussion of research, go to Appendix 2: Research.

Another method of development comes from the informative essay. In writing persuasively, the student writer should remember to include some of the patterns she learned when writing to inform: comparison-and-contrast, exemplification, cause and effect, and description. These patterns can be used effectively to convince the reader.

Building Block: The Conclusion

The final paragraph should ensure that the readers not only remember your argument but are swayed to change their minds and, in the case of persuasion, convinced to act upon their new conviction. To reinforce her position, this student restated her thesis, but instead of stating each point in the thesis, as she had in her introduction, she used only the claim. The method she uses to conclude is inductive: she restates and summarizes the major points she used to support her claim in the essay, and she ends with a concluding sentence that provides an inductive leap into what she believes is the only conclusion the reader can make.

    Therefore, Congress should delay sending forth any bill that
    would tighten federal regulations on air emissions. To date,
    there is insufficient information on the effects of emissions
    from factories, cars, and incinerators to determine their effect
    on health issues. Furthermore, the added financial burden expe-
    rienced by the factories in question would shift to the prices
    charged to the public for items produced by the factories. Fi-
    nally, because of the limited number of qualified personnel
    available to regulate the controls, inequality in the overseeing
    of the process would result in some factories being regulated
    while others remain unsupervised. Thus, until the federal gov-
    ernment provides measurable statistics on health-related prob-
    lems, federal aid to companies to modify their equipment, and
    trained supervisors to ensure compliance by everyone, Congress
    should not create a tightening of federal regulations that are
    unenforceable.

In looking at the student's conclusion, we find no mention of any of the opposition's points. She has devoted her last body paragraph to her strongest point and her conclusion to a summary of all her supporting material. Research in reading theory indicates that most readers remember what they read at the beginning of an article and what they read at the end. If writers remember that and implement that theory in their writing, then a strong closure focusing on the writer's position and eliminating the opposition should leave the writer's argument firmly implemented in the reader's mind.

The Argumentative Example

For their 90-minute final exam, students were given the following prompt to write about in class without the benefit of library or World Wide Web research. Following the prompt is an essay that responds.

Writing Assignment—Final Exam
Disorder in Schools

According to some critics, too many college students have neither the aptitude nor the attitudes needed in college. Therefore, there is a move to tighten the standards for admission. Proponents argue that there are too many students who do not have the prerequisites for going to college, therefore requiring that they take remedial courses before they are admitted into academic courses. They also say that affirmative action does not work because even though students are allowed into the universities, they do not have the background to compete with academically qualified students. They also point out that in many university systems, open admissions allows students to feel little incentive to exert themselves to excel, believing that they can make the grades simply because they were admitted. They also believe that the professors and the taxpayers are wasting time and money on the nonacademically prepared students. On the other hand, opponents of this belief feel that some students are "late bloomers" and will be able to "catch up" with their peers once they are put into a competitive situation. Others feel that it is the student's right to try, and if the student fails, he or she has still learned a valuable lesson. Finally, other opponents believe that community colleges are a form of safety net that allows students to make up deficiencies they may have while pursuing those academic courses at the university level that the students may be qualified to take.

In the essay you are to write, take a position that supports or opposes the issue of tightening the standards for admission into universities. Remember that your audience will be your instructor.

Stronger Standards for Admissions

The issue of admission standards is one which faces universities across the country. Although tax-supported public education has been a privilege enjoyed by America's students for most of the country's history, such education does not imply that all students graduating from high school are qualified under the current admissions standards or even motivated to finish a degree plan. As state budgets tighten and endowment funds gradual decrease, the administrative leaders in such schools are being forced to consider ways to make every dollar as productive as possible in terms of their students' needs. What the opponents of tougher standards argue for is a gradually lessening of admissions standards that would open the country's colleges to a flood of ill-qualified applicants and possibly lay the groundwork for free public education to one day reach the college level. Therefore, America's colleges should tighten its admissions standards as a way to limit the number of unqualified students, to increase the student's responsibility to maintain good grades, and as a way to curb the financial burden both the state and the student share in paying for a college education.

Student qualification for admissions has always been a top priority for colleges. When taken together, national admissions tests, such as SAT and ACT, and high school transcripts are the colleges' main ways to determine how well a student will perform in college. While admissions test reflect the student's abilities to analyze and the skills she mastered, the school transcript indicates the student's ability to perform over an extended period of time. If such skills are lacking and a student would be admitted to the college program, such a move would place a burden on the college to provide remedial courses to bring the student up to acceptable level of performance. Such courses require not only extra faculty to teach the course, but place a strain on the facilities needed, such as classroom space. While programs, such as Affirmative Action, are seen as a way to help some individuals have the opportunity to enter college, such programs also open the way for some students who are not academically qualified to attend a college. Overall, such a weak standards policy could actually frustrate the unprepared student.

Also, a weak policy for admissions would give the student the impression that high grades and consistent performance do not matter in an academic world. If a student with a D+ average was admitted to a college, what is the motivation for that student to excel? If the college left its doors open to most high school students and held them to college standards, then the drop-out rate would leave the school with a bad public image and leave the student with a late start in the job market as well as a poor self-image. The professional image of the college's standing could also be lowered as well, and the college could gain the reputation of being simply a "party" school with no academic foundation. Such an outcome is unacceptable for both student and college.

A more practical reason for tighter admissions standards is the poor use of both faculty effort and tax-payers' funds to educate a poorly qualified student. Colleges employ professors who have spent years gaining an in depth knowledge of their fields, and such knowledge would be wasted or put to poor use if the professor had to "dummy down" or water-down his/her class to an unqualified student. The cost of remedial classes would mean that other academic classes could not be taught in order to make room for such remedial classes. To make up for such a financial burden, the state legislature would have to increase tuition for all college students. Such financial burden would also extend to campus fees because an increased enrollment would put a larger strain on campus facilities, such as parking and general wear and tear of buildings.

Opponents of tighter admissions standards have a clear argument that some students who did not excel in high school are merely "late bloomers." Some students mature later than others, and a tighter admissions policy would definitely hurt a student who developed his/her analytical and concentration skills later in life. Such "late bloomers" may not perform well on standardized tests and may also have poor ACT and SAT scores. Also, colleges do set standards for grade point averages for their degrees which the student must maintain once they are in. Such a competitive atmosphere could act as an added incentive for a student to perform better then he/she has in the past.

Another strong point for lessening admissions standards is the fact that education is still a privilege and a right which the student has. If the student pays a tuition and fee bill instead of receiving a free public education as they did in high school, then he/she assumes the responsibility of his/her actions and decisions. If the student fails, the blame does not fall to the college. Supporters of weaker admissions policies point out that community colleges are available, at the student's own cost, to help in any deficiencies he/she may have while continuing at the college in areas in which the student may be more proficient.

While the arguments for a weaker admissions policy have the student's interest at heart, such arguments do not fit the realities of the academic world. Even though students pay tuition and fees, such payments are no where near the actual cost of maintaining the college-level class. Most of the funds come from the state legislatures which are already burdened with providing other social services to the state. Also, colleges can only maintain facilities for a set number of students, and if the lesser qualified students are allowed in, than the more qualified students are left out. Over time, the quality of service and care at the professional level for the community and the state will suffer. Lastly, colleges are maintained to produce academic excellence, and it is the student's responsibility to reach such levels. By weakening the admissions policies, one weakens the institutions as well and, more importantly, the responsibility of the students to perform and strive for such heights.

A Final Note on Structure

As usual, there is more than one way to write an argumentative or persuasive essay. If the writer finds weak arguments for the opposition, she can place them at the end of the essay instead of at the beginning. For example, in the above essay, the student begins with strong points, builds the argument immediately (gaining credibility), and then adds weak arguments that cannot compete with her material. The conclusion uses elements of the opposition's argument in such a way that they can be dismissed by the reader. Finally, the writer returns with a cause and effect sentence that reveals the problems that can arise by weakening the admissions standards.

• P A R T   T W O •

Multicultural Readings

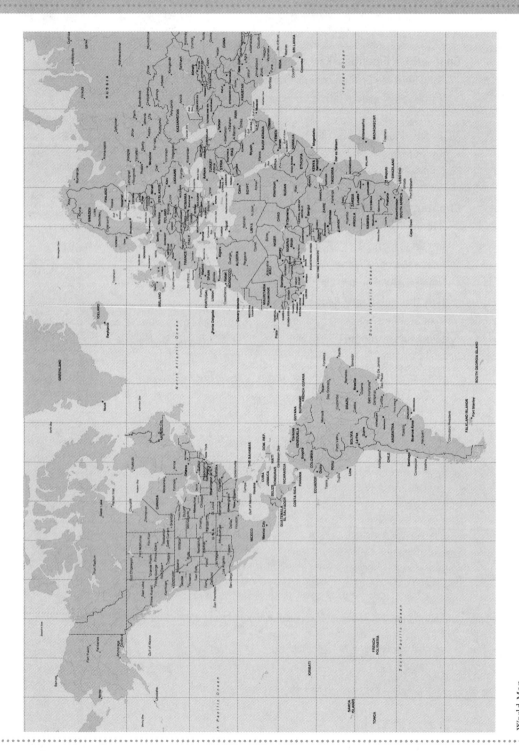

World Map
Source: © 1995 Cartesia Software

Myths and Legends: Stories of Gods, Creation, Man, and Death

Almost all of us can recite the story of the creation of the world; it was probably told to us by our parents or spiritual leaders when we were young. Furthermore, many of us have studied the Greek and Roman stories of gods and goddesses on Mt. Olympus and know of their relationship with mortals. Even though some of us consider these stories to be sacred Truth, these accounts of creation fall into a literary category called **myths:** stories that have their foundation in actual events but that also describe the involvement of mortals with deities and relate supernatural events to explain natural ones. Some myths may seem strange to those who do not belong to the cultures that celebrate those beliefs. For example, those who believe the biblical version of creation may find it difficult to picture their god as a plumed serpent, as did the Aztecs of Mexico.

Creation, however, is not the only mystery that myths attempt to clarify. The idea of death frequently creates feelings of fear in people because of the uncertainty about what lies beyond life. Thus, cultures have provided stories that help their people prepare for the journey or transition between life and death.

An important point that should be kept in mind is that myths are different from **legends.** The former involve the supernatural and mortals interacting with gods. Legends, however, usually focus on historical issues that involve real people or fictional characters such as George Washington, Beowulf, Robin Hood, King Arthur, *La Llorona,* Joan of Arc, and others. Their adventures or misadventures make them into figures of cultural lore that provide lessons of honesty, bravery, chivalry, or even warnings to children and adults on how not to behave.

Before you begin reading any of the creation myths, it would be a good idea to review the story of creation that you learned as you were growing up. Doing so helps you clarify the special points that your culture wants you to remember about the creator and the other individuals involved in the event. Take a few moments before you start reading and think about your own beliefs.

The following world myths have been arranged alphabetically by culture. Most originated from an oral tradition and have been written and summarized by others. Be sure to refer to the maps (pages 000-000) to find the location of each area discussed in the myth.

The Athapascan Story

Western Canada

Introductory Remarks: The Athapascan people are a group of American Indians who live in Alaska, Northwestern Canada, and on the Pacific Northwest coast of the United States.

Pre-Reading Ideas: This myth is based on a belief in a female god. What are your feelings about a female deity who is responsible for the creation of the earth? What characteristics would you use to describe a female god? If you gave her human qualities, you just personified her, an action that helps us identify with deities so that they won't seem so distant or overwhelming.

Vocabulary: Looking up and understanding the following words prior to reading should prepare you for the author's message. Other words will be defined in the margin.

Loom   Athabasca River

1   When Mother Earth was very young, the mountains and the rivers of Her proud body blossomed in the springtime of Her being. She was more than fair to look upon, but Her greatest beauty of all was that part of Her that became the homeland of the Northern Athapascan peoples. . . .

2   It was on this most perfect part of Earth that Asintmah, first woman of the world, appeared at the foot of Mount Atiksa near the Athabasca River. The holy Asintmah walked among the forests that grew upon Earth, gathering branches that had been discarded° by the trees, careful not to tear or wrench away any that might still be growing on the body of the Earth. Joining these branches together Asintmah built the first loom. And upon it she wove the fibers of the fireweed, the willow herb that Earth so favored, weaving them into The Great Blanket of Earth.

3   Once the weaving was completed, Asintmah began her long walk to spread the sacred blanket across the vast body of Earth. . . . Then sitting down beside the edge of the blanket Asintmah began to weave threads of music, singing of all the beauties of Earth, singing songs of how Earth would soon give birth to new lives, beings as perfect as Herself. . . .

discard: to get rid of

4   Suddenly all was quiet. Earth lay still and calm once again. It was in this way that Asintmah knew that the children born of Earth's womb had been delivered. So it was that with the help of the holy Asintmah, the woman who existed before all others, Maiden Earth became Mother Earth. And although this all happened a very long time ago, Athapascan people remember that even now they must care for their aging mother, the one who gave them life, and honor the memory of the woman Asintmah who was with Her in the beginning.

➤ Follow-Up Questions

1. Asintmah is described as the first woman, "the woman who existed before all others." What qualities does she display? What is the significance of her activity of weaving? Do any other creation myths that you know use this craft? If so, who does the weaving?
2. Asintmah is called "holy." What in the context of the myth makes her "holy"?
3. This myth of creation makes no mention of the presence of a heaven or a hell. In no more than three sentences, describe what you think either heaven or hell would be like, bearing in mind that the myth came from the cold regions of Alaska and the Pacific Northwest.

➤ Short Writing Assignments

1. Living in an urban environment makes it difficult to go places that are filled with trees and quiet vistas. Find a place where you can be quiet in nature—a river, the woods, a public park when few people are there—and spend some time sitting and quietly listening to the sounds made by the birds, the wind, the grass, the leaves. Write a **descriptive paper** that recounts your experience. Remember to use all of your senses, rather than relying just on sight. Also describe your feelings.
2. The Athapascan **myth** may differ in many ways from your own beliefs. Choose two or three areas, such as description of deity or order of creation, and write an essay describing how your beliefs **compare and contrast** with the Athapascans' **myth.**

➤ Extended Writing Assignments

1. Many cultures rely on oral or spoken tradition to relate their own myths. However, one problem with oral tradition is that because the stories are memorized, many are lost. Write an essay relating a favorite story of your family or group of friends so that it will not be lost or forgotten.
2. Think of a favorite memory you have about an event in your life and write down a brief description. Then talk to as many people as you can who were involved with the incident and find out what they remember about the event. Then write an essay explaining how each person's recollection of the event is different and similar to your own.

Oannes, the Fish

Babylonian Myth

Introductory Remarks: The Babylonians were an ancient and civilized culture that prospered from 1900 to 1100 BC. Their society was divided into three classes: the patricians, consisting of free men and women; the plebians or common people; and the slaves. The king of Babylonia created the code by which they lived, and it established standards for morals, class, gender relationships, and religion. It was the most important contribution made by Mesopotamia to the civilized world.

Pre-Reading Ideas: There are many classical tales using the convention of the helpful animals who appear when human beings are stranded or in trouble. This myth, however, goes beyond the tales and offers an amphibian who teaches humanity many things. Consider how knowledge was spread among ancient people. Have you ever wondered how people survived before the inventions we know today? How did cooking food come about? Sewing? How did ancient civilizations develop? Read the following myth and see what kinds of answers it provides.

Vocabulary: Looking up and understanding the following words prior to reading should prepare you for the author's message. Other words will be defined in the margin.

Babylon   subjoined   articulate   compile   amphibious

1   In the first year there appeared from that part of the Erythræan Sea which borders upon Babylonia, an animal endowed with reason, by name Oannes, whose whole body (according to the account of Apollodorus) was that of a fish; that under the fish's head he had another head, with feet also below similar to those of a man, subjoined to a fish's tail. His voice, too, and language were articulate and human; and a representation of him is preserved unto this day. This being was accustomed to pass the day among men, but took no food at that season; and he gave them an insight into letters and sciences, and arts of every kind. He taught them to construct cities, to found temples, to compile laws, and explained to them the principle of geometrical knowledge. He made them distinguish the seeds of the earth, and showed them how to collect fruits; in short, he instructed them in everything which could tend to soften manners and humanize lives. From that time, nothing material has been added by way of improvement to his instructions. When the sun had set, this being, Oannes, retired again into the sea, and passed the night in the deep, for he was amphibious.

➤ Follow-Up Questions

1. Draw what you believe the fish Oannes looks.
2. What types of knowledge does Oannes give to humans? Does he sound god-like?
3. Why does Oannes not remain constantly with humans? Is there any correlation between his physical form and his return to the sea at night?

➤ Short Writing Assignments

1. In a short essay, discuss how knowledge and reason, such as that which Oannes gives to humans, can "soften manners and humanize lives."
2. In paragraph form, describe what you would consider the single most important invention of the last fifty years that has helped to "humanize" the society, and explain the reasons for your choice.

➤ Extended Writing Assignments

1. Research the mythology of another culture and find two other examples of animals which are both intelligent and helpful to humans. Then prepare a report which **compares and contrasts** the figures, the physical form, powers, and types of help given to human beings.
2. Research the culture of Babylon to determine the cultural background or significant cultural aspects which would account for the ideas represented in this myth of Oannes. Consider such ideas as fish/sea, the construction of cities, and "geometrical knowledge," to name a few. Explain your findings in a report.

The Hebrew Creation Story

from Genesis

Introductory Remarks: In 1536 William Tyndale, the first man to translate the Scriptures from Hebrew and Greek into English, was burned at the stake for "willfully perverting the meaning of the Scriptures" and for presenting "untrue translations" of the New Testament. Despite these accusations, Tyndale's translations are the basis for most of the subsequent versions of the Bible that have since be published. The major exception was the translation of the New Testament by Roman Catholic scholars who used the Latin Vulgate as their original source. The most well-known and respected version of the Bible is the King James version, published in 1611. Today, countless contemporary versions of the Bible are on bookshelves; with the exception of wording, they convey the same basic message.

Pre-Reading Ideas: If you have a copy of the Bible, regardless of its age or version, you might want to compare it with the version of the Genesis story that follows. Although the Book of Genesis continues for fifty chapters, the story of creation can be conveyed in chapter 1 and the beginning of 2. This myth was written in approximately 800 BC after the Exodus of the Israelites from Egypt occurred.

Vocabulary: Looking up and understanding the following words prior to reading should prepare you for the author's message. Other words will be defined in the margin.

cleave

....

1   In the beginning God created the heaven and the earth. And the earth was
void: empty   without form, and void°; and darkness was upon the face of the deep. And
space   the Spirit of God was moved upon the face of the waters. And God said, Let there be light: and there was light. And God saw that the light, that it was good: and God divided the light from the darkness. And God called the light Day, and the darkness he called Night. And the evening and the morning were the first day.

firmament: sky   2   And God said, Let there be a firmament° in the midst of the waters, and let it divide the waters from the waters. And God made the firmament, and divided the waters which were under the firmament from the waters which were above the firmament: and it was so. And God called the firmament Heaven. And the evening and the morning were the second day.

3   And God said, Let the waters under the heaven be gathered together unto one place, and let the dry land appear: and it was so. And God called the dry land Earth; and the gathering together of the waters called he Seas: And God saw that it was good. And God said, Let the earth bring forth grass, the herb yielding seed, and fruit tree yielding fruit after his kind, whose seed is in itself, upon the earth: and it was so. And the earth brought forth grass, and herb yielding after his kind, and tree yielding fruit, whose seed was in itself, after his kind: and God saw that it was good. And the evening and the morning were the third day.

4   And God said, Let there be lights in the firmament of the heaven to separate the day from the night; and let them be for signs, and for seasons, and for days, and years: and let them be for lights in the firmament of the heaven to give light upon the earth: and it was so. And God made the two great lights; the greater light to rule the day, and the lesser light to rule the night: he made the stars also. And God set them in the firmament of the heaven to give light upon the earth, and to rule over the day and over the night, and to divide the light from the darkness: And God saw that it was good. And the evening and the morning were the fourth day.

5   And God said, Let the waters bring forth abundantly the moving creature that hath life, and fowl that may fly above the earth in the open firmament of heaven. And God created great whales, and every living creature that moveth, which the waters brought forth abundantly, after their kind, and

every winged fowl after his kind: and God saw that it was good. And God blessed them, saying, Be fruitful, and multiply, and fill the waters in the seas, and let fowl multiply in the earth. And the evening and the morning were the fifth day.

6   And God said, Let the earth bring forth the living creature after his kind, cattle, and creeping thing, and beast of the earth after his kind: and it was so. And God made the beast of the earth after his kind, and cattle after their kind, and every thing that creepeth upon the earth after his kind: and God saw that it was good.

7   Then God said, Let us make man in our image, after our likeness: and let them have dominion over the fish of the sea, and over the fowl of the air, and over the cattle, and over all the earth, and over every creeping thing that creepeth upon the earth. So God created man in his own image, in the image of God created he him; male and female created he them. And God blessed them, and God said unto them, Be fruitful, and multiply, and replenish the earth, and subdue it: and have dominion over the fish of the sea, and over the fowl of the air, and over every living thing that moveth upon the earth.

8   And God said, Behold, I have given you every herb bearing seed, which is upon the face of all the earth, and every tree, in the which is the fruit of a tree yielding seed; to you it shall be for meat. And to every beast of the earth, and to every fowl of the air, and to everything that creepeth upon the earth, wherein there is life, I have given every green herb for meat: and it was so. And God saw everything that he had made, and, behold, it was very good. And the evening and the morning were the sixth day.

9   Thus the heavens and the earth were finished and all the host of them. And on the seventh day God ended his work which he had made; and he rested on the seventh day from all his work which he had made. And God blessed the seventh day, and sanctified° it: because that in it he had rested from all his work which God created and made.

sanctified: made it holy

10   These are the generations of the heavens and of the earth when they were created in the day that the Lord God made the earth and the heavens, and every plant of the field before it was in the earth, and every herb of the field before it grew: for the Lord God had not caused it to rain upon the earth, and there was not a man to till the ground. But there went up a mist from the earth, and watered the whole face of the ground. And the Lord God formed man of the dust of the ground and breathed into his nostrils the breath of life; and man became a living soul.

11   And then the Lord God planted a garden eastward in Eden; and there he put the man whom he had formed. And out of the ground the Lord God made to grow every tree that is pleasant to the sight, and good for food; and the tree of life also in the midst of the garden and the tree of the knowledge of good and evil.

12   And a river went out of Eden to water the garden; and from thence it was parted, and became into four heads. . . . And the Lord God took the man,

and put him into the garden of Eden to dress it and to keep it. And the Lord God commanded the man, saying, Of every tree of the garden thou mayest freely eat: but of the tree of the knowledge of good and evil, thou shall not eat of it: for in the day that eatest thereof thou shalt surely die.

13   And the Lord God said, It is not good that the man should be alone; I will make him an help meet for him. And out of the ground the Lord God formed every beast of the field, and every fowl of the air; and brought them unto Adam to see what he would call them: and whatsoever Adam called every living creature, that was its name thereof. And Adam gave names to all cattle, and to the fowl of the air, and to every beast of the field; but for Adam there was not found an help meet for him. And the Lord God caused a deep sleep to fall upon Adam, and he slept: and he took one of his ribs, and closed up the flesh instead thereof; and the rib, which the Lord God had taken from man, made he a woman, and brought her unto the man. And Adam said, This is now bone of my bones, and flesh of my flesh: she shall be called Woman, because she was taken out of Man. Therefore shall a man leave his father and his mother, and shall cleave unto his wife: and they shall be one flesh. And they were naked, the man and his wife, and were not ashamed.

➤ Follow-Up Questions

1. There is argument that the use of the word "day" in this creation myth should be read as a symbolic term rather than taken literally. In other words, it is a word that stands for something else, much like the color red on a traffic signal is symbolic of the command to stop. What are your feelings about this kind of reading? Do you agree or disagree and why?
2. Why do you think Adam could not eat of the "tree of the knowledge of good and evil"?
3. Describe the deity in this myth. Does this deity resemble or differ from any of the other deities read about in this chapter? If so, which ones and how are they similar or different?

➤ Short Writing Assignments

1. Because creation myths have often been handed down in a language that is not the original, there has been concern over reading them literally. As a result, many arguments have arisen over the centuries. The Hebrew version of creation presented here is clearly not the latest; if you compare it to more contemporary editions, you will find it is quite different. The meaning, however, is maintained. Write a brief paper in which you take a **position** on whether this or any version of a creation myth should be read literally.
2. In this myth, as opposed to the American Indian myths, the relationships between God and the animals and between human beings and the animals are clearly different. Write an **informative** paragraph identifying the relationships and discussing what this means about human beings' feelings toward animals in each story, and how you feel about each relationship.

➤ Extended Writing Assignments

1. Genesis recounts two different versions of the creation of man and woman. The first version simply states, "So God created man in his own image, in the image of God he created him; male and female created he them. " The second version involves the creation of Eve from Adam's rib. Write an essay in which you take a position on why the second creation myth is the one most used today and how this second version affects society's views of men and women.
2. Either attend a religious service of your choice or watch a religious program on television; then write an essay that describes the religious views and myths of the service or program and what the main theme or focus of such preaching was.

The Legend of the Jackal and the Color Blue

Hindu Legend

Introductory Remarks: References to Hinduism are made in the following legend as well as in Linda Koffel's poem "Blue Skin" (Chapter 5: Education), in which the narrator also wants blue skin. What do you know about the Hindu religion? Do a little background research in the library or on the Internet to find information about Krishna before you read this legend. See if you can find a picture representing the deity and bring it to class for discussion.

Pre-Reading Ideas: To have power is one thing, but to use power wisely is quite another. What kind of a leader would you make if you suddenly discovered that because of some characteristic that you accidentally acquired, you were now considered not only powerful but godlike? That is the dilemma of the main character in this legend. Before you read the story, write down three things you would do if you had unlimited power. There is an old saying: Be careful of what you wish for; it might come true. After you have determined what three things you would do or change with unlimited power, write a short response explaining what the effects of these changes or acts would be.

Vocabulary: Looking up and understanding the following words prior to reading should prepare you for the author's message. Other words will be defined in the margin.

indigo	shakàl	anointed	homage	consequence

1   There is in the city of Ujayani a shakàl, who, going one night for his pleasure beyond the limits of the town, fell into a pot of indigo; and, unable to rise out of it, lay in it as if he were dead. In the morning the owner of the

indigo pulled him forth and threw him out of the room, then he, concealing himself, ran away into the forest. Perceiving that he was of a dark-blue color, he thus thought within himself: "Am I now of a divine color—the color of Crishna! What greatness, therefore, may I not attain!"

2   Having, accordingly, summoned the rest of the shakàls, he said to them: "the deity of this wood has himself anointed me sovereign of it with the juice of celestial° herbs. See my holy color! To-day, therefore, I must begin the discharge of my duty; and by my command justice shall be administered in the forest." The beasts, perceiving his distinguishing color, fell prostrate° and paid homage saying, "As the king commands!"—and there was supreme dominion° conferred on him by all the animals of his race. Soon after, when he had also assembled a herd of lions, tigers, and other beasts deceived by his appearance, he despised his species, and dismissed all the shakàls, who were much afflicted with their disgrace. But an old shakàl arose among them and said: "Be not grieved; I promise you relief. We who know him are driven from him; but, as he seeks to ruin us, I must contrive to destroy him. The lions, tigers, and the rest imagine from his blue hide that he is a monarch°; but be it our care that he may be detected. Thus may we effect° our purpose: One evening, when you are all collected before him, set up a loud cry. When he hears it, his nature will prompt him to join it; for whatever is natural to anyone can hardly be discontinued: should a dog be made king, he would still gnaw leather. The tigers, lions, and the rest, knowing his voice, will destroy him." This being done, the consequence followed.

celestial: heavenly

prostrate: spread out on the ground in submission and awe

dominion: sovereignty

monarch: ruler

effect: orchestrate

➤ Follow-Up Questions

1. How does the shakàl acquire his new appearance? Why would this new look make him appear as a king?
2. Do all the animals believe that the shakàl should rule them? If not, who becomes his enemy and why?
3. How is the young shakàl's plan to rule overcome in the end? What is his fate?

➤ Short Writing Assignments

1. What would you consider the moral or lesson which the story implies? Explain your answer in paragraph form.
2. Why do you think the young shakàl exiles his own species in the story, once he comes to power? Explain the **causes** of his action in paragraph form.

➤ Extended Writing Assignments

1. Define what you would consider the phrase "own nature" to mean. Then, in essay form, explain your **definition** using specific **examples** to illustrate. You may apply the term to humans, animals, and/or plants in your examples.
2. In the story, the color blue, associated in the Hindu religion with the god Krishna, is used as a symbol to attain power. In essay format, elaborate on three other forms of power individuals use to gain and hold power.

Celebration of the Dead in Mexico

as retold by Carlos Villacis

Introductory Remarks: Quetzalcóatl and the other deities were worshipped by the Aztecs from approximately AD 750 to 1500 or about the time of the arrival of the Spaniards in what is now known as Mexico. Pre-Columbian codices° and stone carvings tell the story of Quetzalcóatl and the human sacrifices made in his honor, but he is primarily known from the pyramid at Teotihuacan.

codices: ancient manuscripts

Pre-Reading Ideas: If you have ever been to a Mexican market, *mercado,* you have probably seen elaborately carved or molded plaques which reproduce the Aztec calendar. The Aztecs had a highly civilized society with a definite government and established religious rituals. When the Spaniards arrived in the mid-1500s, the Aztecs did not recognize them as an invading army. Instead, because of the feathers in the helmet that Hernan Cortés was wearing, the Aztecs mistook him for the returning Quetzalcóatl, and he and his men were mistakenly greeted warmly. The Conquest, on the other hand, destroyed the Aztec society, instituted the Spanish government, and brought Christianity to the Indians. From this set of events, many legends have been created, but the myth that follows discusses the Aztec view of creation and death and its contemporary celebrations.

In the late 1970s and early 1980s, the celebration of the Day of the Dead in Mexico became a magnet for tourism. In the United States, art galleries and museums began to display exhibits about the ofrendas° built to honor the dead. Mexican *ofrendas* and the celebration itself are part of an enormous feast, especially in small towns of south and central Mexico, whereas in the United States, the celebrations are more family-oriented and quiet events.

ofrendas: altars

Vocabulary: Looking up and understanding the following words prior to reading should prepare you for the author's message. Other words will be defined in the margin.

Aztecs	Mesoamerican	Nahuatl	statures	maize

1   The Day of the Dead has roots in the pre-Hispanic civilization of the Aztecs and prior Mesoamerican cultures. According to the Aztecs and their creation myth told in their language of Nahuatl, we owe our mortality to a mistake or accident that befell one of the most revered deities° of the Aztec pantheon°, Quetzalcóatl, the feathered serpent. The myth reveals that there had been four worlds or suns. The present universe is the fifth sun, *El Quinto Sol,* which is eventually supposed to be destroyed by earthquakes. The first was destroyed by showers, the second by wind, the third by fire, and the fourth by a flood. At the end of the four suns, the dead wanted to reinhabit

deities: gods or goddesses

pantheon: a temple dedicated to all gods

the earth, and because the gods of the Nahuatl myth were concerned about repopulating the new earth or *quinto sol,* Quetzalcóatl, the ruler of the second sun, went to retrieve the bones and ashes of our predecessors and take them from Mictlan to Tamoanchan, the paradise of the Aztecs. Quetzalcóatl had to travel to the ninth and last level of Mictlan, the realm of the dead, where the gods, Mictlantecuoltl and Mictlancihuatl, were the keepers of the bones. After meeting the stringent° conditions imposed by the two gods of the ninth under-world, Quetzalcóatl convinced them to give him the bones so he could take them to Tamoanchan. Unfortunately, on the way to the paradise of the Aztecs, he stumbled and dropped the bones, which were scattered and nibbled by quail. Once Quetzalcóatl reached the paradise of the Aztecs, Tamoanchan, the bones were ground by Cihuacoatl, the Earth goddess, and fertilized with Quetzalcóatl's blood. When Quetzalcóatl tried to reassemble and reshape the bones, he did it haphazardly°, accounting for the different statures of people. A new race of human beings emerged, but they were mortal because of the damage done by the quail.

stringent: strict

haphazardly: lacking order, randomly

2   Once he created mankind, Quetzalcóatl discovered that they had noth-ing to eat. So he turned himself into an ant and made his way into the side of a mountain. There he stole a grain of maize that the ants had hidden. From this seed, the crops of corn were grown that became the sustenance° for his people.

sustenance: food

3   Furthermore, death as well as creation is also an important issue, as those who die move to the supernatural realm based on the way they died. For example, those who died a normal death were destined to travel to the ninth underworld. Since it took four years for the souls to reach Mictlan, the survivors buried the deceased with personal belongings and food for the trip. During the first four years after the death of the loved one, special rites were performed by the living to honor and help the dead arrive at his or her final destination. Additonally, the Aztecs had festivals during each of the eighteen months of their calendar honoring their gods. One of these festivals, Miccail-huitontli, was celebrated specifically for the children and known as the Feast of the Little Dead Ones. The other festivals, Miccailhuitl or Tlaxochimaco and Xocot Luetzi, were specifically for the adults who died and were known as the Feast of the Adult Dead or the Offering of the Flowers and The Fruit Falls, respectively. Eventually these festivals were made to coincide with the Catholic Church dates of All Saints' Day and All Souls' Day, thus allowing the indigenous° people to continue their rituals under the guidance of the Church.

indigenous: original inhabitant

4   Today, in Mexico and in many places in the United States where *El Dia de los Muertos* is celebrated, *ofrendas* or altars are set up before and on No-vember 2nd, the official All Souls' Day or Day of the Dead. These displays or altars are elaborate and are a way of honoring and celebrating the dearly de-parted. While many Americans who do not understand the ritual see it as morbid°, the Mexicans/Mexican-Americans, as well as members of other Latin American countries, believe it is a communion° between the living and the dead. Thus, many of the articles displayed were favorites of the relatives, such

morbid: gloomy, pertaining to death

communion: communication, sharing thoughts

pan de muerto:
sweet bread
decorated with
symbols
honoring the
dead

calaveras:
skeletons

as fruits, books, drinks, dishes, candles, and pan de muerto°, while other decorations include papier-mâché calaveras° and sugar skulls. For those who go to visit the dead and who find themselves missing items, the streets leading to the cemeteries are lined with vendors selling everything from food to flowers to other items to be used on the altars.

➤ Follow-Up Questions

1. Why did Quetzalcóatl go to Mictlan? In what way is Quetzalcóatl responsible for caring for humanity?
2. Much like the retelling of the Hebrew myth of creation in a way that is termed the *Fortunate Fall*, Quetzalcóatl experiences a "fortunate fall" while he is carrying the bones of the ancestors. Explain how the partial destruction of the bones by the quail can be considered good rather than bad.

➤ Short Writing Assignments

1. Mexicans and Mexican Americans frequently design and construct altars on which they place pictures of a special person who has died. The Day of the Dead is, for them, a special time to celebrate and honor the dead. Many individuals outside the culture do not understand the custom, and they find it morbid. Talk with people who celebrate the observance and respectfully ask them about the decorations, food, drink, and other memorabilia that they have placed on their altars. Be sure to ask the name of the deceased person and the relation to the individuals present. Write a **descriptive** paper about your experience and explain if it has changed your ideas about this type of celebration.
2. In a paragraph, describe an altar that you would set up for a loved one you have lost. In your paragraph, briefly describe the individual and how the articles you chose are important in relation to the individual.

➤ Extended Writing Assignments

1. Talk to someone from a cultural background (other than Mexican or Mexican American) different from your own and ask that person about his or her cultural views concerning the dead. Then write an essay explaining how that culture honors its dead.
2. Research the life of someone other than a family member or friend who has died. You could possibly choose a local or national hero, a major entertainer, a war veteran, or anyone you feel has affected your life or culture. Write an essay explaining why this individual merits being honored.

CONCLUSION

It would be impossible to include every creation myth that has been presented in oral tradition and later written down for posterity. This chapter has attempted to provide a small sampling of myths from across the world and time, which may give you your first taste of crossing borders. Regardless of your culture or your religion, discovering the beliefs of others (for example, the creation concept), sheds light on philosophies that go beyond the immediate subject. For example, what do some societies believe about women? What do other societies believe about the relationship between human beings and animals? What do some societies believe about good and evil? This chapter is a beginning, a small step in discovering hints about larger issues that might clarify the motivation and foundation for the way people from other cultures act.

➤ Further Writing Assignments

Personal Narrative

Recall the time when you learned your creation story. Were you in Sunday School? Were you told by your parent or grandparent? Were you given the story in a children's book? Have you passed on the story to a younger person: your child, a sibling, a niece or nephew, a godchild? Try to recall your reactions. Write a personal narrative about learning about this or other aspects of your culture.

Exposition

If your cultural creation story has not been included in this chapter, write it, and be willing to share it with members of your class so they will know more about your culture.

Analysis

Analyze the myths in this chapter to determine what qualities they have in common and what qualities make them different from each other. You might make a chart or diagram categorizing them under particular headings as part of your prewriting strategy. For example, some are specifically about helpful animals. What are others about? When you have completed finding the points that allow them to be categorized together, you will have begun the process of division and classification. When you have finished organizing the qualities, write a paper that discusses their similarities. You will discover that even though there are similar stories about the creation myth, the cultures have different ways of approaching the topic. Many societies—even though they are far removed from one another—have similar tales.

➤ Suggested Chapter Projects

1. Form a research group and investigate how the various religions represent their gods and myths in art. Then prepare a presentation and/or report which will discuss the illustrations, who the gods and goddesses are, their powers and functions, and how they are similar to and different from some of the deities in this chapter. Your presentation/report may also include the depiction of myths in art as well.
2. In "The Athapascan Story," Asintmah sings of the earth's beauty and the coming birth of humanity. Such music is central to many religions throughout the world. As a research project, investigate the religious music of a chosen religion, paying close atten-

tion to the lyrics, the words, of the music and what function such music has in the services for that religion. You may want to interview the minister or priest of the chosen religion to gain greater insight. If you wish to present your project to the class, you may want to consider bringing in a recording of the songs your report discusses.

3. Research the Internet, finding Web sites and links to Web sites for the religions of a particular country. Talk with your instructor as to the number of sites for the project and the specific information required. Then organize that information into a packet, giving your reader a brief summary of the information contained on each site.

CHAPTER 2

Walden Pond
Source: Elizbeth Rodriguez Kessler, photographer

Youth: Days of Growing Up

Childhood, youth, and growing up are time periods in people's lives we would like to believe are carefree and innocent. In today's society, however, problems tend to begin earlier for children than they did in the mid-1900s. Although there were the thalidomide babies born with severe birth defects because a drug was prescribed to women who were pregnant, today we have babies born addicted to cocaine. In the 1950s, parents were fearful their children would contract polio, but today babies are born with AIDS. The list goes on; however, just as all children do not live carefree lives, neither do all children experience a bleak childhood.

The works in the following chapter provide brief glimpses into the lives of children from various ethnicities. They laugh, they cry, they love, and they grow, developing friendships and learning about life. However, "Kids," by Anne Perrin breaks the personal narrative mode that is especially appropriate for this topic. "Kids" is an observation about children's behavior in public in American society.

This chapter will give you an opportunity to reminisce about your childhood and write about the topic of youth in a variety of ways. Jotting down ideas in a reflective journal could be a good place to begin collecting memories. By approaching this topic from the point of view of special events rather than as a lengthy assignment about your entire life, you should be able to narrow your focus quickly to a special time, happy or sad, that you recall vividly. On the other hand, if you prefer to approach the topic as Perrin does, then you might write an expository essay. Either way, youth is a topic that has various aspects of interest to readers and writers alike.

The School Days of an Indian Girl

Zitkala-Sa

Introductory Remarks: Zitkala-Sa, a teacher, violinist and American Indian rights activist, was of Sioux and white heritage. Sa attended a Quaker school in Indiana and later Earlham College and the Boston Conservatory of Music. She founded the National

Council of American Indians. Her writings include *Old Indian Legends, American Indian Stories*, and she edited the *American Indian Magazine* for many years. Sa was the first American Indian woman to write autobiographical essays without the help of an editor or interpreter.

Pre-Reading Ideas: Being a child alone in an environment where the adults speak a language different from his or hers can make the child feel isolated and afraid. Even when the child attempts to fulfill all the understood requirements and duties of the new environment but lacks the communication skills, the best intentions can be misinterpreted. This selection describes a young Indian child in a community of strangers; each party must try to accommodate the other's inability to communicate. Unfortunately, the child is usually the one who suffers acutely in this kind of situation. Think about moves you have made to a new community, school, city, or country. Write a descriptive paragraph about one person outside your culture who tried to help you feel welcome.

Vocabulary: Looking up and understanding the following words prior to reading should prepare you for the author's message. Other words will be defined in the margin.

brave   iron horse   paleface

The Land of Red Apples

bronzed: made brown from the sun

1   There were eight in our party of bronzed° children who were going East with the missionaries. Among us were three young braves, two tall girls, and we three little ones, Judéwin, Thowin, and I.

2   We had been very impatient to start on our journey to the Red Apple Country, which, we were told, lay a little beyond the great circular horizon of the Western prairie°. Under a sky of rosy apples we dreamt of roaming as freely and happily as we had chased the cloud shadows on the Dakota plains. We had anticipated much pleasure from a ride on the iron horse, but the throngs° of staring palefaces disturbed and troubled us.

prairie: large treeless piece of land, usually covered with grass

throngs: crowds of people

scrutinized: looked at carefully

3   On the train, fair women, with tottering babies on each arm, stopped their haste and scrutinized° the children of absent mothers. Large men, with heavy bundles in their hands, halted near by, and riveted° their glassy blue eyes upon us.

riveted: fastened or firmly fixed

4   I sank deep into the corner of my seat, for I resented being watched. Directly in front of me, children who were no larger than I hung themselves upon the backs of their seats, with their bold white faces toward me. Sometimes they took their forefingers out of their mouths and pointed at my moccasined feet°. Their mothers, instead of reproving such rude curiosity, looked closely at me, and attracted their children's further notice to my blanket. This embarrassed me, and kept me constantly on the verge° of tears.

moccasined feet: feet with moccasines for shoes

verge: edge

5   I sat perfectly still, with my eyes downcast, daring only now and then to shoot long glances around me. Chancing to turn to the window at my side, I

was quite breathless upon seeing one familiar object. It was the telegraph pole which strode by at short paces. Very near my mother's dwelling, along the edge of a road thickly bordered with wild sunflowers, some poles like these had been planted by white men. Often I had stopped, on my way down the road, to hold my ear against the pole, and, hearing its low moaning, I used to wonder what the paleface had done to hurt it. Now I sat watching for each pole that glided by to be the last one.

6   In this way I had forgotten my uncomfortable surroundings, when I heard one of my comrades° call out my name. I saw the missionary standing very near, tossing candies and gums into our midst. This amused us all, and we tried to see who could catch the most of the sweet-meats. The missionary's generous distribution of candies was impressed upon my memory by a disastrous result which followed. I had caught more than my share of candies and gums, and soon after our arrival at the school I had a chance to disgrace myself, which, I am ashamed to say, I did.

comrade: friend, companion

7   Though we rode several days inside of the iron horse, I do not recall a single thing about our luncheons.

8   It was night when we reached the school grounds. The lights from the windows of the large buildings fell upon some of the icicled trees that stood beneath them. We were led toward an open door, where the brightness of the lights within flooded out over the heads of the excited palefaces who blocked the way. My body trembled more from fear than from the snow I trod° upon.

trod: walked

9   Entering the house, I stood close against the wall. The strong glaring light in the large whitewashed room dazzled my eyes. The noisy hurrying of hard shoes upon the bare wooden floor increased the whirring in my ears. My only safety seemed to be in keeping next to the wall. As I was wondering in which direction to escape from all this confusion, two warm hands grasped me firmly, and in the same moment I was tossed high in midair. A rosy-cheeked paleface woman caught me in her arms. I was both frightened and insulted by such trifling°. I stared into her eyes, wishing her to let me stand on my own feet, but she jumped me up and down with increasing enthusiasm. My mother had never made a plaything of her wee° daughter. Remembering this I began to cry aloud.

trifling: of very small importance or value

wee: little

10   They misunderstood the cause of my tears, and placed me at a white table loaded with food. There our party were united again. As I did not hush my crying, one of the older ones whispered to me, "Wait until you are alone in the night."

11   It was very little I could swallow besides my sobs that evening.

12   "Oh, I want my mother and my brother Dawee! I want to go to my aunt!" I pleaded; but the ears of the palefaces could not hear me.

13   From the table we were taken along an upward incline of wooden boxes, which I learned afterward to call a stairway. At the top was a quiet hall, dimly lighted. Many narrow beds were in one straight line down the entire length of the wall. In them lay sleeping brown faces which peeped just out of the coverings. I was tucked into bed with one of the tall girls, because she talked to me in my mother tongue and seemed to soothe me.

The Snow Episode

14   A short time after our arrival we three Dakotas were playing in the snow drifts. We were all still deaf to the English language, excepting Judéwin, who always heard such puzzling things. One morning we learned through her ears that we were forbidden to fall lengthwise in the snow, as we had been doing, to see our own impressions. However, before many hours we had forgotten the order, and were having great sport in the snow, when a shrill voice called us. Looking up, we saw an imperative° hand beckoning° us into the house. We shook the snow off ourselves, and started toward the woman as slowly as we dared.

imperative: expressing a command

beckoning: signaling, calling, directing

15   Judéwin said, "Now the paleface is angry with us. She is going to punish us for falling into the snow. If she looks straight into your eyes and talks loudly, you must wait until she stops. Then, after a tiny pause, say 'No.'" The rest of the way we practiced upon the little word "no."

16   As it happened, Thowin was summoned to judgment first. The door shut behind her with a click.

17   Judéwin and I stood silently listening at the keyhole. The paleface woman talked in very severe tones. Her words fell from her lips like crackling embers, and her inflection° ran up like the small end of a switch. I understood her voice better than the things she was saying. I was certain we had made her very impatient with us. Judéwin heard enough of the words to realize all too late that she had taught us the wrong reply.

inflection: change in pitch or tone of voice

18   "Oh, poor Thowin!" she gasped, as she put both hands over her ears.

19   Just then I heard Thowin's tremulous° answer, "No."

20   With an angry exclamation, the woman gave her a hard spanking. Then she stopped to say something. Judéwin said it was this: "Are you going to obey my word the next time?"

tremulous: trembling as from fear, nervousness or weakness

21   Thowin answered again with the only word at her command, "No."

22   This time the woman meant her blows to smart, for the poor frightened girl shrieked at the top of her voice. In the midst of the whipping the blows ceased abruptly, and the woman asked another question: "Are you going to fall in the snow again?"

23   Thowin gave her bad password another trial. We heard her say feebly, "No! No!"

24   With this the woman hid away her half-worn slipper, and led the child out, stroking her black shorn° head. Perhaps it occurred to her that brute force is not the solution for such a problem. She did nothing to Judéwin nor to me. She only returned to us our unhappy comrade, and left us alone in the room.

shorn: cut or clipped hair

25   During the first two or three seasons misunderstandings as ridiculous as this one of the snow episode frequently took place, bringing unjustifiable frights and punishments into our little lives. . . .

Four Strange Summers

26   After my first three years of school, I roamed again in the Western country through four strange summers.

chaos: infinity of space

27   During this time I seemed to hang in the heart of chaos°, beyond the touch or voice of human aid. My brother, being almost ten years my senior, did not quite understand my feelings. My mother had never gone inside of a schoolhouse, and so she was not capable of comforting her daughter who could read and write. Even nature seemed to have no place for me. I was neither a wee girl nor a tall one; neither a wild Indian nor a tame one. This deplorable situation was the effect of my brief course in the East, and the unsatisfactory "teenth" in a girl's years.

28   It was under these trying conditions that, one bright afternoon, as I sat restless and unhappy in my mother's cabin, I caught the sound of the spirited step of my brother's pony on the road which passed by our dwelling. Soon I heard the wheels of a light buckboard, and Dawee's familiar "Ho!" to his pony. He alighted upon the bare ground in front of our house. Tying his pony to one of the projecting corner logs of the low-roofed cottage, he stepped upon the wooden doorstep.

29   I met him there with a hurried greeting, and, as I passed by, he looked a quiet "What?" into my eyes. . . .

30   "No, my baby sister. I cannot take you with me to the party to-night," he replied. Though I was not far from fifteen, and I felt that before long I should enjoy all the privileges of my tall cousin, Dawee persisted in calling me his baby sister.

31   That moonlight night, I cried in my mother's presence when I heard the jolly young people pass by our cottage. They were no more young braves in blankets and eagle plumes, nor Indian maids with prettily painted cheeks. They had gone three years to school in the East, and had become civilized. The young men wore the white man's coat and trousers, with bright neckties.

muslin: a plain weave cotton fabric

The girls wore tight muslin° dresses, with ribbons at neck and waist. At these gatherings they talked English. I could speak English almost as well as my brother, but I was not properly dressed to be taken along. I had no hat, no ribbons, and no close-fitting gown. Since my return from school I had thrown away my shoes, and wore again the soft moccasins.

32   While Dawee was busily preparing to go I controlled my tears. But when I heard him bounding away on his pony, I buried my face in my arms and cried hot tears. . . .

➤ Follow-Up Questions

1. What incidents on the train does Zitkala-Sa consider rude? What articles of clothing call attention to her?
2. Why do you think the woman stopped whipping Thowin and did not punish the other children?
3. How does Zitkala-Sa's view of how to dress change in the story?

➤ Short Writing Assignments

1. Investigate some of the larger American Indian tribes to see if they have Web sites; prepare a report describing the information they contain.

2. Sign language played a large part in many American Indian cultures. Research your library to find a book illustrating American Indian sign language and prepare a short speech using that system. You should also prepare a written copy of your speech to give to your audience. Your instructor and you can determine the length of the presentation.

➤ Extended Writing Assignments

1. In some parts of the country, it was an acceptable Indian policy for the US government to educate Indian children away from their parents. Research this topic of separation and prepare a report giving specific details as to when this policy was in effect and what was involved in the process.

2. Research the libraries in your area to see if they have either of Zitkala-Sa's books, *Old Indian Legends, American Indian Stories,* or a copy of the *American Indian Magazine,* which she edited. If these materials are not available, visit the Interlibrary Loan (ILL) Office in your library and order a copy of one of these books. If there is not enough time to have ILL get the book(s) for you, see if any other books on Indian legends and stories are on the shelves. Choose two or three legends and/or stories which deal with children and prepare an essay which describes the part children play in such legends or stories, the particular tribe the narrative comes from, and the purpose of the legend or story.

War Games

Black Elk

Introductory Remarks: In 1876, Black Elk, a member of the Oglala Sioux nation, was a child who witnessed the Battle of the Little Bighorn. As his people were gradually wiped out, he rose in prominence, becoming a holy man, but his hopes for his people's survival were also destroyed. Toward the end of his life, he provided an oral history to scholar John C. Neihardt, hoping to preserve the history of his people.

Pre-Reading Ideas: Define what it means to be a man in your culture. After you have written that down, compare your definition with that in a dictionary. How does the dictionary's compare and contrast with your own personal definition? When Black Elk was growing up, he had certain rites of passage to go through to prove his manhood. Are there equivalent rituals that males in your culture must complete? Does society in general require males to display achievements, reach a certain age, or do anything special to indicate manhood? Paul Theroux once compared society's understanding of manhood and masculinity to an ill-fitting coat that all men are required to wear. On some men the coat fits well, but on others, like himself, it didn't. What do you think of the comparison? How does the comparison apply to Black Elk's narrative?

Vocabulary: Looking up and understanding the following word prior to reading should prepare you for the author's message. Other words will be defined in the margin.

Wasichus

1 When it was summer again we were camping on the Rosebud, and I did not feel so much afraid, because the Wasichus seemed farther away and there was peace there in the valley and there was plenty of meat. But all the boys from five or six years up were playing war. The little boys would gather together from the different bands of the tribe and fight each other with mud balls that they threw with willow sticks. And the big boys played the game called Throwing-Them-Off-Their-Horses, which is a battle all but the killing; and sometimes they got hurt. The horsebacks from the different bands would line up and charge upon each other, yelling; and when the ponies came to- *flounder:* to gether on the run, they would rear and flounder° and scream in a big dust, *struggle with* and the riders would seize each other, wrestling until one side had lost all its *stumbling or* men, for those who fell upon the ground were counted dead. *plunging*
movement

2 When I was older, I, too, often played this game. We were always naked when we played it, just as warriors are when they go into battle if it is not too cold, because they are swifter without clothes. Once I fell off on my back *prickly pears:* a right in the middle of a bed of prickly pears°, and it took my mother a long *number of cacti* while to pick all the stickers out of me. I was still too little to play war that summer, but I can remember watching the other boys, and I thought that when we all grew up and were big together, maybe we could kill all the Wasichus or drive them far away from our country.

3 There was a war game that we little boys played after a big hunt. We went out a little way from the village and built some grass tepees, playing we were enemies and this was our village. We had an adviser, and when it got dark, he would order us to go and steal some dried meat from the big people. He would hold a stick up to us and we had to bite off a piece of it. If we bit a big piece we had to get a big piece of meat, and if we bit a little piece, we did not have to get so much. Then we started for the big people's village, crawling on our bellies, and when we got back without getting caught, we would have a big feast and a dance and make kill talks, telling of our brave deeds like warriors. Once, I remember, I had no brave deed to tell. I crawled up to a leaning tree beside a tepee and there was meat hang- ing on the limbs. I wanted a tongue I saw up there in the moonlight, so I climbed up. But just as I was about to reach it, the man in the tepee yelled "Ye-a-a!" He was saying this to his dog, who was stealing some meat too, but I thought the man had seen me, and I was so scared I fell out of the tree *chapped:* and ran away crying. *cracked,*
reddened,
4 Then we used to have what we called a chapped° breast dance. Our *roughened skin* adviser would look us over to see whose breast was burned most from not

having been covered with the robe we wore; and the boy chosen would lead the dance while we all sang like this:

I have a chapped breast.

My breast is red.

My breast is yellow.

And we practiced endurance, too. Our adviser would put dry sunflower seeds on our wrists. These were lit at the top, and we had to let them burn clear down to the skin. They hurt and made sores, but if we knocked them off or cried Owh! we would be called women.

➤ Follow-Up Questions

1. In medieval times, knights jousted by charging at each other with a lance while on horseback. Is there any similarity between the games of the medieval knights and the episodes that Black Elk recounts? If so, how can you account for the similarity?
2. How would society look on the game of stealing food if it occurred today?
3. What is the story's view of women?

➤ Short Writing Assignments

1. Many games and toys sold today are considered violent or capable of influencing children to violence. Choose one game or toy which you consider violent, describe the toy or game, and then explain why you consider it dangerous.
2. Many young people today engage in contests that are dangerous or result in injuries. Write a paragraph describing one or two contests which young people engage in, whether legal or illegal, that are violent in nature and the harm such contests can have.

➤ Extended Writing Assignments

1. Visit a local arcade and watch the people who are playing those games which you consider exceptionally violent. Be sure to take notes on the type of game(s) played, the average age of the players, the body language of the players, and the words they use while playing. You may even want to interview someone you know who plays arcade games you consider to be of a violent nature. Then write a report explaining the exact way such game(s) are violent and the influence playing such games has on its players.
2. Another eyewitness to the Battle of the Little Bighorn is Chief Rain-in-the-Face. His account was retold by Charles A. Eastman (Ohiyesa, Sioux). Research Chief Rain-in-the-Face's account of the Little Bighorn and write a report explaining the military mistakes which Custer made and what the Indian's view is of the battle, making special note of what Chief Rain-in-the-Face is especially proud of in the battle. If you cannot find Chief Rain-in-the-Face's account, then any other Indian account of the battle is acceptable.

Shame

Dick Gregory

Introductory Remarks: As a child, Dick Gregory grew up in the slums of St. Louis, Missouri. His athletic ability in school continued during his years at Southern Illinois University. A politically active entertainer in the civil rights and anti-Vietnam movements, Gregory also ran for the office of president of the United States. He has written three books: *Nigger*, an Autobiography; *Back of the Bus;* and *No More Lies: The Myth and Reality of American History.* The following selection is from *Nigger.*

Pre-Reading Ideas: Sometimes during youth, young people idolize others, make them role models, or hold them to standards the youth aspire to. Sometimes these individuals do not even realize they are the objects of admiration. Frequently a young person finds himself or herself using the idol as a motivational figure even after the youth has lost contact with the hero. Write a brief description of a person you admired strongly as you were growing up. Did that person live up to your expectations as you grew older, or did you discover human flaws? Have you replaced your youthful hero with anyone as you changed? How does the new individual compare and/or contrast with the original? Add a second paragraph comparing and/or contrasting the new person you admire with the original.

Vocabulary: Looking up and understanding the following word prior to reading should prepare you for the author's message. Other words will be defined in the margin.

nappy

1   never learned hate at home, or shame. I had to go to school for that. I was about seven years old when I got my first big lesson. I was in love with a *complected:* little girl named Helene Tucker, a light-complected° little girl with pigtails and *complexioned* nice manners. She was always clean and she was smart in school. I think I went to school then mostly to look at her. I brushed my hair and even got me a little old handkerchief. It was a lady's handkerchief, but I didn't want Helene to see me wipe my nose on my hand. The pipes were frozen again, there was no water in the house, but I washed my socks and shirt every night. I'd get a pot, and go over to Mister Ben's grocery store, and stick my pot down into his soda machine. Scoop out some chopped ice. By evening the ice melted to water for washing. I got sick a lot that winter because the fire would go out at night before the clothes were dry. In the morning I'd put them on, wet or dry, because they were the only clothes I had.

2   Everybody's got a Helene Tucker, a symbol of everything you want. I loved her for her goodness, her cleanness, her popularity. She'd walk down my street and my brothers and sisters would yell, "Here comes Helene," and

I'd rub my tennis sneakers on the back of my pants and wish my hair wasn't so nappy and the white folks' shirt fit me better. I'd run out on the street. If I knew my place and didn't come too close, she'd wink at me and say hello. That was a good feeling. Sometimes I'd follow her all the way home, and shovel the snow off her walk and try to make friends with her Momma and her aunts. I'd drop money on her stoop° late at night on my way back from shining shoes in the taverns. And she had a Daddy, and he had a good job. He was a paper hanger.

stoop: a raised platform or porch at the entrance of a house

3   I guess I would have gotten over Helene by summertime, but something happened in that classroom that made her face hang in front of me for the next twenty-two years. When I played the drums in high school it was for Helene and when I broke track records in college it was for Helene and when I started standing behind microphones and heard applause I wished Helene could hear it, too. It wasn't until I was twenty-nine years old and married and making money that I finally got her out of my system. Helene was sitting in that classroom when I learned to be ashamed of myself.

4   It was on a Thursday. I was sitting in the back of the room, in a seat with a chalk circle drawn around it. The idiot's seat, the troublemaker's seat.

5   The teacher thought I was stupid. Couldn't spell, couldn't read, couldn't do arithmetic. Just stupid. Teachers were never interested in finding out that you couldn't concentrate because you were so hungry, because you hadn't had any breakfast. All you could think about was noontime, and would it ever come? Maybe you could sneak into the cloakroom and steal a bit of some kid's lunch out of a coat pocket. A bite of something. Paste. You can't really make a meal of paste, or put it on bread for a sandwich, but sometimes I'd scoop a few spoonfuls out of the paste jar in the back of the room. Pregnant people get strange tastes. I was pregnant with poverty. Pregnant with dirt and pregnant with smells that made people turn away, pregnant with cold and pregnant with shoes that were never bought for me, pregnant with five other people in my bed and no Daddy in the next room, and pregnant with hunger. Paste doesn't taste too bad when you're hungry.

6   The teacher thought I was a troublemaker. All she saw from the front of the room was a little black boy who squirmed in his idiot's seat and made noises and poked the kids around him. I guess she couldn't see a kid who made noises because he wanted someone to know he was there.

7   It was on a Thursday, the day before the Negro payday. The eagle always flew on Friday. The teacher was asking each student how much his father would give to the Community Chest. On Friday night, each kid would get the money from his father, and on Monday he would bring it to school. I decided I was going to buy me a Daddy right then. I had money in my pocket from shining shoes and selling papers, and whatever Helene Tucker pledged for her Daddy I was going to top it. And I'd hand the money right in. I wasn't going to wait until Monday to buy me a Daddy.

8   I was shaking, scared to death. The teacher opened her book and started calling out names alphabetically.

9   "Helene Tucker?"

10   "My Daddy said he'd give two dollars and fifty cents."

11   "That's very nice Helene. Very, very nice indeed."

12   That made me feel pretty good. It wouldn't take too much to top that. I had almost three dollars in dimes and quarters in my pocket. I stuck my hand in my pocket and held onto the money, waiting for her to call my name. But the teacher closed her book after she called everybody else in the class.

13   I stood up and raised my hand.

14   "What is it now?"

15   "You forgot me."

16   She turned toward the blackboard. "I don't have time to be playing with you, Richard."

17   "My Daddy said he'd . . ."

18   "Sit down, Richard, you're disturbing the class."

19   "My Daddy said he'd give . . . fifteen dollars."

20   She turned around and looked mad. "We are collecting this money for you and your kind, Richard Gregory. If your Daddy can give fifteen dollars you have no business being on relief°."

relief: welfare; money, food, or other help given to those in poverty or need.

21   "I got it right now. I got it right now, my Daddy gave it to me to turn in today, my Daddy said . . ."

22   "And furthermore," she said, looking right at me, her nostrils getting big and her lips getting thin and her eyes opening wide, "we know you don't have a Daddy."

23   Helene Tucker turned around, her eyes full of tears. She felt sorry for me. Then I couldn't see her too well because I was crying, too.

24   "Sit down, Richard."

25   And I always thought the teacher kind of liked me. She always picked me to wash the blackboard on Friday, after school. That was a big thrill, it made me feel important. If I didn't wash it, come Monday the school might not function right.

26   "Where are you going, Richard?"

27   I walked out of school that day, and for a long time I didn't go back very often. There was shame there.

28   Now there was shame everywhere. It seemed like the whole world had been inside that classroom, everyone had heard what the teacher had said, everyone had turned around and felt sorry for me. There was shame in going to the Worthy Boys annual Christmas Dinner for you and your kind, because everybody knew what a worthy boy was. Why couldn't they just call it the Boys Annual dinner, why'd they have to give it a name. There was shame in wearing the brown and orange and white plaid mackinaw° the welfare gave to 3,000 boys. Why'd it have to be the same for everybody so when you walked down the street the people could see you were on relief? It was a nice warm mackinaw and it had a hood, and my Momma beat me and called me a little rat when she found out I stuffed it in the bottom of a pail full of garbage way over on Cottage Street. There was shame in running over to Mister Ben's at the end of the day and asking for his rotten peaches, there was shame in asking Mrs. Simmons for a spoonful of sugar, there was shame in running out

mackinaw: a short double-breasted coat of heavy woolen fabric, often plaid

to meet the relief truck. I hated that truck, full of food for you and your kind. I ran into the house and hid when it came. And then I started to sneak through alleys to take the long way home so the people going into white's Eat Shop wouldn't see me. Yeah the whole world heard the teacher that day, we all know you don't have a Daddy.

29   It lasted for a while, this kind of numbness. I spent a lot of time feeling sorry for myself. And then one day I met this wino° in a restaurant. I'd been out hustling° all day, shining shoes, selling newspapers, and I had goo-gobs of money in my pocket. Bought me a bowl of chili for fifteen cents, and a cheeseburger for fifteen cents, and a Pepsi for five cents, and a piece of chocolate cake for ten cents. That was a good meal. I was eating when this old wino came in. I love winos because they never hurt anyone but themselves.

wino: a person addicted to wine

hustling: aggressively making a living

30   The old wino sat down at the counter and ordered twenty-six cents worth of food. He ate it like he really enjoyed it. When the owner, Mister Williams, asked him to pay the check, the old wino didn't lie or go through his pocket like he suddenly found a hole.

31   He just said: "I don't have no money."

32   The owner yelled: "Why in hell you come in here and eat my food if you don't have no money? That food cost me money."

33   Mister Williams jumped over the counter and knocked the wino off his stool and beat him over the head with a pop bottle. Then he stepped back and watched the wino bleed. Then he kicked him. And he kicked him again.

34   I looked at the wino with blood all over his face and I went over. "Leave him alone, Mister Williams. I'll pay his twenty-six cents."

35   The wino got up, slowly, pulling himself up to the stool, then up to the counter, holding on for a minute until his legs stopped shaking so bad. He looked at me with pure hate. "Keep your twenty-six cents. You don't have to pay, not now. I just finished paying for it."

36   He started to walk out, and as he passed me, he reached down and touched my shoulder. "Thanks, sonny, but it's too late now. Why didn't you pay it before?"

37   I was pretty sick about that. I waited too long to help another man.

➤ Follow-Up Questions

1. What specifically is Gregory ashamed of in the story?
2. What charitable efforts does Gregory himself do in the story? Are they successful?
3. Why do you think Gregory is so influenced by Helene Tucker?

➤ Short Writing Assignments

1. In a paragraph, explain how Gregory views the idea of "relief" in the story? In your efforts to answer this question, you may want to consider the motivation behind his own perspective.
2. Pretend that you were Gregory's teacher that day in school when donations were asked for the Community Chest. Rewrite the scene the way you would have handled the situation.

➤ Extended Writing Assignments

1. Look on the Internet or in your library and gather information regarding a national relief organization, such as the Red Cross, or an international organization such as the United Nation's efforts to aid children [UNICEF]. Write an essay explaining the efforts at relief that the organization is involved in and the extent of their efforts.

2. Gregory makes a very clear point in his narrative that he looked to the educational system to help him not just with education, but with such basic human needs as food. From your own observations, describe what you think the educational system should provide for its students' welfare. In considering these efforts, be sure that your plans are realistic and workable.

Black Suede Shoes

Roberta Orona-Cordova

Introductory Remarks: Born in Albuquerque, New Mexico, Roberta Orona-Cordova has an extensive career in writing, both as a writer and as an instructor. Orona-Cordova received her Bachelor of Arts degree in Rhetoric from the University of California at Berkeley in 1976, her Master of Arts degree in Speech and Communication Studies from San Francisco State University and her Master of Fine Arts in Screenwriting from UCLA. She has written several screenplays, including "Viva la Vida: The Story of Frida Kahlo," written and directed a narrative short film "Rosie," and written a collection of short stories, *Letters to My Daughter So I Can Sleep*. The following story is from that collection.

Pre-Reading Ideas: Sharing clothes among same-sex siblings can be an issue that raises arguments in families or it can be something that sisters and/or brothers do easily. However, when one sibling works hard to earn the money to buy a special article of clothing, there is sometimes a sense of possession and pride that accompanies wearing it. If a sibling wears it without permission and damages it, the anger that erupts upon discovering the event can be quite destructive emotionally and psychologically. Consider the following short story. It is one that does not provide a conventional conclusion. What would have happened if you had borrowed a piece of clothing from your sibling and unintentionally damaged it? Create an ending that would have been appropriate if you had been in Rosie's position.

Vocabulary: Looking up and understanding the following word prior to reading should prepare you for the author's message. Other words will be defined in the margin.

suede

1   My big sister Rita worked as a carhop and she used all her money to buy clothes, beautiful clothes. Rita, Daddy, and I lived in a two-room apartment behind a big house on South Broadway. The same place we lived when Sammy Baca came knocking at my door with a corsage in his hand, and I let him stand there forever and ever because the house was dark inside. It was the third time the Public Service Company turned off our electricity for non-payment.

2   Rita. Everyone said she looked like Elizabeth Taylor, and I wanted to be just like her with long, natural curly eyelashes, jet-black hair, a perfectly narrow nose, and size D-cup bra. Imagine. Rita kept her latest fashions under lock and key and in a portable closet, and Daddy and I stuffed our clothes in the one chest of drawers the three of us shared.

3   "Can I borrow your black suede shoes, Rita?" I begged.

4   "Not on your life," she snapped back. "Never."

5   Rita could be mean sometimes, but it only made me look up to her more. I was trying to be nice and so I asked first, but little did she know I saw her hide the closet key under her panties and bras in the top drawer. Rita went to work that day assured that her little sister couldn't get her hands on those black suede shoes.

6   Jerry Silva was a juvenile delinquent, but he was still my best friend. He came over just when I was about to steal the key to Rita's closet.

7   "Do you and Anna want to go with us to the show today?" he bragged.

8   "We're going window-shopping downtown, Jerry," I answered. "You're dangerous to hang out with, anyway," I added.

9   "Yeah, you know how I am. Adventure follows me, huh?"

10   I wanted to show off Rita's black suede shoes now that I knew how to get my hands on them. Why would I wear them to sit in a dark movie house where no one could see me?

11   Sister Rita was six years older than I, but thank goodness I had big feet, and we wore the same shoe size.

12   After Jerry left, I opened the closet that held Rita's precious, hard-earned clothes. All her shoes were lined up in pairs across the bottom of the closet. Rita was smart. She placed a long strand of thread on top of and across all her shoes. I knew Rita set this trap for me, but I carefully lifted the thread and removed her brand new black suedes.

13   Suddenly there was a knock at the door. I jumped.

14   "It's hot outside. Maybe we should go to the movies, just to stay cool," Anna said, as I let her in the apartment.

15   "Heck no. Let's go dream about the clothes we're going to buy som day."

16   "Hey, when'd you get those killer shoes?" Anna asked with a little envy.

17   "Yesterday," I answered proudly.

excursion: trip   18   Anna and I were on our way home from our boring excursion° downtown when we saw that crazy Jerry and his side-kick, Stan. They were across the street from us on South Broadway. Stan was carrying a cardboard box, and Jerry was tossing one fresh egg after another up in the air, letting each one land on the hot pavement.

looney: slang meaning crazy

19 "There's that looney° Jerry Silva," Anna said pointing across the street.

20 "Yeah, but there's never a dull moment when he's around."

21 "He has a crush on you, Rosie. Watch out."

22 "You'd never guess after he kissed me last night."

23 "You let him?" Anna asked, shocked. "I thought you were just friends."

24 "We were up on the roof of his house, counting the stars, and he leaned over and planted a kiss on my mouth. A French kiss."

25 "Ugh!" Anna said.

26 "No, it felt good. Really it did."

27 Anna was still making a face when I heard a slight crack at my feet. Splat! I looked down and one of Rita's black suede shoes was splattered with egg yolk.

28 "Spit! My sister's gonna kill me," I yelled.

29 "I thought you said they were your shoes."

30 "Shut up. I'm going to murder that Jerry Silva!"

31 Raw eggs were flying at us one right after another. Jerry and Stan were having a field day using us as targets. Splash. Swoosh. Crack. An egg hit the other shoe, then my dress, then my shoulder. The eggs kept coming at us like machine-gun fire. Around the base of the tree were big mud clods. I filled the two pockets in front of my dress and stood ready. Anna was armed, too.

32 Jerry and Stan crossed the street and headed toward us, all the while throwing their ammunition°. When they stepped on the curb we were ready.

ammunition: any material used to defend or attack

ammo: ammunition

33 "Fire!" I yelled. "Don't stop until you slaughter them!"

34 "Hey, look out," Jerry said. "They've got ammo°."

35 "Rosie's mad as a bulldog," Stan said, laughing his head off. They held the big cardboard box in front of their faces for protection. I kept throwing clods until my pockets were empty.

36 "You bums," Anna screamed. "You ruined Rosie's shoes."

37 "We had to get rid of the eggs we borrowed from Creamland Dairy," Stan said, sarcastically.

38 "You're gangsters," I said. "We should turn you in."

39 "No, you won't. Remember the bicycles we borrowed last summer at the Acapulco swimming pool? Remember, when we didn't have bus money?" Jerry said threateningly.

40 "I hate you guys," I shouted as I ran across the street toward my apartment.

41 "Poor Rosie," I heard Anna say after me. "She's really in trouble."

42 I was scared. I mean really scared. Both the left and right suede shoe were covered with eggs.

43 "What am I going to do?" I thought. When I entered the house, I immediately found a rag, wet it and rubbed and rubbed the yucky yellow yolk off the shoes.

44   "Nooooo! Ruined! Noooo!"

45   I dried the shoes the best I could, set them at the bottom of the closet, put the thread carefully on top of and across all the shoes again, just as it was before my excursion. I stared and stared at those suedes, and they looked like the ugliest shoes I ever saw. I closed the door, pressed the small lock closed, and put the key back in its hiding place.

46   That night when Rita came home from work, she climbed in bed with me and went right to sleep. I lay awake with my eyes wide-open and prayed to the Blessed Virgin.

47   "Make her forgive me. Please don't let her kill me, please Virgin Mary, please. Amen." I fell asleep with a glimmer of hope.

48   "My shoes! My shoes!" Rita yelled, shaking me awake the next morning. "You ruined my brand new shoes. How did you find the key? How?" she cried.

bewildered:
completely
confused

49   "What key?" I asked, acting bewildered° as I sat up in bed.

50   "You know what key," she said. "This key, you brat. You had no right. No right."

51   "What's the matter with you two," Daddy asked, as he came into the room.

52   "My shoes, Dad. She doesn't even care she ruined my favorite shoes." Rita turned on me again.

53   "You're a thief. I didn't give you permission, did I?"

54   "I don't know what you're talking about. I never wore those ugly shoes."

55   "Settle down," Daddy said. "She told you she didn't wear them."

56   "How could I? You had the door locked. I didn't. I promise, I didn't," I swore.

57   "Now you're a liar and a thief. You're going to pay for this. You'll see. You're going to pay," Rita yelled back.

58   "I swear I didn't do it. Cross my heart and hope to die," I said making the sign of the cross over my chest.

59   "Oh, you're swearing, huh? Swear on our mother's grave. Swear."

60   "I swear, huh . . . I'm not swearing on anybody's grave. You can't trick me."

61   "See Dad? See? She's guilty."

tenant: a person
who rents and
occupies a
house, land, and
so forth

62   Daddy walked toward the bathroom we shared with the tenant° in the adjoining apartment.

63   "When I come out I don't want to hear another word, or I'll take the belt to both of you, you hear?" and he meant it.

64   I lay back on the bed and covered my face with the blanket and pretended to go back to sleep. I listened to my sister crying her heart out, and I felt like she was stabbing me with her tears.

➤ Follow-Up Questions

1. Why would Rita put her favorite clothes under lock and key?
2. Why would Jerry Silva and Stan act so cruelly?
3. Do you think the father's reactions were appropriate?

➤ Short Writing Assignments

1. The idea of punishment for wrongdoing is part of the background for this story. Write a paragraph explaining what you feel is the worst form of punishment that Orona-Cordova describes.
2. In a short essay, describe the types of amusements open to young teenagers in your area during the daytime hours. Be as detailed as possible as to location and types of activities.

➤ Extended Writing Assignments

1. **Research** the laws in your area regarding the regulation of child labor. Your investigation should consider the age at which one can work, the number of hours, types of supervision, and restrictions in the work area for young workers. Explain your findings in essay format.
2. Interview the parents of children of all ages to discover the types of excuses children give for the wrongs they commit. Also keep a record of the punishments for these behavioral problems. Then report your findings in a **division and classification** essay.

Kids

Anne Perrin

Introductory Remarks: Born and raised in Houston, Texas, Anne Perrin is of French and German heritage. Second in a family of six siblings, Perrin understands what it is like to travel during summer vacations with young brothers and sisters who have various needs that must be met. As an adult, Perrin now travels extensively, reading critical works in her areas of expertise: Early American literature, especially James Fenimore Cooper and the early environmentalists and nature writers; feminist literature; and the Chicana novelist and critic, Emma Perez. A doctoral candidate at University of Houston, Perrin has spent years teaching composition and literature courses both at the university and community college level. In addition to her short stories, she continues to write satirical social commentary on her observations of family life, rude drivers, recreational vehicles, and other annoying aspects of the landscape.

Pre-Reading Ideas: The object of taking a vacation is to "get away from it all." The only problem is that during the summer, thousands of other families are on the road also trying to escape constant contact with other people and other people's children. However, if vacationers decide to visit the well-known spots that they are told to visit—theme parks, national parks, the shore, the Grand Canyon, and so forth—it is inevitable that they will run into tired, hungry, and grumpy children as well as adults. Unfortunately, crowds and lack of routine lead to a less than perfect vacation regardless of how many plans are made to avoid the pitfalls. Think of the last vacation you took during the summer. Was it the perfect time you were promised by some ad for a special place? Write a descriptive paragraph explaining what happened. After you write it, determine how it compares with "Kids."

Vocabulary: Looking up and understanding the following words prior to reading should prepare you for the author's message. Other words will be defined in the margin.

piece de résistance   Rockies   Walden Pond   Thoreau

....

1   If you have ever traveled by car across this country and visited some of the historic sites and parks that are the touchstones of the American-Way, you were probably exposed to a dilemma° which presses down on the American traveler like an elephant stomping on a grape. For me, my first encounter occurred on a 5,000-mile journey across the US from Texas up to Canada, over to the East coast, and then back to Texas. The trip was meant to revive° the spirits by allowing me to get as close to the wilderness areas of America and Canada as my urban° mentality would allow. What the trip actually did was to place me face to face with that most formidable° of all enigmas°, the child-traveler, and to reaffirm a suspicion I have always had about children.

2   You quickly discover on such a long road trip that motel pools do not translate to cool rest on a summer evening and lazy adult conversation with your traveling friends. That fantasy is what the ad execs for the motel chains con° you into thinking you'll get in their Internet ads. No, sir. What a pool represents and what Holiday Inn, La Quinta, and any other motel chain with any brains at all fails to put in their Internet ads is that a motel pool is a kid-magnet in liquid form. No, change that to "a screaming, rousing, let-me-get-all-my-cooped-up-frustration-out-by-yelling-at-absolutely-no-one-and-nothing-for-4-hours" kid-magnet, which will drive any sane adult right over the edge, especially if that adult actually believed those Internet photos and was gullible° enough to ask for a "pool view." Five weeks of nightly yelling sessions will do it — no jury would convict. I hold the firm belief that the traveling parents of America send their kids to the pools of America's motels to keep from killing them after an all-day drive. I mean, how many American parents feel as if they have sunk into a death spiral after 8 hours of "Mom, I have to go," "Mom, I don't want to _____ [fill in the blank]," and that all-time clincher, sure-fire guarantee of a four-lane change and total lock-up on the anti-lock breaking system, the proverbial°, "Mom, I have to throw up, NOW!" a dread, superseded° only by the even more dreaded, "Mom, I THREW UP!", or even worse, the silent heave° into the front seat.

3   I will give those parents credit though; they are in the process of teaching their children manners. I have found that children, for the most part, do say "Excuse me" and a host of other polite, politically correct buzz terms. However, what the parents of America fail to explain to their children is that such phrases should not be mumbled to total strangers through a mouth full of soggy Sugar Frosted Flakes. Nor does the mumbling give them carte

dilemma: a situation requiring a choice between equally undesirable alternatives

revive: renew, refresh

urban: of the city

formidable: powerful

enigma: puzzling or inexplicable person or situation

con: convince by deception, exaggeration manipulation

gullible: easily deceived or cheated

proverbial: having become the object of common mention

superseded: set aside in effectiveness

heave: to throw up, vomit

carte blanche: unconditional authority

blanche° to then reach across, reach over, step on, or take food which the adult was about to take, or, worse yet, return food the kids found they didn't like back to their table. After 8 continuous hours of Nintendo background noise, the parents are now in such a psychotic state that they are totally oblivious to the whole breakfast drama.

4   Of course, from the kids' points of view, maybe *they* are the ones who are exercising control. Maybe the continuous repetition of "Don't _____ [fill in the blank] by parents results in an accumulation° of pressure in a kid similar to water rising behind a dam. Probably the most miserable kid I ever saw on that road trip was in Plymouth, Massachusetts, in a gift shop at the Plymouth Village site. The gift shop was very trendy, very interesting, and very cluttered, with only about 1½ feet of space in the aisles and it was packed with people. In jostling to get to the check-out counter, I turned around and saw a father pushing his daughter in a wheelchair; the girl, who was about 12 years old, had no legs. You could tell by the dejected°, bored, frustrated expression on her face versus the exuberance° on his face that this was his idea. I really felt for that kid because her father had placed her in such an awkward position. She knew it, and he was in "La La-Land," totally oblivious. It took them 15 minutes to go 10 feet, and the people literally had to press up next to total strangers just to make room. It was then that I came to realize that fidgeting and bickering are the most prominent forms of retaliation° known to kiddom. What's a parent going to do—take away the Nintendo that night? They might as well stand in front of a Mack truck and get it over with quick. Nintendo is the parents' goal at the end of the day, the light at the end of a long, whining tunnel, an oasis of activity designed to occupy kids so that the adults can calm their nerves and enjoy their exhaustion. I envisioned a minimum of 4 hours of whining later that night at the local Holiday Inn for that father, at least.

5   When my companion and I finally made it out of that gift shop and to the historically restored village of Plymouth, we sought out each nook and cranny as if we were on a divine mission. On coming out of one of the restored homes, we came upon one of the "historic characters" shelling peas into a wooden bowl. Two children, a girl and her little brother, stared, fascinated at what was coming out of those green pods. Their parents, brochures° and village maps in hand, had realized that their children had broken routine and that such a disaster called for immediate intervention°. From the walkway, the parents began calling the kids to come see all the artifacts° at the next home. No use. As I watched, those kids, in a show of American freedom, sat down beside that village character and began shelling peas into the bowl. They were still at it when we passed the house a while later. I firmly believe that those small green peas equaled blissful hours of Nintendo later that night for those parents.

6   As I said earlier, my travels that summer confirmed what I have always suspected about kids. I was reminded of this view in what to an American wilderness lover like myself is considered the breathing heart of American nature, the center pull on the individual's love of self, and the point of calm and

accumulation: a building up of

dejected: a feeling of depression

exuberance: state of enthusiasm

retaliation: act of returning like for like

brochures: pamphlets or leaflets

intervention: act of coming between, mediate

artifact: man made object from an earlier time or cultural stage

spiritual bonding in a world of glitzy Internet.com. I'm talking about Walden Pond here. No need for majestic Rockies or clear, shallow running rivers dotted galore like country gingham with fly fishermen. Walden is the calm in a sea of technology, the resting place of the soul on its journey to wherever, the *pièce de résistance* of human versus society. Such were my delusions° on approaching Thoreau's woods after hauling myself across the US and doing battle with the whining, complaining, rude, crying, sniveling children of America. I was about to re-attain harmony, purge° my soul of distress, walk in peace. What I found was a pond in the woods with about one-quarter of it cordoned off° as a rowdy swimming area for the neighborhood kids for the summer, complete with a whistle-blowing lifeguard and watchful parents lining the small, narrow beach like so many stranded whales. I stood at the roadside taking in the whole scene, my mouth dropped opened like a largemouth bass° about to suck in a worm. I did try to ignore it all as my companion and I plunged as quickly as we could down the path that surrounds the pond. But even though the woods and distance drowned out a good part of the swimmers' noises and the blasts from the lifeguard's whistle, we were never totally out of the sounds of others. My companion and I found the site of Thoreau's cabin, and, true to tradition, each of us tossed a small stone on a growing pile of stones and small boulders placed there by other, similar travelers of nature. What was so disturbing was that someone, whose name I will not mention to avoid undue embarrassment, felt the need to place not only a good-sized boulder on top the pile, but to paint his name in white letters on the rock. Talk about missing the point here. Anyway, my friend and I walked Thoreau's woods that day, and it was somewhat peaceful, despite the distant splashes and shouts of the swimmers and the incessant° whistle-blowing of the lifeguard.

7   At the end of our walk, we arrived back at the swimming area where we had started just in time to hear a blast on the lifeguard's whistle and her shouting for everyone to get out of the pond for a 15-minute break. Peace and calm descended momentarily on those woods, and this was the view I wanted as my last glimpse of Walden, so I quickly turned to leave. As we began to walk to the car, I became aware of the lifeguard's whistle becoming louder and more frequent and shouts coming from her and another woman. I really didn't want to spoil my last view of the quieter side of Walden Pond, but curiosity got the better of me, and I turned to see what was the matter. I was too far from the area to tell if it was a boy or a girl. What I did see was that a kid did not want to come in; he/she wanted to stay in the pond—that was where she/he wanted to be. What this kid had done was to duck under the ropes surrounding the swimming area and in a mad, hell-bent-for-leather, give it all you got, no holds barred, go for broke effort was making a beeline for the middle of that pond. The sun glistened on those little arms which moved like a Ferris wheel gone maniac, and water sprayed like a broken fire hydrant from the kicking. That kid didn't give a damn about whistles, parents, rules, boundaries, ropes, maps, Nintendo, or anything else. It was glorious. It confirmed what I always suspected about kids. I'm glad I looked back.

delusion: false belief or opinion

purge: clean or purify

cordoned off: enclosed

bass: edible, fresh water fish

incessant: non-stop

➤ Follow-Up Questions

1. Describe the types of behavior which Perrin finds annoying. What do the adults do in the story to annoy the children?
2. What would you consider the most frustrating event which Perrin finds on her trip?
3. In Thoreau's writings about Walden Pond, one of his main ideas deals with simplicity in one's lifestyle. Why does Perrin think that the individual who painted the large boulder at Walden "miss[ed] the point"?

➤ Short Writing Assignments

1. Perrin never does specifically state what she "always suspected about kids." In a short essay take a **position** on what you believe is Perrin's ultimate view of children and support your ideas with specific examples from the story.
2. One of the techniques used in the essay deals with the use of gendered pronouns. Perrin describes the last kid in the story, the swimmer, first as "he/she" and then as "she/he," making it quite clear in the story that she could not tell what the sex of the swimmer is. Think for a moment about how you feel about this technique. Also consider how both sexes are often represented by "he" or "man" in writings, such as in the statement, "Since the dawn of man. . . ." Write an essay explaining your view of this technique and of society's way of marginalizing or minimizing women through its use of pronouns.

➤ Extended Writing Assignments

1. Pretend that you are given unlimited money, but, like most individuals, you only have a limited amount of vacation time. Plan a trip that can take no longer than two weeks. Then write a **descriptive** essay about your trip, detailing where you plan to go and what you would like to see. Your trip can be as fantastic and futuristic as you wish.
2. One of Perrin's reasons for going to Thoreau's woods was to escape the urban environment. However, many people, because of circumstances, plan vacations within a short space and time, often staying within their own community and benefiting from the local events and amusements offered. Write a descriptive essay in which you take a local vacation, detailing the activities and the benefits from this type of vacation.

CONCLUSION

It is easy to see from the selections in this chapter that growing up, regardless of a child's culture, is not always easy. Poverty, expectations, isolation, language barriers, and other problems are frequently obstacles that mar the innocence of youth. How children overcome these difficulties and survive can be an inspiration to those who read their narratives.

➤ Further Writing Assignments

Personal Narrative

Rites of passage or initiation rites—sometimes formal and traditional, and sometimes informal—can mark the movement of a child into maturity. For example, when a girl turns fifteen in the Latino culture, she might be given a birthday party called a *quinceañera*. She is officially introduced into society and at one time was considered ready for marriage. Getting a driver's license frequently signals a male's independence. Think about a rite of passage you experienced that indicated that you had matured or changed. Write a **descriptive** paper that tells your story and what you learned from the experience.

Exposition

Many people complain that this is a more permissive era in child raising. Girls are wearing makeup at younger ages than before. Boys are drinking and staying out later at earlier ages also. The point of the complaint is that boys and girls no longer have anything to look forward to because they do "older" activities at such a young age. Write a **comparison-and-contrast** essay, discussing how child-rearing today is similar to and/or different from the way your parents or grandparents were raised. You might want to interview your parents and/or grandparents or individuals from that generation to get information for the paper.

A variation on this topic is that children are more materialistic than they were in the past. Explore this topic through comparison-and-contrast, and draw conclusions from your discoveries for the topic you write about.

Analysis

Read several of the works in this chapter to find a common idea. Determine how each author addresses the theme and write an essay that analyzes at least two articles for the common theme. For example, several of the authors refer to playing in their essays. Look for others.

Argumentation

Refer to the expository topic above and choose a side that you believe in and want others to believe about raising children. Write an **argumentative** essay using points that support your position and points from your opposition that you can refute. Are children, in fact, being raised more permissively than they were in the past?

➤ Suggested Chapter Projects

1. Watch cartoons and read comic books not only from today's market but as far back as you can to determine how children are portrayed, the themes these programs and stories offer, and the levels of violence portrayed. Then write a report comparing and contrasting the views of children's programs and literature in the past with that of today.
2. Many of the stories in this chapter deal with problems of growing up and the successful ways children very often solve these problems. Interview an older adult, asking him or her what issues were encountered when growing up and how successful

he/she was at solving them. In your interviews, consider the cultural and social forces working on these adults to determine if things have really changed that much. Then prepare a report describing the individual and explaining your findings about growing up in a former time.

3. Acculturation occurs when an individual moves between two cultures; this type of situation can occur when a new immigrant must learn the language and customs to survive in a new country but actually prefers his old cultural base. Assimilation occurs when a person completely embraces a new culture because he/she desires the new customs and language rather than those of his or her former culture. Interview a person who has moved to America and is now dealing with American culture and issues such as language, dress, gender, food, and education, to name a few topics. Discuss your findings in an essay that describes the culture of the persons interviewed and the specific areas of difficulty. Then take a **position** in your paper about whether you believe, based on evidence, that the individual is attempting to acculturate or assimilate.

4. Many areas of the country have locations within communities where various cultures perform their rituals and ceremonies, such as the Day of the Dead, Pow Wows, the Chinese New Year, and a St. Joseph's table. **Research** your community's local papers and magazines to find out where such ceremonies are occurring and attend as many as possible, making sure to document the event with photography, if permitted, brochures, notes regarding the customs, and interviews with participants. Then prepare a presentation to the class, complete with handouts describing the event(s) and explaining its/their cultural significance to that particular community.

CHAPTER 3

You Can't Go Home Again
Source: *The Los Angeles Times*

Home and Family:
The Ambiguous Environment

The American novelist Thomas Wolfe wrote, "You can't go home again," and that declaration has raised many issues of what going home means. If you no longer live in your parents'/guardians' home, think back to the first time you returned home for at least an overnight stay. Had you been living on your own for a while? Maybe in a dorm or with friends? Alone? When you went home for the visit, were you expected to follow the "house rules"? However, you had moved beyond being accountable to others because you had been living responsibly and independently, and you couldn't return to the role of the child. For others of us, when we go home, things aren't as we remember them. Everything seems smaller or slower or not quite as exciting. The people—friends, relatives, teachers, ministers, and others—have changed. Look at the *Peanuts* cartoon on page 132.

Although this is a humorous treatment of the subject of going home to see an old friend, it can be quite true. Still some of us discover that we have changed while everything else has remained static.

The works in this chapter are similar to those in Chapter 2, because home and family are topics that lend themselves to personal narratives. Agnes Herman describes how even the love and comfort parents give their children are not enough to keep the family from having to face serious conflict. Similarly, Barbara Cain provides views of family life as it is constructed and destroyed, as she explores the effect of divorce on older children. The poem by Cathy Song describes a young woman's duties and relationship with her mother, and Syble Simon describes the plight of a homeless woman in her short story. Terrell Dixon, on the other hand, provides us with a view of our non-human neighbors and what is happening to them as urban dwellers cross another border and encroach upon their territory.

Writing opportunities abound in this chapter and can even be combined with something you might have written based on the material in Chapter 2. Home and family, like youth, can spark many memories, but they can also inspire investigation into changes in the family, homelessness, cultural differences, the return of children to the home after college, and other interesting topics that lead to exposition, comparison-and-contrast, and cause and effect writing.

Squatting

Syble Simon

Introductory Remarks: Born and raised in Palestine, Texas, Syble Simon moved to Houston to attend Texas Southern University where she graduated with a Bachelor of Arts and Master of Arts degree. Simon has worked as a magazine editor, and she writes fiction and poetry. She is currently writing her first novel, *Turmoil: Acrimonious Assumptions.*

Pre-Reading Ideas: The stereotype that many people have of "homeless" individuals is usually quite negative. Think about the men and women you have seen sleeping on sidewalks, waiting in lunch lines outside shelters or churches, or asking for money on the streets. What assumptions have you and others made about their lives and how does society encourage those beliefs? Those who do not know the kinds of problems people who live in shelters have had frequently assume that the residents are shiftless and have no desire to improve their living conditions. Others believe that the "homeless" have no education and simply want to live off the charity of others. In the past two decades, however, the state of the economy has been such that many men and women with good jobs have simply gotten into trouble with debt and have lost their homes and, in some cases, their families. The stereotypes are far from the life described in the following short story.

Vocabulary: Looking up and understanding the following words prior to reading should prepare you for the author's message. Other words will be defined in the margin.

receptionist	mishap	affluent	innovator	immaculate

1 I know the Lord works in mysterious ways, and I remember a whole lot of things told to me. One particular saying was, "If you make one step, He'll make two," and I'm a firm believer in that verse, adage°, cliché° or whatever you want to call it. Let me introduce myself. My name is Saffia Sound. I was once known as a statistic, an African American homeless woman. I never take anything for granted, but people have taken me that way, especially my drug-addicted husband. He's a sad case, but that's another story.

adage:
a traditional saying
cliché:
a frequently or over-used phrase or saying

2 I have been down and out for well over two and a half years. That doesn't sound like a long time, but it is when experiencing these hardships day by day. Many times I think I am depicting the song written by Bobby

Womack, "Harry Hippie." You know, like he wrote that song just for me, or at least to remind me, "I'd like to help a (wo)man when (s)he's down, but I can't help him much if (s)he's sleeping on the ground."

3   Life is so funny. A rose garden was never promised to any of us, but we were all given a will, and it is up to us to make the right decisions. Social ills come in all kinds of forms. One major ill for young people is fornication°. One does the right thing to stop fornicating and marry for better or worse. This is what I did. But it seemed to me things only got worse. I was totally losing it. *It,* meaning everything. I lost my job, my home and my kids, and I kept losing until I finally lost my mind. I was completely insane. That's what society confirmed.

fornication: sexual intercourse

4   "She's crazy, and those kids don't deserve to go through the hell she is going through. Please award my grandchildren to me." My mother pleaded to the courts, and of course, she was given the children. But I'm grateful; at least they weren't awarded to the State.

5   I am educated, however. I got a job as a receptionist for a podiatrist° making $5 an hour. My boss was a cheapskate°, and a no-nonsense perfectionist°. One day I was an hour late for work. She forgave me and told me not to make it a habit. Then one evening my husband didn't pick me up at all, making me stay at work an hour past closing. I finally called a cab and asked her for an advance of $5 to pay for the cab. She didn't take too kindly to that, but she gave it to me anyway. I was late the next day and commenced° to confess to her that my husband had a major drug problem.

podiatrist: a foot doctor

cheapskate: a stingy person

perfectionist: a person who demands that things be perfect

commenced: started

6   She smiled at me and said, "I appreciate your honesty and admire your boldness for telling me your problem, but I can no longer employ you. You have too many problems that will eventually overwhelm you. If you know like I know, you'll get out while you're ahead. Good luck and may God bless you." She handed me a check for $200 and locked the door behind me.

7   "What does she know," I thought. "She's never been married, and probably never will be." I shrugged my shoulders, folded my check and walked the long way home.

8   This was the initial mishap of being a devoted wife, of loving some tangible° being more than I loved myself. I lost job after job, home after home, family and friends, and as I mentioned earlier my sanity.

tangible: something you can touch

9   BAM!!! Out on the street, under a bridge, a shelter here and a shelter there. I was pitiful, sorrowful. I went from agency to agency trying to receive help, but my estranged° spouse always fixed that for me. Yeah, fixed it so I wouldn't get a damn thing. I didn't have an address and my senses were slowly depleting°. Finally the police ushered° him out of my life, and I had to deal with myself.

estranged: separated

depleting: to decrease

ushered: to escort

10   One afternoon I took a bus ride to view the city to try to clear my mind so I could think. I came upon an affluent section of the city and decided to get off. The scenery was serene and pleasant; there was hardly anything out of place. It was really a normal place; it just looked fantasy-like because my life hadn't been so normal.

11   I was sitting at the bus stop, just sitting mind you, imagining and getting lost in my dreams because I sure as hell wasn't going anywhere. Suddenly a dignified° maid walked up to the stop, complaining in her native tongue. She saw me and started ranting in English, declaring she no longer had a job because her employers were leaving the country for six months and her services were no longer needed except for watering the plants, getting the paper, and taking the mail, which would be junk mail because they would forward all important mail. She had just walked from the beautiful Tudor-style mansion hidden in the forest of dogwood and crape myrtle trees on the busy boulevard lined with other trees and similar houses.

dignified:
stately

12   "The nerve of these rich people. I've worked for them one year, established myself and to give me a blow like this is unheard of. Madame actually asked me to water her stupid plants and bring in the junk mail, and they only give me one month of severance pay°. They expect for me to work for no pay for five more months. I don't think so!" She was venting°; she had to tell somebody, and I was her victim. "Well, I've got news for them," she continued, "I won't do nothing of the sort." She took a key off her ring and walked over and threw it in the trash can.

severance pay:
final wages after
an employee
leaves a job

venting:
releasing one's
emotions

13   The bus came and she bid me farewell, got on the bus and went on with her life.

14   As she exited her life, I was about to enter mine. After the bus roared by, I sat and I looked around as if I were waiting for the place to clear, which I was. There was not a soul in sight, except for the Almighty. I said a little prayer and asked God to let His will be done.

15   I walked over to the trash can. It was half full, so I assumed the key would be easy to reach. Wrong. The more I dug, the more things shifted and I literally heard the key hit the bottom of the barrel. This was one of those cement trash cans that the city controlled. I started to think that God didn't want me to do what I had planned and was forbidding me to get the key. I was disheartened. I apologized to God for having such mischievous° thoughts and plans.

mischievous:
playfully
annoying

sanitation:
garbage

16   All of a sudden, a city sanitation° truck pulled up to the empty trash. A tall, caramel-colored, lean, yet muscular man stepped down.

17   "How are you today, m'am?" he asked.

18   "I'm so glad you came by. I would be doing a lot better if you would please get my key out of the trash when you empty it." I lied. My mouth started speaking involuntarily. "I was throwing away my trash and mistakenly threw it in there." I continued as I stepped toward him.

19   "No problem. I'll get it for you," he responded, as he flashed his beautiful set of pearly whites°.

pearly whites:
slang expression
for teeth

fiddled around:
aimless
movement

20   He lifted the heavy can and put the trash on the sidewalk and fiddled around°.

21   "Here's your key," he said as he made two steps and politely handed it to me.

22   I wanted so badly to say thank you for giving me the key to my life, but I just said, "Thank you so much. You are so kind. Let me help you pick this stuff up."

23   "Never mind," he said. "I can do it. Have a nice day." Then he winked and got back on the truck to continue his job.

24   Now I know this sounds bad, but sometimes a person has to do what she has to do. This brings to mind the saying, "God helps those who help themselves." And I am about to help myself to these people's house. Don't think I'm a user because I'm not. I am an innovator. At least that is what I want to think of myself as.

25   After I got back to the shelter, I decided to keep my new plan to myself. I shared space with three other females. I only got along with Trudy; the other two say they don't care for me because I think I'm so "damn smart and holy." They say this because I don't accompany them on their wrongdoings. Therefore, we only share our living arrangements.

26   Trudy, on the other hand, is soft, too passive. Actually she is young and scared. She has that passion to always want to fit in, to be part of the in-crowd. She is sweet but needs some guidance. I talk to her when I really need to talk. For instance, I'd talk to her about my children and my family. I was never close to her or anyone at that place. It just wasn't the thing to do.

contemplated:
thought about

27   For three weeks I contemplated° a plan. It was hell keeping this secret in, but I managed. I was sitting at the front desk answering the phone one morning and a nice lady called to inquire about the location of the shelter because she had a load of clothes and items that she wanted to drop off. I gave her the address and tried to give her easy directions.

28   "I know exactly where that is. Thank you. I should be there shortly. And may I ask who I am speaking with?" she asked.

enunciating:
speaking,
pronouncing
clearly

29   "Yes. My name is Saffia Sound." I answered enunciating° so she wouldn't think I was saying Sophia.

30   "Oh! What a lovely name! Is that short for Sapphire?"

31   "No." I laughed.

32   In less than an hour a poised, casually dressed white lady with a chignon° sashayed° into the shelter. She had shopping bags from Lord & Taylor, Saks Fifth Avenue and Neiman Marcus filled with clothes and shoes. I came from around the desk to help her with her charity.

chignon:
a smooth twist
or roll of hair
worn at the nape
of the neck

sashayed:
to walk or move
easily

33   "You must be Saffia, or is it Sapphire now?" she asked as she smiled at me with laughing eyes.

34   "Yes, I'm Saffia. How did you guess?" I asked.

35   "It's the accent. You have a distinctive and lilting voice, sort of a Southern comfort." She gave me a look like *what are you doing here anyway.* She could tell I was a resident because of my clothes. You know, I was mixed matched. She looked me up and down. It was kind of embarrassing. I felt ashamed. "We're about the same size. I wear a size 8. I think you do, too. Let's go through these bags before the others do, especially the employees. I know they go through stuff before they hand them over. We'll just beat them to the punch today." She was very nice and friendly.

36   "I don't think we should do this," I declared. "I could get in trouble."

37   "Aren't these my clothes?" she asked sarcastically.

38   "Well, yes."

39   "Well, what's the problem. I'm giving *you* something special." She reached in the bags and brought out beautiful dresses, skirts, blouses, slacks, jeans, and shoes. She began to sort them out as if she were shopping for herself or at least matching outfits together as if she were packing for a trip. "Here are the nicest outfits in the bunch. Put them on just to make yourself feel pretty because you really are a pretty lady and you deserve more. These shoes are a size 9. You choose the pairs you like."

40   "Thank you, Mrs. huh. I'm sorry. . . ." I said before she cut me off.

41   "Call me Elle. Now I've got to run. I've got a flight to catch, but you take care of yourself. Oh yeah, I have a leather duffel in the car. Come get it to put your clothes in. Don't leave them on that desk," she warned me. "Bring them with you!"

42   Two days passed after I met Elle. I woke up, brushed my teeth and took a shower with a piece of soap the size of a thin-strip Band-Aid™. I swear, those people who run these shelters do nothing but steal. I dressed in a pair of nice jeans that still had the starched freshness and a nice brown short-sleeved sweater, combed my hair in a high ponytail and glided some Vaseline on my lips to give my face a youthful innocence. I then gathered all my belongings and packed them in the big brown leather duffel bag Elle had given me. I looked all around the place and was grateful I had a place to lay in from the temperamental weather, but I had been there too long. It was time to move on. I went down stairs, out the front door, and I never looked back. I didn't want to ever go there again.

43   I felt in my pocket for the key. It was pinned inside my pocket as though I were a child forbidden not to lose it or else I'd be in trouble.

44   The bus came and opened its door. I hesitated at first, but the man behind me told me to hurry up. I got on and rode to my new destination, scared but determined to make a new life for myself.

45   The house was sitting beautiful as usual. Walking up the winding driveway, I began to pray. I started to cry. I unpinned the key, walked around to the side entrance that led to the kitchen because I figured the maid wouldn't have the front door key. And POWDOW! The key fit the familiar lock, and the door opened. The kitchen was immaculate. The house was immaculate yet quiet and lonely. I found the guest bedroom, unpacked and laid down to take a nap, for I was tired.

46   Later that week, I went job hunting using the address and got a job. I got a job at a prestigious law firm being a receptionist, of course. This led to bigger and better things for me. I house sat for two months, found my own place and continued my new great life.

47   When I left the big house on that busy boulevard, I left it immaculate as I found it, and I also left that beautiful golden key with a single card saying THANK-YOU.

➤ Follow-Up Questions

1. Saffia admits in the story that she lost her "sanity" for a time in her life. Point out specific thoughts and/or actions from the story that could represent those times when Saffia lost touch with reality.

2. Where in the story do you think Saffia had a turning point in her life?
3. What is Saffia's attitude about her life and career at the end of the story, as opposed to the beginning?

➤ Short Writing Assignments

1. Saffia initially presents her troubles through the music she knows, first referencing Bobby Womack, then indirectly referring to Anne Murray's song about life resembling "a rose garden." Think about and listen to the songs currently popular; then write a short essay describing some of the metaphors or symbols for life and its problems that are used in these songs.
2. Often people, whether female or male, remain in relationships which are destructive to them, not only in terms of physical violence but often in the negative attitudes such relationships can have on a person. In a short essay, discuss what you believe to be the **causes** for people remaining in such relationships.

➤ Extended Writing Assignments

1. Research a shelter in your area, whether it is a woman's shelter, a homeless shelter, a safe haven for teens or others in need. Your information can come from such sources as brochures, Web sites, interviews or a tour of the shelter. Prepare a report for your class in which you give a physical description of the facility, the services it provides, and a description of the benefits it provides to the community.
2. Does Saffia commit a crime in the story by staying in the house, despite the fact that she left it as she found it? Would you consider this action a positive way to get on the right footing? If not, discuss realistic opportunities available to someone such as Saffia which your community offers, taking into account as many opportunities as possible, and write a **division and classification** essay explaining these options.

Landscapes of Home: Thoughts on Urban Nature

Terrell Dixon

Introductory Remarks: Terrell F. Dixon teaches literature and the environment at the University of Houston with a special emphasis on urban nature. He has published widely on a variety of environmental literature subjects, and he has edited two books: *Being in the World: An Environmental Reader for Writers* (with Scott Slovic) and *City Wilds: Essays and Short Stories about Urban Nature*. Originally from Oklahoma, Dixon received his doctorate in English from the University of Indiana in Bloomington.

Pre-Reading Ideas: The idea of diversity of population takes on a different meaning if you consider exactly who your neighbors are. Have you ever stepped outside in the morning to find your pet's food bowl empty? If you believe it is one of the neighborhood strays taking advantage of your pet's leftovers, you might walk out late at night or peek through a window. You might discover an opossum or a raccoon dining by moonlight. The following essay raises questions about how we think about our non-human neighbors and how we treat the land that was once their homes, before humanity and progress invaded their territory. It also brings up issues of language, which can convey a particular attitude toward the world around us. As you read this essay, focus not only on the visual landscape and description, but also on the sounds that are suggested.

Vocabulary: Looking up and understanding the following word prior to reading should prepare you for the author's message. Other words will be defined in the margin.

metropolis

1   Home for me is the city of Houston, Texas. I live in the Montrose area, an old neighborhood on the edge of downtown. As the city has grown into a giant metropolis of more than four million people sprawling over hundreds of square miles, the Montrose has managed to maintain areas of quiet beauty. There are huge, old live oak trees whose long branches and thick foliage° stretch across yards and streets, providing an almost continuous canopy° of green. Some older homes, many built over eighty years ago, still survive: a rare thing in a city that, like many, forgoes preservation to embrace wide-open development. The people who live in the Montrose are diverse. We take pride in our inclusive neighborhood, one where gays and straights, yuppies and hippies, painters, poets, and lawyers, musicians and accountants, browns, blacks, and whites are all at home.

2   This neighborhood invites us to walk. Unlike the new, far-flung suburbs metastasizing° their way through the landscape, built without sidewalks and with streets and attitudes that discourage foot traffic, the shaded sidewalks of Montrose encourage sauntering°. It's an invitation I accept often. What draws me on these walks is not just the chance to talk with my human neighbors, nice though that can be. It is the chance to observe the nearby flora and fauna°, to see what is going on with the other inhabitants of the neighborhood: the trees, flowers, birds, and animals. That prospect creates a sense of expectancy, an eagerness to know what the day's walk will bring.

3   Once it brought a mother raccoon and two young ones on the sidewalk ahead of me, strolling sedately, peacefully at home in the center of the city at 5:30 on a Saturday morning. Another morning it was a big raccoon seated on a fence, its masked eyes watching me carefully as I studied it. There is also an occasional opossum, off-white and very shy. One played dead at my approach, behaving in a way that explains where we get the term "playing possum." Sometimes a resonant° drumming above my head calls attention to the bright red head-patch and black-and-white ladder-like back of a neighborhood hairy woodpecker. Cardinals with big red crests

Margin notes:

foliage: leaves of a plant collectively

canopy: a cover formed by the leafy upper branches of the trees in a forest

metastasizing: spreading as if by disease

sauntering: walking leisurely

flora and fauna: plants and animals of a particular region

resonant: echoing

and beaks appear all year; goldfinches earn their name as their chest feathers grow gold in March; and brilliantly colored scarlet tanagers, warblers, and vireos visit in the spring.

4 Some of the best places to become acquainted with this nearby nature are those rare openings in the steady succession of human homes, those places that we have been taught to call "vacant lots." One favorite place like this in my neighborhood, situated between a small apartment complex and an old two-story house, was left alone long enough to develop into a small forest of unpruned° trees and a dense undergrowth of bushes and grasses and flowers. This pocket of city wildness has been home to rabbits and tree frogs, sphinx moths, dragonflies, and swallowtail butterflies. A red-tailed hawk used to place itself near the top of a nearby oak tree, staring intently down into the trees on the lot. On spring nights, I listened to the soft, descending notes of a screech owl and looked hard at the tree branches until I finally found its outline. One year, on moonlight nights, the plumed head of a white-crowned night heron stood out in silhouette° over its nest, dark against the night sky.

unpruned: allowed to grow unchecked, wild

silhouette: profile

mutant: a new type of organism

5 Then one day it all changed. Like some mutant° mushroom, a big red-and-white sign appeared on the curb proclaiming a "Vacant Lot for Sale . . . Suitable for Townhouse Development." In months the trees, plants, and wildlife were gone, and "Three Luxury Townhouses . . . Priced to Sell in the $350,000's," had taken their place. The expensive townhouses crowded every inch of the lot, and they sold quickly.

6 This is not a unique story; similar things happen every day in cities across the country, but it does tell us something about our culture. We are accustomed to seeing land, especially urban land, only in terms of human habitat and financial gain. Our concept of home is species specific°. Other species, those without down payments, credit cards, or bank accounts seldom come into consideration. It is not so much that we Americans are at heart anti-nature; it is rather that we have fallen into bad habits. We have become accustomed to reserving our innate biophilia—our basic love of nature, our compassion for other living things—for nature outside our cities (or for those increasingly overwhelmed formal, manicured° parks within them), burying any concern for the nature in our neighborhoods beneath the bottom line.

species specific: in this case, referring to the human race

manicured: trimmed and cut meticulously

7 I believe that this is beginning to change, albeit slowly. Now that over eighty percent of Americans live in cities, the nature of our cities becomes increasingly important to more of us. Even as urban nature disappears, we Americans are becoming more aware of it and more ready to protect it. Two things could help accelerate this protection of urban nature. One is to watch our language. Without thinking much about it, we use words in ways that reinforce a narrow view of those urban landscapes. Our usual term for places like the one in my neighborhood, for example, is "empty lot" or "vacant lot." Such terms suggest that the land itself is without meaning or value when it is an undeveloped wild place and thus 'only' a place for nature. We can begin to help change our cities by calling these places by different names, to designate them in terms that emphasize their value as "open spaces," "urban wild

solidify: to unite firmly

incentive: something that encourages action

places," or "habitat spaces." Such names would eventually solidify° our changing view of these places: we would become less inclined to let development destroy them. Over time, perhaps, our government could find ways to provide financial incentives° such as tax credits to support those who seek to protect such small wild parts of our home landscapes. My hope is that with such a name change, we could begin to protect and expand these pocket open spaces, maybe even connect such sites into larger areas so that other animals, those less at home with humankind than raccoons and screech owls, could also live comfortably in our cities.

8   My second suggestion complements the first. What we need most is a basic change in how we see the relationship between cities and the natural world. For decades we have usually thought of "nature" as something "out there," beyond the city limits sign, a rural farm, a national park, or wilderness area. This false and destructive concept of a border is changing, but to speed up that process, I propose that we deliberately set out to expand and update our concept of the nature walk. We tend to relegate nature walks to a long-ago time, to view them as something that occupied our nineteenth-century ancestors but which has little relevance to city life today.

9   Nature walks, however, can and should take place in our urban neighborhoods. Once we get out of our subways, buses, and automobiles and get past the idea that the only reason to walk in our cities is heart-healthy aerobic exercise, we become free to notice the urban plants and animals with whom we share our lives. Once we start paying attention to them, we will be on our way to protecting and expanding those easily lost pockets of city wilds, to creating neighborhoods that are more inclusive of the natural world. As urban nature walkers, we can, without leaving our neighborhoods for the country or the wilderness, begin to connect with the natural world: its beauty, its unpredictability, and its evocations° of a larger life beyond our day-to-day human concerns. This, too, we will find, is good for the heart.

evocation: calling forth

➤ Follow-Up Questions

1. List the kinds of wildlife Dixon saw in his neighborhood before progress took over the "vacant lot."
2. How does Dixon use the term "border" in this essay? Is it how you would normally think of it?
3. Dixon's concluding sentence ends on a thought that he began in the paragraph. How is it an appropriate ending?

➤ Short Writing Assignments

1. In an essay that Annie Dillard, another environmental writer, wrote, she recommends that the way to see the wildlife of a particular area is to go to a secluded spot, and sit very still for an hour or so. Do not take a book, do not take snacks, and do not become impatient. Simply sit in the midst of nature and allow the residents to appear to you. Go to a quiet spot where nature is not intruded upon by humanity or progress and follow Dillard's recommendations. Using all your senses—vision, hearing, smell, taste,

and touch—see what you discover. Write a descriptive paragraph recording everything that you observe. Be sure to indicate where you went and how long you stayed.

2. Your own backyard or patio can be a small animal world. Take some time to observe your non-human neighbors either in the early morning hours or late one evening. Don't forget to observe the insects that might be crawling around, also. Write a descriptive paragraph recording what you see and hear. Include all the human noises you observe. Record the time of day you completed your observation.

➤ Extended Writing Assignments

1. Find a spot that you pass daily or every other day on your way to class or work or other location. Take some time to observe it one day and record what you see. It might be a manicured flower garden, a crack in the sidewalk, a patch of untended grass or other part of the environment. Take a few minutes to look at it closely every day that you pass it. At first you won't see change, but as time goes by, you will begin to see differences in the spot. Record your observations every day that you walk by the spot. You are keeping a nature journal. You might see an anthill beginning, a new plant growing or dying, a new bloom, or damage done by someone who has walked by. Simply record the observations and after about a month, write a description of your "nature spot" and how it has changed. It will be very much like writing a character analysis, but this will be a nature analysis. You might also want to record your feelings about the changes you see, especially if your spot was in some way damaged by others who walk by it without noticing what they do.

2. Go to one of the local state forests or nature preserves in your community and find a well-traveled spot. Sit on a bench or beneath a tree and observe the people who go to the site. Watch their activity and write a descriptive passage that explains what they did, how they acted, what they commented on, and their general attitude toward this preserved area. Are their activities what you expected? If they had children with them, did they attempt to point out anything special to them or teach them anything about the site? Stay long enough to watch three or four different groups. After you write the **description,** write an **expressive** paragraph, reflecting on how you felt about their behavior.

The Youngest Daughter

Cathy Song

Introductory Remarks: Born in Hawaii of Chinese and Korean parents, Cathy Song has written poetry that is strongly influenced by her cultures and by the Hawaiian landscape. Although she was born in and now lives in Honolulu, she graduated from Wellesley College and Boston University. Song has published two collections of poetry, *Picture Bride* and *Frameless Windows, Squares of Light.* "The Youngest Daughter" appeared in *The Best of Bamboo: The Hawaii Writers' Quarterly.*

Pre-Reading Ideas: Many cultures assign the responsibility of caring for an aging parent to a child in a particular birth order. For example, in the novel, *Like Water for Chocolate,* readers discover that the youngest daughter will be prevented from marrying so that she can care for her mother until her mother's death. Even though the two women in the poem, "The Youngest Daughter," appear to have a close relationship, they both recognize that the narrator is not completely satisfied with her responsibilities. Think about the role the senior members of society have and the role their children must assume. How do different cultures treat their elderly? How has the creation of assisted living centers helped families with senior members? Have they had a negative impact on the families? How do you perceive your responsibilities toward aging members of your family?

Vocabulary: Looking up and understanding the following words prior to reading should prepare you for the author's message. Other words will be defined in the margin.

rice paper   parched   migraine   graveled   flaccid   insulin

The sky has been dark
for many years.
My skin has become as damp
and pale as rice paper
5   and feels the way
mother's used to before the drying sun
parched it out there in the fields.

Lately, when I touch myself,
my hands react as if
10   I had just touched something
hot enough to burn.
My skin, aspirin-colored,
tingles with migraine. Mother
has been massaging the left side of my face
15   especially in the evenings
when it flares up.

This morning
her breathing was graveled,
her voice gruff with affection
20   when I took her into the bath.
She was in a good humor,
making jokes about her great breasts,
floating in the milky water
like two walruses,
25   flaccid and whiskered around the nipples.
I scrubbed them with a sour taste
in my mouth, thinking:
six children and an old man
have sucked from these brown nipples.

30 I was almost tender
   when I came to the blue bruises
   that freckle her body,
   places where she has been injecting insulin
   for thirty years, ever since
35 I can remember. I soaped her slowly,
   she sighed deeply, her eyes closed.

   In the afternoons
   when she has rested,
   she prepares our ritual of tea and rice,
40 garnished° with a shred of gingered° fish,
   a slice of pickled turnip,
   a token for my white body.
   We eat in the familiar silence.
   She knows I am not to be trusted,
45 even now planning my escape.
   As I toast to her health
   with the tea she had poured,
   a thousand cranes° curtain the window,
50 fly up in a sudden breeze.

garnished: decorated

gingered: prepared for cooking with ginger, a spicy, pungent root of a plant

crane: large, wading bird, with long legs, bill, and neck

➤ Follow-Up Questions

1. What specific health issues does the speaker in the poem mention? Which ones does the mother have?
2. Make a list of the cultural references or markers in the poem that indicate the Chinese and Korean background of the poet.
3. The narrator in the poem has mixed feeling about her mother; how would you describe their relationship?

➤ Short Writing Assignments

1. In stanza 1 of the poem, the speaker talks about her problem by using such physical **symbols** as a "dark" sky, paper, and physical pain, but in the last stanza, she mentions "escape" and then describes how the cranes "fly up." Write a paragraph explaining how the narrator's attitude about her situation changes or develops in the poem.
2. Emotional issues in one's life or even life changes can often lead to physical problems. For example, the poem's narrator refers to migraine headaches that perhaps result from being confined to a tradition from which she sees little hope of escaping. Choose one or two types of changes that one may have to encounter in life, and in a short essay explain the physical and emotional effects such changes may have on an individual.

➤ Extended Writing Assignments

1. Writers often rely on colors and shades to indicate the mood or emotions they wish to show in the work. For example, Song refers to a "dark" sky at the poem's beginning to set an initial tone of despair for her poem. Think about two or three colors and/or shades which you may have read about in literature or encountered in your everyday life, and in an extended essay identify those colors and/or shades, explaining the moods and emotions which they create and how they are used in literature, ads, or wherever they occur.

2. One often sees the time that he/she grows up in as the most important, despite the fact that later generations may think of such a period as old-fashioned. One way of preserving these past times is to create a time capsule. Write an essay describing the items that you would put into such a box to preserve an overall view of your generation, and explain the significance of each article.

A Parent's Journey Out of the Closet

Agnes G. Herman

Introductory Remarks: Agnes Herman was born in New York City in 1922 and graduated from the University of Michigan and Columbia University. She was the founder of the Union of American Hebrew Congregations programs on the Changing Jewish Family and the Synagogue.

Pre-Reading Ideas: Because the act of disclosing that one's sexuality differs from that of a heterocentric society is so difficult, the individual who announces his or her non-conforming sexual orientation must face issues that are personally painful. Frequently, being immersed in that emotional and psychological struggle prevents the son or daughter from clearly seeing what kind of impact the announcement will make on the parents, even if the parents are not homophobic. While the son or daughter may have been carrying knowledge of his or her different sexual orientation for years, the shock of the disclosure is usually not met with ease and composure. Most parents need some time to adjust to the revelation, and despite the knowledge that their child needs them for support or comfort or acceptance, they must sometimes struggle with their initial feelings before they can reach out to help. Some never do. Others, however, make the "journey out of the closet," sometimes taking as long as it did for the gay son or lesbian daughter.

Vocabulary: Looking up and understanding the following words prior to reading should prepare you for the author's message. Other words will be defined in the margin.

Bar mitzvah	**Passover**	**rabbi**	**lured**	**seder**
Kaddish	**cantorial**	**myth**	**sexual orientation**	**alienation**

1   When we agreed to adopt seven-month-old Jeff, we knew that his life as a member of a Jewish family would begin the moment we brought him to our home. We celebrated that joyous homecoming with appropriate religious ritual, with blessings recited by Jeff's rabbi father as our gurgling, happy baby teethed on his infant kiddush cup° and enjoyed his challah°. There in the warmth of our extended family circle of grandparents, an aunt, an uncle, and the Temple Board, our small son passed comfortably through his bris°, his initial Jewish milestone. There would be many more.

kiddush cup: cup that wine is poured into at Sabbath prayer

challah: ceremonial twisted egg bread loaf used at Sabbath dinner

bris: circumcision

decry: public disapproval

2   By the time he was two, Jeff ate an ice-cream cone without spilling a drop; his face came out of the sticky encounter clean. At five, he watched other kids play ball in the alley, standing aside because he had been told not to play there. Besides, he seemed more comfortable playing with the little girl next door. There were awkward moments as he began to grow up, such as the times when the baseball bat, which his father insisted upon, was not comfortable in his hands, but the rolling pin, which his father decried°, was. His grandmother, whom he adored, remarked, "Jeff is too good."

archaic: from an older or ancient time

3   I knew she was right, and privately I felt a nagging fear I could hardly express to myself. Was Jeff a "sissy"? That archaic° term was the only one I dared whisper to myself. "Gay" only meant "lively and fun-loving"; "homosexual" was a label not to be used in polite society and certainly never to be mentioned in the same sentence with a child's name. Such a term would certainly stigmatize° a youngster and humiliate a family.

stigmatize: mark in disgrace

reluctant: unwilling

4   Jeff continued to be an eager volunteer in the kitchen and a reluctant° participant on the ball field. We fought the former and pressed to correct the latter, frustrating our son while we all grew tense. As to our silent fears, we repressed° them.

repressed: to hold back on purpose

5   Jeff developed reading problems in school. We worried, but accepted the inappropriate assurance offered by his teacher. "He is such a good boy—don't confuse him with counseling." We bought it, for a while. As the reading problems continued, Jeff did enter therapy and was helped to become less anxious and learn how to read all over again. At our final parental consultation with the psychiatrist, I hesitantly asked, "Doctor, I often worry that Jeff is effeminate°. What do you think?" I held my breath while he offered his reassurance: "There is nothing wrong with your son. He is a sensitive boy—not aggressive or competitive. So he likes girls! In a few years you will be worrying about that for other reasons."

effeminate: having female characteristics

6   Jeff looked forward eagerly to religious school. He accompanied his dad, helped around the temple, and received many kudos°. He was quick, efficient, and willingly took instructions. In later years, even after his father was no longer in the pulpit, Jeff continued his role as a temple volunteer. He moved chairs and carried books; later he changed fuses, focused spotlights, and handled sound equipment. Jeff was comfortable; it was "his" temple. Other children there shared his interests and became his friends, later forming the temple youth group. . . .

kudos: praise

7   During confirmation and youth group years, Jeff seemed to be struggling to be like his peers. Temple became the center of his life. He worked

and played there, dated, went steady, and attended meetings and dances. He shared with no one—not his parents, his friends, or his rabbi—his own feelings of being "different."

8   When Jeff was sixteen, we moved from New Rochelle to Los Angeles. It was a difficult move for him, cutting off relationships and sources of recognition and acceptance. As we settled into our new home, Jeff began to explore the San Fernando Valley, enrolled in high school, and tried to make new friends. At our insistence, he attended one meeting of the local temple youth group, but felt rejected by the youngsters there. That marked the unfortunate beginning of Jeff's disenchantment° with synagogues and withdrawal from family religious observations and celebrations.

disenchant- ment: freedom from illusion

acclimated: to become used to

9   Jeff gradually acclimated° to his new environment. He took Amy, a Jewish girl his own age, to the senior prom; he cruised Van Nuys Boulevard on Wednesdays with Ann. He was always on the move—coming home to eat, shower, change clothes, and zip out again. We blamed it on the fast pace of California and the novelty of having his own "wheels"; first a motorcycle, and then a car. There were several accidents—none serious, thank heavens! Again, in retrospect, the furious struggle with his identity must have played a part in his fast-paced behavior. At the time, though, we buried our heads in the sand, believing that Jeff was merely behaving like every other teenager.

10   After high school, the pace seemed to slow down a bit. So when Jeff was nineteen and we decided to leave him in charge for six months of our sabbatical° world tour, we had no hesitation. Conscientious and cautious, he could handle the cars and the checkbook. He would continue in college and be available to his sister Judi, also attending college. We flew off to Europe and Israel, confident and secure.

sabbatical: an extended period of time for leave from work for rest

11   When an overseas call came three months later in Jerusalem, my heart beat fast, and my sense of well-being faltered slightly. "Everything is fine, no problem. I have quit college. Now don't get excited . . . I want to go to business school and study interior design. Jobs are plentiful; I know a guy who will hire me the minute I graduate."

12   Jeff had always shown a creative flair for color and design. He constantly rearranged our furniture, changing one room after another. All this raced through my mind as I held the phone, separated from him by 9,000 miles. Erv and I looked at each other, wished Jeff luck, and told him to write the check for his tuition.

surly: gruff

furtively: secretly

cantorial: pertaining to the official songs or chants of prayers

appropriated: taken for oneself without permission

ashen: pale

13   When we finally returned home, Jeff was obviously depressed. His answers to our questions were surly°, clipped, and evasive. Behaving unlike his usual loving self, he ran in and out of the house silently, furtively°, always in a hurry. He seemed uninterested in our trip and was clearly trying to avoid us.

14   One day during Passover, Erv was searching for a favorite cantorial° record that Jeff often appropriated°. He checked Jeff's record collection and poked among the torn jeans. Speechless and ashen°, Erv returned to the breakfast room and dropped a book into my lap: *Homosexuality in Modern Society.* "This was hidden in Jeff's room." My heart raced and skipped.

Confrontation:
an open conflict
of opposing
ideas

Confrontation° was finally at hand, not only with Jeff, but with my own fears as well.

15   Then our son came through the front door on the run: "I'm late . . . can't stop . . . talk to you later."

16   The tone of our response and expressions on our faces stopped him mid-flight. "Son, stand still! Something is going on, you are not yourself! Are you in trouble? Drugs, maybe? Is one of your girlfriends pregnant? Or, are you, is it possible that you are . . . homosexual?"

17   I waited, trembling. The faces of my beloveds were creased with anger and worry. I could barely breathe.

18   "Yes, I am gay." A simple sentence, yet I did not understand. Nothing was "gay"!

19   We asked in unison, "What does that mean?"

20   "I am homosexual," he explained. After long minutes of uncomfortable conversation, we sent Jeff on his way with "we'll talk later." I ran from the room to what was to become my comfort zone, the cool tile of the bathroom floor, and I cried my eyes out. I guess Erv went to work. All we can recall now is that neither of us could face the reality right then.

21   That evening and the next, we did an enormous amount of soul-searching. What did I, a social worker, know about homosexuality? What did my husband, the rabbi, know? Our academic credentials° were impressive—professionally we were both well-trained to help other people in pain. But in our personal distress, we felt helpless.

credentials:
documents,
degrees that give
an individual
authority

22   Everything I had ever heard about homosexuality destroyed all my dreams about our son's future. He would never marry and have children. His warmth, caring, good looks, and so many other wonderful traits would not be passed along to a son or daughter, a grandchild. We wondered whether we could keep him in our family circle, or would we lose him to "that other world" of homosexuality, a world that was foreign to us.

23   We wracked ourselves with self-blame—what did we do wrong? I accepted all the myths° about homosexuality. First, the myth of the strong mother—I was a strong mother, but what mother doesn't overexert her influence on her children? Second, the myth of the absent father—Erv spent so much time crisscrossing the country, berating° himself for not being at home enough. Third was the myth of seduction—had someone lured Jeff into this awful lifestyle? And then finally, I believed the myth of "the cure"—that the right therapist could change Jeff's sexual orientation.

myths: belief or
stories often
untrue, unproven
or false

berating:
scolding angrily

24   We did seek help from a therapist. He was patient, caring, and accepting of Jeff and his lifestyle. He helped us begin to sort out myth from reality and guided us through a tangled web of grief, pain, and disappointment. He gently destroyed our unrealistic hope of "changing" Jeff. Our abiding love for our son was, of course, the key to this difficult yet hopeful journey. . . .

25   Jeff sought help, too. At nineteen, he admitted that there was much that he wanted to know about himself. During that time, he offered a comment

that we gratefully accepted: "Please stop blaming yourselves. It is not your fault that I have grown up gay." With those words, Jeff erased our most devastating, yet unspoken, anxiety.

26 Time moved along for all of us. We grieved the loss of deeply held expectations for our son's life. We experienced inner turmoil. Jeff struggled to make peace with himself. We learned to support one another.

27 Over time, we came to understand that a child who is homosexual needs no less understanding, support, and acceptance than one who is heterosexual. Clearly our gay son has the same needs that his straight sister has: for empathy and patience, for security and success, for caring and love. Rejection is difficult for both our children, yet perhaps more so for our gay child. Society has taught him that he will experience less validation° and more unnecessary pain. He, and all of us who love him, are vulnerable° to that pain.

validation:
acceptance

vulnerable:
easily hurt or
wound

intrinsic:
essential in
nature

28 It became clear that Jeff's sexual orientation was only one part of his life. There remained the ordinary concerns and controversies intrinsic° to raising any child. Jeff rode the roller coaster of financial and vocational problems. We provided advice, which he sometimes accepted, and loans, which he often repaid. Jeff's married sister behaved in much the same manner. . . .

29 During all this time, it never occurred to us to turn to the Jewish community for support, though we knew its resources well. We kept our concerns about Jeff's lifestyle to ourselves: We were in the closet. A child's homosexuality was not something one discussed in 1969 and throughout the 1970s. And sharing intimacies with others was not our way—these were matters we had to work out ourselves. . . . And we decided alone, together, to tough out our son's homosexuality, confront it, embrace him, and then face the world together.

30 I recall sitting with close friends one evening. Naturally, the conversation turned to our kids. At one point, someone said, "I think we have something in common." We all agreed, but even then, none of us could articulate° it. In fact, on the way home, Erv asked, "Are you sure their oldest son is gay?"

articulate:
express clearly
and precisely

31 Finally, we came "halfway out," sharing only with family. We found almost unanimous acceptance; affection for Jeff did not falter. But it was seventeen long years before we went public in the Jewish community. Even during the years when my husband was deeply involved in supporting the establishment of a gay outreach synagogue in Los Angeles, when he was busy teaching others that Judaism must not turn its back on any of its children, we did not share our son's homosexuality with the Jewish public.

32 I "came out" for us, with Jeff's permission, in 1986, with an article in *The Reconstructionist,* a national Jewish magazine. The response was overwhelming. Support from rabbis, lay leaders, and friends poured in from around the country. Even at that late date, comfortable as we had become with Jeff's lifestyle, we found those messages heartwarming and reassuring. . . .

solace: comfort
in a time of
sorrow

33 There are Jewish parents who shut out their gay and lesbian children and erect a wall of alienation. There is little solace° in that course of action, or in believing that their child can be "changed" to heterosexuality. Those who reject the person rather than accept the reality, or who chase fantasies rather than learning facts, deserve our compassion and understanding. . . .

Kaddish:
mourner's prayer

34   Some parents actually chant Kaddish° for their "wayward" children. For us our Jewish dedication to family left no room for such behavior. Disappointment hurts, but is curable. Alienation, on the other hand, can kill relationships, love, and family.

35   We Jewish parents love our offspring, sometimes desperately. We can survive the shock of learning that a son is gay, or a daughter is lesbian. Eventually we can find that love will crumble the walls of alienation and that time is an ally. Our children, too, can learn to be patient with us as we grow.

36   Would we have done anything differently? Yes. We would have paid heed to the "flashing lights," the warnings of parenthood. We would have helped our son as early as possible to like himself and make peace with himself. And when he did break the news to us in 1969, I wish we would have been wise enough to hug our beloved son and say, "We love you very much. Let's talk about it."

37   When strangers ask me today if our son is married, I do not hesitate to explain, "He is not. He is gay." We are out of the closet. It has been a long road, but well worth it.

➤ Follow-Up Questions

1. What are some of the everyday activities that Jeff goes through that are similar to other kids growing up?
2. How did Jeff's parents react to his statement that he is gay?
3. What changes in personality does Jeff appear to go through in the narrative?

➤ Short Writing Assignments

1. Many communities have organizations which help support gays and lesbians and sponsor their political concerns. Write a paragraph or short essay describing one such organization either in your own community or a national organization, its history, and the efforts it makes to support the gay and lesbian community.
2. Herman states that she had a sense that her son may have been gay early in his life because he acted "effeminate." Such a statement assumes that certain behavior in young children is "gay." Is this a stereotypical way to view how young people are supposed to act in society? Write a short essay explaining your **position** on specific types of behavior in children and if such behavior can be seen as indicating a form of sexuality or just the natural way a child behaves.

➤ Extended Writing Assignments

1. One of the reasons Herman has concern for her son is because he might face discrimination from those socially, and in some cases, violently opposed to homosexuality. Form a small research group and investigate the discrimination policies which exist in your own school, possibly at a workplace, and even in your own city government. Then write a report that both explains such policies and states your group's position with

respect to the fairness of such policies or lack of such policies. If your group cannot reach a consensus, then each member of the group is to write an additional paragraph to the report explaining his/her points of agreement or disagreement with the policies the group discovered.

2. Often young gay and lesbian teenagers have no one to discuss their own issues with in private. Research various resources available to teenagers, especially those that offer help to gay and lesbian teens or to those who merely want to talk about their sexuality. Such research can include the Internet, library, and community re-sources. Then prepare a report for the class that **describes** these organizations, their purpose, and your **evaluation** of how effective their support is to the gay and lesbian community.

Older Children and Divorce

Barbara Cain

Pre-Reading Ideas: The percentage of divorces rose greatly in the twentieth century, with approximately fifty percent of all marriages ending before the death of a spouse. In the February 19, 2001, issue of *Time* magazine, Josh Tryangiel notes that marriages in ". . . California of 10 years or more are classified as 'long term'" (88) according to California divorce law. When most people hear of a couple's divorce, they think immediately of custody and the impact on the small children in the family. Few people be-yond the immediate family, however, consider the psychological and emo-tional trauma divorce might have on older children, individuals in college who are still considered dependents but are also mature and self-sufficient. How should they be expected to react and respond? Should special coun-seling be available to them or should they be expected to assume an adult demeanor and accept their parents' decision just as they are expected to accept other changes in their lives? Should parents look toward adult chil-dren for support and help during the divorce and subsequent adjustments? Because adult children are "mature" and can take care of themselves, their needs and problems frequently go unacknowledged. Barbara Cain, how-ever, provides insights into the feelings of college-age children whose par-ents underwent a midlife divorce while the children were college students.

Vocabulary: Looking up and understanding the following words prior to reading should prepare you for the author's message. Other words will be defined in the margin.

sanguine**vulnerable****estranged****interloper****apprehension**

1   They were more sanguine about Laura. She was, after all, in college and on the far side of growing up. They said she had loosened her tether° to the family and was no longer hostage to the twists of their fate. They allowed that

tether: rope or chain

she would be shaken for a time by their divorce, but insisted that before long she would find her balance and regain her stride. Her younger brothers, on the other hand, were a constant source of nagging concern. At home and in the eye of the storm, they were in closer range and at higher risk. But Laura, they said, was less vulnerable. Not to worry, Laura would be fine.

2   So go the prevailing attitudes toward college-age children of a midlife divorce. Moreover, these assumptions appear to be shared by social scientists and cultural tribunes° who have rigorously° investigated the impact of divorce on younger children but have, nevertheless, overlooked the plight° of a college-age population, even though statistics show increased incidence of divorce during midlife, thereby involving greater numbers of young adult offspring.

3   In an effort to narrow this gap in the literature, a study was launched in 1984 at the University of California at San Diego and the University of Michigan at Ann Arbor—in which 50 college students between the ages of 18 and 26 were interviewed by this writer, who reported the findings in the journal *Psychiatry* in May 1989. There were obvious differences among the students, their families and each individual divorce process, but recurrent° themes and threads of discourse° wove themselves within and across the interviews with striking regularity.

4   Perhaps the most consistent among them were the students' initial reaction to news of their parents' divorce. All but three in the study recalled an immediate state of shock followed by a lingering sense of disbelief. Even those who grew up amid a turbulent marriage were incredulous° when a separation was announced.

5   "I shouldn't have been surprised," a 20-year old woman reflected. "I used to hear them argue night after night. I used to hear Mom cry and Dad take off in the car. I used to lie awake until he came back, but he always did come back, so I just assumed they would carry on like that for the rest of their lives."

6   Others who had observed their parents slowly disengage° solaced° themselves with the belief that though a marriage of two decades might inevitably lose its luster° it would not necessarily lose its life. "Sure, I noticed them drift apart," a 21-year-old woman remarked. "But then I surveyed the marriages in our neighborhood, and nobody was exactly hearing violins, so I relaxed and told myself that Mom and Dad were like every other couple who had spent half their lives in one relationship."

7   An unexpected finding was that more than half the youngsters surveyed had glorified the marriage preceding its breach°, claiming theirs was "the all-American family," their parents were "the ideal couple"—and "the envy of everyone they knew."

8   "I mean I wasn't exactly naive about divorce," a 19-year-old woman explained. "Half my friends grew up with a single parent, but my Mom and Dad were considered Mr. and Mrs. Perfect Couple. So when they split up, all our friends were just as freaked out as I was."

9   When the veil of denial began to lift and reality took hold, these young adults experienced a profound° sense of loss. They felt bereft° of the family of

---

tribunes: those who uphold or defend the rights of the people

rigorously: strictly

plight: a distressing condition

recurrent: to happen repeatedly

discourse: communication

incredulous: unbelieving

disengage: disconnect

solaced: comforted

luster: newness, shininess

breach: break, split

profound: very deep

bereft: deprived

denude: to strip or make bare

symbolized: represented

relief: clarity

interloper: intruder

virtually: almost real

evicted: asked to leave

ushered: led

calamities: disasters

unprecedented: never before known

preoccupation: absorbed in the thought of

cynics: those who believe that people act only for selfish reasons

subterfuge: something hidden

certifiably: guaranteed

impaired: weakened

opprobrium: cruel power

conduit: a passageway

pejoratives: bad words

self-indulgent: selfish

hypocritical: a person whose actions belie stated beliefs

fury: violent anger

fait accompli: an act that has already happened

upbraided: to find fault with

childhood, the one in the photo album, the one whose members shared the same history, the same humor, the same address. Many described in graphic detail the wrenching pain when the family house was sold, when the furniture was divided and delivered to two separate addresses, neither of which "would ever be home."

10 "Nothing really sank in," explained a 20-year-old man, "until I watched the movers denude° the house I lived in for most of my life. And then I sat on the bare floor and stared at the marks on the wall which outlined the places where our furniture used to be. And I cried until I couldn't see those borders anymore." Clearly the dismantling of the family house symbolized° in stark relief° the final dismantling of the family itself.

11 As each parent began living with new partners, the young adults surveyed said that they felt estranged from the resented interloper° and displaced by the new mate's younger (often live-in) children. Others felt virtually° evicted° from the parents' new homes, which simply could not accommodate two sets of children during over-lapping visits.

12 "When neither Mom nor Dad had room for me during spring break," a 19-year-old man recalled, "it finally hit me that I no longer had a home to go back to and, like it or not, I'd better get my act together because it was 'Welcome to the adult world, kid, you're now completely on your own.' "

13 Because the divorce represented the first sobering crisis in their young adult lives, many in the study believed it marked the end of an era of trust and ushered° in a new apprehension about life's unforeseen calamities°. They reported an unprecedented° preoccupation° with death, disease, and crippling disabilities. They became self-described cynics°, and began scanning relationships for subterfuge°. "I used to believe what people said," a 22-year-old woman recalled. "I used to trust my roommates. I used to trust my boyfriends, and now I know I also used to be certifiably° 'judgment impaired°.' "

14 Striking among this age group was the way in which harsh moral opprobrium° became the conduit° through which anger toward parents was expressed. Pejoratives° like irresponsible, self-indulgent°, and hypocritical° punctuated the interviews.

15 "You accept as an article of faith that your parents will stay together until they die," explained a thoughtful 20-year-old woman, "and then they pull the rug out from under you and you want to scream out and ask 'How can you break the very rules you yourselves wrote?' "

16 Many described being gripped by an unforgiving fury° toward parents who they felt had deprived them of a home, a family, and that inseparable parental pair they had assumed would always be there, together, at birthdays, holidays, and vacations at home. Furthermore, they viewed these losses to have been preventable, hence they deeply resented learning of the decision when it was a *fait accompli*°. And they upbraided° their parents for excluding them from a process they might have otherwise reversed.

17 "Why didn't they tell me they were having trouble?" one young woman asked in barely muted exasperation. "If I had known, I would have helped them find a marriage counselor. If they were unhappy then why didn't they

do something about it? My dad spent more time fixing his car than he ever did his marriage."

18   Most in the study blamed the parent who initiated° the break and relentlessly° hectored° that parent for explanations. "Every day I'd ask my mother 'Why,'" one young woman recalled, "and no answer ever made sense. They sounded so feeble, and so absolutely wrong."

19   The young adults surveyed were most staggered by the apparent moral reversals in their parents' behavior. In stunned disbelief, a 20-year-old woman discovered her "buttoned up, bible-carrying" mother in bed with a man two years older than her son. Another student witnessed his ambitious, seemingly conscience-ridden father walk away from his family and his lucrative° law firm for destinations unknown. As though looking through lenses badly out of focus, many gazed upon parents they no longer recognized and struggled over which image was false, which authentic°.

20   "Was the old Mom just hiding under the real one that was coming out now?" a 21-year-old man wondered. "Was that tender, loving person all a lie? Was I just not seeing what I didn't want to see? And if that's true, then how am I supposed to trust what I think I see now?"

21   Upon observing their mothers' unbridled sexuality, several young women withdrew from romantic relationships, retreated to solitary study, became abstemious° and, in Anna Freud's° words, declared war on the pursuit of pleasure.

22   In sharp contrast, others plunged into hedonism,° flaunting° their indulgences,° daring their parents to forbid activity that mirrored their own. A 20-year-old woman launched a series of sexual liaisons° with older married men. A 19-year-old moved in with a graduate student after knowing him for 10 days. And a 22-year-old male dropped out of school to deal in drugs.

23   In response to their parents' apparent moral inversion°, a small subgroup temporarily took refuge in a protective nihilism°, reasoning that illusions that never form are illusions that never shatter. "Since their breakup I don't pin my hopes on anything anymore," a disenchanted young man declared: "And I no longer have a secret dream. What will be will be. Since I can't change any of that, why even try and why even care?"

24   . . . Several said they feigned° an affectionate tie to the rejected parent simply because of financial need. "Between you and me," a spunky 19-year-old man confessed, "I can't wait until I'm self-supporting, so then I won't have to humor my father with a phony song and dance every time my tuition is due." And a number reported that their overt° condemnation of their father cost them a long-enjoyed relationship with paternal° grandparents as battle lines between "his" and "her" side of the family were drawn.

25   Remarks such as these suggest that, whatever else, these college-age youngsters are better able than younger children to remove themselves from the internecine° warfare and resisted colluding° with the parent "spurned" in excoriating° the parent blamed.

26   In sharp contrast to younger children of divorce who frequently hold themselves responsible for the separation, the young adults surveyed did not reveal even the slightest traces of guilt or blame. Though most were certain

initiated: started, began

relentlessly: without stop

hectored: gave a hard time to

lucrative: profitable

authentic: real

abstemious: moderate in eating and drinking

Anna Freud: daughter of psychoanalyst, Sigmund Freud

hedonism: living for pleasure and happiness

flaunting: making obvious

indulgences: permissiveness

liaisons: relationships

inversion: reversal

nihilism: rejection of all things

feigned: pretended, faked

overt: obvious

paternal: on the father's hereditary side

internecine: conflict within a group

colluding: conspiring

excoriating: severely denouncing

lamented:
grieved

chided: scolded

estrangement:
separation

disabuse: free
from error

apocalyptic:
prophetic

legacy: a gift
handed down

they had not caused their parents' divorce, several lamented° having failed to prevent it. A 19-year-old woman believed that had she managed her mother's domestic chores more effectively, her mother would not have ended her marriage in favor of her career. And a 21-year-old woman chided° herself for not noticing her parents' estrangement°: "Sometimes I still wonder if I had paid more attention to *them,* maybe we would all still be *us.*"

27   And because each youngster in the study was living away from home at the time of the separation, many believed that their parents had literally "stayed together for the sake of the children." Indeed, several parents did not disabuse° their children of this notion. When a 20-year-old man accused his father of being foolishly headstrong in abruptly ending his 25-year marriage, his father informed him that he had wanted to end his marriage for more than 20 years but had waited until his son was grown and gone.

28   . . . Perhaps the most uniform finding in this study was the radically altered attitudes toward love and marriage held by many following their parents' divorce.

29   When a young woman's parents separated soon after their 20th anniversary, she created her own theory of marriage: "People marry in order to have children, and parenthood is what holds a marriage together. When children are grown and gone, marriage no longer has a reason for being and couples will then drift apart and the marriage will slowly die. If couples stay together even after their last child leaves home, then they are truly in love and they are the lucky few."

30   . . . With rare exception, most in the study feared they were destined to repeat their parents' mistakes, a concern frequently reinforced by the parents themselves. "You're attracted to the same kind of charming Don Juan who did me in," one mother admonished. "Beware of the womanizer just like your father or you'll be dumped in your 40's, just like me." Many of the youngsters deeply resented these apocalyptic°, cautionary tales. Others felt burdened by having to wrestle with the ghosts of their parents' past. "Most people meet, fall in love and marry," a 21-year-old lamented, "but I have to find someone who convinces my mother he's not my father and then he has to fit the job description of a saint."

31   . . . Whether or not the profound sense of loss, the disillusionment, the revised attitudes toward love and marriage remain an enduring legacy° of parental divorce for college-age youngsters, only future studies can determine. It should be noted, however, that most of these youngsters unsuccessfully disguised a deep and abiding wish to marry, to have children and to recapture the family of childhood—the one in the picture frame, animated, intertwined, and inseparable.

➤ Follow-Up Questions

1. Why would someone assume that an older, college-age child would respond differently to the divorce of his or her parents or guardians from a younger child?
2. What do you consider the two most negative responses of older children to divorce cited in the article?
3. What are some of the parents' or guardians' responses to their own divorce?

➤ Short Writing Assignments

1. Cain refers to several types of behavior that older children resort to in response to divorce. Do you feel that such behavior is a passive, emotional response to the situation, or could the divorce merely be a cover-up or excuse used by the older child for such behavior?

2. While Cain's article displays the many negative effects divorce has, many view the process as a positive step in one's life. Use information in the article and/or from interviewing others who have been through a divorce to write a paragraph or short essay defending the process of divorce.

➤ Extended Writing Assignments

1. Form a research group and investigate Cain's findings. Interview as many individuals as you can who are older children of divorce. Be sure to have a representative sample for your investigation; that is, try to have as many young men as women, different educational backgrounds, and so forth. Then write an essay explaining your findings and stating whether your research group found Cain's **argument** valid or not.

2. Appearance is often confused with reality; in Cain's article, some older children question whether their parents had been deceiving them, because after the divorce the parent exhibited new types of behavior. In an essay, **describe** what you believe to be the two or three major indicators of how one can determine the "real" person; give specific **examples** to illustrate how the indicators can be used.

CONCLUSION

Although the cliché "Home is where the heart is" may be true, home may not always be the safest place. The works in this chapter describe homes that provide security, support, and comfort, but they also present examples of danger, instability, and dependence. The home as a political issue is not often considered, but the problem of homelessness is becoming more common. Readers will find that they might not identify with the home and family situations they read about, but they will discover ways of living they might have never considered before.

➤ Further Writing Topics

Personal Narrative

The terms *home* and *family* have different meaning for different people. Some cultures practice opening their homes to extended families. In giving priority to the welfare of the family, adults will take aging parents, other siblings, children a family cannot care for, or others into the home on a temporary or permanent basis. Some cultures are reluctant to send aging family members to nursing homes, preferring to care for the relative at home. Write a descriptive narrative discussing your experiences within an extended family. If you do not come from an extended family, write a descriptive narrative describing your family.

Exposition

Polygamy, or the practice of having multiple wives and families, was once considered a legal practice in the United States under certain conditions, but it is now illegal. The impact of polygamy on wives, children, and society has been investigated and written about. Write a brief **research** paper that discusses some aspect of polygamy.

Analysis

Three of the works in this chapter describe the relationship between children and their parents. Using "The Youngest Daughter" by Cathy Song, "A Parent's Journey out of the Closet" by Agnes Herman, and/or "Older Children and Divorce" by Barbara Cain, write an **analytical** paper that **compares and/or contrasts** parents' relationships with their parents.

Argumentative

Using the topic for the **personal narrative,** write an **argumentative** essay about the benefits or the problems that arise from an extended family. Do you support or oppose extended families?

➤ Suggested Chapter Projects

1. Prepare a project that shows how the American culture represents the idea of the family in various media. Your project should consider as many examples and cultural viewpoints as possible, including those from TV, music, the arts, and religion, among others. As a conclusion, prepare a report of your findings and what you believe is the typical family image presented to the American public.
2. The idea of family and family values is often appropriated or used as a propaganda tool, as a way to influence someone to agree with a viewpoint, such as showing a family picnic to sell hotdogs or cars. Research how the family situation is appropriated by advertisement and/or other social institutions as a way to promote commercial products, such as fashion, music, and food. You may also want to consider such institutions as political campaigns which show candidates holding babies. Consolidate your findings in a report that you will present to the class which **describes** how such appropriation occurs, the motivation behind such efforts, and your position on why such campaigns or ads choose the family as a way to get what they want.
3. While several articles in this chapter address problems with home and family, other issues, such as health care for family members, are also important. Choose one such issue and investigate the resources which are available in your community to address this problem. You may want to consider such resources as church groups, community programs, state and federal agencies, and even Internet sites. Then prepare a **letter** to either your state representative or senator in which you describe the problem in your community, detail your findings, and request further assistance for your community. A copy of your letter will be turned in to your instructor; the original is to be mailed to the representative or senator in your district.

4. There have been several excellent films presenting the difficulties gay men and lesbians have coping with or disclosing their identity to their families and society. Watch a movie such as *The Matthew Shephard Story, Philadelphia, The Band Played On, But I'm a Cheerleader*, or *In and Out*, and write a paper explaining the **causes** of the problems gay men and lesbians have in society as seen in the movie or the **effects** of the gay men's and lesbians' disclosure of their sexual orientation on their families.

CHAPTER 4

Reflection
Source: PhotoDisc AA009587

Identity: Self, Dreams, and Breaking Society's Rules

D o you remember when you first started defining yourself? You were quite young when you first uttered your name, held up three or four fingers to show your age, and later announced importantly that you wanted to be a nurse, firefighter, police officer, or teacher. Today, things are more complex, and not only have your career options expanded, but the beliefs you hold have also broadened. Take a few minutes to write in your journal. Define yourself. Answer questions such as Who am I? What are my dreams and goals? Who is important to me? These questions identify you to yourself; other questions can include topics such as plans for the future, ideas about your current family and friends, the goals you hold for yourself, what your beliefs are now, and how much you like who you are.

Once you have looked introspectively and once you have defined what you believe, you will be able to move forward to identify with or explore other people's positions and beliefs. This chapter will explore how characters and authors see themselves in relation to their family, friends, and society. In most pieces a struggle will be apparent as the desires of significant others conflict with the dreams, goals, and identity each speaker wants to pursue. How each author resolves the struggle is important. Sandra Cisneros, Henry Louis Gates, Jr., and Lois Gould examine the importance of a name for a young person. Marcus Bleeker looks introspectively at life as an African-American and explains the role his white father had in helping him develop pride in his ethnicity. Finally, Linda Rader Overman travels to Chiapas, Mexico, and through observation of the indigenous people and reflective writing discovers her own narrative.

If you have not yet taken time to begin solidifying the goals, beliefs, and values that create your identity, this chapter will give you an opportunity to do so. Although some people begin this activity early in their lives, other people are happy to go wherever life leads them. That you have enrolled in this class indicates that you have begun thinking ahead and preparing for a future you and/or your parents/guardians may have set. To discover that you disagree with those goals is not bad, but to be unable to define your own goals probably means you are still deciding. You have many choices available to you based on your abilities, interests, and time. If you are uncertain, your institution provides career counselors, interest inventories, and other tools to help narrow your choices. Constructing your identity, emphasizing particular talents, and developing personal and professional skills are exciting steps to becoming the kind of person you wish to be.

My Name

Sandra Cisneros

Introductory Remarks: Born in Chicago, Illinois, Sandra Cisneros grew up having a great respect for books and later for writing. Growing up with six brothers and in a household where her mother was a homemaker who had "never finished high school," and her father was an upholsterer who had "thrown away his college education," Cisneros felt different from her fellow students in the University of Iowa graduate writing program. Unable to identify with others in the program whom she describes as being "from the best schools in the country" and as "ha[ving] been bred as fine hothouse flowers," Cisneros finally found her voice and began "to write a series of autobiographical sketches [that her] classmates could not write about," and ". . . *The House on Mango Street* was born."

Pre-Reading Ideas: In this short chapter from her novel, Cisneros describes an eleven-year-old youngster who is thinking deeply about who she is and where she came from. She knows the story of her great-grandparents, and she knows that she doesn't want to follow the path that her namesake followed, but she is curious about what her great-grandmother did with her life. Do you know any stories about your ancestors? Do you think it is important to know stories from the past to understand who you are today?

1   In English my name means hope. In Spanish it means too many letters. It means sadness, it means waiting. It is like the number nine. A muddy color. It is the Mexican records my father plays on Sunday mornings when he is shaving, songs like sobbing.

2   It was my great-grandmother's name and now it is mine. She was a horse woman too, born like me in the Chinese year of the horse—which is supposed to be bad luck if you're born female—but I think this is a Chinese lie because the Chinese, like the Mexicans, don't like their women strong.

3   My great-grandmother. I would've liked to have known her, a wild horse of a woman, so wild she wouldn't marry. Until my great-grandfather just threw a sack over her head and carried her off. Just like that, as if she were a fancy chandelier. That's the way he did it.

4   And the story goes she never forgave him. She looked out the window her whole life, the way so many women sit their sadness on an elbow. I wonder if she made the best with what she got or was she sorry because she

couldn't be all the things she wanted to be. Esperanza. I have inherited her name, but I don't want to inherit her place by the window.

5   At school they say my name funny as if the syllables were made out of tin and hurt the roof of your mouth. But in Spanish my name is made out of a softer something, like silver, not quite as thick as sister's name—Magdalena—which is uglier than mine. Magdalena who at least can come home and become Nenny. But I am always Esperanza. I would like to baptize myself under a new name, a name more like the real me, the one nobody sees. Esperanza as Lisandra or Maritza or Zeze the X. Yes. Something like Zeze the X will do.

➤ Follow-Up Questions

1. Esperanza clearly does not like her name. However, she talks about other issues besides her name. One is culture. She says that the Chinese and the Mexicans "don't like their women strong." Is she talking about all members of the culture? If not, to whom is she referring?
2. Esperanza appears to admire her great-grandmother, but she also criticizes her. How does Esperanza wish to be different from her and why?
3. Esperanza wants to change her name to Zeze the X. How would that change her identity? In how many ways?

➤ Short Writing Assignments

1. Esperanza talks about the sound of English as opposed to the sound of Spanish. Write a descriptive paragraph or short essay in which you detail some of the specific sounds from each language. Then conclude your writing with a statement as to which language you prefer and why.
2. How do you feel about your name? Has it caused you any troubles in your life? Do you have a nickname that your family or friends gave you? Do you like it or have you ever tried to change your name? Write a journal entry discussing your feelings about your name.

➤ Extended Writing Assignments

1. In contemporary American society, names that give no hint as to gender or nationality are being adopted by parents for their children. Look for examples of these names among your classmates, friends, or coworkers. Talk to them about how they feel about their names. Write a short **informative** paper that discusses the names, their origins, the people's feelings about their names, and how others react to them when the strangers first hear the name. Also, read the next story and see if the reactions in public are similar to or different from those recorded in the story.
2. One of the most exciting times in many parents' lives occurs after they discover that they will have a baby. They start thinking about what they will name their child. Many options are considered: naming the child after a parent, relative, or a character they read about in a book. Sometimes they will look in baby books for names that sound good together. Sometimes they will create their own names that are unique. What are your considerations in naming a future child? Would you consider how the name will

sound to his or her peers? Would you give your child a nickname? If possible, talk to your mother and to other people and ask what they considered when they named their child or children. Write an informative paper describing the different methods employed to name babies.

What's in a Name?

··

Henry Louis Gates, Jr.

Pre-Reading Ideas: How important is it to you that people know your name? Have you ever felt insulted if someone calls you by the wrong name accidentally? In the following personal narrative, a child learns the ugliness of racial prejudice when he discovers that an older white man in his community refuses to take the time to learn the difference between one African-American and another, preferring to call them all by the same name. Individual differences are first acknowledged when people can distinguish you from those around you. Your own identity is part of your self-esteem and your self-confidence. Most people take great care in constructing their own characteristics by which they can be recognized, and to be placed in a group of people who are considered indistinguishable from one another is to become invisible, anonymous, and insignificant. Visibility is an important part of life for many people; how do you ensure that you are known to your professors, friends, co-workers, and others around you?

Vocabulary: Looking up and understanding the following words prior to reading should prepare you for the author's message. Other words will be defined in the margin.

affluent	**Riley**	**Sugar Ray**	**Jackie Robinson**

··

1   I had forgotten the incident completely, until I read Trey Ellis's essay, "Remember My Name," in a recent issue of the *Village Voice* (June 13, 1989). But there, in the middle of an extended italicized list of the by-names of "the race" ("the race" or "our people" being the terms my parents used in polite or

reverential: deep respect

reverential° discourse, "jigaboo" or "nigger" more commonly used in anger, jest, or pure disgust) it was: "George." Now the events of that very brief exchange return to mind so vividly that I wonder why I had forgotten it.

2   My father and I were walking home at dusk from his second job. He

moonlighted: to work at an additional job after one's regular job

"moonlighted"° as a janitor in the evenings for the telephone company. Every day but Saturday, he would come home at 3:30 from his regular job at the paper mill, wash up, eat supper, then at 4:30 head downtown to his second job. He used to make jokes frequently about the union official who moonlighted. I never got the joke, but he and his friends thought it was hilarious. All I knew was that my family always ate well, that my brother and I had new clothes to wear, and that all of the white people in Piedmont, West Virginia, treated my parents with an odd mixture of resentment and respect that even we understood at the time had something directly to do with a small but certain measure of financial security.

3   He had left a little early that evening because I was with him, and I had to be in bed early. I could not have been more than five or six, and we had stopped off at the Cut-Rate Drug Store (where no black person in town but my father could sit down to eat, and eat off real plates with real silverware) so that I could buy some caramel ice cream, two scoops in a wafer cone, please, which I was busy licking when Mr. Wilson walked by.

4   Mr. Wilson was a very quiet man, whose stony, brooding, silent manner seemed designed to scare off any overtures° of friendship, even from white people. He was Irish, as was one-third of our village (another third being Italian), the more affluent among whom sent their children to "Catholic School" across the bridge in Maryland. He had white straight hair, like my Uncle Joe, whom he uncannily° resembled, and he carried a black worn metal lunch pail, the kind that Riley carried on the television show. My father always spoke to him, and for reasons that we never did understand, he always spoke to my father.

overture: offer

uncannily: extraordinarily

5   "Hello, Mr. Wilson," I heard my father say.

6   "Hello, George."

7   I stopped licking my ice cream cone, and asked my Dad in a loud voice why Mr. Wilson had called him "George."

8   "Doesn't he know your name, Daddy? Why don't you tell him your name? Your name isn't George."

9   For a moment I tried to think of who Mr. Wilson was mixing Pop up with. But we didn't have any Georges among the colored people in Piedmont; nor were there colored Georges living in the neighboring towns and working at the mill.

10   "Tell him your name, Daddy."

11   "He knows my name, boy," my father said after a long pause. "He calls all colored people George."

ensued: followed

rent: a tear in a fabric

12   A long silence ensued°. It was "one of those things," as my Mom would put it. Even then, that early, I knew when I was in the presence of "one of those things," one of those things that provided a glimpse, through a rent° curtain, at another world that we could not affect but that affected us. There would be a painful moment of silence, and you would wait for it to give way to a discussion of a black superstar such as Sugar Ray or Jackie Robinson.

13   "Nobody hits better in a clutch than Jackie Robinson."

14   "That's right. Nobody."

15   I never again looked Mr. Wilson in the eye.

➤ Follow-Up Questions

1. Describe Gates's father.
2. If you had been Gates's father, what would you have said to your son about Mr. Wilson's comment?
3. Who are Sugar Ray and Jackie Robinson, and why are they so important to Gates's community?

➤ Short Writing Assignments

1. Watching a parent or guardian in an embarrassing situation is often difficult for the child as well as for the adult. Think back to a situation in which your parent or guardian endured a difficult and embarrassing event and then write a personal narrative describing the event, how the adult handled the situation, and your own emotional reactions at the time and now.

2. According to Gates, his narrative was a response to a specific word that held great emotional meaning to him, "George." Think about your own lifetime and consider a specific word, whether positive or negative, which holds great personal significance for you. Then prepare a paragraph identifying the word and explaining how it is significant to you. If you cannot think of a specific word, possibly a short phrase is important, such as "It's a girl!"

➤ Extended Writing Assignments

1. Gates asks a simple but very powerful question in his title. Exactly "What's in a Name"? Write an essay explaining how you would respond to this question, taking into account the multiple ways a "name" identifies who a person is, whether positively, negatively, or simply as a way to conduct one's life, such as "doctor."

2. Gates points out in his essay how humor was a way to cope in a world often devoid of anything humorous at all. Watch several comedy programs that employ comedy as a way to cope with life's problems and also as a way to break through social barriers so that cultures have a common ground on which to come together. If you feel that a comedian was ridiculing a culture, make note of how the comment could be taken negatively. Then prepare an essay explaining the various subjects that the comedians made fun of and how such humor acted as a way to join rather than divide a community or cultures.

X: A Fabulous Child's Story

Lois Gould

Introductory Remarks: Lois Gould published this story as a children's book in 1978; however, it presents some important adult ideas about identity.

Pre-Reading Ideas: This story could also be printed in Chapter 8, Misconceptions: Stereotypes, Prejudice, and War. When you begin reading that chapter, you may want to refer to this story again for further discussion. Now, however, we can look at this "children's story" from a more academic viewpoint. If we take it in that context, we could call this an example of **satire,** a style of writing that blends a criticism of society or institutions with wit and humor so as to improve them. You may have read "A Modest Proposal" by Jonathan Swift, in which he satirically recommends that to stem the rise of hunger in England, children who are a year old should be "offered in sale to the persons of quality and fortune through the kingdom, always advising the mother to let them suck plentifully in the last month, so as to render them plump and fat for a good table." Of course, Swift did not intend for this "modest" suggestion to be taken seriously, and, instead, was offering a critical commentary about the British government. Gould's satire is not quite so shocking in its suggestion, but it does make readers stop and think about how parents help to construct the identity not only of their own children but also of those with whom their children associate.

Stop before you read the story and take a personal inventory. Are you dressed in a way that indicates your gender? Are your clothes a reflection of what society says is proper for you? Do you send a message about who you are when people look at you? In Lois Gould's story, as well as in Sandra Cisneros's, each author discusses the topic of how children feel about themselves and their identity.

Vocabulary: Looking up and understanding the following words prior to reading should prepare you for the author's message.

biceps   mischievous

1   Once upon a time, a Baby named X was born. It was named X so that no-body could tell whether it was a boy or a girl.

2   Its parents could tell, of course, but they couldn't tell anybody else. They couldn't even tell Baby X—at least not until much, much later.

3   You see, it was all part of a very important Secret Scientific Xperiment, known officially as Project Baby X.

4   This Xperiment was going to cost Xactly 23 billion dollars and 72 cents. Which might seem like a lot for one Baby, even if it was an important Secret Scientific Xperiment Baby.

5   But when you remember the cost of strained carrots, stuffed bunnies, booster shots, 28 shiny quarters from the tooth fairy . . . you begin to see how it adds up.

6   Long before Baby X was born, the smartest scientists had to work out the secret details of the Xperiment, and to write the *Official Instruction Manual* in secret code, for Baby X's parents, whoever they were. These parents had to be selected very carefully. Thousands of people volunteered to take thousands of tests, with thousands of tricky questions.

7   Almost everybody failed because, it turned out, almost everybody wanted a boy or a girl, and not a Baby X at all.

8   Also, almost everybody thought a Baby X would be more trouble than a boy or a girl. (They were right, too.)

9   There were families with grandparents named Milton and Agatha, who wanted the baby named Milton or Agatha instead of X, even if it *was* an X.

10   There were aunts who wanted to knit tiny dresses and uncles who wanted to send tiny baseball mitts.

11   Worst of all, there were families with other children who couldn't be trusted to keep a Secret. Not if they knew the Secret was worth 23 billion dollars and 72 cents—and all you had to do was take one little peek at Baby X in the bathtub to know what it was.

12   Finally, the scientists found the Joneses, who really wanted to raise an X more than any other kind of baby—no matter how much trouble it was.

13   The Joneses promised to take turns holding X, feeding X, and singing X to sleep.

14   And they promised never to hire any baby-sitters. The scientists knew that a baby-sitter would probably peek at X in the bathtub, too.

15   The day the Joneses brought their baby home, lots of friends and relatives came to see it. And the first thing they asked was what kind of baby X was.

16   When the Joneses said, "It's an X!" nobody knew what to say.

17   They couldn't say, "Look at her cute little dimples!"

18   On the other hand, they couldn't say, "Look at his husky little biceps!"

19   And they didn't feel right about saying just plain "kitchy-coo."

20   The relatives all felt embarrassed about having an X in the family.

21   "People will think there's something wrong with it!" they whispered.

22   "Nonsense!" the Joneses said cheerfully. "What could possibly be wrong with this perfectly adorable X?"

23   Clearly, nothing at all was wrong. Nevertheless, the cousins who had sent a tiny football helmet would not come and visit any more. And the neighbors who sent a pink-flowered romper suit pulled their shades down when the Joneses passed their house.

24   The *Official Instruction Manual* had warned the new parents that this would happen, so they didn't fret about it. Besides, they were too busy learning how to bring up Baby X.

25   Ms. and Mr. Jones had to be Xtra careful. If they kept bouncing it up in the air and saying how *strong* and *active* it was, they'd be treating it more like a boy than an X. But if all they did was cuddle it and kiss it and tell it how *sweet* and *dainty* it was, they'd be treating it more like a girl than an X.

26   On page 1654 of the *Official Instruction Manual,* the scientists prescribed: "plenty of bouncing and plenty of cuddling, *both*. X ought to be strong and sweet and active. Forget about *dainty* altogether."

27   There were other problems, too. Toys, for instance. And clothes. On his first shopping trip, Mr. Jones told the store clerk, "I need some things for a new baby." The clerk smiled and said, "Well, now, is it a boy or a girl?" "It's an X." Mr. Jones said, smiling back. But the clerk got all red in the face and said huffily, "In *that* case, I'm afraid I can't help you, sir."

28   Mr. Jones wandered the aisles trying to find what X needed. But everything was in sections marked BOYS or GIRLS: "Boys' pajamas" and "Girls' Underwear" and "Boys' Fire Engines" and "Girls' Housekeeping Sets." Mr. Jones went home without buying anything for X.

29   That night he and Ms. Jones consulted page 2326 of the *Official Instruction Manual*. It said firmly: "Buy plenty of everything!"

30   So they bought all kinds of toys. A boy doll that made pee-pee and cried "Pa-Pa." And a girl doll that talked in three languages and said, "I am the Pres-i-dent of Gen-er-al Mo-tors."

31   They bought a storybook about a brave princess who rescued a handsome prince from his tower, and another about a sister and brother who grew up to be a baseball star and a ballet star, and you had to guess which.

32   The head scientists of Project Baby X checked all their purchases and told them to keep up the good work. They also reminded the Joneses to see page 4629 of the *Manual*, where it said, "Never make Baby X feel *embarrassed* or *ashamed* about what it wants to play with. And if Baby X gets dirty climbing rocks, never say, 'Nice little Xes don't get dirty climbing rocks'."

33   Likewise, it said, "If X falls down and cries, never say, 'Brave little Xes don't cry.' Because, of course, nice little Xes *do* get dirty and brave little Xes *do* cry. No matter how dirty X gets, or how hard it cries, don't worry. It's all part of the Xperiment."

34   Wherever the Joneses pushed Baby X's stroller in the park, smiling strangers would come over and coo: "Is that a boy or a girl?" The Joneses would smile back and say, "It's an X." The strangers would stop smiling then and often snarl something nasty—as if the Joneses had said something nasty to *them*.

35   Once a little girl grabbed X's shovel in the sandbox, and zonked X on the head with it. "Now, now, Tracy," the mother began to scold, "little girls mustn't hit little—"and she turned to ask X, "Are you a little boy or a little girl, dear?"

36   Mr. Jones, who was sitting near the sandbox, held his breath and crossed his fingers.

37   X smiled politely, even though X's head had never been zonked so hard in its life. "I'm a little X," said X.

38   "You're a *what?*" the lady exclaimed angrily. "You're a little b-r-a-t, you mean!"

39   "But little girls mustn't hit little Xes, either!" said X, retrieving the shovel with another polite smile. "What good's hitting, anyway?"

40   X's father finally X-haled, uncrossed his fingers, and grinned.

41   And at their next secret Project Baby X meeting, the scientists grinned, too. Baby X was doing fine.

42   But then it came time for X to start school. The Joneses were really worried about this, because school was even more full of rules for boys and girls, and there were no rules for Xes.

43   Teachers would tell boys to form a line, and girls to form another line.

44   There would be boys' games and girls' games, and boys' secrets and girls' secrets.

45   The school library would have a list of recommended books for girls and a different list for boys.

46   There would even be a bathroom marked BOYS and another one marked GIRLS.

47   Pretty soon boys and girls would hardly talk to each other. What would happen to poor little X?

48   The Joneses spent weeks consulting their *Instruction Manual*.

49   There were 249 and one-half pages of advice under "First Day of School." Then they were all summoned to an Urgent Xtra Special Conference with the smart scientists of Project Baby X.

50   The scientists had to make sure that X's mother had taught X how to throw and catch a ball properly, and that X's father had been sure to teach X what to serve a doll's tea party.

51   X had to know how to shoot marbles and jump rope and, most of all, what to say when the Other Children asked whether X was a Boy or a Girl.

52   Finally X was ready.

53   X's teacher had promised that the class could line up alphabetically, instead of forming separate lines for boys and girls. And X had permission to use the principal's bathroom, because it wasn't marked anything except BATHROOM. But nobody could help X with the biggest problem of all— Other Children.

54   Nobody in X's class had ever known an X. Nobody had even heard grown-ups say, "Some of my best friends are Xes."

55   What would other children think? Would they make Xist jokes? Or would they make friends?

56   You couldn't tell what X was by its clothes. Overalls don't even button right to left, like girls' clothes, or left to right, like boys' clothes.

57   And did X have a girl's short haircut or a boy's long haircut?

58   As for the games X liked, either X played ball very well for a girl, or else played house very well for a boy.

59   The children tried to find out by asking X tricky questions, like "Who's your favorite sports star?"

60   X had two favorite sports stars: a girl jockey named Robyn Smith and a boy archery champion named Robin Hood.

61   Then they asked, "What's your favorite TV show?" And X said: "Lassie," which stars a girl dog played by a boy dog.

62   When X said his favorite toy was a doll, everyone decided that X must be a girl. But then X said the doll was really a robot, and that X had computerized it, and that it was programmed to bake fudge and then clean up the kitchen.

63   After X told them that, they gave up guessing what X was. All they knew was they'd sure like to see X's doll.

64   After school, X wanted to play with the other children. "How about shooting baskets in the gym?" X asked the girls. But all they did was make faces and giggle behind X's back.

65   "Boy, is *he* weird," whispered Jim to Joe.

66   "How about weaving some baskets in the arts and crafts room?" X asked the boys. But they all made faces and giggled behind X's back, too.

67   "Boy, is *she* weird," whispered Susie to Peggy.

68   That night, Ms. and Mr. Jones asked X how things had gone at school. X tried to smile, but there were two big tears in its eyes. "The lessons are OK," X began, "but. . . ."

69   "But?" said Mr. Jones.

70 "The Other Children hate me," X whispered.

71 "Hate you?" said Mr. Jones.

72 X nodded, which made the two big tears roll down and splash on its overalls.

73 Once more, the Joneses reached for their *Instruction Manual.* Under "Other Children," it said:

74 "What did you Xpect? Other Children have to obey silly boy-girl rules, because their parents taught them to. Lucky X—you don't have rules at all! All you have to do is be yourself.

75 "P.S. We're not saying it'll be easy."

76 X liked being itself. But X cried a lot that night. So X's father held X tight, and cried a little, too. X's mother cheered them up with an Xciting story about an enchanted prince called Sleeping Handsome, who woke up when Princess Charming kissed him.

77 The next morning, they all felt much better, and little X went back to school with a brave smile and a clean pair of red and white checked overalls.

78 There was a seven-letter-word spelling bee in class that day. And a seven-lap boys' relay race in the gym. And a seven-layer-cake baking contest in the girls' kitchen corner.

79 X won the spelling bee. X also won the relay race.

80 And X almost won the baking contest, Xcept it forgot to light the oven. (Remember, nobody's perfect.)

81 One of the Other Children noticed something else, too. He said: "X doesn't care about winning. X just thinks it's fun playing boys' stuff *and* girls' stuff."

82 "Come to think of it," said another one of the Other Children, "X is having twice as much fun as we are!"

83 After school that day, the girl who beat X in the baking contest gave X a big slice of her winning cake.

84 And the boy X beat in the relay race asked X to race him home.

85 From then on, some really funny things began to happen.

86 Susie, who sat next to X, refused to wear pink dresses to school any more. She wanted red and white checked overalls—just like X's.

87 Overalls, she told her parents, were better for climbing monkey bars.

88 Then Jim, the class football nut, started wheeling his little sister's doll carriage around the football field.

89 He'd put on his entire football uniform, except for the helmet.

90 Then he'd put the helmet *in* the carriage, lovingly tucked under an old set of shoulder pads.

91 *Then* he'd jog around the field, pushing the carriage and singing, "Rockabye Baby" to his helmet.

92 He said X did the same thing, so it must be okay. After all, X was now the team's star quarterback.

93 Susie's parents were horrified by her behavior, and Jim's parents were worried sick about his.

94 But the worst came when the twins, Joe and Peggy, decided to share everything with each other.

95   Peggy used Joe's hockey skates, and his microscope, and took half his newspaper route.

96   Joe used Peggy's needlepoint kit, and her cookbooks, and took two of her three baby-sitting jobs.

97   Peggy ran the lawn mower, and Joe ran the vacuum cleaner.

98   Their parents weren't one bit pleased with Peggy's science experiments, or with Joe's terrific needlepoint pillows.

99   They didn't care that Peggy mowed the lawn better, and that Joe vacuumed the carpet better.

100   In fact, they were furious. It's all that little X's fault, they agreed. X doesn't know what it is, or what it's supposed to be! So X wants to mix everybody *else* up, too.

101   Peggy and Joe were forbidden to play with X any more. So was Susie, and then Jim and then *all* the Other Children.

102   But it was too late: The Other Children stayed mixed-up and happy to be free, and refused to go back to the way they'd been before X.

103   Finally, the parents held an emergency meeting to discuss "The X Problem."

104   They sent a report to the principal stating that X was a "bad influence," and demanding immediate action.

105   The Joneses, they said, should be *forced* to tell whether X was a boy or a girl. And X should be *forced* to behave like whichever it was.

106   If the Joneses refused to tell, the parents said, then X must take an Xamination. An Impartial Team of Xperts would Xtract the secret. Then X would start obeying all the old rules. Or else.

107   And if X turned out to be some kind of mixed-up misfit, then X must be Xpelled from school. Immediately! So that no little Xes would ever come to school again.

108   The principal was very upset. X, a bad influence? A mixed-up misfit? But X was an Xcellent student. X set a fine Xample! X was Xtraordinary!

109   X was the president of the student council. X had won first prize in the art show, honorable mention in the science fair, and six events on field day, including the potato race.

110   *Nevertheless,* insisted the parents, X is a Problem Child. X is the Biggest Problem Child we have ever seen!

111   So the principal reluctantly notified X's parents and the Joneses reported this to the Project X scientists, who referred them to page 85769 of the *Instruction Manual*. "Sooner or later," it said, "X will have to be Xamined by an Impartial Team of Xperts.

112   "This may be the only way any of us will know for sure whether X is mixed up—or everyone else is."

113   At Xactly 9 o'clock the next day, X reported to the school health office. The principal, along with a committee from the Parents' Association, X's teacher, X's classmates, and Ms. and Mr. Jones, waited in the hall outside.

114   Inside, the Xperts had set up their famous testing machine: the Super-psychiamedicosocioculturometer.

115   Nobody knew Xactly how the machine worked, but everybody knew that this examination would reveal Xactly what everyone wanted to know about X, but were afraid to ask.

116   It was terribly quiet in the hall. Almost spooky. They could hear very strange noises from the room.

117   There were buzzes.

118   And a beep or two.

119   And several bells.

120   An occasional light flashed under the door. Was it an X ray?

121   Through it all, you could hear the Xperts' voices, asking questions, and X's voice, answering answers.

122   I wouldn't like to be in X's overalls right now, the children thought.

123   At last, the door opened. Everyone crowded around to hear the results. X didn't look any different; in fact, X was smiling. But the Impartial Team of Xperts looked terrible. They looked as if they were crying!

124   "What happened?" everyone began shouting.

125   "*Sssh,*" ssshed the principal. "The Xperts are trying to speak."

126   Wiping his eyes and clearing his throat, one Xpert began: "In our opinion," he whispered—you could tell he must be very upset—"in our opinion, young X here—."

127   "Yes? Yes?" shouted a parent.

128   "Young X," said the other Xpert, frowning, "is just about the *least* mixed-up child we've ever Xamined!" Behind the closed door, the Superpsychiamedicosocioculturometer made a noise like a contented hum.

129   "Yay for X!" yelled one of the children. And then the others began yelling, too. Clapping and cheering and jumping up and down.

130   "*SSSH!*" SSSHed the principal, but nobody did.

131   The Parents' Committee was angry and bewildered. How *could* X have passed the whole Xamination?

132   Didn't X have an *identity* problem? Wasn't X mixed up at *all*? Wasn't X *any* kind of a misfit?

133   How could it *not* be, when it didn't even *know* what it was?

134   "Don't you see?" asked the Xperts. "X isn't one bit mixed up! As for being a misfit—ridiculous! X knows perfectly well what it is. Don't you, X?" The Xperts winked. X winked back.

135   "But what *is* X?" shrieked Peggy and Joe's parents. "*We* still want to know what it is!"

136   "Ah, yes," said the Xperts, winking again. "Well, don't worry. You'll all know one of these days. And you won't need us to tell you."

137   "What? What do they mean?"

138   Jim's parents grumbled suspiciously.

139   Susie and Peggy and Joe all answered at once. "They mean that by the time it matters which sex X is, it won't be a secret anymore!"

140   With that, the Xperts reached out to hug Ms. and Mr. Jones. "If we ever have an X of our own," they whispered, "we sure hope you'll lend us your instruction manual."

141   Needless to say, the Joneses were very happy. The Project Baby X scientists were rather pleased, too. So were Susie, Jim, Peggy, Joe, and all the Other Children. Even the parents promised not to make any trouble.

142   Later that day, all X's friends put on their red and white checked overalls and went over to see X.

143   They found X in the backyard, playing with a very tiny baby that none of them had ever seen before.

144   The baby was wearing very tiny red and white checked overalls.

145   "How do you like our new baby?" X asked the Other Children proudly.

146   "It's got cute dimples," said Jim. "It's got husky biceps, too," said Susie.

147   "What kind of baby is it?" asked Joe and Peggy.

148   X frowned at them. "Can't you tell?" Then X broke into a big mischievous grin. "*It's a Y!*"

➤ Follow-Up Questions

1. Satire is a technique in writing which uses humor to point out a social problem or situation which needs to be addressed. Can you find an example of satire in the story? If so, please explain.

2. Why were the Other Children's parents displeased with X when it went to school? There are several reasons stated in the story.

3. How did you feel about the ending of the story? What is the irony° in the ending? Do you know what gender the first child is? The gender of the second baby? What makes you think you know?

irony:
incongruity between what is said or done and what is true or expected

➤ Short Writing Assignments

1. In contemporary society parents are able to know the sex of their child before the child is born. Would you want to know this? What is the point of finding out in advance? Write an informative paper that describes reasons for knowing the sex of the child before it is born. Do you agree with the reasons?

2. The term *gender* refers to those cultural markers or behaviors which one is taught to perform to conform to one's sex. Research various public representations of gender, such as advertisements in magazines and on billboards. Then report your findings in an informative paper that identifies the specific gender codes for either males or females in your community. Conclude your report with your own evaluation of these codes.

➤ Extended Writing Assignment

1. Many people believe that the term *sex* is the biological term that distinguishes males from females and that *gender* is a term that shows how we construct our "masculine" and "feminine" personalities. For example, many people believe that women are not women unless they are mothers and that real men must fight to settle a dispute. List

several qualities that you believe are particularly "masculine" and "feminine." Are these characteristics that individuals are born with or characteristics that society has told us are definitions of man or woman? Write a paper in which you **define** your culture's view of gender and then defend/support or oppose your culture's beliefs. **Evaluate** that view from your own perspective.

2. Find a friend or acquaintance who is from a different culture. Discuss the characteristics that that culture uses to define men and women. Write a **comparison and contrast** paper that discusses your culture's gender construction in relation to your friend's.

My Father's Black Pride

Marcus Bleeker

Pre-Reading Ideas: The subject of interracial marriage has been a topic of controversy for decades. In fact, marriage in America was once limited to couples of the same race. Marriage has since been redefined, and individuals of different races are now legally allowed to intermarry. One of the main problems cited for opposing interracial marriages was the difficulties children produced by the marriage would have to face. Today children of "mixed marriages" are quite common. Read the article, "Ground Zero of the New California," in the Preface to see how interracial families live in Riverside, California.

How close are you to your father emotionally? The father-son relationship has always been considered important in growing up and in the development of the son. When the son physiologically reflects the mother's culture rather his father's, problems can arise. See how Marcus Bleeker and his father overcame the obstacles involved in growing up a child of mixed ancestry.

Vocabulary: Looking up and understanding the following words prior to reading should prepare you for the author's message. Other words will be defined in the margin.

Afrocentric   **Max Roach**   **Miles Davis**

1   I am black. My mother is black. My father is white. This wouldn't necessarily be important, but we live in a country where conflict runs deep between blacks and whites. We live in a country where white male slaveholders casually disavowed° the black children they had sired°. We live in a country where the worst of human traits—laziness, violence, and irrationality—are seen as defining characteristics of those of African descent. This makes my being a mixed-race person whose ethnic identity is black somewhat complicated. There is a dissonance° between who I say I am—a proud black man trying to do something positive with his life—and who society says I am. Yet I feel strong, and I embrace my black heritage. I've often reflected on how I learned to keep my positive self-image. The answer is, my white father.

disavowed: disowned

sired: fathered

dissonance: lack of agreement

2   With my olive-colored skin, hazel eyes, and curly hair, I've been taken for Hispanic or Middle Eastern. In fact, in addition to being black, I am Jewish. And my father taught me to be proud of that heritage as well. When bullies at school demanded "Are you black or white?" there was no confusion. When I ran home and asked my father, he said, "Tell them you are African-American." That was in the early 1970s and it was a term I wouldn't hear again until the Afrocentric movement of the 1990s made it fashionable again.

3   It wasn't that my father wanted me to deny my Jewish roots, it's just that he knew we live in a society where my African heritage would define me socially. He didn't want me to seem ashamed of my black roots. My father knew that love and hopes for an ideal world in the distant future would be no *panacea*° for the bigotry and small-mindedness I would encounter in my lifetime. He didn't want me, my brother, or my sister to be unprepared for racism.

panacea: cure-all

4   And so, my father, a writer and avid reader, lined my shelves with books about black American culture, African culture, and Jewish culture. He encouraged me to think, to come up with my own ideas. A simple question posed to him was sure to be followed by his search for a book on the subject, with articles and additional materials to follow. In this way he gave me not only his opinion, but also the keys to how he arrived at that opinion. Knowing that I had those keys, too, he thought that I could evaluate his opinion and come up with my own. He encouraged me to determine what being black meant to me.

5   In the predominantly white suburb near Princeton, N.J., where I grew up, my father knew that I needed to know black men. So when I started playing drums at age 14, my father took me to jazz clubs. He encouraged me to talk to the musicians and get their autographs. This introduction led to my decision to become a professional musician, and also filled my home with a black male presence. Jazz was more than a *genre*° of music; it instructed me in the cool posture of black me—Max Roach's shades, Miles Davis's scowl, and his always stylish threads. It also instructed me in a kind of heroism. These men were geniuses who created America's only enduring art form despite its best efforts to stifle and ignore them.

genre: category

6   My father also hired James, a black 16-year-old, who became my favorite baby-sitter. My father gave me book knowledge and taught me to have an open mind; James showed me how to deal with people on a practical level. My father was gentle, but James taught me that as a black man, you have to be ungentle sometimes. You have to speak up for yourself. James never let me walk away from a confrontation without speaking my mind.

7   During the summers, my parents sent me to my mother's family in Virginia. My cousins—especially Jeffrey, who is seven years older than I—helped me become a mature black man. Jeffrey taught me to treat women with respect, through his example as well as through his words. These are lessons my father had taught me also, but he hoped that my summer visits down South would reinforce those values by being transmitted by black men of my generation.

8   In college, I counseled children from mixed backgrounds. I could see the emptiness in some of the kids either who didn't have a black parent around—usually a father—or whose parents weren't in agreement about how much emphasis should be put on black culture. Often these children would grow up in a predominantly white environment with a negative view of their black fathers or of black culture in general. I realized how fortunate I was to have both parents and to have a father who encouraged me to develop as a black person while never making me feel that I was any less his son because of my blackness.

9   In many ways what my father taught me about manhood was not related to color. He taught me that, ultimately, I determined through my behavior what a black man is. My father taught me to be a gentle man, to use my mind and not my fists. He taught me the value of education and encouraged me to ask questions. My father exposed me to black men who lived up to these universal ideals of manhood, and thereby emphasized that blacks shared in that tradition. All these things have made me the man, the black man, I am today.

10   My father and I are now the closest we have ever been. Of course, there are race-related topics, things I feel, that he will never be able to understand. I know that there are probably people who meet my father and see just another white man. But I know that there are things he has learned from me and my brother that have given him an insight into black masculinity that most white men will never experience. In this way, we have taught each other. Our relationship epitomizes° a reality that is so rarely seen—a black man and a white man who are not adversaries°. Who are more than father and son. They are men who love each other very deeply.

epitomizes:
serves as a
perfect example

adversaries:
enemies

➤ Follow-Up Questions

1. Explain what Bleeker means by "universal ideals of manhood." Does one have to be a certain culture to practice them?
2. What did Bleeker discover about other children who had been raised in "mixed" backgrounds? How were their experiences similar to or different from Bleeker's?
3. In addition to being African-American, Bleeker was also Jewish, but he did not discuss this aspect of his ancestry. Why do you think he omitted developing it? Do you get a sense that it was part of his life at all? As a reader do you feel uncomfortable that the author left out an explanation of part of his life or are you satisfied with what he wrote?

➤ Short Writing Assignments

1. There has been a lot of controversy over interracial adoptions. What are the objections to adopting children who are not of the same culture as the adopting parents? What are the points that support interracial adoptions? Complete a prewriting exercise by listing as many points that support and oppose mixed-family adoptions. Take a position that supports or opposes a mixed-family adoptions and write a paper about it.

primary source:
first hand
information:
letters,
recordings,
personal
journals,
interviews

2. What combination of cultures do you have in your ancestry? Do you celebrate the characteristics of each heritage? Does the culture include knowing and/or speaking a language that is different from English? If so, do you know and/or speak it? Do you know your ancestry? Complete some primary source° research to find out more about

your heritage. Ask your mother and father about your relatives and their place of origin. Draw a family tree in your **journal,** and write a **description** of your family history. Share it with the class.

➤ Extended Writing Assignments

1. Research your local library and/or the Internet for examples of cultural artists in such fields as graphic design, painting, and sculpture. Choose a cultural identity that is different from your own. Then narrow your focus to one particular individual and prepare a report for the class that includes a brief background of the artist, samples of his/her work, and an explanation of the cultural aspects found in the work. A brief handout for your audience should accompany your oral presentation and a written report for your instructor.
2. Bleeker finds music to be a very moving cultural experience which he associates with the black community. Listen to various selections from different types of music associated with the black community, such as jazz, gospel, and rap. Narrow your focus to one type and investigate the origins of such music, the main artists, its themes, and its cultural significance. Compose a report that explains your findings.

Project Chiapas

Linda Rader Overman

Introductory Remarks: A self-defined Latina, Mexicana, and Chicana, Linda Rader Overman is an instructor who teaches Freshman Composition in the English Department and in the Chicano Studies Department at California State University at Northridge. She also works in the University's Writing Lab, helping students improve their writing skills. Graduating with her Master of Arts in English, Overman is also completing her Master of Fine Arts degree in Creative Writing in the Writing Consortium through California State University at Chico. Overman's work has appeared in *Willa: Journal of the Women in Literature and Life Assembly, Voices* and *onthebus.*

Pre-Reading Ideas: Sometimes individuals have to go on a quest before they recognize who they are. The quest may be in search of something other than themselves, as it frequently is in heroic literature and even in contemporary Mexican-American literature, or it may be an internal quest where the individual is seriously looking introspectively to discover who he or she is. This narrative takes the readers to Chiapas, Mexico (see map), where the speaker worked with the men and women there. Notice how the author uses Spanish woven into her English narrative. This use of two languages sometimes confuses students who do not know the foreign language; however, it usually adds depth and meaning to the work that cannot be fully translated into English. If you do not know Spanish, have someone explain what the terms mean beyond the translation provided.

Vocabulary: Looking up and understanding the following words prior to reading should prepare you for the author's message. Other words will be defined in the margin.

Chiapas, Mexico   Ladino

1   *Chiapas Journal of Memory—3.28.97*

2   *Sitting on top of El Templo de la Cruz among these Mayan ruins in Palenque, the oversized white, hand-embroidered shirt I purchased from a Mayan woman a few days ago wraps itself over my breasts, into the crevices underneath. It sticks along the length of my spine and it remains moist from the screeching humidity of this place and I am not surprised. This is where I want to be. Sitting on these stone steps, shells of what once was, I feel a connection that transcends time, myself, what I might have been, what I was, or perhaps what I am now. Quizas. I find my own deepest creative feeling in this remote jungle is not only Woman going back through the ages, she is myself discovering my own inner worlds, where my present one seems so* pathetically°

pathetically: pitifully

inadequate.

trapezoidal: four-sided with two parallel and two non-parallel sides

accessible: easy to reach

palisade: a fence for defense

3   *I look past the* trapezoidal° *complex of El Palacio, covered with anthills of foreign tourists speaking French, Spanish, and German who climb these steps, snap photographs, gulp down bottled water, and wipe away the perspiration from their faces. I see into the distance beyond these thirty-seven acres cleared and* accessible° *to visitors, beyond the green of the jungle, beyond the patches of farmland, beyond the sphere of the earth, and I comprehend just why the ancient rulers from this natural* palisade° *believed they were all powerful. They must have felt as I do now, like I'm sitting on top of the world where no one can touch me.*

4   Coming from Los Angeles, where Mexicana/Chicana is synonymous with the label of an historically under-represented group, in Chiapas, suddenly, I was a member of the historically oppressive group. Ladinos historically have marginalized the Mayan Indians and continue to do so today." ¡Andale bruta! Que te pasa, correte y trae la señora su toalla ahorita. ¡Estúpida!" The few minutes I spent watching a young Mayan servant girl being given a tongue-lashing by her Ladino employer, in the hotel I was staying at in San Cristobal, made me painfully aware of five hundred years of oppression suffered by these Indians. It was something I did not want to face, did not want to remember. It was knowledge I had stuffed away inside of me and wanted no part of. But traveling and journal writing in Chiapas during an English class trip, in order to study Mayan literature in whatever form I chose to appropriate it from, forced me to confront another story, the discovery of my own cuento.

5   *Suddenly I hear the calling of birds, birds I do not know the names of. The music they sing is like nothing I have heard at home in any forest. At first I'm not sure if it's the birds or the howler monkeys, but they are not so very near. They are smart and stay away from the throngs of people that invade this place during Semana Santa. Foreigners, all of them, all of us, and all of me.*

Although I am the daughter, granddaughter, and great-granddaughter of a Mestiza, I too am a foreigner in my own land. This country is some part of what I am, yet for so long I was not allowed to admit to my connections to it by a mother who wanted to protect me from suffering the racial epithets° *hurled at her during a painful adolescence. But now that disconnection is falling away and reconnections are merging in union with the rhythms of this rain forest, in the heat that thaws my memory and soaks my oversized white, hand embroidered shirt. Estoy empapada completamente, pero no me muevo, aqui me quedo.*

epithets: words or phrases of abuse or contempt

6   *Clearly I'm on a journey in time and space. Answering la llamada de la aventura, I travel, although I sit here on this age-old stone. I have not traveled nearly far enough, yet. I am compelled by the* spectre° *of my indigenous great-grandmother. She appears to me as a young black-haired beauty standing outside her hacienda in Puebla, staring toward the hills watching for her husband's return. She was barely sixteen when she married Antonio Morales. By the age of twenty-one she was dead, leaving three small children motherless. My grandmother, Maria, was only six years old when, calling for her mother one day, who had fallen ill, she was told by a servant "Está muerta."*

spectre: ghost

7   *Sleep comes and I try to shake it off. I lie down on the cold harshness of the stone steps. I stretch out my legs. My head rests on my backpack. Mosquitos buzz around my ear. I wave them off. Half asleep I begin to see other sights and hear other sounds, still in the jungle but far away from here. I think about the women. All those women dressed in red and white huipiles and black cortes. "No nos olvidas," they cried and I can't. Displaced, homeless, and hungry refugees, their men in prison or murdered by their enemies, the Mexican government, the women keep reappearing, the whole group of thirty or was it fifty? They almost look as if they are wearing uniforms while sitting, waiting, and watching our group of fifteen college students, as we climb out of the white Ford pickup truck. We are all so happy to unwedge ourselves from the mass of crowded bodies and backpacks crammed into the back. We never did learn whose truck it really was. Juan Díaz, our Tzotzil translator, in the municipality of El Bosque, said he had a truck to take us to Las Delicias about one hour away, but no* chauffeur°. *Armando, one of our group answers, "Pues tenemos un grupo de chauffeurs aqui, señor," Juan smiles, "ah, pues vamanos entonces." We arrive in Las Delicias, a small hamlet about an eight-hour drive in the mountains northwest of San Cristóbal on a mission to take testimony from this group of expulsados, kicked out of their village two weeks earlier by La Seguridad Publica, the men in blue, the state police. Briefed by the Human Rights Center, back in San Cristóbal, in proper* protocol° *among the Maya, we bring nothing to offer these desplasados, as we must not single anyone out. If we don't have enough provisions for 60 families, then we must not cause* divisiveness° *by favoring anyone with food, water, or medicine. Something they have little of and need desperately. Something we have more of than we need.*

chauffeur: driver

protocol: customs and regulations

divisiveness: feelings of discord

8   We arrived at this refugee camp believing ourselves to be a group of intellectuals sent by California State University Northridge to do research and

gather data for the term papers we were expected to write out of this experience. We were ready and felt ourselves to be completely prepared by the previous two months of study on the Mayan condition, and on the political upheaval from the Zapatista Revolution with its current tensions. We had our journals. We were armed and eager to write.

9   *There are over a hundred people milling around between those of us in front of the main assembly building up on a little hill where we wait and the open area below us where the women wait. We are all waiting for something to happen. I watch the women who wait still, so many of them sitting together in orderly fashion like schoolgirls. The littler girls stay together, some by their mothers' side. Other little babies are in rebosos which are slung around their mothers' shoulders, nursing, sleeping, clutching the warmth of the body that carries them. These females of all ages are so beautiful with their long hair in braids, as they stand and sway in a sea of red and white while the day's heat melts us all. They move as if possessed by one body, one mind alone. And I move . . . weaving the fabric of a canto constructed out of a cuento of my own—as these women have woven the very shirts that now cling to their breasts and the crevices underneath.*

➤ Follow-Up Questions

1. What was Overman's purpose(s) in visiting Chiapas?
2. What elements of oppression, both racial and political, does Overman find in Chiapas and the surrounding countryside?
3. Why does Overman feel such a closeness to the country and people of Chiapas? Consider the full article before you answer.

➤ Short Writing Assignments

1. After reading the narrative, determine what you think Overman means by the terms *Woman* and the *women* as used in her narrative. Then in a short essay **compare and contrast** the meanings of the two terms, giving specific **examples** to illustrate.
2. Research your library or a travel agency to discover texts and/or brochures that picture the geographical areas which Overman refers to in her **narrative.** Then prepare a **descriptive** paragraph detailing your findings.

➤ Extended Writing Assignments

1. Research the political upheaval which Overman refers to in her narrative, the "Zapatista Revolution with its current tensions" in Mexico. Prepare a report of your findings that both explains the political situation and discusses whether the tensions have been resolved or not.
2. Overman makes reference to the Human Rights Center in San Cristóbal. Research another human rights organization which is currently active anywhere in the world. Prepare a report explaining the functions of the organization, one area where it is currently active, and the problems it is trying to alleviate.

CONCLUSION

There is a current philosophical debate being waged about whether a person constructs his or her identity or whether a person is born with certain characteristics that make that person who he or she is. In Sandra Cisneros's story and Henry Louis Gates, Jr.' s, personal narrative, the authors discuss how their names identify them in certain ways. Lois Gould, however, shows how a name like "X" disturbs society's expectations of what the person is or should be. Gender, race, and sexual orientation are no longer based on either-or choices but can be seen as fluid and changing in their characteristics. The debate about identity will continue as long as cultures profess certain beliefs and individuals accept or reject those beliefs.

➤ Further Writing Assignments

Personal Narrative

Write a personal narrative that tells the story of your name. Were you named after a family member or after a famous public or historical figure? Is it unusual? How does your name or nickname contribute to your personality? Some cultures believe that every twenty-one years, a person enters a new phase of his or her life and has the opportunity to change names. Given this opportunity, what would you change to? Why? Organize these questions into a coherent personal narrative.

Expository

Ursula Le Guin wrote a short story, "She Unnames Them," in which Eve "unnames" all the animals Adam named. Without a name, the narrator suggests that expectations based on names/identity are destroyed. The terms race and gender provoke a variety of responses from people with some having clearly defined views, others having no feelings about the terms, and others arguing that they are artificial and do not exist. Choose one term, race or gender, and write an **expository** essay that describes the attitudes people from different generations and different ethnicities hold toward the term. You will have to interview people, so be very specific in your question. Choose people from your age group, your parents' age group, and your grandparents' age group. Draw conclusions about your findings.

Analytical

Marcus Bleeker and Linda Rader Overman both construct their identity based on a particular criterion. Write a paper analyzing one or both of these essays to determine what qualities each author uses and how each feels about that identity.

Argumentative

Using the ideas elicited in the **personal narrative** assignment, write an **argumentative** essay on a position supporting an inborn or a constructed identity. Take into consideration issues such as culture, society, advertisements, fashion, language, and so forth.

➤ Suggested Chapter Projects

1. Watch the movie *Pleasantville, 10,000 Men Named George,* or any other video production available in your area, making note of the cultural issues it addresses that you see reflected in the society around you. Then choose one major cultural issue and in a report, explain the issue you have chosen, discuss the problem as detailed in both the movie and society, and offer a realistic way, in your conclusion, to lessen or remove the problem.

2. Part of this chapter is about "Self and Dreams"; the stories in one way or another are about individuals who had a lifetime to fulfill their dream or to reflect on the effects of their childhood. But, because of illnesses, many individuals do not have the time or even the ability to develop their life's goals. Investigate a program in your area, such as the Make-a-Wish Foundation or the Sunshine Kids, that has the goal of fulfilling the wishes of terminally ill children. Then prepare a report describing the organization, its goals, the process it goes through to fulfill the wish of a very sick child, and any future plans for the organization.

3. As a service project, visit a facility which helps the elderly through such efforts as therapy and daytime activities, and in your investigations interview both facility members and their elderly visitors and patients to gain an insight into both the facility's view of its program and the patients'. Then prepare an oral report, supported by handouts, brochures if available, and photographs, that describes the facility, its services, and the patients themselves, their background, and purposes for coming to the facility. Conclude your report with an overall **evaluation** of the program based on specific criteria that you see as important and how such a facility is of benefit to your community. Examples of facilities to consider would be senior programs offered by a YMCA, a church facility, and a senior day-care program.

C H A P T E R   5

Glacier National Park
Source: Anne Perrin, photographer

Education: How My Religion and Culture Influence Me

A recent catchphrase in education circles has been the importance of helping students become "lifelong learners." In other words, teachers, instructors, and professors should help students discover the joy of learning so that they will maintain a curiosity about everything around them. There are students in their seventies, eighties, and even nineties who continue to attend courses in community colleges and universities. Education, however, is not limited to the classroom. It is available with almost every event we are involved in, every new person we meet, many televisions shows we watch, each new job we take, and so forth. In other words, opportunities to learn are all around us if we just notice them and take advantage of them.

If you look closely at the titles in this chapter, none of them have anything to do with the traditional concept of education. Instead, the authors and poets in this chapter describe experiences that promote learning from religion and culture, how these two forces that surround us teach us about others, about life, and even about ourselves. Valdes-Rodriguez begins the chapter with an essay that expresses the importance of a white mainstream America learning the differences among ethnicities it does not belong to rather than lumping all cultures with similar characteristics together. The next three works discuss how religion informs and teaches the writers about spirituality as well as about themselves: "I Am a Catholic," "Blue Skin," and "In the Park." So, however, brings a different perspective to education in her short narrative: gender. Finally, Barbara Ehrenreich's essay is a combination of personal narrative and exposition in which she begins with her own experiences and expands her view to include a global perspective.

If you could teach other people one thing about yourself, your religion, or aspects of your culture, what would you choose? How would you do it? Sometimes a process paper works well in teaching others. Sometimes an expository or comparison-and-contrast paper helps readers learn. The latter could present new information against ideas the reader is already familiar with, making learning new ideas easier. Think about a topic you would like to teach someone about and consider the best way or ways to present it. Think also about what method you prefer when you are reading about something new. By teaching others something you are already familiar with, you learn it even better and you not only share your knowledge, but you reinforce your own learning skills.

Crossing Pop Lines:
Attention to Latinos Is Overdue, But Sometimes Off-Target

Alisa Valdes-Rodriguez

Pre-Reading Ideas: Nothing, not even pop culture, seems to be immune from the problem of stereotyping, making general assumptions about a person or group. In some cases, Asian youngsters are stereotyped as being able to excel in math and science. Even though that might be a positive characteristic, it still presents a burden to the individual who feels he or she must live up to that expectation. Consider then how it must feel if you are assumed to be a member of a certain ethnic group but you don't belong to it. First, your public identity is created for you as being someone you are not. Second, you have to assert your own identity without hurting or being disrespectful toward the group you do not belong to. Finally, you realize that in some cases, the public won't listen to you because they want to believe certain things about you. See how popular recording artists deal with this problem in the following essay.

Vocabulary: Looking up and understanding the following words prior to reading should prepare you for the author's message. Other words will be defined in the margin.

exotic   phenomenon   cliché   vying   genre   Yoruba

phenomenal:
extraordinary

1   First, the well-known facts: Puerto Rican pop star Ricky Martin is enjoying phenomenal° success with his first English-language album, and more Latino pop artists, such as Enrique Iglesias, are vying to do the same. This has led the U.S. media—including a *Time* magazine cover story—to trumpet a new "Latin crossover phenomenon."

2   Now, the lesser-known facts.

3   One: many of the so-called crossover artists are American by birth, including Martin. But the pervasive° impression in the media and in the culture at large is that these artists are exotic foreigners. Example? *USA Today* calling Martin's sounds "south-of-the-border," even though residents of his native Puerto Rico have been United States citizens since 1917, and the island's signature musical genre, salsa°, was invented in the 1960s in a city south of the Connecticut border: New York.

pervasive:
spreading
everywhere

salsa:
a Caribbean
musical form

4   Two: even though in the pop music business "crossover" generally means switching genres, Martin's music—pop by any standards—has not

changed, only the language he sings in. He is not, as some publications have
posited°, a salsa singer.

posited:
suggested

5   For Martin and others, the only real "crossover" is their language; it's an
unusual category, and one that French-speaking Canadian Celine Dion managed to avoid. Latinos, even those U.S.-born like Martin, are not afforded the
same leeway°.

leeway: extra
space or time

6   Shakira, for example, is a Colombian rock singer whose style has been
compared to Alanis Morissette; her "crossover" album will consist of translations of rock songs she has recorded in Spanish. Enrique Iglesias sings syrupy
ballads in the tradition of Air Supply; it's a formula that will likely work as
well for him in English. And Martin's music, while injected occasionally with
percussive° instruments, is no more or less "Latin" than that of, say, Puff
Daddy, who also uses Spanish phrases.

percussive:
pertaining to
striking musical
instruments to
make tones

R & B: Rhythm
and Blues

irrelevant:
unimportant

7   All of this has led East Harlem's Marc Anthony, who records salsa in
Spanish and R & B° dance music in English, to declare "crossover" irrelevant°,
venturing to say the term has only been applied to these artists because they
are Latinos on the mainstream charts, not because they perform Latin music
on the mainstream charts.

8   While no one denies that focusing the mainstream media spotlight on
Latino musicians and singers is overdue, the recent storm of coverage has ex-
posed an abysmal° ignorance about the complexity, diversity and reality of
Latinos and Latin music.

abysmal:
extremely or
hopelessly bad

frenzy:
excitement

9   Lost in the frenzy° to cover "crossover" artists have been two simple
facts: Latino artists do not necessarily perform in Latin music genres; and Latin
music is not always performed by Latinos.

nascent: new

10   In the case of Jennifer Lopez, who is often lumped into this nascent°
category, the only "crossover" is in the minds of a media establishment
oblivious° to the fact that she is a Bronx native who has recorded her debut°
album of commercial pop songs in her "native tongue": English. Yes, Lopez
has two Spanish-language pop songs on the album, but artists from Madonna
to Bon Jovi have been recording in Spanish for release in Latin America for
years, and yet no one has called them crossover artists.

oblivious:
unaware

°*debut:*
introductory

11   Beyond the assumptions about Latino-Americans seeming somehow foreign, there is another, more unsettling bit of stereotyping being done in the
media about the new "crossover stars."

12   Clichéd adjectives are used over and over in the mainstream press in
general but take on a different connotation when used to describe artists such
as Martin, Lopez, Anthony and others. Words such as "hot," "spicy," and "pas-
sionate" are taken, one assumes, from the flavors of Mexican cuisine° and
outdated stereotypes of the "Latin lover."

°*cuisine:* food

13   Particularly upsetting is the media's propensity° to comment on certain
body parts when writing about Latino artists, namely hips and rear ends. *Entertainment Weekly* labeled Martin "hot hips." And the vast majority of stories
on Lopez refer to her hind side. This is no mere coincidence; several academics have shown direct links between the view European settlers took of the

°*propensity:*
tendency, habit

indigenous:
native

American land and indigenous° peoples, both of which were seen as wild, sexual and, in their view, in need of taming.

14   Speaking of hot: According to *Billboard* magazine, Ricky Martin is a "hot tamale°." This phrase appears several times, and is ridiculous because Martin hails from Puerto Rico, where the local cuisine includes neither chili peppers nor tamales, both of which come from Mexico. The recent *TV Guide* cover story on Martin made it only three paragraphs before calling the singer "spicy," and a few paragraphs later made reference to his wiggling hips.

tamale: a
Mexican food
that has a
chicken, pork,
bean, chili, or
coconut filling
surrounded by a
spicy corn-meal
coating and
wrapped in corn
husks

15   According to the New York *Daily News,* Martin is "red hot," while the *Atlanta Constitution* calls him "hot stuff." The *Seattle Times* says Martin is "incendiary°" (give them credit for consulting a thesaurus, at least). The list goes on and on. Even the *New York Times* has not been immune° to the stereotyping; the headline of its recent concert review of Chayanne—a singer who appeared in the film "Dance with Me" alongside Vanessa Williams and who has plans to release an English-only album soon—read: Amor (Those Hips!) Passion: (Those Lips!).

incendiary:
arousing
discontent or
strife

immune: not
susceptible

innuendo:
indirect
derogatory
remark

16   When it comes to Lopez, the coverage is even more troubling, tainted with sexism and sexual innuendo° in addition to ignorance. Lopez was called "salsa-hot" by the *Hartford Courant.* Like Martin, Lopez is Puerto Rican; once more, on that island, salsa is to be danced, not eaten. The New York *Daily News* calls Lopez a "hot tamale." Even in Canada the stereotypes, and mistakes, persist: The *Ottawa Citizen* called Lopez "a hot-blooded Cuban."

17   Marc Anthony is so disgusted with the "heated coverage" he and others are getting in the mainstream press—he has been called "red hot" by the *Boston Herald* and "white-hot" by the New York *Daily News*—that he has started refusing to do some interviews. He jokingly told his publicist that he will "jump off a bridge" if he is called "hot" or "spicy" by one more publication.

Too Complex to be Lumped as "Latin Music"

18   To understand why this type of writing is so offensive, one must be familiar with the complex reality of Latinos and the dozens of musical genres that have been lumped into the amorphous° "Latin music" category.

amorphous:
without form

19   Most of the thirty million Latinos in the U.S. speak English as their primary language. Beyond that, they are as racially and economically diverse as the entire U.S. population. While many people continue to believe that all Latinos are "brown," this is simply not true.

20   In fact, the history of the U.S. is parallel to that of Latin America: The Native American inhabitants were "conquered" by Europeans; many Native Americans were killed in the process, and Africans were "imported" to replace them as slaves. Documents from slave ships show that fully 95% of the Africans brought to the Americas as slaves went to Latin America, according to historians.

21   Brazil is home to the largest African American population on Earth, and five of every six Dominicans is of African descent. My father's birth was dedicated to the Yoruba god Obatala, as were those of most other white kids in

his neighborhood in Cuba; he has often said that to be a Caribbean Latino is to be African, regardless of color.

22   At this moment, there are plenty of black Latinos succeeding in mainstream American pop music, but few, if any, ever get mentioned in the Latin crossover write-ups. In some instances, this is due to the artist's decision not to make his or her background known. But in other cases, as in the exclusion° of R & B crooner° Maxwell, who is half Puerto Rican, it's due mostly to reluctance° on the part of both the English and Spanish media to include blacks in the discussion at all.

exclusion: failure to include

crooner: smooth singer

reluctance: unwillingness

23   Pop singer Usher is half Panamanian. Other Puerto Ricans include TLC rapper Lisa "Left Eye" Lopes, "Ghetto Superstar" singer Mya—who has recorded in Spanish—and rappers Fat Joe and Big Pun. And Mariah Carey, who describes her father as a black Venezuelan and who routinely includes Spanish singles on her albums for import to Latin America, is also absent from the crossover discussion.

24   With one notable exception in the *New York Times* last month, merengue singer Elvis Crespo has been left out of the crossover equation too, even though he is probably the only Latin artist who currently qualifies in the traditional sense of the term. Crespo currently has two Spanish-language albums on the Billboard 200 mainstream chart.

executives: those with authority in an organization

25   Some music executives°, including Sony Music Chairman and CEO Thomas D. Mottola, have said outright that they are excited about Martin and other crossover candidates because these artists fill the role of the white male pop star that has been vacant since the glory days of George Michael.

26   While a white Latino is just as Latino as a brown or black one, it unfortunately seems that in the world of American pop culture, Latinos are still only palatable° as long as they appeal to a mainstream, Caucasian standard of beauty. Jennifer Lopez seems to have figured this one out: Her naturally wavy, dark brown hair has been lightened and straightened, and her once-fuller body has been whittled° down by a fitness guru° to something virtually indistinguishable from the lean, muscular Madonna.

palatable: acceptable

whittled: cut down

guru: mentor

27   All of this brings us to the ungainly truth no one seems to want to embrace in this country: Simply, there is no such thing as a singular "Latino," and efforts, no matter how well-intentioned, to classify 30 million racially, economically and educationally diverse individuals as one unity is ignorant—and irresponsible.

ostensibly: appearing to be

28   The term "Hispanic" was invented by the U.S. Census Bureau in the 1970s in order to classify a group of Americans ostensibly° linked through a common language—Spanish. Hispanics, or Latinos, don't exist in Latin America where people identify themselves by nationality, class, and race—just like here. "Latinos" have been invented in the U.S. for the convenience of politics and marketing, overlooking considerable cultural differences and complexity that can make your head spin.

clave: hand held sticks or blocks hit together to produce music

29   Think about this: Much of what we call "Mexican food" today is really Native American food; the unifying "Latino" language, Spanish, is a European import, just like English; the backbone of salsa music, the clave° rhythm,

tambora: double drums

comes from West Africa, as does merengue's two-headed tambora° drum; Mexican norteno and banda music is rooted in Germany and Poland . . . but Cajuns in Louisiana who play essentially the same stuff in French are not Latinos. Got that?

anathema: hated or loathed

capitalist: that which invests money in business

lasso: rope in

elusive: hard to see or find

chronicle: tell the story

snippet: a small piece

30   Complexity! It is anathema° to good capitalist° marketing plans which promise big bucks to whomever can lasso° the elusive° buyers of the world. And yet history is complex—all of ours—and journalists owe it to everyone to accurately chronicle° the history of our world and one of its most powerful cultural forces: music.

31   We leave you with a sadly typical example of the comedy and tragedy of simplification of Latinos and Latin music. It happened, of all places, at a recent Los Angeles Dodgers game. As each Dodger goes to bat, the scoreboard lists personal facts, including the player's favorite band. A snippet° from said band is then played over the loudspeakers. Two Dominican players both listed the New Jersey-based merengue group Oro Solido as their favorite. Yet when one came up to the plate, the folks in charge of the public address system chose instead to play . . . Ricky Martin!

32   To many a Dominican, the exchange of Martin for Oro Solido could be seen as a slap in the face; first, merengue is the official national dance of the Dominican Republic. Secondly, there is a long history of tension between Puerto Ricans and Dominicans over class and citizenship issues. In this context, replacing Oro Solido with Martin was not only ignorant, but possibly even insulting. But to know this means to study history. It means entertaining complex thought. And that, in a trend-driven pop culture obsessed° with simple marketing categories and the almighty dollar, is apparently too much work.

obsessed: overly preoccupied

➤ Follow-Up Questions

1. What problems does Valdes-Rodriguez discuss in relation to performing artists such as Ricky Martin and Jennifer Lopez?
2. What points does Valdes-Rodriguez make about the reality that all Latinos are not "'brown'"?
3. Valdes-Rodriguez makes a point of comparing and contrasting Latino performers with what she terms the "mainstream American culture," but she never actually defines that term in the essay. Based on your own observations, how would you define that term?

➤ Short Writing Assignments

1. Valdes-Rodriguez notes that many cultural signs or markers are misused when describing a performer, such as calling Ricky Martin a "hot tamale" when he is actually of Puerto Rican descent, a culture which is not associated with the "tamale." Choose a performer who you feel is representative of a culture and investigate the cultural signs which are associated with that performer; the individual can come from any cultural background. Then prepare an essay in which you describe such signs; in your conclusion, judge whether such cultural signs misrepresent the performer or not.

2. In her article, Valdes-Rodriguez discusses many cultural artists from the Latino community and their representation in the performing arts, such as music. But one of the problems with such representation is what Valdes-Rodriguez terms "the complexity, diversity, and reality of Latinos and Latin music." Form a small research group and investigate this "complexity" by interviewing members of different cultures which are included under the term Latino. How do these individuals feel about this generic or all-inclusive term being applied to their specific culture? Then prepare a report that explains the various cultural concerns and/or benefits which these individuals discussed. Conclude your essay with a position in which you determine if an all-inclusive term such as *Latino* is a positive or negative way to view this cultural "diversity."

➤ Extended Writing Assignments

1. Part of Valdes-Rodriguez's argument criticizes those writers who label a performer by "body parts," such as Ricky Martin being described as "'hot hips.'" Could the performer's style actually encourage this type of description or are the artists being **stereotyped?** Investigate various ways a cultural artist, such as Ricky Martin or Jennifer Lopez, is represented in the mainstream culture using such vehicles as music videos, performances, album covers, and promotional photographs. Then prepare a **position** paper in which you determine whether the artist is catering to a preconception of how mainstream American culture wants a performer to act or whether the artist, as Valdes-Rodriguez suggests, is being misunderstood and misrepresented.

2. Investigate a particular culture outside the United States regarding the perception of masculine and feminine, terms that denote these gender roles, and how individuals in this culture dress and act. Then assume the role of a music industry executive and create a superstar for the American public based on your findings. In your written report, describe each particular cultural sign you would include and why.

I Am a Catholic

Anna Quindlen

Introductory Remarks: The *New York Times* columnist Anna Quindlen is a writer who not only writes personal narratives to examine fundamental issues; she also writes about controversial issues such as euthanasia° to make readers confront their own basic beliefs. Quindlen is also a novelist, as well as a Pulitzer Prize-winning columnist and a Catholic.

euthanasia:
mercy killing

Pre-Reading Ideas: Regardless of religious background, many people have found themselves in conflict with the teachings of their church. For example, many people believe their religion is wrong to impose dietary restrictions or the practice of using female clothing that covers the face and body completely. Other individuals follow faithfully their church's dogma and spread their beliefs to their children from one generation to the next. Can individuals claim membership in an institution that they do not fully believe in or support or in one with laws they do not observe? Should religions attempt to change and remain current with the popular culture, or should they maintain the original foundation and laws on which they were built? Quindlen implicitly poses these questions in her essay. Before you begin reading, answer these questions in a personal journal entry to clarify your standing about religion and its place in society and/or in your life.

Vocabulary: Looking up and understanding the following words prior to reading should prepare you for the author's message. Other words will be defined in the margin.

Dominus vobiscum	*Et cum spiritu tuo*	**bona fides**
Kyrie eleison	*Confiteor dei*	**ordination**	**misogyny**
tenets	**Baltimore Catechism**	**confessional**	**fast**

1   *Dominus vobiscum. Et cum spiritu tuo.* These are my bona fides: a word, a phrase, a sentence in a language no one speaks anymore. *Kyrie eleison. Confiteor dei.* I am a Catholic. Once at a nursing home for retired clergy, I ate lunch with a ninety-year-old priest, a man who still muttered the Latin throughout the English Mass and ate fish on Fridays. When he learned how old I was, he said with some satisfaction, "You were a Catholic when being a Catholic still meant something."

2   What does it mean now? For myself, I cannot truly say. Since the issue became material to me, I have not followed the church's teaching on birth control. I disagree with its stand on abortion. I believe its resistance to the or-

manifestation: outwardly visible sign

dination of women as priests is a manifestation° of a misogyny that has been with us much longer than the church has. Yet it would never have occurred to my husband and me not to be married in a Catholic church, not to have our children baptized. On hospital forms and in political polls, while others leave the space blank or say "none of your business," I have no hesitation about giving my religion.

3   We are cultural Catholics. I once sneered at that expression, used by

introspective: characterized by thinking about oneself

Jewish friends at college, only because I was not introspective° enough to understand how well it applied to me. Catholicism is to us now not so much a system of beliefs or a set of laws but a shared history. It is not so much our faith as our past. The tenets of the church which I learned as a child have ever since been at war with the facts of my adult life. The Virgin Birth. The Trinity. The Resurrection. Why did God make me? God made me to know Him, to love Him, and to serve Him in this world and to be happy with Him forever in the next. I could recite parts of the Baltimore Catechism in my sleep. Do I believe those words? I don't know. What I do believe are those guidelines that do not vary from faith to faith, that are as true of Judaism or Methodism as they are of Catholicism: that people should be kind to one another, that they should help those in need, that they should respect others as they wish to be respected.

4   And I believe in my own past. I was educated by nuns, given absolution by priests. My parents were married in a Catholic church, my grandparents

Leatherette:
material made to
look like leather

grille: a grating
or gate

Shabbat: Jewish
Sabbath

cassocks: long
clothing worn by
participants in a
church service

Extreme Unction:
last rites

and mother buried from one. Saturday afternoons kneeling on Leatherette° pads in the dim light of the confessional, listening for the sound of the priest sliding back the grille° on his side. Sunday mornings kneeling with my face in my hands, the Communion wafer stuck to the roof of my dry mouth. These are my history. I could no more say I am not Catholic than say I am not Irish, not Italian. Yet I have never been to Ireland or Italy.

5   Some of our Jewish friends have returned to the ways of their past, to Shabbat° without automobiles and elevators, to dietary laws and the study of Hebrew. We cannot do the same. There is no longer a Latin Mass, no Communion fast from midnight on. Even the inn is gone from the Bible; now Mary and Joseph are turned away from "the place where travelers lodged."

6   The first time my husband and I went to midnight mass on Christmas Eve in our parish church, we arrived a half-hour early so we could get a seat. When the bells sounded twelve and the priest came down the center aisle, his acolytes in their child-size cassocks° walking before him, the pews were still half empty. We were thinking of a different time, when the churches were packed, when missing Mass was a sin, when we still believed that that sort of sin existed—sins against rules, victimless sins.

7   There are more families coming to that church now, families like us with very small children who often have to leave before the Gospel because of tears, fatigue, temper tantrums. (I remember that, when I was growing up, my family's parish church was shaped like a cross, and one of the short arms was for the women with babies. It had a sheet of glass walling it off and was soundproof. And through the glass you could see the babies, as though in a movie with no audio, their little mouths round, their faces red. Inside that room, the noise was dreadful. But missing Mass was a sin.)

8   I think perhaps those families are people like us, people who believe in something, although they are not sure what, people who feel that in a world of precious little history or tradition, this is theirs. We will pass down the story to our children: There was a woman named Mary who was visited by an angel. And the angel said, "Do not be afraid" and told her that though she was a virgin she would have a child. And He was named Jesus and was the Son of God and He rose from the dead. Everything else our children learn in America in the late twentieth century will make this sound like a fairy tale, like tales of the potato famines in Ireland and the little ramshackle houses with grape arbors on hillsides in Italy. But these are my fairy tales, and so, whether or not they are fact, they are true.

9   I was born a Catholic and I think I will die one. I will ask for a priest to give me Extreme Unction°, as it was given to my mother, and to her mother before her. At the end, as in the beginning, I will ask for the assistance of the church, which is some fundamental part of my identity. I am a Catholic.

➤ Follow-Up Questions

1. What does Quindlen mean when she says that she is one of the "cultural Catholics"?
2. How did her religion change from when she was younger?

3. Despite the many changes in her religion, why does Quindlen still choose to identify herself as a Catholic?

➤ Short Writing Assignments

1. Quindlen makes note of the many rituals and beliefs which she was taught as a child but has since begun to doubt. Write an **informative** paragraph explaining a cultural or religious belief which you had difficulties following when you were growing up.
2. Quindlen's article does not go into depth about the **causes** of the changes in her religion. Write a paragraph that speculates on the causes for such changes in religious rituals.

➤ Extended Writing Assignments

1. Investigate a particular religious community in your area. Such research should include interviews with the religious authorities and members of the congregation of various age groups. Also, plan a visit to the religious facilities. Then prepare a report which describes the religious community, its meaning to the community, the services it provides, and relevant comments from its congregation.
2. Religions, such as Catholicism, very often baptize or admit individuals into their membership when the individuals are infants. Such a decision, made by the parents or guardians, eliminates the individual's choice of which religion he/she will follow. Write a position paper in which you argue for or against such a practice. In considering this position, interviews with individuals who were admitted as infants into a church's membership as well as with religious leaders should be considered.

Blue Skin

Linda Koffel

Introductory Remarks: Poet, essayist, journalist, and photographer, Linda Koffel has had varied experiences, writing for a business as well as a literary audience. As a young student, Koffel won the National Council of Teachers of English Award for excellence in writing and has also won awards from the Daughters of the American Revolution for her writing. She began her professional writing career as a journalist, writing for *The Dolphin,* a newspaper for the US Navy. She also wrote and anchored a news program in New London, Connecticut. Koffel has written over 1,600 poems and has published many in literary journals such as *Midtown Review* and *Southwest Review.* She has just finished a full-length book of poetry inspired by the poet-saints of India and is currently working on a series of poems about Tibet.

Pre-Reading Ideas: In Hinduism, Krishna, an incarnation of the deity Vishnu, is one of the major gods: the creator, Brahma; the preserver, Vishnu; and the destroyer, Shiva. Krishna was born to human parents, but because he is a deity, he had powerful abilities even from birth. Krishna is usually depicted as playing a flute with a less than serious attitude toward life while Vishnu is sometimes depicted as sleeping and dreaming of creating the universe. Krishna was born with blue skin and is quite handsome. In the poem, the narrator, even though expressing a "wish," a "yearn[ing]" and an "ache" for the blue skin of Krishna, presents a sense of inner peace and self-assurance found in the Hindu belief in Karma and reincarnation and ultimately in Moksha or freedom from rebirth when the Hindu soul merges back into its origin: God. The last stanza changes somewhat. How is it different from the rest of the poem?

Vocabulary: Looking up and understanding the following words prior to reading should prepare you for the author's message.

porcelain   **blemish**   **ceramic**   **cerulean**

In my solemn hours,
I wish for blue skin—
The skin of Krishna,
Surprising, gleaming,
5 Porcelain skin,
A skin that shows no defects
that will not blemish,
only crack like a ceramic egg
and let my true self
10 flow through and puddle out
like yolk.

In my quiet repose,
I yearn for blue skin.
The skin of Krishna
15 Deep blue, cerulean blue,
Sapphire blue skin
Skin blue with feeling—
Skin that will not decay,
But will stand against time,
20 Centuries ago and centuries ahead.

In my deep resignation,
I ache for blue skin
The skin of Krishna.
I ache for the plastic clay skin of a doll,
25 The skin of a beautiful blue doll,
A doll that moves hands and feet,
But can't be crushed,
Only left in a box covered with earth.

➤ Follow-Up Questions

1. What physical characteristics does the poem's narrator associate with blue skin?
2. Consider the fact that the poem is written from the first-person "I" viewpoint. Also consider that one usually asks for what one does not have. Based on these two concepts, what could you say about the narrator of the poem?
3. How are the poem's last two lines significant when one thinks of what blue skin means to the narrator?

➤ Short Writing Assignments

1. The poem's narrator shows a subtle shift in attitude towards blue skin. Line 2 uses the word "wish," which changes in line 13 to "yearn," and finally in line 22 to "ache." Write a paragraph in which you describe how the narrator's feeling change as the poem progresses.
2. Two powerful lines in the poem are line 9, "and let my true self," and line 27, "But can't be crushed." Write a paragraph analyzing what you think the poet is trying to say about the narrator's existence in the world.

➤ Extended Writing Assignments

1. The Pre-Reading Ideas in the Introduction to this poem note that Krishna has "powerful abilities," but the narrator only asks for a beautiful appearance. Which would you prefer? Compose a **personal** essay in which you make such a decision and detail how such a choice could aid you in life.
2. Research the religious art of Hinduism. Such investigation should consider the figures in the painting, how they are positioned in relation to each other, and even in some cases the colors used for each figure. You may want to consult both an art instructor and a representative of the Hindu religion to provide insight. Then prepare an **informative** report which explains your findings, making special note of the religious significance of such art.

In the Park

Maxine Kumin

Introductory Remarks: Poet, novelist, essayist, and children's book writer, Maxine Kumin has been a prolific writer. In 1973 she won the Pulitzer Prize, and she has published eleven books of poetry.

Pre-Reading Ideas: Although there are those who do not find comfort in religion, it can sometimes offer ideas that help prepare the believer for death. Thomas Paine, an American author who wrote in the eighteenth century, noted in his work *The Age of Reason* how differently each religion is constructed yet how each has the same goal. Here Maxine Kumin reveals two completely different religious denominations and their approach to death.

Not only do different religions have varying philosophies about death, so do different cultures. Talk to members of your class or friends who are from different cultures and ask them about their beliefs about death. How are they similar to or different from yours?

Vocabulary: Looking up and understanding the following words prior to reading should prepare you for the author's message. Other words will be defined in the margin.

Buddhist	Old Testament	Noah	crossovers	Devil	zealot
Glacier Park	Moses	Samuel	Hell	atheist	

You have forty-nine days between
death and rebirth if you're a Buddhist.
Even the smallest soul could swim
the English Channel in that time
5 or climb, like a ten-month-old child,
every step of the Washington Monument
to travel across, up, down, over or through
—you won't know till you get there which to do.

He laid on me for a few seconds
10 said Roscoe Black, who lived to tell
about his skirmish°

skirmish: quick fight

with a grizzly bear
in Glacier Park. *He laid on me
not doing anything. I could feel
15 his heart beating against my heart.*
Never mind *lie* and *lay,* the whole world
confuses them. For Roscoe Black you might say
all forty-nine days flew by.

I was raised on the Old Testament.
20 In it God talks to Moses, Noah,
Samuel, and they answer.
People confer° with angels. Certain

confer: to talk with

animals converse with humans.
It's a simple world, full of crossovers.
25 Heaven's an airy Somewhere, and God
has a nasty temper when provoked°,

provoked: angered

but if there's a Hell, little is made of it.
No longtailed Devil, no eternal fire,
and no choosing what to come back as.
30 When the grizzly bear appears, he lies/lays down
on atheist and zealot. In the pitch-dark
each of us waits for him in Glacier Park.

➤ Follow-Up Questions

1. Kumin mentions several powerful forces in her poem. What are they and what types of strength does she note?
2. In the poem, the relation between the spiritual and physical worlds is described as a "simple world." How would you explain this idea, based on the poem?
3. Nature, represented in the poem through the grizzly bear, has a particular view of humans. Looking especially at the last several lines of the poem, how would you describe this view?

➤ Short Writing Assignments

1. Write a paragraph that describes a monumental force, such as the grizzly bear, which could be considered god-like.
2. Many people have had an event in their life in which they were faced with an enormously powerful force and escaped. Examples could be near-accidents in a car or narrowly avoiding a vicious dog. Write a **descriptive** paragraph which gives your account of such an incident. Conclude your writing with a personal comment of whether or not you attached any religious significance to the event or its outcome.

➤ Extended Writing Assignments

1. Research one of the major national parks in America, such as Glacier National Park or Yellowstone National Park. Such investigation should include the location of the park, the services it offers visitors, the geographical features located within it, and the dangers or warnings that visitors must abide by to avoid danger. Then prepare a written report that describes such details and conclude your report with a reference to the problems that human intrusion has imposed on the park itself.
2. Research a religion other than your own to discover the figure(s) of power, the god(s) and/or goddess(es), and what position(s) such figures hold in the religion. Then write a report describing such deity/deities and their significance.

The Color Yellow: Education

Connie Ching So

Pre-Reading Ideas: The role of women in many cultures still remains that of wife and mother, caretaker and historian. Consequently, in many cases, education is reserved for males who assume the role of husband and provider. Today, however, many young women in traditionally male-dominated cultures are rejecting or delaying their roles of wives and mothers. Even in communities where financial burdens on the families make supporting a woman through her years of higher education difficult or impossible, women are applying for financial aid, working part-time and full-time jobs, and going to school. So remembers a personal experience within her family that displays not only cultural but generational attitudes in one Asian family toward educating women.

Vocabulary: Looking up and understanding the following word prior to reading should prepare you for the author's message. Other words will be defined in the margin.

aptitude

1   *The belief that women should not receive much education, in conjunction with the fact that most Chinatown immigrants are from poor families probably explains why the median level of education for Chinatown women was a grade school education.*

2   During the early period of my childhood, while you and dad worked, grandma took care of all of us. One afternoon, while grandma was preparing dinner, oldest sister walked into the kitchen to get a drink of water. As oldest sister sipped her water, grandma turned to her and told oldest sister that we— the females—should all get jobs to put little brother through college. She recounted how difficult it was to put Youngest uncle through college. But oldest sister felt differently. Oldest sister was in sixth grade and many of her teachers had commented on her aptitude for mathematics and science. Grandma's advice insulted oldest sister.

3   Oldest sister told all of us what grandmother said and concluded that it was little brother's fault. I don't know when it began, but as long as I can remember, oldest sister resented little brother.

4   That same day, we told father what grandmother said. He told us to ignore her while you, mother, said, "We don't have the money to put all of you through school." Meanwhile, you told us you only had the opportunity to complete elementary and some middle school while dad completed middle school. You added that it was a great amount of education for people caught in the war in China. But your response seemed irrelevant° to us.

irrelevant:
not important

5   Oldest sister was determined to go to college. In the seventh grade, she began working as a waitress in Chinatown. Later she joined the Seattle Work Training Program for lower-income students and worked at the University of Washington's research laboratories. Second sister followed in her footsteps and worked; so did third sister and so did I, the fourth sister, as well as little sister and little brother. Eventually, we all went to college on scholarships. When that happened, no one was disappointed. It was economics. Not gender. On the contrary, I recall that one of your biggest disappointments occurred when second sister gave up engineering for marriage and domestic life. You quarreled with her. You screamed. You cried. You kept saying, "What a waste of money. We should have saved it." Then she reminded you that you never spent a cent on any of our educations. Then you said, "It's not the money. It's the opportunity."

➤ Follow-Up Questions

1. Why does the oldest sister resent her little brother?
2. What is the difference in attitude between the grandmother's view of education and gender and that of the father and mother in the story?
3. What does the mother mean at the end when she states that "'It's not the money. It's the opportunity'"?

➤ Short Writing Assignments

1. Interview several students about their family's attitude toward education. Be sure to include questions about their parents' and grandparents' education, and keep accurate records of any questions asked and answers given. Then prepare an **informative** report that explains the various views about the meaning of education people hold today.
2. Television and movies often present a view of college that is very different from reality. View a TV program or film that has a college setting and take notes as to the different aspects of college life it shows. Then write a short essay **comparing and contrasting** the program or film with the realities of your experiences and observations in college.

➤ Extended Writing Assignments

1. Many students work to afford higher education. To discover the different problems such students face, interview several students who combine work and education. Then prepare an **informative** report that explains your findings.
2. **Research** the sources within your school to find out the options for scholarships and financial aid offered through the state, federal programs, and private endowments. Then prepare an **informative** presentation to the class that **classifies** the monies available and the various requirements needed, both academic and administrative, to apply for such aid. Your should prepare a brief handout for your audience and a written report for your instructor.

Cultural Baggage

Barbara Ehrenreich

Pre-Reading Ideas: If you were asked to define or identify yourself ethnically, what would you say? We are frequently asked to do this when we fill out medical forms, insurance applications, job applications, census questionnaires, and other forms requiring personal information. In some cases, friends, acquaintances, and even strangers make assumptions about our heritage based on physical, cultural markers: skin color, shape of facial features, hair texture, and so forth. However, sometimes those who do not know may guess incorrectly. Barbara Ehrenreich may surprise you with her answer to a friend's question, "'And what is your ethnic background, if I may ask?'" What would your response be?

Vocabulary: Looking up and understanding the following words prior to reading should prepare you for the author's message. Other words will be defined in the margin.

ethnic	WASP	ecumenism	Disraeli	Elijah
heritage	ethnic chauvinism		clans	ecumenical

ancestors: those from whom one comes, such as grandparents, great-grandparents, and so forth

warrant: allow for

1 An acquaintance was telling me about the joys of rediscovering her ethnic and religious heritage. "I know exactly what my ancestors° were doing 2,000 years ago," she said, eyes gleaming with enthusiasm, "and I can do the same things now." Then she leaned forward and inquired politely, "And what is your ethnic background, if I may ask?"

2 "None," I said, that being the first word in line to get out of my mouth. Well, not "none," I backtracked. Scottish, English, Irish—that was something, I supposed. Too much Irish to qualify as WASP; too much of the hated English to warrant° a "Kiss Me, I'm Irish" button; plus there are a number of dead ends in the family tree due to adoptions, missing records, failing memories and the like. I was blushing by this time. Did "none" mean I was rejecting my heritage out of Anglo-Celtic self-hate? Or was I revealing a hidden ethnic chauvinism in which the Britannically derived serve as a kind of neutral standard compared with the ethnic "others"?

ethnicity: characteristics of a particular cultural group

trampled: abused

venerable: respected

locales: places

militant: active and aggressive

sweetbreads: the thymus or pancreas of a young animal used for food

tartans: plaid fabrics

flaxen-haired: blond

half-clad: half-dressed

3 Throughout the '60s and '70s, I watched one group after another-African-Americans, Latinos, Native Americans-stand up and proudly reclaim their roots while I just sank back ever deeper into my seat. All this excitement over ethnicity° stemmed, I uneasily sensed, from a past in which *their* ancestors had been trampled° upon by my ancestors, or at least by people who looked very much like them. In addition, it had begun to seem almost un-American not to have some sort of hyphen at hand, linking one to more venerable° times and locales°.

4 But the truth is, I was raised with none. We'd eaten ethnic foods in my childhood home, but these were all borrowed, like the pasties, or Cornish meat pies, my father had picked up from his fellow miners in Butte, Mont. If my mother had one rule, it was militant° ecumenism in all matters of food and experience. "Try new things," she would say, meaning anything from sweetbreads° to clams, with an emphasis on the "new."

5 As a child, I briefly nourished a craving for tradition and roots. I immersed myself in the works of Sir Walter Scott. I pretended to believe that the bagpipe was a musical instrument. I was fascinated to learn from a grandmother that we were descended from certain Highland clans and longed for a pleated skirt in one of their distinctive tartans°.

6 But in "Ivanhoe," it was the dark-eyed "Jewess" Rebecca I identified with, not the flaxen-haired° bimbo Rowena. As for clans: Why not call them "tribes," those bands of half-clad° peasant and warriors whose idea of cuisine

rampaging:
erupting into
violently
uncontrollable
behavior

forebears:
ancestors

seder:
ceremonial
Jewish dinner at
the beginning of
Passover

matzoh: Jewish
ceremonial bread

secular: people
not connected
with religion

eluded: escaped

Manischewitz:
kosher Jewish
wine

progenitors:
ancestors

disillusioned: to
lose one's beliefs

Orthodox
Judaism:
traditional
Jewish religion

epiphany:
a sudden
understanding

ritual: a specific
way of
performing a
religious act

strain: the group
of descendants
of a common
ancestor

spewed: poured
forth violently

was stuffed sheep gut washed down with whisky? And then there was the sting of Disraeli's remark—which I came across in my early teens—to the effect that his ancestors had been leading orderly, literate lives when my ancestors were still rampaging° through the Highlands daubing themselves with blue paint.

7   Motherhood put the screws to me, ethnicitywise. I had hoped that by marrying a man of Eastern European–Jewish ancestry I would acquire for my descendants the ethnic genes that my own forebears° so sadly lacked. At one point, I even subjected the children to a seder° of my own design, including a little talk about the flight from Egypt and its relevance to modern social issues. But the kids insisted on buttering their matzohs° and snickering through my talk. "Give me a break, Mom," the older one said. "You don't even believe in God."

8   After the tiny pagans had been put to bed, I sat down to brood over Elijah's wine. What had I been thinking? The kids knew that their Jewish grandparents were secular° folks who didn't hold seders themselves. And if ethnicity eluded° me, how could I expect it to take root in my children, who are not only Scottish-English-Irish, but Hungarian-Polish-Russian to boot?

9   But, then, on the fumes of Manischewitz°, a great insight took form in my mind. It was true, as the kids said, that I didn't "believe in God." But this could be taken as something very different from an accusation—a reminder of genuine heritage. My parents had not believed in God either, nor had my grandparents or any other progenitors° going back to the great-great level. They had become disillusioned° with Christianity generations ago—just as, on the in-law side, my children's other ancestors had shaken off their Orthodox Judaism°. This insight did not exactly furnish me with an "identity," but it was at least something to work with: We are the kind of people, I realized—whatever our distant ancestors' religion—who do *not* believe, who do not carry on traditions, who do not do things just because someone has done them before.

10   The epiphany° went on: I recalled that my mother never introduced a procedure for cooking or cleaning by telling me, "Grandma did it this way." What did Grandma know, living in the days before vacuum cleaners and disposable toilet mops? In my parents' general view, new things were better than old, and the very fact that some ritual° had been performed in the past was a good reason for abandoning it now. Because what was the past, as our forebears knew it? Nothing but poverty, superstition and grief. "Think for yourself," Dad used to say. "Always ask why."

11   In fact, this may have been the ideal cultural heritage for my particular ethnic strain°-bounced as it was from the Highlands of Scotland across the sea, to the Rockies, down into the mines and finally spewed° out into high-tech, suburban America. What better philosophy, for a race of migrants°, than "Think for yourself"? What better maxim°, for a people whose whole world was rudely inverted every 30 years or so, than "Try new things"?

12   The more tradition-minded, the newly enthusiastic celebrants of Purim° and Kwanza° and Solstice°, may see little point to survival if the survivors

carry no cultural freight—religion, for example, or ethnic tradition. To which I would say that skepticism°, curiosity and wide-eyed ecumenical tolerance are also worthy elements of human tradition and are at least as old as such notions as "Serbian" or "Croatian," "Scottish" or "Jewish." I make no claims for my personal line of progenitors except that they remained loyal to the values that may have induced° all of our ancestors, long, long ago, to climb down from the trees and make their way to the open plains.

13   A few weeks ago, I cleared my throat and asked the children, now mostly grown and fearsomely smart, whether they felt any stirrings of ethnic or religious identity, etc., which might have been, ahem°, insufficiently nourished at home. "None," they said, adding firmly, "and the world would be a better place if nobody else did, either." My chest swelled with pride, as would my mother's, to know that the race of "none" marches on.

➤ Follow-Up Questions

1. List the ethnic backgrounds which Ehrenreich claims and then briefly discuss how she can claim no ethnic background at all.
2. What specific religious identity does Ehrenreich acquire from her grandparents and parents?
3. " 'Think for yourself' " and " 'Try new things' " become two new maxims or basic truths which Ehrenreich proposes for her new identity. How do these two statements support her claim?

➤ Short Writing Assignments

1. Consider all the questions you would ask to discover an individual's own ethnic origins. Then, using your list of questions, interview a fellow classmate to discover his/her origins. Try to be as thorough as possible because you can only talk to this person once. Then, in class, review your notes and write a paragraph that describes that individual's origins as thoroughly as possible in the time given.
2. Think about all the food you eat and all the music you listen to in one week. Then write a short **descriptive** essay that **classifies** all the different cultural backgrounds associated with such food and music.

➤ Extended Writing Assignments

1. Ehrenreich notes that during the 1960s and 1970s many cultural groups were instrumental in increasing public awareness of oppression. Research a cultural organization, such as LULAC or the NAACP, to gain information as to its background, specific purposes and goals, and the services it offers to its community. Then prepare an **informative** report that explains each of these areas.
2. Ehrenreich's title, "Cultural Baggage," implies her idea that culture may have a negative side in contemporary life, that it is baggage or weight which one carries around. Take a **position** on such a view and write an essay supporting your **argument.**

CONCLUSION

From this chapter, readers can see various ways individuals learn. Education is not limited to books and classrooms; rather, it is an experience that can be indulged in as long as a person maintains a wonder and curiosity about the world around her. This kind of education is based on experiences, self-motivated exploration of interesting topics, and an understanding of people who practice cultural values and rituals different from the observer's. Because few people live in an isolated enclosure, apart from radio, television, newspapers, or other people, it is difficult not be exposed to new ideas and not to learn about things surrounding them. The secret is to keep an open, interested, and inquiring mind.

➤ Further Writing Topics

Personal Narrative

In some cases, students who enter higher education are the first in their family to do so. In other cases, students in higher education might come from families who have planned for their children's education since their birth. And then there are students who, for different reasons, chose to delay their education until a later time in life. Write a personal narrative describing your situation as a student, including how you arrived here and what your educational goals are that will help you prepare for the future.

Expository

Choose a cultural tradition or ritual different from your own (Chanukah, Kwanza, Christmas, Passover, death rituals, and so forth) and research it. Look up its history, noting any changes made in its observation, the way it is observed, its duration, and any features associated with it (special foods, clothing, dietary laws, prayers, songs, and so forth). Dedicate part of your paper to a comparison-and-contrast of the researched ritual or tradition with one in your culture that is similar to it. If you have none that are similar, explain why.

Analysis

Using Alisa Valdes-Rodriguez's article, "Crossing Pop Lines" or Barbara Ehrenreich's personal narrative, "Cultural Baggage," write a summary analysis. Using the two poems, Linda Koffel's "Blue Skin," Maxine Kumin's "In the Park" and Anna Quindlen's personal essay, "I Am a Catholic," explain the characteristics of each religion the writers discuss and what each means to the writer.

Argumentation

Using Anna Quindlen's personal narrative, "I Am a Catholic," write an argumentative essay agreeing or disagreeing with the belief that one can't be Catholic or any other religion without accepting all rituals and beliefs. In other words, you will write an argumentative paper that supports or rejects the belief that one can claim membership in a religion and accept only those aspects that appeal to him or her.

➤ Suggested Chapter Projects

1. Understanding a culture other than your own or one which you are exposed to regularly can be a difficult process. But what if you could create a culture, one that included food, fashion, language, geographical location, and religion? Assume you have found an alien planet in another galaxy or even another universe, and you must now report your findings to your supervisors on your home planet. Prepare your report, describing not only your alien planet but its culture as well.

2. Assume that you are in charge of a United Nations banquet, and that your job is to make sure that the food and service are "politically correct." You may serve only culturally acceptable food to each delegate, and you must be careful not to seat delegates from warring nations next to each other. Choose any ten nations that are members of the United Nations, and in a report, identify the countries, the dinner—including dessert!—and who would sit next to whom.

3. Many times the border between countries shifts, and when this happens, such as in a treaty, residents of the area who once thought they were citizens of one country suddenly find themselves citizens of a different nation. Consider how such a shift in national identity would affect an individual and his/her family tradition. You may possibly know individuals who have gone through such a situation; if so, you may want to interview them to find out their viewpoints. Then write an essay that discusses the effects such a transformation had on them.

CHAPTER 6

Crossing Borders in the Classroom
Source: © Barbara Stitzer/PhotoEdit

Language: Communication with Myself and Others

C ommunication with the world begins with the first cry an infant gives at birth, announcing his or her arrival. Communication continues as the child learns the language, develops language skills, and refines his or her methods of communication. If you've ever watched small children, you discovered that they have a silent language that appears understood until someone violates the code and a peal of anger or distress signals a caretaker that a problem has arisen. Language, while apparently a part of our daily routine, can become controversial when it fails or refuses to conform to the standards required of it. Speaking a language different from that of the country in which one resides can pose problems with simply getting along in daily activities.

The pieces in this chapter discuss the difficulty of trying to communicate and succeed when a person does not know the language of his environment. Bárbara Mujica describes the hardships students undergo while learning. Richard Rodriguez describes what it means to grow up bilingual and be deprived of his family language suddenly and completely so he will be able to learn to speak English more easily. On a different note, Carol Tarvis looks at the differences in a language based on gender. Maya Angelou takes her reader to a small rural town removed in time where dialect is spoken and everyone understands one another.

Language is a controversial topic that rouses anger and defiance in many. Because it is an outward sign of one's cultural heritage sometimes in a country different from one's birth, speakers are reluctant to give it up. On the other hand, residents of the host country frequently feel resentful that their country must make accommodations for non-native English speakers. Language scholars and educators understand that speakers of a different language are not uneducated in their own language, but they have difficulty holding the second-language speakers to the same standards as English speakers in the classrooms. This topic is one that sparks interesting debates and argumentative papers. It also lends itself to personal narratives from individuals whose primary language is not English. As you read the following works, see whether you identify with any of the problems the writers encounter. Write a brief entry in your journal, describing your feelings about English if it is not your native language, or your feelings about making English the official language of the United States, before you begin reading these works.

The Struggle to Be an All-American Girl

Elizabeth Wong

Introductory Remarks: Originally interested in journalism as a career, Elizabeth Wong graduated from University of Southern California. After growing up in Los Angeles, Wong moved to New York City and attended New York University's Tisch School of the Arts, where she began writing plays, including *Kimchee and Chitlins: A Serious Comedy about Getting Along* and *Letters to a Student Revolutionary*. Wong also writes articles that appear in newspapers such as the following one, published in the *Los Angeles Times*.

Pre-Reading Ideas: There have been many heated debates about the role of cultural loyalty as opposed to assimilation into the dominant society. While cultural loyalty involves maintaining the traditions, values, and language of an individual's heritage, assimilation means replacing traditions, values, and language with those of the host culture. While some people see this as an either-or situation, where one is either a member of his or her culture or a member of the dominant society, other people argue that acculturation is a compromise. Through acculturation an individual does not sacrifice all of his or her family beliefs but is able to work and live comfortably within the dominant culture. Examine Wong's attitudes in her piece.

Vocabulary: Looking up and understanding the following words prior to reading should prepare you for the author's message. Other words will be defined in the margin.

kowtow   painstakingly   ideographs   disassociate

1   It's still there, the Chinese school on Yale Street where my brother and I used to go. Despite the new coat of paint and the high wire fence, the school I knew ten years ago remains remarkably, stoically° the same.

stoically: without showing emotion or pain

2   Every day at 5 p.m., instead of playing with our fourth- and fifth-grade friends or sneaking out to the empty lot to hunt ghosts and animal bones, my brother and I had to go to Chinese school. No amount of kicking, screaming, or pleading could dissuade° my mother, who was solidly determined to have us learn the language of our heritage.

dissuade: to convince someone not to do something

3   Forcibly, she walked us the seven long, hilly blocks from our home to school, depositing our defiant tearful faces before the stern principal. My only memory of him is that he swayed on his heels like a palm tree, and he always

clasped his impatient twitching hands behind his back. I recognized him as a repressed maniacal° child killer, and knew that if we ever saw his hands we'd be in big trouble.

maniacal: having characteristics of a maniac or insane person

4   We all sat in little chairs in an empty auditorium. The room smelled like Chinese medicine, an imported faraway mustiness. Like ancient mothballs or dirty closets. I hated the smell. I favored crisp new scents. Like the soft French perfume that my American teacher wore in public school.

5   There was a stage far to the right, flanked by an American flag and the flag of the Nationalist Republic of China, which was also red, white, and blue but not as pretty.

6   Although the emphasis at the school was mainly language—speaking, reading, writing—the lessons always began with an exercise in politeness. With the entrance of the teacher, the best student would tap a bell and everyone would get up, kowtow, and chant, "Sing san ho," the phonetic for "How are you, teacher?"

7   Being ten years old, I had better things to learn than ideographs copied painstakingly in lines that ran right to left from the tip of a *moc but,* a real ink pen that had to be held in an awkward way if blotches were to be avoided. After all, I could do the multiplication tables, name the satellites of Mars, and write reports on *Little Women* and *Black Beauty.* Nancy Drew, my favorite heroine never spoke Chinese.

8   The language was a source of embarrassment. More times than not, I had tried to disassociate myself from the nagging loud voice that followed me wherever I wandered in the nearby American supermarket, outside Chinatown. The voice belonged to my grandmother, a fragile woman in her seventies who could outshout the best of the street vendors°. Her humor was raunchy°, her Chinese rhythmless, patternless. It was quick, it was loud, it was unbeautiful. It was not like the quiet, lilting romance of French or the gentle refinement of the American South. Chinese sounded pedestrian°. Public.

vendors: sales people

raunchy: vulgar

pedestrian: very common

9   In Chinatown, the comings and goings of hundreds of Chinese on their daily tasks sounded chaotic° and frenzied°. I did not want to be thought of as mad, as talking gibberish. When I spoke English, people nodded at me, smiled sweetly, said encouraging words. Even the people in my culture would cluck and say that I'd do well in life. "My, doesn't she move her lips fast," they would say, meaning that I'd be able to keep up with the world outside Chinatown.

chaotic: completely confused

frenzied: acting wildly

10 My brother was even more fanatical° than I about speaking English. He was especially hard on my mother, criticizing her, often cruelly, for her pidgin° speech—smatterings of Chinese scattered like chop suey in her conversation. "It's not 'What it is,' Mom," he'd say in exasperation. "It's 'What *is* it, what *is* it!'" Sometimes Mom would leave out an occasional "the" or "a," or perhaps a verb of being. He would stop her in mid-sentence: "Say it again, Mom. Say it right." When he tripped over his own tongue, he'd blame it on her: "See, Mom, it's all your fault. You set a bad example."

fanatical: extreme enthusiasm

pidgin: combination of two languages spoken as one

11 What infuriated° my mother most was when my brother cornered her on her consonants, especially "r." My father had played a cruel joke on Mom

infuriated: angered

by assigning her an American name that her tongue wouldn't allow her to say. No matter how hard she tried, "Ruth" always ended up "Luth" or "Roof."

12   After two years of writing with a *moc but* and reciting words with multiples of meanings, I finally was granted a cultural divorce. I was permitted to stop Chinese school.

13   I thought of myself as multicultural. I preferred tacos to egg rolls; I enjoyed Cinco de Mayo° more than Chinese New Year.

14   At last, I was one of you; I wasn't one of them.

15   Sadly, I still am.

Cinco de Mayo:
Fifth of May,
Mexican
Independence
Day

➤ Follow-Up Questions

1. In the first half of the essay, what is Wong's view of the Chinese school and her mother's idea of going there? Choose specific words to justify your answer.
2. Much of the essay focuses on languages in different cultures. Why do you think language is so important? List very specific reasons, both from the article and from your own experiences.
3. In what ways were Wong's brother and father cruel or insensitive to her mother? Based on the brother's and father's actions, what would you determine to be their view of learning Chinese?

➤ Short Writing Assignments

1. Why is it such a switch for Wong that she would end the article with the idea that "Sadly, I still am"? Write a paragraph responding to this last statement in view of Wong's essay.
2. In a short **descriptive** essay point out the specific characteristics you would consider as encompassing the "All-American Girl" or the "All-American Boy."

➤ Extended Writing Assignments

1. Each generation involved in the immigration and settlement process has its own set of issues to deal with when coming to a new country. The first generation has to leave the old country and traditions they have grown up with; the second generation, those children born to the first generation, face their own issues dealing with both the old and the new. In an essay, take a **position** as to which generation has the more difficult task and make note of specific reasons for your **argument.**
2. Wong mentions her appreciation for the "romance of French" and how she favored the Mexican celebration of Cinco de Mayo over the Chinese New Year. Does this give some indication that even "All-American Girls/Boys" favor certain qualities of other cultures over those of traditional America? In an essay, take a position about whether Americans view other cultures as superior to theirs in certain areas; give specific **examples** to support your discussion. You might consider such areas as precision instruments, fashions, food, or even the cars most valued in America.

Aria: Public and Private Language

Richard Rodriguez

Introductory Remarks: A Mexican-American writer, Richard Rodriguez has won acclaim as well as notoriety for his first major publication, *Hunger of Memory: The Education of Richard Rodriguez*. It was followed ten years later by *Days of Obligation: An Argument with My Mexican Father.* Both works are autobiographical. Rodriguez also writes essays of social criticism and is a frequent speaker about language and multicultural education.

Pre-Reading Ideas: One of the major components of culture is language. If a person lives in a country other than that of his or her heritage, it is quite likely that he or she will speak the language of the host country. However, if the person lives in a community that values the ability to speak the language of the heritage, he or she must decide whether to learn the new language. Sometimes knowledge of the heritage language slows down a child's ability to learn in school if the heritage language is different from the language of the dominant culture. Consequently, children may be encouraged to learn to speak the dominant culture's language. This is not to say that a child is deficient in his or her ability to learn. It simply means that he or she has learned a language system that might interfere with the language used to teach students in school. Knowing a second language has been acknowledged as helping the speaker in his or her analytical skills. However, when a child's parents are told that it is in his or her best interest to speak the dominant culture's language in the home, a feeling of discomfort and separation may be felt. Richard Rodriguez learned Spanish first and was encouraged by his teachers and his parents to speak English in the home to help him in his schoolwork. In the following essay, Rodriguez shares his feelings about having to give up his family language.

Vocabulary: Looking up and understanding the following words prior to reading should prepare you for the author's message. Other words will be defined in the margin.

institution	disadvantaged	barrio	bilingual	*gringos*

1   I remember to start with that day in Sacramento—a California now nearly thirty years past—when I first entered a classroom, able to understand some fifty stray English words.

2   The third of four children, I had been preceded to a neighborhood Roman Catholic school by an older brother and sister. But neither of them had revealed very much about their classroom experiences. Each afternoon they returned, as they left in the morning, always together, speaking in Spanish as they climbed the five steps of the porch. And their mysterious books, wrapped in shopping-bag paper, remained on the table next to the door, closed firmly behind them.

executives:
senior level
individuals who
hold power and
authority in an
organization

3   An accident of geography sent me to a school where all my classmates were white, many the children of doctors and lawyers and business executives°. All my classmates certainly must have been uneasy on that first day of school—as most children are uneasy—to find themselves apart from their families in the first institution of their lives. But I was astonished.

impersonal:
lacking human
emotion and
warmth

4   The nun said, in a friendly but oddly impersonal° voice, "Boys and girls, this is Richard Rodriguez." (I heard her sound out *Rich-heard Road-ree-guess.*) It was the first time I had heard anyone name me in English. "Richard," the nun repeated more slowly, writing my name down in her black leather book. Quickly I turned to see my mother's face dissolve in a watery blur behind the pebbled glass door.

endorsed:
approved

5   Many years later there is something called bilingual education—a scheme proposed in the late 1960s by Hispanic-American social activists, later endorsed° by a congressional vote. It is a program that seeks to permit non-English speaking children, many from lower-class homes, to use their family language as the language of school. (Such is the goal its supporters announce.) I hear them and am forced to say no: It is not possible for a child—any child—ever to use his family's language in school. Not to understand this is to misunderstand the public uses of schooling and to trivialize° the nature of intimate° life—a family's 'language.'

trivialize:
to make
unimportant

intimate: very
personal

6   Memory teaches me what I know of these matters; the boy reminds the adult. I was a bilingual child, a certain kind—socially disadvantaged—the son of working-class parents, both Mexican immigrants.

optimism: hope

7   In the early years of my boyhood, my parents coped very well in America. My father had steady work. My mother managed at home. They were nobody's victims. Optimism° and ambition led them to a house (our home) many blocks from the Mexican south side of town. We lived among *gringos* and only a block from the biggest, whitest houses. It never occurred to my parents that they couldn't live wherever they chose. Nor was the Sacramento of the fifties bent on teaching them a contrary lesson. My mother and father were more annoyed than intimidated° by those two or three neighbors who tried initially to make us unwelcome. ('Keep your brats away from my sidewalk!') But despite all they achieved, perhaps because they had so much to achieve, any deep feeling of ease, the confidence of 'belonging' in public was withheld from them both. They regarded the people at work, the faces in crowds, as very distant from us. They were the others, *los gringos.* That term was interchangeable° in their speech with another, even more telling, *los americanos.*

intimidated:
scared

interchangeable:
to use one thing
in the place of
another

8   I grew up in a house where the only regular guests were my relations. For one day, enormous families of relatives would visit and there would be so many people that the noise and the bodies would spill out to the backyard and front porch. Then for weeks, no one came by. (It was usually a salesman who rang the doorbell.) Our house stood apart. A gaudy yellow in a row of white bungalows. We were the people with the noisy dog. The people who raised pigeons and chickens. We were the foreigners on the block. A few

neighbors smiled and waved. We waved back. But no one in the family knew the names of the old couple who lived next door; until I was seven years old I did not know the names of the kids who lived across the street.

9   In public my father and mother spoke a hesitant, accented, not always grammatical English. And they would have to strain—their bodies tense—to catch the sense of what was rapidly said by *los gringos*. At home they spoke Spanish. The language of their Mexican past sounded in counterpoint° to the English of public society. The words would come quickly, with ease. Conveyed through those sounds was the pleasing, soothing, consoling reminder of being at home.

counterpoint:
point that is
contrasted with
one before it

10   During those years when I was first conscious of hearing, my mother and father addressed me only in Spanish; in Spanish I learned to reply. By contrast, English *(inglés),* rarely heard in the house, was the language I came to associate with *gringos.* I learned my first words of English overhearing my parents speak to strangers. At five years of age, I knew just enough English for my mother to trust me on errands to stores one block away. No more.

11   I was a listening child, careful to hear the very different sounds of Spanish and English. Wide-eyed with hearing, I'd listen to sounds more than words. First, there were English *(gringo)* sounds. So many words were still unknown that when the butcher or the lady at the drugstore said something to me, exotic polysyllabic sounds would bloom in the midst of their sentences. Often, the speech of people in public seemed to me very loud, booming with confidence. The man behind the counter would literally ask, "What can I do for you?" But by being so firm and so clear, the sound of his voice said that he was a *gringo;* he belonged in public society.

12   I would also hear then the high nasal notes of middle-class American speech. The air stirred with sound. Sometimes, even now, when I have been traveling abroad for several weeks, I will hear what I heard as a boy. In hotel lobbies or airports in Turkey or Brazil, some Americans will pass, and suddenly I will hear it again—the high sound of American voices. For a few seconds I will hear it with pleasure, for it is now the sound of *my* society—a reminder of home. But inevitably—already on the flight headed for home—the sound fades with repetition. I will be unable to hear it anymore.

13   When I was a boy, things were different. The accent of *los gringos* was never pleasing nor was it hard to hear. Crowds at Safeway or at bus stops would be noisy with sound. And I would be forced to edge away from the chirping chatter above me.

14   I was unable to hear my own sounds, but I knew very well that I spoke English poorly. My words could not stretch far enough to form complete thoughts. And the words I did speak I didn't know well enough to make into distinct sounds. (Listeners would usually lower their heads, better to hear what I was trying to say.) But it was one thing for *me* to speak English with difficulty. It was more troubling for me to hear my parents speak in public: their high-whining vowels and guttural consonants; their sentences that got stuck with 'eh' and 'ah' sounds; the confused syntax°; the hesitant rhythm of

syntax: the
grammar rules of
a language

sound so different from the way *gringos* spoke. I'd notice, moreover, that my parents' voices were softer than those of the *gringos* we'd meet.

15   I am tempted now to say that none of this mattered. In adulthood I am embarrassed by childhood fears. And, in a way, it didn't matter very much that my parents could not speak English with ease. Their linguistic difficulties had no serious consequences. My mother and father made themselves understood at the county hospital clinic and at government offices. And yet, in another way, it mattered very much—it was unsettling to hear my parents struggle with English. Hearing them, I'd grow nervous, my clutching trust in their protection and power weakened.

16   There were many times like the night at a brightly lit gasoline station (a blaring white memory) when I stood uneasily, hearing my father. He was talking to a teenaged attendant. I do not recall what they were saying, but I cannot forget the sounds my father made as he spoke. At one point his words slid together to form one word—sounds as confused as the threads of blue and green oil in the puddle next to my shoes. His voice rushed through what he had left to say. And, toward the end, reached falsetto° notes, appealing to his listener's understanding. I looked away to the lights of passing automobiles. I tried not to hear anymore. But I heard only too well the calm easy tones in the attendant's reply. Shortly afterward, walking toward home with my father, I shivered when he put his hand on my shoulder. The very first chance that I got, I evaded his grasp and ran on ahead into the dark, skipping with feigned°, boyish exuberance°.

17   But then there was Spanish, *Español:* my family's language. *Español:* the language that seemed to me a private language. I'd hear strangers on the radio and in the Mexican Catholic church across town speaking in Spanish, but I couldn't really believe that Spanish was a public language, like English. Spanish speakers, rather, seemed related to me, for I sensed that we shared—through our language—the experience of feeling apart from *los gringos*. It was thus a ghetto° Spanish that I heard and I spoke. Like those whose lives are bound by a barrio, I was reminded by Spanish of my separateness from *los otros, los gringos* in power. But more intensely than for most barrio children—because I did not live in a barrio—Spanish seemed to me the language of home. (Most days it was only at home that I'd hear it.) It became the language of joyful return.

18   A family member would say something to me and I would feel myself specially recognized. My parents would say something to me and I would feel embraced by the sounds of their words. Those sounds said: *I am speaking with ease in Spanish. I am addressing you in words I never use with los gringos. I recognize you as someone special, close, like no one outside. You belong with us. In the family.*

19   (Ricardo.)

20   At the age of five, six, well past the time when most other children no longer easily notice the difference between sounds uttered° at home and words spoken in public, I had a different experience. I lived in a world magi-

falsetto: very high-pitched sounds

feigned: pretended, fake

exuberance: characterized by lots of energy

ghetto: a slum community

uttered: spoken

compounded: to form by combining parts

poised: hovering as if in the air

cally compounded° of sounds. I remained a child longer than most; I lingered too long, poised° at the edge of language—often frightened by the sounds of *los gringos,* delighted by the sounds of Spanish at home. I shared with my family a language that was startlingly different from that used in the great city around us.

gradations: changes by stages

21   For me there were none of the gradations° between public and private society so normal to a maturing child. Outside the house was public society; inside the house was private. Just opening or closing the screen door behind me was an important experience. I'd rarely leave home all alone or without reluctance. Walking down the sidewalk, under the canopy° of tall trees, I'd warily° notice the—suddenly—silent neighborhood kids who stood warily watching me. Nervously, I'd arrive at the grocery store to hear there the sounds of the *gringo*—foreign to me—reminding me that in this world so big, I was a foreigner. But then I'd return. Walking back toward our house, climbing the steps from the sidewalk, when the front door was open in summer, I'd hear voices beyond the screen door talking in Spanish. For a second or two, I'd stay, linger there, listening. Smiling, I'd hear my mother call out, saying in Spanish (words): 'Is that you Richard?' All the while her sounds would assure me: *You are home now; come closer; inside. With us.*

canopy: a covering overhead

warily: without trust

22   '*Sí,*' I'd reply.

23   Once more inside the house I would resume (assume) my place in the family. The sounds would dim, grow harder to hear. Once more at home, I would grow less aware of that fact. It required, however, no more than the blurt of the doorbell to alert me to listen to sounds all over again. The house would turn instantly still while my mother went to the door. I'd hear her hard English sounds. I'd wait to hear her voice return to soft-sounding Spanish, which assured me, as surely as did the clicking tongue of the lock on the door, that the stranger was gone.

cloistered: hidden away

24   Plainly, it is not healthy to hear such sounds so often. It is not healthy to distinguish public words from private sounds so easily. I remained cloistered° by sounds, timid and shy in public, too dependent on voices at home. And yet it needs to be emphasized: I was an extremely happy child at home. I remember many nights when my father would come back from work, and I'd hear him call out to my mother in Spanish, sounding relieved. In Spanish, he'd sound° light and free notes he never could manage in English. Some nights I'd jump up just at hearing his voice. With *mis hermanos* I would come running into the room where he was with my mother. Our laughing (so deep was the pleasure!) became screaming. Like others who know the pain of public alienation°, we transformed the knowledge of our public separateness and made it consoling—the reminder of intimacy. Excited, we joined our voices in a celebration of sounds. *We are speaking now the way we never speak out in public. We are alone—together,* the voices sounded, surrounded, to tell me. Some nights, no one seemed willing to loosen the hold sounds had on us. At dinner, we invented new words. (Ours sounded Spanish, but made sense only to us.) We pieced together new words by taking, say, an English verb

sound: utter

alienation: separation from

lacquered: polished

and giving it Spanish endings. My mother's instructions at bedtime would be lacquered° with mock-urgent tones. Or a word like *sí* would become, in several notes, able to convey added measures of feeling. Tongues explored the edges of words, especially the fat vowels. And we happily sounded that military drum roll, the twirling roar of the Spanish *r*. Family language: my family's sounds. The voices of my parents and sisters and brother. Their voices insisting: *You belong here. We are family members. Related. Special to one another. Listen!* Voices singing and sighing, rising, straining, then surging°, teeming° with pleasure that burst syllables into fragments of laughter. At times it seemed there was steady quiet only when, from another room, the rustling whispers of my parents faded and I moved closer to sleep.

surging: rushing forth

teeming: swarming

➤ Follow-Up Questions

1. How does Rodriguez's brother and sister's reaction to school differ from his?
2. Describe the efforts of Rodriguez's parents to establish a new life in America. What were their neighbors' reactions?
3. What is the overall effect of Rodriguez's initial inability to learn formal English?

➤ Short Writing Assignments

1. In a short essay, explain how Rodriguez **defines** "bilingual" and what his opinion of such a system is. Conclude your essay with your own **evaluation** of how effective such a system can be.
2. Compose a short **comparison-and-contrast** essay that examines Rodriguez's view of private and public langauge.

➤ Extended Writing Assignments

1. Research the beginning of bilingual education in your area or generally in the United States. Then prepare a report that explains the reasons for incorporating such a system within the schools and identifying those students who should receive such benefits. Conclude your essay with an **evaluation** of whether such a system is successful.
2. Consider Rodriguez's statement regarding "the public uses of schooling," then think about you own educational experiences and the course(s) you have to take. How do such requirements conform to what a "public" education should be? For example, why would a history major be required to take a course or two in science? Then write an **argumentative** essay in which you defend the reasons education is considered a "public" institution and how that concept influences the courses you take.

To Succeed, Learn in English

Bárbara Mujica

Introductory Remarks: Educated in the United States at UCLA and New York University, where she graduated with her PhD, as well as internationally at the University of Mexico and the Sorbonne in Paris, Bárbara Mujica understands the important role language plays in education. In addition to being a professor of Spanish at Georgetown University, Mujica is a bilingual author who has written books and articles including critical studies of Spanish literature and prose fiction. The following essay displays her belief in mainstreaming second-language students as soon as possible.

Pre-Reading Ideas: When tourists visit a country where the dominant language is different from their primary language, communication problems can arise. To attempt to be understood, individuals frequently use gestures and body language for clarification. Sometimes, however, each speaker becomes frustrated and raises his or her voice, seemingly assuming that the listener will understand better if the language is shouted. This scenario loses its humorous side when necessity requires successful communication. Thus, the debate rages in education as well as in the legal system about the best way for students to learn to speak English. If you have ever had to try to speak with someone who doesn't know your language, you understand the challenges that arise for both speakers. And if you are an English as a Second Language student, you know the disadvantages you face in the classroom.

Vocabulary: Looking up and understanding the following words prior to reading should prepare you for the author's message. Other words will be defined in the margin.

proficiency   immersed   longitudinal

1   The White House response to Senator Robert Dole's call to make English the official language of the United States was high on knee-jerk political correctness and low on common sense. White House spokeswoman Ginny Terzano said Dole's proposal was "not realistic because so many young students don't speak English, and in order to communicate with their teachers and reach full competency in their courses, they have to be taught in Spanish" or other languages. Actually, a longitudinal study published in October 1994 by the New York City Board of Education shows that the opposite is true. Students who are taught in English from the beginning have higher scores in reading and math than those taught in their native language.

2   New York City employs two methods to teach LEP (limited English proficiency) students. Bilingual education uses the student's native language for content instruction. This means students spend most of the day in classes taught in their native language. ESL (English as a second language) uses English as the medium of instruction, but students are not simply immersed in the language. Instead, they are taught by a specially trained instructor who uses "controlled" or limited English to introduce new aspects of the language systematically.

3   The longitudinal study demonstrates that students who receive ESL instruction fare° far better than those taught primarily in their native language. A

fare: experience

comparison of the three-year exit rates for students in ESL and bilingual programs shows that those who receive ESL instruction test out faster and in higher percentages than those who receive instruction in their native language, regardless of the grade in which they entered school. For example, 79.3 percent of the children who entered ESL programs in kindergarten tested out, while only 51.5 percent of those who received their education in their native languages did. Likewise, 72.9 percent of the ESL students who entered programs in the first grade tested out, while only 38.5 of those in bilingual programs did. For students who entered LEP programs in the ninth grade, 91.6 percent of those in native-language instruction classes still hadn't tested out after three years, as compared with 78.1 percent of those in ESL classes.

4   Furthermore, children who had been in ESL classes tested higher in English and math once they exited LEP programs than those who had received native-language instruction. Of the LEP students who entered in kindergarten or the first grade, 49 percent of those who had been in ESL classes eventually read at grade level, while only 32 percent of those who had been in bilingual classes performed that well. In math, the statistics are even more impressive. Of the children who entered in kindergarten or the first grade, more than 69 percent of those who had been in ESL classes eventually performed at grade level or above, as opposed to 54 percent of those who had been in bilingual classes.

barrage: an overwhelming amount

mitigating: giving excuses for

5   Naturally, the study provoked a barrage° of criticism from the highly political and vocal bilingual lobby, which prompted the New York City Board of Education to issue a paper in November 1994 mitigating° the findings of the study and ignoring the distinction between students in ESL and bilingual education programs. Rather than exit rates, this paper focuses on the achievement of LEP students *during* the period in which they are in bilingual or ESL classes. The authors show that although the scores of LEP students were below average on the English-language test, their scores in all areas showed improvement; they point out that in math, there were insufficient data on the progress of LEP students to draw valid conclusions.

6   However, a report on citywide mathematics test results in New York in the spring of 1995 deals more fully with the math scores of the 26,248 students who were examined the previous school year in Chinese, Spanish, or Haitian Creole. According to this document, only 16.6 percent of these children were performing at or above grade level in mathematics. Although this figure represents an improvement of 1.1 percent over the scores of the previous year, it discredits the argument that native-language instruction keeps students performing at grade level in subject areas. Although LEP students are *improving* faster than the national norm, they continue to *perform* far below the norm.

7   Several other studies also demonstrate that LEP students taught in English do just as well or better than those taught in their native language. In El Paso, Texas, a longitudinal evaluation shows that young children in the "bilingual immersion" program, which uses English as the language of instruction from the first day of the first grade, actually do better in math and reading

than those taught in their native language. In addition to bilingual immersion, many other new programs that combine English with subject-area instruction have been developed.

8   Clearly, it is not necessary to teach LEP children in their native language, and doing so may actually be detrimental° to their academic achievement. Furthermore, by isolating children into language ghettos in school, we discourage contact with English-speaking youngsters who could facilitate° newcomers' socialization into American society and contribute to their mastery of English. It is simply common sense that students who are taught in English will learn the language more quickly and qualify for mainstreaming earlier than those who are not. And it is common sense to use methods that produce positive results in the classroom.

detrimental: damaging

facilitate: help

➤ Follow-Up Questions

1. Why would the New York City Board of Education ignore its own findings in the 1994 study and only look to performance "during the period in which students are in bilingual or ESL classes," instead of to "exit rates"?
2. Where was the study conducted? Do you think that the same results would occur if the study were done in another area of the country? If so, why?
3. What reason does Mujica give at the end for favoring ESL over bilingual classes?

➤ Short Writing Assignments

1. If you were on the school board, which course of action would you prefer, ESL or bilingual classes for students with language difficulties? Write a short essay defending your decision with specific points.
2. Mujica gives some very important statistics in written form. But often such information is presented as graphs, which can take many forms, such as bar graphs or pie graphs. Reread the paragraph regarding the "longitudinal study," then represent the information in the form of graphs; the style of the graph is your choice. Explain why you chose the graph you used.

➤ Extended Writing Assignments

1. Form a research group, then investigate the language policies in a school district in your area. If your area has more than one district, you may want to consider researching at least two districts for **comparison.** Once you have the information you need regarding number of students, types of programs, and success and failure rates, prepare a report explaining your findings. Conclude your report with a group **evaluation** of whether you favor ESL, LEP, or another program currently being used in your area.
2. Mujica uses the term "language ghettos" in school. Decide whether this designation has any negative **connotations.** You may want to interview language instructors and students with a variety of language skills to help determine the term's meaning. Then prepare an essay **defining** what such a term means and whether it implies a negative or positive image.

Champion of the World

Maya Angelou

Introductory Remarks: Born and raised in the American South, Maya Angelou overcame racial adversity in a segregated area of the country. Angelou has become a well-known poet, novelist, and performer who read her poem "On the Pulse of Morning" at President Bill Clinton's 1993 inauguration. One of Angelou's best-known works, *I Know Why the Caged Bird Sings,* has won her enormous acclaim, and the following narrative is an excerpt from that autobiography.

Pre-Reading Ideas: The topic of sports, whether it is football, soccer, ice hockey, or boxing, creates feelings of excitement in the spectators as well as in the participants. Regardless of the level of competition, little league, high school, college/university, or professional, those involved become experts in how the game should be played and even feel a personal investment in the teams and/or opponents. "Champion of the World" focuses on the impact of the event on those who sit listening to the broadcast, far removed physically but personally connected to Joe Louis when he fought to defend his title of World Heavy Weight Champion against a white contender in the 1930s.

Vocabulary: Looking up and understanding the following words prior to reading should prepare you for the author's message. Other words will be defined in the margin.

wedge	**clinch**	**contender**	**maimed**
cracker	**uppercut**	**lynching**	**Joe Louis**

1   The last inch of space was filled, yet people continued to wedge themselves along the walls of the Store. Uncle Willie had turned the radio up to its last notch so that youngsters on the porch wouldn't miss a word. Women sat on kitchen chairs, dining-room chairs, stools, and upturned wooden boxes. Small children and babies perched on every lap available and men leaned on the shelves or on each other.

apprehensive: nervous

2   The apprehensive° mood was shot through with shafts of gaiety, as a black sky is streaked with lightning.

cracker: an offensive term used to refer to a poor white person living in rural parts of the south-eastern U.S.

3   "I ain't worried 'bout this fight. Joe's gonna whip that cracker° like it's open season."

4   "He gone whip him till that white boy call him Momma."

5   At last the talking finished and the string-along songs about razor blades were over and the fight began.

cackled: laughed

6   "A quick jab to the head." In the Store the crowd grunted. "A left to the head and a right and another left." One of the listeners cackled° like a hen and was quieted.

7   "They're in a clinch, Louis is trying to fight his way out."

8   Some bitter comedian on the porch said, "That white man don't mind hugging that niggah now, I betcha."

9   "The referee is moving in to break them up, but Louis finally pushed the contender away and it's an uppercut to the chin. The contender is hanging on, now he's backing away. Louis catches him with a short left to the jaw."

10   A tide of murmuring assent° poured out the door and into the yard.

assent: agreement

11   "Another left and another left. Louis is saving that mighty right. . . ." The mutter in the Store had grown into a baby roar and it was pierced by the clang of a bell and the announcer's "That's the bell for round three, ladies and gentlemen."

12   As I pushed my way into the Store I wondered if the announcer gave any thought to the fact that he was addressing as "ladies and gentlemen" all the Negroes around the world who sat sweating and praying, glued to their "Master's voice."

13   There were only a few calls for RC Colas™, Dr. Peppers™, and Hines™ root beer. The real festivities would begin after the fight. Then even the old Christian ladies who taught their children and tried themselves to practice turning the other cheek would buy soft drinks, and if the Brown Bomber's° victory was a particularly bloody one they would order peanut patties and Baby Ruths, also.

Brown Bomber: nickname for Joe Louis

14   Bailey and I laid coins on top of the cash register. Uncle Willie didn't allow us to ring up sales during a fight. It was too noisy and might shake up the atmosphere. When the gong rang for the next round we pushed through the near-sacred quiet to the herd of children outside.

15   "He's got Louis against the ropes and now it's a left to the body and a right to the ribs. Another right to the body, it looks like it was low. . . . Yes, ladies and gentlemen, the referee is signaling but the contender keeps raining blows on Louis. It's another to the body, and it looks like Louis is going down."

16   My race groaned. It was our people falling. It was another lynching, yet another Black man hanging on a tree. One more woman ambushed and raped. A Black boy whipped and maimed. It was hounds on the trail of a man running through slimy swamps. It was a white woman slapping her maid for being forgetful.

17   The men in the Store stood away from the walls and at attention. Women greedily clutched the babes on their laps while on the porch the shufflings and smiles, flirtings and pinching of a few minutes before were gone. This might be the end of the world. If Joe lost we were back in slavery and beyond help. It would all be true, the accusations that we were lower types of human beings. Only a little higher than apes. True that we were stupid and ugly and lazy and dirty and, unlucky and worst of all, that God Himself hated us and ordained° us to be hewers° of wood and drawers° of water, forever and ever, world without end.

ordained: ordered

hewers: choppers

18   We didn't breathe. We didn't hope. We waited.

drawers: those who bring up

19   "He's off the ropes, ladies and gentlemen. He's moving towards the center of the ring." There was no time to be relieved. The worst might still happen.

20   "And now it looks like Joe is mad. He's caught Carnera with a left hook to the head and a right to the head. It's a left jab to the body and another left to the head. There's a left cross and a right to the head. The contender's right eye is bleeding and he can't seem to keep his block up. Louis is penetrating every block. The referee is moving in, but Louis sends a left to the body and it's an uppercut to the chin and the contender is dropping. He's on the canvas, ladies and gentlemen."

21   Babies slid to the floor as women stood up and men leaned toward the radio.

22   "Here's the referee. He's counting. One, two, three, four, five, six, seven. . . . Is the contender trying to get up again?"

23   All the men in the store shouted, "NO."

24   "—eight, nine, ten." There were a few sounds from the audience, but they seemed to be holding themselves against tremendous pressure.

25   "The fight is over, ladies and gentlemen. Let's get the microphone over to the referee. . . . Here he is. He's got the Brown Bomber's hand, he's holding it up. . . . Here he is. . . ."

26   Then the voice, husky and familiar, came to wash over us—"The winnah, and still heavyweight champeen° of the world . . . Joe Louis."

champeen:
slang for
champion

27   Champion of the world. A Black boy. Some Black mother's son.

28   He was the strongest man in the world. People drank Coca-Colas like ambrosia and ate candy bars like Christmas. Some of the men went behind the Store and poured white lightning° in their soft-drink bottles, and a few of the bigger boys followed them. Those who were not chased away came back blowing their breath in front of themselves like proud smokers.

white lightning:
homemade
alcoholic drink

29   It would take an hour or more before people would leave the Store and head home. Those who lived too far had made arrangements to stay in town. It wouldn't do for a Black man and his family to be caught on a lonely country road on a night when Joe Louis had proved that we were the strongest people in the world.

➤ Follow-Up Questions

1. What specific techniques does Angelou skillfully use to keep the tension in her narrative?
2. What link does Angelou make between Joe Louis and the black community?
3. Angelou balances the elements of glory and cruel reality within her narrative. What would be considered examples of such balances?

➤ Short Writing Assignments

1. Does race still play as important a part in sports as it did in the 1930s? Write a paragraph taking a **position** on this topic and support your **argument** with specific **examples.**
2. Compose a brief **persuasive** essay that proposes reasons why sports play such an important part in the American culture today.

➤ Extended Writing Assignments

1. Many major sports heroes today make even more money through their endorsement of products and services than through their playing. Should such a policy be continued? Write a **position** paper elaborating your ideas on this topic. Consider in your essay the fact that many fans of sports heroes are young people who often come from families who cannot afford the high prices of some commodities.

2. Form a research group to investigate the Louis fight. Your **research** should consider such sources as old newspapers and magazines, as well as personal narratives from those, like Angelou, who may remember the fight and how his/her community responded to Louis's victory. Consider how the fight was received by different sources and why, as well as the accuracy of Angelou's memory of the fight. Explain your findings in a report.

How Friendship Was "Feminized"

Carol Tarvis

Introductory Remarks: A graduate of Brandeis University with her undergraduate degree and the University of Michigan with her doctorate, Carol Tarvis has written books as well as numerous essays that have appeared in the *New York Times* and elsewhere. Among her works are *The Female Experience, Anger: The Misunderstood Emotion,* and others.

Pre-Reading Ideas: The differences between the genders have been explored, researched, explained, debated, and generally discussed by authorities in the field as well as by everyday people. That doesn't mean that any conclusions that can help us understand each other better have been reached. Rather, individual differences usually cloud the issues even more. However, researchers have generalized that women *tend* to act in a particular way in given circumstances, whereas men *tend* to behave in another way in the same situation. Thus, how each gender behaves in homosocial settings as opposed to heterosocial settings and how masculine and feminine characteristics overlap or do not overlap in those settings are of special concern for Tarvis in this article. An interesting experiment might be to observe groups of friends without letting them know they are being observed in social settings and determine whether gender has an influence on behavior.

Vocabulary: Looking up and understanding the following words prior to reading should prepare you for the author's message. Other words will be defined in the margin.

Damon and Pythias   Hamlet and Horatio   Laurel and Hardy
Butch Cassidy and the Sundance Kid   Lone Ranger and Tonto
camaraderie   Scarlet O'Hara

1   Once upon a time and not so very long ago, everyone thought that men had the great and true-blue friendships. The cultural references stretched through time and art: Damon and Pythias, Hamlet and Horatio, Butch Cassidy and the Sundance Kid. The Lone Ranger never rode off with anyone but Tonto, and Laurel never once abandoned Hardy in whatever fine mess he got them into.

2   Male friendships were said to grow from the deep roots of shared experience and faithful camaraderie, whereas women's friendships were portrayed as shallow, trivial, and competitive, like Scarlet O'Hara's with her sisters. Women, it was commonly claimed, would sell each other out for the right guy, and even for a good time with the wrong one.

3   Some social scientists told us that this difference was hard-wired, a result of our evolutionary history. In the early 1970's, for example, the anthropologist° Lionel Tiger argued in "Men in Groups" that "male bonding" originated in prehistoric male hunting groups and was carried on today in equivalent pack-like activities: sports, politics, business and war.

4   Apparently, women's evolutionary task of rummaging° around in the garden to gather the odd yam or kumquat° was a solo effort, so females do not bond in the same way. Women prattle° on about their feelings, went the stereotype, but men act.

5   My, how times have changed. Today, we are deluged° in the wave of best-selling books that celebrate female friendships—*Girlfriends, Sisters, Mothers and Daughters,* and its clever clone, *Daughters and Mothers.* The success of this genre° is partly because the book market is so oriented° to female readers these days.

6   But it is also a likely result of two trends that began in the 1970's and 1980's: Female scholars began to dispel° the men-are-better stereotype in all domains° and women became the majority of psychotherapists°. The result was a positive reassessment of the qualities associated with women, including a "feminizing" of definitions of intimacy and friendship.

7   Accordingly, female friendships are now celebrated as the deep and abiding ones, based as they are on shared feelings and confidences. Male friendships are scorned° as superficial, based as they are on shared interests in, say, the Mets° and Michelle Pfeiffer°.

8   In our psychologized culture, *intimacy* is defined as what many women like to do with their friends: talk, express feelings, and disclose worries. Psychologists, most of whom are good talkers, validate° this definition as the true measure of intimacy. For example, in a study of "intimacy maturity" in marriage, published in the *Journal of Personality and Social Psychology,* researchers equated "Most mature" with "most verbally expressive." As a woman, I naturally think this is a perfectly sensible equation, but I also know it is an incomplete one. To label people mature or immature, you also have to know how they actually behave toward others.

9   What about all the men and women who support their families, put the wishes of other family members ahead of their own or act in moral and considerate ways when conflicts arise? They are surely mature, even if they are

anthropologist: an individual involved in the study of human beings

rummaging: searching

kumquat: a small orange-colored citrus fruit

prattle: talk in a childish way

deluged: flooded

genre: category

oriented: directed

dispel: get rid of

domains: areas

psychotherapists: those who treat individuals with mental illness

scorned: to treat as worthless

Mets: New York baseball club

Michelle Pfeiffer: a contemporary film actress

validate: approve

inarticulate:
unable to speak

companionable:
to be with
another person

worrisome:
causing worry

stoicism: not
showing pain or
emotion

reminisced:
spoke of the past

ruminating:
thinking deeply
about

invert: reverse

inarticulate° or do not express their feelings easily. Indeed, what about all the men and women who define intimacy in terms of deeds rather than words: sharing activities, helping one another or enjoying companionable° silence? Too bad for them. That's a "male" definition, and out of favor in these talky times.

10   Years ago, my husband had to have some worrisome° medical tests, and the night before he was to go to the hospital we went to dinner with one of his best friends, who was visiting from England. I watched, fascinated, as male stoicism° combined with English reserve produced a decidedly unfemale-like encounter. They laughed, they told stories, they argued about movies, they reminisced°. Neither mentioned the hospital, their worries, or their affection for each other. They didn't need to.

11   It is true that women's style of intimacy has many benefits. A large body of research in health psychology and social psychology finds that women's greater willingness to talk about feelings improves their mental and physical health and makes it easier to ask for help.

12   But as psychologists like Susan Nolen-Hoeksema of Stanford University have shown, women's fondness for ruminating° about feelings can also prolong depression, anxiety and anger. And it can keep women stuck in bad jobs or relationships, instead of getting out of them or doing what is necessary to make them better.

13   Books and movies that validate women's friendships are overdue, and welcome as long as they don't simply invert° the stereotype. Playing the women-are-better game is fun, but it blinds us to the universal need for intimacy and the many forms that friendship takes. Maybe men could learn a thing or two about friendship from women. But who is to say that women couldn't learn a thing or two from them in exchange?

➤ Follow-Up Questions

1. What are some of the stereotypes of men and women which Tarvis addresses in the opening part of her essay?
2. Does Tarvis distinguish between female and male intimacy?
3. What would be considered the positive and negative forms of feminine intimacy?

➤ Short Writing Assignments

1. Gender is a set of behaviors which society constructs for the individual. A review of men's and women's fashions in dress and hair in the 1700s or 1800s reveals many of the changes that have occurred. Likewise, many changes have occurred just within the last fifty years. Choose either an extended historical period or a more recent time and compare and contrast the style of dress and hair for either men or women. Then write a **comparison-and-contrast** essay that details your findings.
2. Tarvis identifies several literary and popular culture friendships, such as Hamlet and Horatio, and Scarlet O'Hara and her sisters. In a paragraph, identify two females who have a strong friendship in either literature or pop culture and explain why you think they are successful and respected by society.

➤ Extended Writing Assignments

1. Set up your own research project to determine the accuracy of Tarvis's article. Choose one of her statements regarding the behavior of men or women. Then observe individuals in an everyday setting such as restaurants, grocery stores, or shopping malls to test this theory. Also interview a sample of the population, for example, people from a variety of ages and an equal number of men and women. Then prepare an oral presentation that explains your findings, including a brief handout for your audience and a written report for your instructor.

2. View a past television program which involves friendship, such as *I Love Lucy,* and any television programs that have aired within the last five years. Make a note of the elements that bond the friends together, how the friends help each other and/or cause trouble for each other, and the ways in which they handle stress in the relationship. Then prepare a **comparison-and-contrast** paper in which you detail your findings. Conclude your essay by taking a position as to which single quality is the most beneficial to a relationship.

CONCLUSION

Language is a growing and evolving component of any culture. Every generation and every new "age" (the Age of Technology, the Space Age, and so forth) leave indelible marks on the vocabulary, either adding new words or changing existing meanings. Parents and children have consistently had communication problems as long as parents fail to grow with the language and children fail to explain new meanings to their parents. Communication becomes even more difficult for non-native speakers, who must learn not only the literal meanings of words but slang, idioms, and clichés that add interesting elements to language. For example, think of the following expressions and how they might be (mis)understood by non-English speakers: "The whole kit and kaboodle"; "There are many ways to skin a cat"; and "Keep an eye out." Think about the Jerry Seinfeld commercial in which Seinfeld is trying to entertain a British audience but fails until he tours the surrounding countryside, talks to the residents, and learns the language. He returns to the stage, delivers a punchline, and makes the British audience laugh while Americans, and possibly others, are left (as some might say) clueless. Again, the composition adage that tells the writer "Know your audience" is applicable to many areas of life.

➤ Further Writing Topics

Personal Narrative

Ralph Waldo Emerson, a nineteenth-century essayist and philosopher wrote, "To be great is to be misunderstood." Unfortunately, to be misunderstood does not guarantee greatness, but instead probably ensures we will get into trouble. Think of a time when something you said was completely misunderstood and nothing you could say to explain helped the situation. How did you finally make yourself clear? What happened?

Exposition

Go to a grocery store or a large discount store on a Saturday, when many families go shopping. Select a family that you will follow at a discreet distance as they shop and observe their use of language—verbal as well as nonverbal. Try not to let the family know you are observing them so they will behave naturally. Write a **descriptive** essay explaining language usage between adults and children in public.

Analysis

Elizabeth Wong and Richard Rodriguez discuss the difficulties they had with public and private language. Write an **analytical** essay that **compares and contrasts** how each author dealt with the problem.

Argumentation

There have been many attempts in many states to make English the official language of the United States. Investigate what this means to non-English speakers. Take a **position** on whether English should be made the official language of the United States and write an essay attempting to **persuade** your readers to share your position.

➤ Suggested Chapter Projects

1. Several articles in this chapter deal with the interrelationship between language and cultural acceptance. Often what one individual sees as the immigrant's inability to speak a new language results from the sound patterns the immigrant learned in his/her native culture. Choose a language other than the one(s) you already know. Investigate both the written letters used in the language and the sounds of those letters. You may find that some languages do not use "letters": at times what appear as letters are actually symbols representing whole words. Find what you consider to be ten variations between this new language and standard English; such variations can come in the form of sound, how the character is formed, a difference in punctuation, or other distinctions. Prepare a report that **compares and contrasts** the two language systems and be prepared to demonstrate orally to the class how such language characteristics sound.

2. Many issues involved with assimilating or acculturating to a new society or culture are the result of differences between what is expected and what is the reality in the new society. Interview several immigrants or foreign visitors to America to find out their expectations prior to coming to the United States and then what they found to be the reality. You may want to ask them what helped to create their expectations, such as movies and magazines they may have seen in their native country. Prepare a report that compares and/or contrasts three of the main views of America and the actualities that were found.

3. Since the invention of the mechanized clock, the issue of regulated time has been a possibility in the world. However, some cultures move in a different time-frame. Even in America, industries such as farming, are on a different schedule than, for example, the Internal Revenue Service, or the average worker. Consider the different views of time that operate now in the United States or in another culture. Then write a report explaining at least three different views of time, how such time is allocated for work, play, religion, or other activities. Conclude your report with your own **evaluation** of how you think the American culture truly regulates and values time.

CHAPTER 7

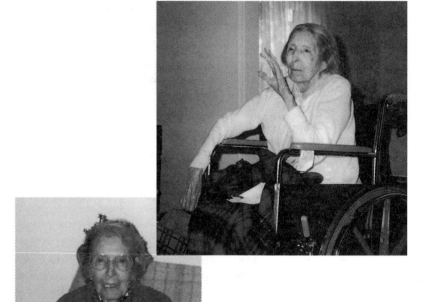

A Solitary Life
Source: Elizabeth Rodriguez Kessler, photographer

Relationships: Living with Others

Research shows that from birth, human beings need socialization. They need to be touched, talked to, and played with so they can grow, develop, and learn social skills. Failure to do this results in emotional retardation, lack of self-esteem, paranoia, antisocial behavior, and, in extreme cases, death. Yet not all socialization results in positive relationships. Parents and guardians are regarded as a source of safety and strength, but they are sometimes the people who violate their own children as well as others. On a lesser but still important scale, when children grow into adults, they can have difficulty accepting others and find themselves in conflict with others who disagree with their beliefs.

May Sarton writes a personal narrative celebrating the joys of living alone. Sandra Cisneros and Martin Espada use fiction and poetry to describe the effects of child abuse. Sojourner Truth delivers a highly charged yet gracefully charming feminist speech about her rights as a woman. Finally, R. Watson discusses life and death in his poem.

The material in this chapter brings up some interesting ideas to explore and research. Human beings enjoy being social, so why would anyone choose to live alone? Interviewing men and women of various generations about living alone could provide some interesting information about relationships, especially if the interviewees are in committed relationships but choose to or must live apart. Another topic of interest might be the changing roles of men and women over the years. In addition, the rising incidence of child abuse says something about our society. Researching the topic could uncover some surprising information about how individuals justify child abuse. On a lighter note, have you ever wondered what happened on the day you were born? Were you born during a historical moment? On an important day? Researching your birth date or a grandparent's birth date might reveal some interesting facts.

The Rewards of Living a Solitary Life

May Sarton

Introductory Remarks: May Sarton was born in Belgium but moved to the United States, where she became a citizen, at the age of twelve. One of her numerous essays, "The Rewards of Living a Solitary Life," has become a well-known piece. Sarton also wrote poetry and fiction and received numerous awards. In addition to her career as a writer, Sarton also taught writing.

Pre-Reading Ideas: Human beings are generally social creatures. They prefer to have companionship and participate in social, religious, and academic functions that involve being with others. Although there are times when we need to be alone for a while for whatever reason, most of us do not care for the idea of living alone. Finding oneself without someone to share ideas with, eat meals with, or even sit in silence with can create feelings of abandonment or extreme loneliness. There are others, however, who prefer solitude, who find that being alone is not the same as being lonely, and who find the presence of others inhibiting and distracting. If you have ever lived alone, you probably fit somewhere between the two extremes, being neither a hermit nor feeling anxiety-ridden without human contact. The following essay describes Sarton's solitary life of twenty years and her feelings about her solitude. Do you have any friends or know of other literary or historical figures who prefer the solitary life? How do they compare with Sarton?

Vocabulary: Looking up and understanding the following words prior to reading should prepare you for the author's message. Other words will be defined in the margin.

gregarious   bliss   acutely

acquaintance: a person one knows

1   The other day an acquaintance° of mine, a gregarious and charming man, told me he had found himself unexpectedly alone in New York for an hour or two between appointments. He went to the Whitney and spent the "empty" time looking at things in solitary bliss. For him it proved to be a shock nearly as great as falling in love to discover that he could enjoy himself so much alone.

2   What had he been afraid of, I asked myself? That, suddenly alone, he would discover that he bored himself, or that there was, quite simply, no self there to meet? But having taken the plunge, he is now on the brink° of adventure; he is about to be launched° into his own inner space, space as immense°, unexplored, and sometimes frightening as outer space to the astronaut. His every perception° will come to him with a new freshness and, for a time, seem startlingly original. For anyone who can see things for himself with a naked eye becomes, for a moment or two, something of a genius. With another human being present vision becomes double vision, inevitably°. We are

brink: edge
launched: sent forth or sent out
immense: large
perception: awareness

inevitably: unavoidable

impact: influence

diffused: widely spread out

busy wondering, what does my companion see or think of this, and what do I think of it? The original impact° gets lost, or diffused°.

3   "Music I heard with you was more than music." Exactly. And therefore music *itself* can only be heard alone. Solitude is the salt of personhood. It brings out the authentic flavor of every experience.

4   "Alone one is never lonely: the spirit adventures, walking / In a quiet garden, in a cool house, abiding single there."

5   Loneliness is most acutely felt with other people, for with others, even with a lover sometimes, we suffer from our differences of taste, temperament, mood. Human intercourse° often demands that we soften the edge of perception, or withdraw at the very instant of personal truth for fear of hurting, or of being inappropriately° present, which is to say naked, in a social situation. Alone we can afford to be wholly whatever we are, and to feel whatever we feel absolutely. That is a great luxury!

intercourse: communication between individuals

inappropriately: not correctly

6   For me the most interesting thing about a solitary life, and mine has been that for the last twenty years, is that it becomes increasingly rewarding. When I can wake up and watch the sun rise over the ocean, as I do most days, and know that I have an entire day ahead, uninterrupted, in which to write a few pages, take a walk with my dog, lie down in the afternoon for a long think (why does one think better in a horizontal° position?), read, and listen to music, I am flooded with happiness.

horizontal: flat or level with the ground

7   I am lonely only when I am overtired, when I have worked too long without a break, when for the time being I feel empty and need filling up. And I am lonely sometimes when I come back home after a lecture trip, when I have seen a lot of people and talked a lot, and am full to the brim with experience that needs to be sorted out.

8   Then for a little while the house feels huge and empty, and I wonder where my self is hiding. It has to be recaptured slowly by watering the plants, perhaps, and looking again at each one as though it were a person, by feeding the two cats, by cooking a meal.

9   It takes a while, as I watch the surf blowing up in fountains at the end of the field, but the moment comes when the world falls away, and the self emerges again from the deep unconscious, bringing back all I have recently experienced to be explored and slowly understood, when I can converse again with my hidden powers, and so grow, and so be renewed, till death do us part.

➤ Follow-Up Questions

1. Why would Sarton begin her essay with someone else's experiences with solitude instead of her own?
2. What causes Sarton to feel lonely?
3. After feeling lonely, how does Sarton recover her appreciation of solitude and her sense of "self"?

➤ Short Writing Assignments

1. **Define** your own view of what it means to be lonely and explain your view in paragraph form. End your essay by considering if one can be lonely in a room full of people.
2. In a short essay, **describe** two or three jobs that require an employee to work alone. In your discussion, **analyze** the pros and cons of such jobs.

➤ Extended Writing Assignments

1. The idea of the lone American as a cultural hero extends back to the frontier days; often the tradition involved only men, who were represented as the lone frontiersman or cowboy. **Research** the movies or literature to find one such "lone hero" and investigate the qualities that make the individual an American hero. You may consider a hero or heroine from pop culture for your research.
2. Has the computer contributed to the trend of being alone? Explain your response to this question in an **argumentative** essay that gives specific **examples** to support your ideas.

What Sally Said

Sandra Cisneros

Introductory Remarks: For information about Cisneros, see "My Name," in Chapter 4: Identity.

Pre-Reading Ideas: Physical abuse and sexual abuse of children are crimes, and many victims suffer at the hands of people they trust and love: fathers, mothers, aunts, uncles, ministers, neighbors, Boy Scout leaders, and so forth. Unfortunately, the crime is frequently hidden because the child loves the individual who abuses him or her, is threatened with more extensive physical harm, or is simply ashamed and feels guilty about his or her role in the incident(s). At other times, if the individual who molests the child is the father, the mother may not believe or want to believe the child, thereby further covering up the abuse. Cisneros writes realistically about a young girl with an abusive father whose crime escalates as time passes and who is allowed to continue the abuse. Laws have been passed requiring adults such as teachers, counselors, neighbors, and others to report suspected incidents of child abuse; however, this does not always happen. Just as the child is afraid to say anything, sometimes the adults are fearful of getting involved or afraid for the safety of their own family. Surprisingly, some adults feel that child abuse is not wrong, believing that they are responsible for disciplining their child as they see fit. The issues of physical abuse and sexual abuse of children are sensitive issues and ones people feel are controversial.

lard: fat from hogs

1   He never hits me hard. She said her mama rubs lard° on all the places where it hurts. Then at school she'd say she fell. That's where all the blue places come from. That's why her skin is always scarred.

2   But who believes her. A girl that big, a girl who comes in with her pretty face all beaten and black can't be falling off the stairs. He never hits me hard.

3   But Sally doesn't tell about the time he hit her with his hand just like a dog, she said, like if I was an animal. He thinks I'm going to run away like his sisters who made the family ashamed. Just because I'm a daughter, and then she doesn't say.

4   Sally was going to get permission to stay with us a little and one Thursday she came finally with a sack full of clothes and a paper bag of sweetbread her mama sent. And would've stayed too except when the dark came her father, whose eyes were little from crying, knocked on the door and said please come back, this is the last time. And she said Daddy and went home.

5   Then we didn't need to worry. Until one day Sally's father catches her talking to a boy and the next day she doesn't come to school And the next. Until the way Sally tells it, he just went crazy, he just forgot he was her father between the buckle and the belt.

6   You're not my daughter, you're not my daughter. And then he broke into his hands.

➤ Follow-Up Questions

1. What images does Cisneros present of the mother in the story?
2. What excuses does the father give in the story to justify his actions? Are these reasons acceptable?
3. Is the father sincere in his display of remorse?

➤ Short Writing Assignments

1. Often when school officials and teachers suspect a student is being abused, they are frustrated by the student's denial of such incidents. Make a list of the excuses school officials and teachers hear from students who cover up abuse in one way or another. Also, add to your list those signs, such as bruising, which these adults should be aware of.
2. In paragraph form, write your own response to Sally's statement that her father "never hits me hard."

➤ Extended Writing Assignments

1. Research the issue of abuse to determine the reasons why individuals abuse others on a continual basis. Explain your findings in an **informative** essay.
2. Assume that you are Sally's teacher, and one day, in a conversation about her bruises, she tells you that her father doesn't "hit me hard." Write a dialogue between you and your student Sally to show how you would handle the situation.

When the Leather Is a Whip

Martin Espada

Introductory Remarks: Award-winning poet, editor, and literature professor, Martin Espada has written five books of poetry, including his two most recent publications *City of Coughing and Dead Radiators* and *Imagine the Angels of Bread.* He is the editor of *Poetry Like Bread: Poets of the Political Imagination.*

Pre-Reading Ideas: When a child experiences physical or sexual abuse, the memories linger with the child for the rest of his or her life. Although the pain will eventually fade, the experience has long-lasting and far-reaching effects on the victim as well as on those with whom the victim lives as an adult. Espada's poem depicts not the experience his wife underwent but one small way he must deal with her memory. Despite the lack of graphic detail, Espada creates a sense of horror and fear in many readers as the reminder of physical or sexual abuse appears in even the smallest detail of daily life.

```
    At night
    with my wife
    sitting on the bed,
    I turn from her
  5 to unbuckle
    my belt
    so she won't see
    her father
    unbuckling
 10 his belt.
```

➤ Follow-Up Questions

1. How would you describe the type of man the woman in the poem has married?
2. What is the implication of the man turning away from his wife to remove his belt?
3. In such a condensed poem, each word is significant. Pick out three or four words that you feel are most significant to the poem and briefly explain why

➤ Short Writing Assignments

1. Create a pamphlet that you would distribute to elementary school children to help them avoid abuse of any kind, whether verbal, physical, sexual, or possibly even self-abuse, such as eating too much candy.
2. One of the issues regarding abuse is how to get the victim to report the crime or incident. One of the issues involved is the sex of the victim. Do you feel that women or

men are more likely to report an abuse crime? Write a paragraph that takes a **position** of this issue and support your **argument** with specific **examples.**

➤ Extended Writing Assignments

1. Victims of abuse often return either to their abuser or to a person with the same type of personality, thus beginning the abusive cycle all over again. **Research** the causes of such behavior by the victims to discover why they have difficulty breaking the cycle. Then prepare a report that explains the **causes and effects** of abuse.

2. Recovery and healing are very important parts of the overall process to help a victim of abuse, both for the physical and psychological damage. Form a research group to discover the types of recovery programs in your area. For this project, you should consider self-abuse, in the form of drugs, alcohol, or gambling, as possible avenues of research. Then prepare a report that **divides** the programs in your community into specific kinds and **classifies** the services they provide. Conclude your essay with your own **evaluation** regarding the effectiveness of such programs.

Ain't I a Woman?

Sojourner Truth

Introductory Remarks: Sojourner Truth was a slave who escaped her owners and began to travel (sojourn) and spread her messages of truth. As a speaker, she was an outspoken advocate of women's rights. In 1851, while slavery was still legal in many states, Truth attended the Women's Rights Conference, where she delivered the following speech to an audience composed mainly of white women; Elizabeth Cady Stanton°, who was in the audience, wrote it down.

Elizabeth Cady Stanton: a social reformer who fought for womens' right to vote

Pre-Reading Ideas: Think about what you know about feminism. Frequently, those who don't know its history or its proponents are familiar with only the militant groups that incite political conflict. Others, however, are familiar with leaders such as Elizabeth Cady Stanton who led the fight for women's right to vote so that one-half of the American adult population would no longer be silenced. Among those who spoke out for the enfranchisement° of women was Sojourner Truth, a woman who would have to wait until women gained suffrage° before her voice could be legally recognized. Read her speech aloud and listen for the rhythm and the beauty of her language, especially clauses like, "That's it, honey" and the concluding sentence.

enfranchisement: admission into citizenship

suffrage: voting rights

Vocabulary: Looking up and understanding the following words prior to reading should prepare you for the author's message. An additional word will be defined in the margin.

racket   **out of kilter**   **last**

'twixt: between

1   Well, children, where there is so much racket there must be something out of kilter. I think that 'twixt° the negroes of the South and the women of the North, all talking about rights, the white men will be in a fix pretty soon. But what's all this here talking about?

2   That man over there says that women need to be helped into carriages, and lifted over ditches, and to have the best place everywhere. Nobody helps me into carriages, or over mud-puddles, or gives me the best place! And ain't I a woman? Look at me! Look at my arm! I have ploughed and planted, and gathered into barns, and no man could head me. And ain't I a woman? I could work as much and eat as much as a man—when I could get it—and bear the last as well! And ain't I a woman? I have borne thirteen children, and seen them most all sold off to slavery, and when I cried out with my mother's grief, none but Jesus heard me! And ain't I a woman.

3   Then they talk about this thing in the head; what's this they call it? [Intellect, someone whispers.] That's it, honey. What's that got to do with women's rights or negro's rights? If my cup won't hold but a pint and yours holds a quart, wouldn't you be mean not to let me have my little half-measure full?

4   Then that little man in black there, he says women can't have as much rights as men, 'cause Christ wasn't a woman! Where did your Christ come from? Where did your Christ come from? From God and a woman! Man had nothing to do with Him.

5   If the first woman God ever made was strong enough to turn the world upside down all alone, these women together ought to be able to turn it back and get it right side up again! And now they is asking to do it, the men better let them.

6   Obliged to you for hearing me, and now old Sojourner ain't got nothing more to say.

➤ Follow-Up Questions

1. Describe Truth's response to the idea that women need to be "helped," "lifted," and given the "best."
2. Does Truth feel that women are the intellectual equal of men?
3. Truth refers to her audience at the beginning as "children." By using such a term, what relationship does she establish with her audience and how is this an effective strategy for her speech?

➤ Short Writing Assignments

1. **Research** the Internet for the Web sites of organizations for women, such as the National Organization for Women, to see what issues they are currently addressing. Then write a short essay explaining such issues and what actions the organizations are suggesting.
2. Make a list of female personalities who are the main anchors for a variety of television programs. Try to list as many as possible. Then review your research to determine

what types of programs these women lead and when they are aired. For example, how significant is it for a woman to anchor a major newscast for a large network, such as CNN or NBC, if her program only airs at 3:00 a.m.? Then prepare a short essay that **evaluates** your findings as to the equality for women in television broadcasting.

➤ Extended Writing Assignments

1. Putting a woman metaphorically on a "pedestal," that is, idealizing her, comes at a price. Consider the effects of idealizing or romanticizing women when, in reality, women face the usual problems of everyday life in terms of jobs, family, laws, health issues, and educational efforts. Compose an essay that identifies three main **effects** of such idealization and/or romanticization of women.
2. Do women enjoy complete equal rights with men in American society? You may want to **research** opportunities in the workplace, education, military, and law before preparing your essay. In your report, take a definite **position** and defend your **argument** with specific examples.

The Nail Star Revisited

R. Watson

Introductory Remarks: R. (Randall) Watson has been the recipient of numerous prizes, some of which include the Chelsea Award in poetry, as well as grants from InPrint Inc. and the Cultural Arts Council of Houston and Harris County. His poems and essays have appeared in, among others, *ArtLies*, *The Georgia Review*, *The North American Review*, *Shenandoah*, and *The Western Humanities Review*. His work has also recently been translated into Spanish. "The Nail Star (Revisited)" first appeared in *Chelsea*. He received his BA from Sarah Lawrence College in 1981, his MFA from the University of Montana in 1986, and his PhD from the University of Houston in 1995. He currently teaches composition, creative writing, American literature, as well as other literature courses at Houston Community College and the University of Houston.

Pre-Reading Ideas: Have you ever wondered what happened on the day you were born? In the following poem, the narrator lists the events that took place on the day of his or her birth. From the perspective of relationships and living with others, this poem describes the way people live among others privately and in society. The birth of the narrator was only one of the many events that happened on that particular day, and it signaled the beginning of a relationship with his mother and others that he does not discuss, choosing instead to concentrate only on those activities outside himself. Can what happened on the day one is born have an impact on one's life? While the following poem discusses only situations involving individuals, think of the global events, war, famine, cures for diseases, peace agreements, and so forth, which involve relationships among many people, that which could ultimately affect everyone. Do some research to find out what significant events occurred on your birth date. Did they have any impact on your life or future?

Vocabulary: Looking up and understanding the following words prior to reading should prepare you for the author's message. Other words will be defined in the margin.

arthritis   succubus

The day I was born a streetlamp plunged
hissing into the sea. The head mechanic
at Faber's Auto Repair collapsed in the heat,
the desk clerk at the Oconee Hotel spun
5 two shining bullets in the chambers of his heart,
his cheap-blue, three-piece suit
as pale as his faded eyes.
It was the day two teenage lovers timed
the lights on Main Street with their eyes closed,
10 when women swam out into the sea
until the strength in their muscles failed
then floated back, a day when trees stood
ankle deep in ash, and junkies waited
patiently on the impatient lines of people
15 wanting death. It was the day
children with arthritis wept, wiping their eyes
with newsprint. When men with black hair
set off flares at night, revealing nothing
but themselves, and Chevron stations
20 lit up red like flags that spared
no one, the attendants' silhouettes°
hunched up behind the cars like dusk.
It was the day the syllables broke
and sentences slumbered at the curb,
25 the day my eyes, blinded
by the magic of my mother's blood,
opened, fluent in esperanto°, the day the midwife
sucked my mouth and nostrils clean
with a kiss. Outside I could hear
30 insects moving in the damp shadows, sensed
a face in a mirror, turn, ashamed, away
from itself, the televisions weeping,
wiring hidden in the walls
beginning to heat up and to burn,
35 starting, like all fires, at the core
and moving outwards, breaking at last
from its sheath into flame, a succubus

silhouettes:
outlines

esperanto:
a language
invented in 1887
for international
use

assuming form, rising inside me,
her pale arms as thin as an uncooperative vein,
40 her hand in mine, our tattooed forearms
full of roses straining to hold light.

➤ Follow-Up Questions

1. Based on the information in the poem, what do you determine to be the year the poem's narrator was born?
2. What are the tones or feelings Watson creates in the poem? Identify specific words or phrases that helped create such feelings.
3. Which would you consider the three most striking **images** in the poem, and what do you think is Watson's strategy for using them?

➤ Short Writing Assignments

1. The rose is traditionally a **symbol** for romantic love and/or a beautiful woman. Consider how Watson employs the rose **image** in the poem. Then write a short essay describing how he wishes his readers to consider the rose image.
2. Research a particular day's events in newspapers and/or magazines, considering all sections of the sources, not just the political news. Then compose your own poem, starting with the line, "The day I wrote this poem. . . . "

➤ Extended Writing Assignments

1. Catalogue (make a list) of the images Watson uses in lines 1 through 28 and again in lines 30 through 41. Note what the images are and classify them according to whether they are **concrete** or **abstract** representing emotions, mysticism, or imagination. Then write an essay describing how Watson moves his reader's imagination from the **concrete** to the real, to a more illusive or fantasy world, using specific images from the poem as **examples.** Conclude your essay with what you feel is the narrator's final view of his or her birth.
2. Look at the images of the women in the poem. Birth is a time often focused on mother and child, but after reviewing the poem's female figures, decide how important such a "mother image" is to the work and what other types of female images the poem contains. Then prepare an essay that explains your **analysis.**

CONCLUSION

As May Sarton points out in her essay, it's sometimes easier and more rewarding to live alone than it is to live with others. However, we cannot completely escape living in and being a part of society, and because of that, we frequently have to make accommodations for others so we can avoid conflict and live in relative harmony with each other. Unfortunately, public and private relationships are not always good for each person involved, and the works in this chapter clearly explain that.

➤ Further Writing Topics

Personal Narrative

Sometimes writing about difficult situations helps the writer cope with unresolved feelings and bring closure to a particular event. Think about a relationship you have had or are in that was not/is not all you expected it to be. Tell your story from the first-person point of view, allowing all the memories to spill out on the page. Sometimes writing it at different times helps you remember things you might have forgotten. After you have recorded everything, go back and organize the narrative into a **chronological** pattern. You may omit incidents that are too painful, too private, or that you simply do not want to share with others.

Exposition

Using Sojourner Truth's speech, "Ain't I a Woman?" write a declaration of your identity as a(n) _____. List and develop the characteristics that define you as the person you declare you are. Avoid using her self-definition of woman.

Analysis

Using May Sarton's narrative, "The Rewards of Living a Solitary Life," determine her **thesis** and the points she uses to construct her **argument**. Write a **summary analysis** of her essay. Remember that your thesis is a reflection of her argument not an **assertion** of your opinion.

Argumentation

Living with others can bring both joy and pain, but living alone also can bring the joy of self-sufficiency and the sadness of loneliness. Each way of life has its rewards and drawbacks. Choose one lifestyle and write an **argumentative** essay supporting your choice over the other.

➤ Suggested Chapter Projects

1. While most of us have relationships with other human individuals, we frequently maintain one with a pet. In our relationship with the world of animals we often create changes in the animal that we may not even be aware of. Choose a registered breed of dog or cat and **research** how the animal has been "designed" over time. To determine how such design or change in physical features has developed, find a picture of the animal twenty to fifty years ago and compare it to the standards of the breed today. Then research the physical problems such "designing" through breeding now causes the animal. Write a report in which you explain the standards of the breed you chose to research, its changes over an extended period of time, and some of the physical problems such breeding now causes the animals.
2. Accuracy in reporting is a must for any newscast, but if the anchorperson is not perceived as trustworthy, then the information given may not be well received by the

public. Watch a wide variety of news programs to determine the many points, both obvious and subtle, which give credibility to the program. Consider the exact dress of the anchorperson and his/her hair cut as well as the desk used, whether the person stands or sits, the backdrop of the program, the efficiency of switching from anchor to video, and so forth. Then determine those qualities which best represent "honest reporting" and explain these features in an essay, citing specific examples to support. Conclude your essay with an **evaluation** of whether the sex of the anchorperson is a major factor or not, all other factors being equal.

3. The issue of gender identity is central to many of the pieces in this chapter and within this textbook. The arguments involving this issue move, basically, between two poles, masculine and feminine. What if there were a third gender; not one that was a combination of the two that already exist or one that was totally neutral in all respects, but, literally, a third form of gender. Compose a **descriptive** essay that details the social construction of such a gender: how it acts in public and in private, its "traditional roles" in the family, how it should dress, what pronoun should be used, and so forth.

CHAPTER 8

L.A. Riots
Source: © Michael Newman/PhotoEdit

Misconceptions: Stereotypes, Prejudice, and War

Stereotypes, prejudice, and war are ugly elements society has been burdened with since individuals became aware of the differences between themselves and others. Ethnic cleansing, religious conflicts, desires to expand a country's borders, and other issues have led to pain, brutality, and extermination of large groups of people. But on a less global scale, stereotypes and prejudice exist on a daily, common level. Hate crimes target individuals because they belong to certain ethnicities or because they practice alternative lifestyles. In the recent past, James Byrd was a victim, brutally murdered because he was African-American. Matthew Shepard was beaten and left to die because he was gay. Yet there are individuals who strongly believe that passage of a hate crimes law does more harm than good.

This chapter addresses the misconceptions that people have about others. Even if the misconception is as seemingly complimentary as attributing talent and intelligence to Asians, as Felicia Lee discusses in her article "Model Minority," it is still an example of giving attributes to individuals because they belong to a certain group. Frank Chin and Liliana Heker provide views somewhat different but no less disturbing. In Chin's short story and Heker's personal narrative, each author describes children victimized by members of their own heritage. Albert Camarillo in his "Zoot Suit Riots" describes what happens when a group retaliates against injustice that appears to be supported by police and city government. Lini Kadaba, on the other hand, writes an expository essay discussing the survival of fast-food chains like McDonald's in countries where residents do not eat beef because of dietary laws or prefer other foods over beef.

Writings arising from this chapter can begin from highly charged emotional feelings, especially if you have ever received insulting remarks based on your race, gender, religion, sexual orientation, or age. Beyond the personal narrative is also the opportunity to write letters to the editor about incidents concerning hate crimes or argumentative articles about racism, sexism, agism, or homophobia in the workplace, in housing, in the classroom, and in other places. Another controversial topic that lends itself to misconceptions is affirmative action. That topic could also provide research material to support a strong argumentative essay. Take some time before you begin reading the works in this chapter to consider your feelings and/or experiences with any of these examples of prejudice and write about them in your journal.

Donald Duk and the White Monsters

Frank Chin

Introductory Remarks: Playwright and novelist Frank Chin has been writing since the 1960s. He graduated from the University of California at Berkeley and was the first Chinese-American to have a play produced on the New York stage. The following piece is from his novel, *Donald Duk* Chin is widely known as an angry protestor, one who attacks the sinister villain stereotype of the Asian male, criticizes the failure of mainstream publishers to publish Asian male writers, critiques the misrepresentation and devaluing of the traditional Asian culture by other Asian writers, and attempts to create images of strong, independent Asian males. Chin is clearly a controversial writer who feels the need to disturb and confront the public's false beliefs and to poke fun at and see humor in the elements of ethnic identity.

Pre-Reading Ideas: Growing up as a member of a heritage different from the dominant society can leave one vulnerable to racial discrimination. However, having to confront bullies and gang members from one's own ethnic group makes growing up twice as difficult. Although humor is suggested in this novel's excerpt as one method of confronting harassment, it is frequently only a temporary remedy. Yet fighting is not always the answer, either. Many schools are trying to combat the problem of bullies on campus. What suggestions do you have for helping to eliminate the problem?

Vocabulary: Looking up and understanding the following words prior to reading should prepare you for the author's message. Other words will be defined in the margin.

Fred Astaire	Ginger Rogers	Lawrence Ferlinghetti
Barbara Stanwyck	Rita Hayworth	Br'er Rabbit
Confucian	Zen introverted	victimization

1   Who would believe anyone named Donald Duk dances like Fred Astaire? Donald Duk does not like his name. Donald Duk never liked his name. He hates his name. He is not a duck. He is not a cartoon character. He does not go home to sleep in Disneyland every night. The kids that laugh at him are very smart. Everyone at his private school is smart. Donald Duk is smart. He is a gifted one, they say. No one in school knows he takes tap dance les-

sons from a man who calls himself "The Chinese Fred Astaire." Mom talks Dad into paying for the lessons and tap shoes.

2   Fred Astaire. Everybody everywhere likes Fred Astaire in the old black-and-white movies. Late at night on TV, even Dad smiles when Fred Astaire dances. Mom hums along. Donald Duk wants to live the late-night life in old black-and-white movies and talk with his feet like Fred Astaire and smile Fred Astaire's sweet lemonade smile.

3   The music teacher and English teacher in school go dreamy eyed when they talk about seeing Fred Astaire and Ginger Rogers on the late-night TV. "Remember when he danced with Barbara Stanwyck? What was the name of that movie . . . ?"

4   "Barbara Stanwyck?"

5   "Did you see the one where he dances with Rita Hayworth?"

6   "Oooh, Rita Hayworth?"

7   Donald Duk enjoys the books he reads in school. The math is a curious game. He is not the only Chinese in the private school. But he is the only Donald Duk. He avoids the other Chinese here. And the Chinese seem to avoid him. This school is a place where the Chinese are comfortable hating Chinese. "Only the Chinese are stupid enough to give a kid a stupid name like Donald Duk," Donald Duk says to himself. "And if the Chinese were that smart, why didn't they invent tap dancing?"

8   Donald Duk's father's name is King. King Duk. Donald hates his father's name. He hates being introduced with his father. "This is King Duk, and his son Donald Duk." Mom's name is Daisy. "That's Daisy Duk, and her son Donald." Venus Duk and Penny Duk are Donald's sisters. The girls are twins and a couple of years older than Donald.

9   His own name is driving him crazy! Looking Chinese is driving him crazy! All his teachers are making a big deal about Chinese stuff in their class because of Chinese New Year coming on soon. The teacher of California History is so happy to be reading about the Chinese. "The man I studied history under at Berkeley authored this book. He was a spellbinding lecturer," the teacher throbs. Then he reads, "The Chinese in America were made passive and nonassertive by centuries of Confucian thought and Zen mysticism°. They were totally unprepared for the violently individualistic and democratic Americans. From their first step on American soil to the middle of the twentieth century, the timid, introverted Chinese have been helpless against the relentless victimization by aggressive, highly competitive Americans.

10   "One of the Confucian concepts that lends the Chinese vulnerable° to the assertive ways of the West is 'the mandate of heaven.' As the European kings of old ruled by divine right, so the emperors of China ruled by the mandate° of heaven." The teacher takes a breath and looks over his spellbound class. Donald wants to barf pink and green stuff all over the teacher's teacher's book.

11   "What is he saying?" Donald Duk's pal Arnold Azalea asks in a whisper.

12   "Same thing as everybody—Chinese are artsy, cutesy, and chicken-dick," Donald whispers back.

mysticism: the belief that direct knowledge of ultimate reality is attainable through immediate intuition or insight

vulnerable: capable of being hurt

mandate: a command from an authority

13   Oh, no! Here comes Chinese New Year again. It is Donald Duk's worst time of year. Here come the stupid questions about the funny things Chinese believe in. The funny things Chinese do. The funny things Chinese eat. And "Where can I buy some Chinese firecrackers?"

14   And in Chinatown it's *Goong hay fot choy* everywhere. And some gang kids do sell firecrackers. And some gang kids rob other kids looking for fire-crackers. He doesn't like the gang kids. He doesn't like speaking their Chi-nese. He doesn't have to—this is America. He doesn't like Chinatown. But he lives there.

15   The gang kids know him. They call him by name. One day the Frog Twins wobble onto the scene with their load of full shopping bags. There is Donald Duk. And there are five gang boys and two girlfriends chewing gum and swearing and smirking. The gang kids wear black tanker jackets, white tee shirts, and baggy black denim jeans. It is the alley in front of the Chinese Historical Society Museum. There are fish markets on each side of the China-town end of the alley. Lawrence Ferlinghetti's famous City Lights Bookstore is at the end that opens on Columbus Street. Suddenly there are the Frog Twins in their heavy black overcoats. They seem to be wearing all the clothes they own under their coats. Their coats bulge. Under their skirts they wear several pairs of trousers and slacks. They wear one knit cap over the other. They wear scarves tied over their heads and shawls over their shoulders.

16   That night, after he is asleep, Dad comes home from the restaurant and wakes him up. "You walk like a sad softie," Dad says. "You look like you want everyone to beat you up."

17   "I do not!" Donald Duk says.

18   "You look at yourself in the mirror," Dad says, and Donald Duk looks at himself in his full-length dressing mirror. "Look at those slouching shoulders, that pouty face. Look at those hands holding onto each other. You look scared!" Dad's voice booms and Donald hears everyone's feet hit the floor. Mom and the twins are out in the hall looking into his open door.

19   "I am scared!" Donald Duk says.

20   "I don't care if you are scared," Dad says. His eyes sizzle into Donald Duk's frightened pie-eyed stare. "Be as scared as you want to be, but don't look scared. Especially when you walk through Chinatown."

21   "How do I look like I'm not scared if I *am* scared?" Donald Duk asks.

22   "You walk with your back straight. You keep your hands out of your pockets. You don't hunch your shoulders. Think of them as being down. Keep your head up. Look like you know where you're going. Walk like you know where you're going. And you say, 'Don't mess with me, horsepuckie! Don't mess with me!' but you don't say it with your mouth. You say it with your eyes. You say it with your hands where everybody can see them. Any-body gets two steps in front of you, you zap them with your eyes, and they had better nod at you or look away. When they nod, you nod. When you walk like nobody better mess with you, nobody will mess with you. When you walk around like you're walking now, all rolled up in a little ball and hid-ing out from everything, they'll get you for sure."

23   Donald does not like his Dad waking him up like that and yelling at him. But what the old man says works. Outside among the cold San Francisco shadows and the early morning shoppers, Donald Duk hears his father's voice and straightens his back, takes his hands out of his pockets, and says "Don't mess with me!" with his eyes and every move of his body. And, yes, he's talking with his body the way Fred Astaire talks, and shoots every gang kid who walks toward him in the eye with a look that says, "Don't mess with me." And no one messes with him. Dad never talks about it again.

24   Later, gang kids laugh at his name and try to pick fights with him during the afternoon rush hour, Dad's busy time in the kitchen. Donald is smarter than these lowbrow beady-eyed goons. He has to beat them without fighting them because he doesn't know how to fight. Donald Duk gets the twins to talk about it with Dad while they are all at the dining room table working on their model airplanes.

25   Dad laughs. "So he has a choice. He does not like people laughing at his name. He does not want gangsters laughing at his name to beat him up. He mostly does not want to look like a sissy in front of them, so what can he do?"

26   "He can pay them to leave him alone," Venus says.

27   "He can not! That is so chicken it's disgusting!" Penelope says.

28   "So, our little brother is doomed."

29   "He can agree with them and laugh at his name," Dad says. "He can tell them lots of Donald Duk jokes. Maybe he can learn to talk that quack-quack Donald Duck talk."

30   "Whaaat?" the twins ask in one voice.

31   "If he keeps them laughing," Dad says, "even if he can just keep them listening, they are not beating him up, right? And they are not calling him a sissy. He does not want to fight? He does not have to fight. He has to use his smarts, okay? If he's smart enough, he makes up some Donald Duck jokes to surprise them and make them laugh. They laugh three times, he can walk away. Leave them there laughing, thinking Donald Duk is one terrific fella."

32   "So says King Duk," Venus Duk flips. The twins often talk as if everything they hear everybody say and see everybody do is a dialog in a memoir they're writing or action in a play they're directing. This makes Mom feel like she's on stage and drives Donald Duk crazy.

33   "Is that Chinese psychology, dear?" Daisy Duk asks.

34   "Daisy Duk inquires," says Penelope Duk.

35   "And little Donnie Duk says, *Oh, Mom!* and sighs."

36   "I do not!" Donald Duk yelps at the twins.

37   "Well, then, say it," Penelope Duk says. "It's a good line. So *you* you, you know."

38   "Thank you," Venus says.

39   "Oh goshes, you all, your sympathy is so . . . so . . . so literary. So dramatic," Donald Duk says. "It is truly depressing."

40   "I thought it was narrative," Venus says.

41   "Listen up for some Chinese philosophy, girls and boys," Daisy Duk says.

42   "No, that's not psychology, that's Bugs Bunny," Dad says.

43   "You don't mean Bugs Bunny, dear. You always make that mistake."

44   "Br'er Rabbit!" Dad says.

45   "What does that mean?" Donald Duk asks the twins. They shrug their shoulders. Nobody knows what Br'er Rabbit has to do with Dad's way of avoiding a fight and not being a fool, but it works.

46   One bright and sunny afternoon, a gang boy stops Donald and talks to him in a quacking voice of Walt Disney's Donald Duck. The voice breaks Donald Duk's mind for a flash, and he is afraid to turn on his own Donald Duck voice. He tries telling a joke about Donald Duck not wearing trousers or shoes, when the gangster—in black jeans, black tee shirt, black jacket, black shades—says in perfect Donald Duck voice, "Let's take the pants off Donald Duk!"

47   "Oh Oh! I stepped in it now!" Donald Duk says in his Donald Duck voice and stuns the gangster and his two gangster friends and their three girl-friends. Everything is seen and understood very fast. Without missing a beat, his own perfect Donald Duck voice cries for help in perfect Cantonese *Gow meng ahhh!* and they all laugh. Old women pulling little wire shopping carts full of fresh vegetables stop and stare at him. Passing children recognize the voice and say Donald Duck talks Chinese.

48   "Don't let these monsters take off my pants. I may be Donald Duk, but I am as human as you," he says in Chinese, in his Donald Duck voice, "I know how to use chopsticks. I use flush toilets. Why shouldn't I wear pants on Grant Street in Chinatown?" They all laugh more than three times. Their laughter roars three times on the corner of Grant and Jackson and Donald Duk walks away, leaving them laughing, just the way Dad says he can. He feels great. Just great!

49   Donald Duk does not want to laugh about his name forever. There has to be an end to this. There is an end to all kid stuff for a kid. An end to diapers. An end to nursery rhymes and fairy tales. There has to be an end to laughing about his name to get out of a fight. Chinese New Year. Everyone will be laughing. He is twelve years old. Twelve years old is special to the Chinese. There are twelve years in the Asian lunar zodiac°. For each year there is an animal. This year Donald will complete his first twelve-year cycle of his life. To celebrate, Donald Duk's father's old opera mentor, Uncle Donald Duk, is coming to San Francisco to perform Cantonese opera. Donald Duk does not want Chinese New Year. He does not want his uncle Donald Duk to tell him again how Daddy was a terrible man to name his little boy Donald Duk, because all the *bok gwai*, the white monsters, will think he is named after that barebutt cartoon duck in the top half of a sailor suit and no shoes.

zodiac: the division of the heavens into twelve parts

➤ Follow-Up Questions

1. Why does Donald Duk like Fred Astaire movies?
2. What are the positive and negative aspects of the American school for Donald Duk?
3. What does Donald Duk have to be scared about from his own community? How does he solve this problem?

➤ Short Writing Assignments

1. Chin mentions items from other cultures that the American culture has incorporated into its own cultural system, such as firecrackers. In a paragraph, describe other cultural items from various parts of the world that have become part of the American culture.
2. Donald Duk's father advises his son to look tough but also to use humor to avoid violence and physical harm. Is this good advice? Write a paragraph in which you defend your position on this topic.

➤ Extended Writing Assignments

1. Chin presents, in the character of Donald Duk, a view of the Chinese male that is different from how he is represented in American pop culture, such as in movies. Interview several Asian men to get their views of how Asian men are represented in pop culture. Then, in essay format, **compare and contrast** the view of the Asian man as represented in movies and television with the realities found through your interviews.
2. Choose either "Confuscian thought" or "Zen mysticism" as a research topic. Discover the basic tenets, or beliefs, of your chosen philosophy and explain these beliefs in essay format. Conclude your essay with an **evaluation** of whether Duk was correct in stating that the philosophy is opposed to American individualism.

Those Who Stayed Behind

Mary Margaret Listenberger

Introductory Remarks: Born in Bryan, Texas, Mary Margaret Listenberger grew up near Texas A&M University. Even though her father worked there, he was called into active military service when World War II required that all American men serve their country. Listenberger eventually went to San Antonio, where she trained as a registered nurse at Santa Rosa School of Nursing. She currently lives in Houston. She received her Bachelor of Arts degree from St. Edwards University in Austin, Texas, and has completed some graduate study at St. Thomas University in Houston. After working as a nurse for eighteen years, she left the profession to become a drug abuse and alcoholism counselor.

Pre-Reading Ideas: When we think of World War II—or any war, for that matter—most of us are first concerned about the soldiers who leave home to fight for their country. Because of the nature of war, we frequently do not think about the families and friends who have to live without their husbands, fathers, brothers, and friends, as well as without the women who also go overseas to serve in various capacities. The following narrative describes the effects of World War II on those who stayed behind.

Vocabulary: Looking up and understanding the following word prior to reading should prepare you for the author's message.

rationing

....

1   All our lives changed during World War II. However, my life changed drastically during this time.

2   In 1943, my parents and I lived in a small town, Bryan, Texas, where once all the single men were drafted, the married men with one child followed. My father was the first married man to be drafted. I can still remember the night that he and many others took the train to San Antonio for their basic training. It seemed like the whole town was there to bid farewell to their loved ones and friends. I remember the tears flowing as I kissed Dad good-bye.

3   Except for an aunt who lived twenty-one miles away from Bryan in Hearne, my mother and I were left alone. We were two women—one young and one relatively young—left to survive at a time when the man was the provider of the family. My mother never learned to drive, so my first task at fourteen was to learn to drive on my own. I remember backing the car out of the garage and hitting the corner of the house repeatedly. Both the car and the house remained scarred for the duration. On a trip to College Station to visit my grandson several years ago, my daughter and I drove by the house. Surprisingly, it still stands, and even though it's been repaired, I can see in my mind's eye the damage I did. Mother never got angry with me.

4   During this time, we were placed on rationing for gasoline and sugar. Everyone knew me, so I didn't have any difficulty getting gas because those who didn't drive or didn't need the gas always gave me their extra gas tickets.

5   I will always remember a particular trip we took when I had to drive. One day while I was still fourteen, I became sick and vomited all night. The next day my mother took me to the doctor (I drove), and she was told not to let me eat all day and bring me back that evening. My mother decided that she had to notify my aunt in Hearne. Since we did not have a phone, I had to drive to my aunt's house. While we were there, we ate a hardy supper. On the way home, it started sleeting and the car ran hot, so I had to stop several times. As it happened, I began vomiting again, so my mother made me drive straight to the hospital. The doctor was called, and he wasn't too happy about being called out on an emergency on such a bad night. Needless to say, I had to have an emergency appendectomy and continued to vomit beans and rice during the surgery. I can still hear the doctor fussing at me for having eaten.

➤ Follow-Up Questions

1. Why were the narrator and her mother left alone?
2. Who taught the narrator to drive?
3. What advice did the doctor give the narrator's mother?

➤ Short Writing Assignments

1. Visit a nursing home, a Veterans' Administration Hospital, or other retirement community that provides a home to widows or children of men who served in World War II. Ask permission from the administration of the home to interview one of the widows or children. Ask them to tell you any stories they remember about living through the war without their husband or father. Record the **narrative** and type it up. Be prepared to read it to the class. Also write a short **reflective** paragraph about your experience.

2. Visit a nursing home, a Veterans' Administration Hospital, or other retirement community that provides a home to widows or children of men who served in World War II. Ask permission from the administration of the home to interview one of the widows or children. Ask them to tell you any stories they remember about living through the war without their husband or father. Record the narrative and type it up. Now talk to your parents or grandparent to see if your father, uncle, or grandfather served in the Vietnam War. Ask the wife or the children of the soldier to recount the events surrounding family members who stayed behind in the 1960s. Record their memories and **contrast** them with the memories of the World War II families. Write an essay in which you use both narratives to describe the differences between the time of World War II and the Vietnam War.

➤ Extended Writing Assignments

1. Conduct research on the conditions that existed in the United States for families during World War II. How were lives changed economically and professionally? What happened to the role of women during this time? Write a paper that explains the conditions of the period.

2. Patriotic feeling during the Vietnam War differed greatly from the feelings of patriotism that surrounded World War II. Conduct **research** about the Vietnam War and identify the feelings of young men and women during this time; investigate the **causes** of these feelings; and look for the **effects** of the young people's actions during the war that were manifested immediately after the war and today.

No Beef

Lini Kadaba

Introductory Remarks: Award-winning journalist Lini Kadaba has written for the *Philadelphia Inquirer* since 1986. Her essays have also appeared in the *Philadelphia Inquirer Magazine, Woman's World, Boston Magazine,* and other publications. She has won the Pennsylvania Associated Press Managing Editor's Award, as well as others for her outstanding journalism.

Pre-Reading Ideas: Most Americans take for granted the wide variety of ethnically diverse fast-food and full-service restaurants available around town. There may be a Chinese food restaurant next to an Afghan restaurant beside a fried chicken franchise across the street from a McDonald's drive-through. How many times, however, do we stop to consider how commercialism has affected American restaurants that try to establish themselves in non-Western cultures such as India, Japan, Russia, and other countries with dietary laws that differ from those in the United States. Even some Western European countries such as Germany, Spain, and Norway have special cultural food preferences. Do we also take for granted the value of a "friendly smile" and assume that it has the same value in other countries? The next time you take a bite of a hamburger fixed "your way," consider what that "way" might be in international locales.

Vocabulary: Looking up and understanding the following words prior to reading should prepare you for the author's message. Other words will be defined in the margin.

quintessential   jalapeños   franchises   acculturation

steeped: influence by

jostle: to come into rough contact with

sari: a garment worn by women of India and Pakistan

nary: not a

paradox: a contradiction

1   In this mostly Hindu, tradition-steeped° land with little taste for beef, what is one of the hottest eateries around? McDonald's. On any given night, this city's blue jean-clad hip jostle° with middle-class families, who tow along toddlers and the occasional grandmother—her head modestly covered with a sari°—for a chance to chow down on beefless burgers.

2   Here the Golden Arches sizzle, but with nary° a Big Mac in sight. Out of respect for India's large Hindu population, which shuns the consumption of beef, the Big Mac was replaced by the Maharaja Mac—two all-lamb patties, special sauce, lettuce, cheese, pickles, and onions on a sesame seed bun.

3   It makes for quite a paradox°. Here is the quintessential all-American hamburger joint without any hamburgers and with a decidedly Indian flavor, what with a menu that features lamb burgers (potatoes, peas, sweet corn, carrots, onions, and spices) and Vegetable McNuggets with chili and masala dipping sauces.

4   No matter. Even if this is India's version of American fare, the crowds are eating it up. It's a new craze, said Kilip Odhrani, as his wife, children, and friend's children gobbled McChicken burgers, fish filet sandwiches, Vegetable McNuggets, fries, sodas, and more.

5   The first McDonald's franchises in India opened more than a year ago in New Delhi and Bombay. Since then, New Delhi has added four more and Bombay two, all told serving more than six million customers, according to Brad Trask, spokesman for the Oak Brook, Illinois-based company. McDonald's plans another dozen locations in India by the close of the year.

6   On Christmas Day, a holiday for most Indians, lines four abreast stretched some thirty feet out the door of Bombay's first McDonald's, past the security guard and the life-size Ronald McDonald and through the wrought-iron gates on fashionable Linking Road.

7   The popularity of McDonald's holds true across the world, except, ironically, in the United States, where sales have slumped. McDonald's makes 59 percent of its profit outside the United States, Trask said. In Moscow, where the world's busiest McDonald's opened in 1990, lines still spill out the door.

8   All for a fast burger with a side of fries and a milkshake?

9   "It's not about the hamburgers," said John Stanton, a professor of food marketing at St. Joseph's University. "It's everything else. McDonald's is still an American icon. It stands for everything that is American." Which, it seems, would explain why McDonald can tinker° with its menu, even strike its signature product—the Big Mac—and still pull hordes°.

tinker: a weak attempt to repair

hordes: crowds

10   Other symbols of America also attract groupie-like fans abroad. The Kentucky Fried Chicken restaurant in Bangalore, India, is the place to eat for the in-crowd. And Domino's now delivers in Bombay in thirty minutes or less, attracting the city's upper crust with topings that include jalapeños, pancer (an Indian cheese), lamb, and chicken.

11   In Germany, too, Stanton said, locals pay outrageous prices to satisfy a Big Mac attack. In Bombay, the vegetable burger we sampled was served with a smile and a peppy, "Enjoy your meal," a level of customer service rarely heard in India. The burger was quite tasty but no bargain at thirty-one rupees° about eighty cents, considering that the average Rajiv—India's version of the average Joe—can feed himself for the entire day for about thirty cents.

rupee: basic unit of money in India

12   Still, they come—or at least the well-heeled do.

13   "A lot of these places carry an American message," Stanton said, by way of explanation. But not everyone attributes McDonald's success abroad to its country of origin. According to food historian Elisabeth Rozin, the author of the 1994 *The Primal Cheeseburger*, the meat is the message. "The cheeseburger with all its component parts represents a common denominator eating experience," she said. In her book, she dissects the burger platter, from its juicy, fat-laden beef patty to the icy, effervescent soft drink. "Beef has always had a great deal of panache°." But how does she explain McDonald's popularity in a place like India, which gives new meaning to the ad line "Where's the beef?"

panache: a great deal of nerve

14   The next most valued red meat is lamb, she said. Enter the Maharaja Mac.

15   The appeal of fast food, Rozin said, "is that it not only gives you a quick meal—fills your tummy—but it has to do it in a very familiar, attractive fashion." What's more familiar and attractive than an easy-to-handle bundle consisting of a meat patty topped with melted cheese, crisp lettuce and condiments served up on a fresh bun? Never mind the acculturation of the burger. "That's the nature of the food exchange," she said.

16   Cases in point:

- In Japan, McDonald's has the teriyaki burger, a sausage patty with teriyaki sauce.
- In New Zealand, it has the kiwi burger, which features a fried egg and slice of beet on top of a beef patty. (Surely, that's an acquired taste.)
- In Manila, it has a noodle dish.
- And in Norway, it has the McLox, a salmon sandwich.

17   "I don't think you'll find a more extreme example of cultural sensitivity by McDonald's than in India," Trask said. "The very product we're known for can't be served there." Yet everything else about the experience reeks of

America, or at least foreigners' impression of America—from the assembly line efficiency of service to the broad smiles that accompany every "May I take your order, please?"

modular:
standard units

ambiance: a
special mood
created

zeal:
enthusiasm

cachet:
reputation,
distinguishing
feature

18   The decor is Early Fast Food, modular°, bright, clean, with no concessions to Indian architectural style. The ambiance° is exciting, almost frenzied, as customers surge toward the counter to order their Maharaja Macs and Happy Meals. (Indian customers, it would seem, haven't adopted the American notion of standing in orderly lines with the same zeal° as they have American food.)

19   "In some cases, McDonald's is a place to see and to be seen," Trask said of the restaurant's cachet° abroad. "That's very much the case in India." Consider Aditya Varma, the essence of cool, what with his hip jeans, stylish crop, and jean-clad female friend. The twenty-year-old corporate sales representative for KLM Royal Dutch Airlines, out on the town, agreed that McDonald's offered tasty food and fast service, all with a friendly smile.

20   But what's the real attraction for him? "It's a cool crowd," he said.

➤ Follow-Up Questions

1. What is the difference between the American McDonald's menu and that of India?
2. Why has McDonald's succeeded so well in India?
3. What titles has McDonald's given to its foods to accommodate the culture of the country it is in? What does the "Big Mac" and the "Happy Meal" say about the American culture?

➤ Short Writing Assignments

1. Pretend that you are a McDonald's executive in a new country. Write a short essay identifying and discussing all the factors to consider before your company spends millions in opening its first restaurant.
2. In a short essay, explain what you would consider the **causes** of McDonald's "slump" in the US market.

➤ Extended Writing Assignments

1. **Research** the food habits of a country not mentioned in the article and create a McDonald's menu for that country which is appropriate in terms of food selections and culturally, in terms of naming of the food items. Accompanying your menu should be a short essay that explains the reasons for your decisions.
2. Write an essay that explains the perceptions of America, whether true or not, that make it so "cool" to many foreigners.

Model Minority

Felicia R. Lee

Pre-Reading Ideas: Biases, whether positive or negative, can sometimes be painful to individuals. When children of a particular ethnic group are singled out as especially gifted in math or science, especially talented in computer skills, or having any qualities of a particular stereotype, the children frequently feel that they must live up to other people's unfair expectations of them. When they can't meet the expectations, these children may experience feelings of inferiority, lack of worth, or anger. Think of the preconceived ideas you have about certain groups and where these beliefs stem from. How often do these beliefs reveal themselves in expectations of others and in surprise when the expectations are not fulfilled? Talk to Asian students and ask them how they feel about the high expectations that are usually held of them simply because of their heritage. Speak with others of different nationalities and see if they have similar feelings.

Vocabulary: Looking up and understanding the following words prior to reading should prepare you for the author's message. Other words will be defined in the margin.

docile	perceived	assimilate	reluctant
myth	stoicism	perception	schizophrenic

1   Zhe Zeng, an 18-year-old junior at Seward Park High School in lower Manhattan, translates the term "model minority" to mean that Asian-Americans are terrific in math and science. Mr. Zeng is terrific in math and science, but he insists that his life is no model for anyone.

2   "My parents give a lot of pressure on me," said Mr. Zeng, who recently came to New York from Canton with his parents and older brother. He has found it hard to learn English and make friends at the large, fast-paced school. And since he is the only family member who speaks English, he is responsible for paying bills and handling the family's interactions with the English-speaking world.

3   "They work hard for me," he said, "so I have to work hard for them."

4   As New York's Asian population swells, and with many of the new immigrants coming from poorer, less-educated families, more and more Asian students are stumbling under the burden of earlier émigrés' success—the myth of the model minority, the docile whiz kid with one foot already in the Ivy League°. Even as they face the cultural dislocations of teachers and parents and resentment from some non-Asian classmates.

Ivy League: major universities in the Northwest United States

5   Some students, like Mr. Zeng, do seem to fit the academic stereotype. Many others are simply average students with average problems. But, in the view of educators and a recent Board of Education report, all are more or less victims of myth.

6   "We have a significant population of Chinese kids who are not doing well," said Archer W. Dong, principal of Dr. Sun Yat Sen Junior High School near Chinatown, which is 83 percent Chinese. "But I still deal with educators who tell me how great the Asian kids are. It puts an extra burden on the kid who just wants to be a normal kid."

The Dropout Rate Rises

starkest: most basic

7   Perhaps the starkest° evidence of the pressures these students face is the dropout rate among Asian-American students, which has risen to 15.2 percent, from 12.6 percent, in just one year, though it remains well below the 30 percent rate for the entire school system. In all, there are about 68,000 Asians in the city's schools, a little more than 7 percent of the student population.

mechanism: a means by which a purpose is accomplished

8   Behind these figures, the Board of Education panel said, lies a contrary mechanism° of assumed success and frequent failure. While teachers expect talent in math and science, they often overlook quiet Asian-American students who are in trouble academically.

over-whelmingly: overpowering in effect or strength

usurping: taking over

advocacy: individuals who champion a cause

9   The report also said that Asian students frequently face hostility from non-Asians who resent their perceived success. And although New York's Asian population is overwhelmingly° Chinese, this resentment is fed by a feeling in society that the Japanese are usurping° America's position as a world economic power. Some educators said that because they are often smaller and quieter, Asian students seem to be easy targets for harassment.

10   Teresa Ying Hsu, executive director of an advocacy° group called Asian-American Communications and a member of the board panel, described what she called a typical exchange at a New York City school. One student might say, "You think you're so smart," she said, then "someone would hit a kid from behind and they would turn around and everyone would laugh."

ailments: illnesses

11   Since Asian cultures dictate stoicism, she explained, students in many cases do not openly fight back against harassment or complain about academic pressures. But though they tend to keep their pain hidden, she said, it often is expressed in ailments° like headaches or stomach troubles.

"Acutely Sensitive"

acutely: intensely

12   "We have a group of youngsters who are immigrants who are acutely° sensitive to things other students take in stride, like a door slamming in their face," said John Rodgers, principal of Norman Thomas High School in Manhattan.

13   Norman Thomas, whose student body is about 3 percent Asian, had two recent incidents in which Chinese students were attacked by non-Asian students. The attackers were suspended.

escalated: increased, intensified

14   But tensions escalated° after a group of thirty Chinese parents demanded that the principal, John Rodgers, increase security, and rumors spread that "gangs of blacks" were attacking Chinese. Both incidents, however, were one-on-one conflicts and neither attacker was black. In some cases, Mr. Rodgers said, Chinese students say they are attacked by blacks but that they cannot identify their attackers because all blacks look alike to them.

15   In response to the parents' concern, Mr. Rodgers said, he increased security and brought in a speaker on cross-cultural conflict.

16   Traditionally, Asian parents have not been that outspoken, educators say. While they often place enormous pressures on their children to do well, most Asian parents tend not to get involved with the schools.

17   Lisa Chang, a 17-year-old senior at Seward Park—which is 48 percent Asian—recalled being one of six Asians at a predominantly° black intermediate school.

predominantly: mainly

18   "Inside the school was no big deal," she said. "I was in special classes and everyone was smart. Then I remember one day being outside in the snow and this big black boy pushed me. He called me Chink."

19   "Then, at home, my parents didn't want me to dress a certain way, to listen to heavy metal music," Ms. Chang said. When she told her dermatologist° that she liked rock and roll, the doctor accused her of "acting like a Caucasian."

dermatologist: skin doctor

20   Ms. Chang and other students say there are two routes some Asian students take: they form cliques° with other Asians or they play down their culture and even their intelligence, in hopes of fitting in.

cliques: small, exclusive groups

Wedged Between Two Cultures

21   Most Asian students are acutely aware of being wedged between two cultures. They say their parents want them to compete successfully with Americans but not become too American—they frown on dating and hard rock music. There is also peer pressure not to completely assimilate. A traitor is a "banana"— yellow on the outside, white on the inside.

22   There is anger, too, over the perception that they are nerdy bookworms and easy targets for bullies.

23   "A lot of kids are average; they are not what the myth says," said Doris Liang, 17, a junior at Seward Park. "In math, I'm only an average student and I have to work really hard."

24   Ms. Liang said she sometimes envies the school's Hispanic students.

"Not Make Any Mistakes"

25   "The Hispanic kids, in a way they are more open," she said. "They're not afraid to bring their dates home. If you're Chinese and you bring your date home they ask a lot of questions. My parents only went to junior high school in China, so when we got here they wanted us to do well in school."

26   Nicole Tran, a 15-year-old senior who spent the early part of her life in Oregon, said she believes her generation will be far more assertive°.

assertive: bold, aggressive

27   "We are the minority minority," said Ms. Tran. "We are moving too fast for them," she said of the dominant white culture.

28   Dr. Jerry Chin-Li Huang, a Seward Park guidance counselor, said he believes that Asians in New York are in part experiencing the cultural transformations° common to all immigrants.

trans-formations: changes

29   He notes that more of the new Asian immigrants—whose numbers in New York have swelled 35 to 50 percent in the past five years, to about 400,0000—are coming from smaller towns and poorer, less educated families.

30   It was the early waves of educated, middle-class Asian immigrants whose children became the model minority, Dr. Huang said. Many of the students he sees have problems.

31   For one thing, Dr. Huang said many Asian parents are reluctant to admit that their children need help, even in severe cases. He said he had a schizophrenic Chinese student who began constantly wearing a coat, even on the hottest summer days. The parents were of little help.

32   "I have other children who run away from home because of the pressures," said Dr. Huang. "I had two sisters who had to go to school, then work in the factories, sewing. Their parents could not speak English so they were helping them with the bills. The girls said they barely had time to sleep."

33   Dr. Huang said many non-Asian teachers come to him for his insights because they have few Asian coworkers. Asians are 1.4 percent of all school counselors, 0.8 percent of all principals, and 1.4 percent of all teachers in New York City.

34   Among its recommendations, the task force called for more Asian counselors and teachers.

optimistic:
believes in a
good thing;
hopeful
quota:
maximum
number

35   People like Ms. Hsu, of Asian-American Communications, are optimistic° that the situation for Asian students will improve as students and educators talk openly about it.

36   "I gave a workshop and I talked about the quotas°, the Chinese exclusion act," said Ms. Hsu. "Two black girls came up to me. One said: 'You know, I always thought the Chinese kids were snooty. Now after hearing what you went through I feel you're my brothers and sisters.'"

➤ Follow-Up Questions

1. What are some of the causes for the increase in dropout rates for Asian students?
2. After reading the article, how would you describe the "model" versus the "real" Asian student?
3. How has the movement of Asians into the United States paralleled the traditional immigration pattern of other cultures?

➤ Short Writing Assignments

1. In the article, Lee refers to Asian stoicism. **Research** the meaning of this term; then, in a short essay, define the term and explain what the physical and psychological effects of stoicism in any form would have on a student having difficulties in school.
2. Research the immigration statistics for a foreign country, other than an Asian country, into the United States over the last twenty years. Then prepare a report to be given to the class explaining the amount of increase/decrease, whether the economic and educational levels of the immigrants have changed, and **evaluating,** in your **conclusion,** why the numbers have changed or not over the years.

➤ Extended Writing Assignments

1. Many parents, not just Asian, ignore the problems of their children in school. Research an issue that has the potential for generating student-family problems. A school counselor's office and your library should be able to provide the information. Then prepare a report explaining the problems and also the programs and aid available to lessen the problem for both student and family.

2. One of the problems mentioned in the article is the small number of Asian teachers in the classrooms. This is a problem not just for the Asian community but also for many other minority communities. Contact a school district in your area and investigate the salary and benefits, teaching load, duties, and committee work a new teacher is offered. Then discover the number of minority teachers employed by the district. If possible, interview teachers in the district or at a school you are familiar with to gain their perspective on the issue of cultural representation within the teaching staff. Then, combining the research on the financial benefits and workload of the district and your interviews, prepare a report explaining your findings regarding minority representation within the teaching staff. Conclude your essay by evaluating the representation of minority teachers within the district; that is, is the number sufficient or insufficient and what could be the **cause(s)** for the number? Also include reference to the monies offered by the district, the size of the workload, or other issues not related to finances and teaching requirements.

Zoot Suit Riots

Albert Camarillo

Pre-Reading Ideas: Every era has had a certain popular fashion that marked its wearers with a particular label. For example, the flappers wore distinctively short skirts, tightly fitting little hats, and carried swinging purses. In the 1960s, the hippies preferred torn jeans, mismatched clothes, headbands, long flowing skirts, and flowers. In the 1940s, some Mexican-American males dressed in baggy suits known as zoot suits and used special accessories. During this time period, Los Angeles was especially vulnerable to riots and disturbances because of the war in the Pacific. Unsure about anyone who looked "foreign," residents and police alike were ultrasensitive to "incidents," and triggered irrational and unwarranted actions against individuals who, in some cases, were innocent bystanders. Think of incidents from the recent past when those employed to protect us have reacted with extreme violence, resulting in calls for reform and investigations of police brutality. Audiences frequently polarize—move to one side or the other of an argument—over these incidents. What do you think about the incident described here and others like it?

Vocabulary: Looking up and understanding the following words prior to reading should prepare you for the author's message. Other words will be defined in the margin.

barrio   bravado   xenophobic
clannishness   camaraderie   "reds"

Chicanos:
individuals of
Mexican-
American
descent

1   Nothing has come to symbolize more dramatically the racial hostility encountered by Chicanos° during the 1930s and 1940s than the Sleepy Lagoon case and the Zoot Suit Riots. Both involved Chicano youth in Los Angeles city and county, local police departments, and the judicial system.

high-pompadoured: combed up

allegiance: loyalty

impoverished: poor

alienated: separated

Pachucos: Mexican-American gang members

disdain: contempt

deviants: different from the normal

stigmas: disgraceful marks

internment: to confine during World War II

summarily: quickly, without warning

precipitated: started or caused

indicted: to charge with wrong doing

2   At the heart of these conflicts was the growing attention paid to Chicano youth by the local media. The press focused on *pachucos*, members of local clubs or neighborhood gangs of teenagers (both male and female). They separated themselves from other barrio youth by their appearance—high-pompadoured° ducktail haircuts, tattoos, and baggy zoot suits for boys; short skirts, bobby sox, and heavy makeup for girls—and by their use of *caló*, a mixture of Spanish and English. Their characteristics, according to the press, included unflinching allegiance° to neighborhood territories, clannishness, and bravado. Though other teenagers in cities such as Detroit, Chicago, and New York dressed like their counterparts in wartime Los Angeles, *pachuquismo* became popularly identified with Chicano youth who came of age during the 1930s and 1940s in the Los Angeles area. Predominantly children of migrant parents, these youths matured in an environment in which they saw themselves as neither fully Mexican nor American. Raised in impoverished° barrios and alienated° from a society that discriminated against Mexicans, they identified only with others of their age and experience. Pachucos° constituted a minority among Chicano youth, and they set themselves apart by their disdain° of the public schools, skipping classes and drawing together into neighborhood gangs where they found companionship and camaraderie. To outsiders who relied on the local media for their information, pachucos were perceived not only as marijuana-smoking hoodlums and violence-prone deviants°, but also as un-American. These stigmas° during the early 1940s, particularly during the first two years of a frustrating war for Americans, helped create a climate of repression for pachucos and, by extension, for others in the Chicano community.

3   In the hot summer days of August 1942, most Los Angeles residents had wearied of newspaper reports of setbacks against the Japanese forces in the Pacific. Japanese Americans on the home front had already been relocated to internment° camps, thereby temporarily silencing Californians embittered by Pearl Harbor. Many xenophobic citizens also did not like Mexicans, especially the "foreign, different-looking" pachucos arrested following an incident at Sleepy Lagoon.

4   Sleepy Lagoon, a swimming hole frequented by Chicano youth of East Los Angeles, soon became the symbol of both popular outrage and repression. At a home near the lagoon, where the night before two rival gangs had confronted one another, the body of a young Chicano was discovered. Though no evidence indicated murder, the Los Angeles Police Department summarily° arrested members of the 38th Street Club, the teenage group that had crashed a party the prior evening and precipitated° the fighting.

45   The grand jury indicted° twenty-two members of the club for murder and, according to Carey McWilliams, "to fantastic orchestration of 'crime' and 'mystery' provided by the Los Angeles press seventeen of the youngsters were convicted in what was, up to that time, the largest mass trial for murder ever held in the country." Reflecting on the treatment of the Sleepy Lagoon defendants, the aroused McWilliams stated:

appellate: court that hears appeals

For years, Mexicans had been pushed around by the Los Angeles police and given a very rough time in the courts, but the Sleepy Lagoon prosecution capped the climax. It took place before a biased and prejudiced judge (found to be such by an appellate° court); it was conducted by a prosecutor who pointed to the clothes and the style of haircut of the defendants as evidence of guilt; and was staged in an atmosphere of intense community-wide prejudice which had been whipped up and artfully sustained by the entire press of Los Angeles. . . . From the beginning the proceedings savored° more of a ceremonial lynching° than a trial in a court of justice.

savored: tasted like

lynching: mob hanging

incommunicado: without allowing to communicate

improprieties: wrong doings

6   Concerned Anglo and Chicano citizens, headed by McWilliams, sharply criticized violations of the defendants' constitutional and human rights (such as beatings by police while the youth were being held incommunicado° and the courtroom improprieties° indicated above by McWilliams). They organized the Sleepy Lagoon Defense Committee and, with the support of such groups as the Congreso and UCAPAWA, faced down intimidation by the media and accusations of being "reds" by state senator Jack Tenney and his Committee on Un-American Activities. In 1944 they succeeded in persuading the District Court of Appeals to reverse the convictions, declare a mistrial, and release the defendants from San Quentin prison.

prelude: introduction

43   The Sleepy Lagoon case served as a prelude° to an even more discriminatory episode in wartime Los Angeles—the so-called Zoot Suit Riots of 1943. Racial tensions intensified after the Sleepy Lagoon case, as police continued to arrest large numbers of Chicano youth on a variety of charges. Adding to the unrest were confrontations between military servicemen and Chicano zoot suiters on city streets. Then on June 3, 1943, rumors circulated that Chicanos had beaten sailors over an incident involving some young Mexican women. The newspapers seized on the rumor and soon sailors and marines from nearby bases converged° on the downtown area and on Chicano neighborhoods. There they attacked Chicano youth, regardless of whether they wore zoot suits, beat them, stripped off their clothes, and left them to be arrested by the police who did nothing to interfere with the "military operation." A virtual state of siege existed for Chicanos in Los Angeles as hundreds of servicemen in "taxicab brigades" looked for Mexicans on whom to vent their anger. "I never believed that I could see a thing like that," recalled Josephine Fierro de Bright.

converged: met

I went downtown and my husband and I were standing there and we saw all these policemen hanging around . . . and hundreds of taxis with sailors hanging on with clubs in their hands, bullies just beating Mexicans on Main Street. And we went up and asked a cop to stop it: he says, "You better shut up or I'll do the same thing to you." You can't do a thing when you see people and the ambulances coming to pick them up and nobody is stopping the slaughter. It's a nightmare. It's a terrible thing to see.

rampant:
out of control

The local press continued to feed the hysteria with headlines announcing the sailors' "war" against zoot-suited pachucos. After five days of beatings, mass arrests, and rampant° fear in Chicano communities, military authorities— ordered by federal officials at the request of the Mexican consulate—quelled the riots by declaring downtown Los Angeles off limits to all naval personnel.

7   In the wake of the riots, which also occurred in San Diego and several other communities but with much less violence than in Los Angeles, the Chicano community remained paralyzed with fear of another occurrence. The Mexican government and many local citizens protested the outrages, and Governor Earl Warren appointed a committee composed of clergy, public officials, and other well-known citizens to investigate the incident. Even so, Chicano relations with the police remained tense for many years. Jesse Saldana, a Los Angeles resident who witnessed the riots, articulated° the sentiment of many Chicanos: "Justice is blind; she can't see the Mexicans."

articulated:
spoke about

suppression:
putting an
end to

8   The Zoot Suit Riots climaxed an era of overt hostility against Chicanos in California. Beginning with mass deportations during the early years of the Depression and the violent suppression° of unionization efforts, the 1930s and early 1940s witnessed much sadness and frustration for Chicanos who struggled to keep family and neighborhood from moral and physical deterioration. The irony was that tens of thousands of Mexican fathers and sons were fighting overseas with the U.S. armed forces as their families on the home front were experiencing bigotry and persecution. But this period of depression and repression° also aroused in Chicanos a desire to gain the equality that eluded° them. The post-World War II decades witnessed a new upsurge° of activity and a sense of hope within the Mexican community.

repression:
to keep from
happening by
force

eluded: escape

upsurge:
increase

➤ Follow-Up Questions

1. What are the distinguishing characteristics of the pachucos?
2. How would you describe the Sleepy Lagoon incident?
3. Explain the "irony" of the Zoot Suit Riots of 1943.

➤ Short Writing Assignments

1. **Research** the Committee on Un-American Activities referred to in the article to determine its purposes and what actions it is noted for both during and after World War II. Explain your findings in a short essay.
2. Investigate magazines and newspapers of that era to discover exactly what a zoot suit looks like. You may have a tuxedo store in your area with a sample that would help you. Then, in a short **descriptive** essay, explain what the zoot suit and what its accessories look like.

➤ Extended Writing Assignments

1. Do your own investigation of the Zoot Suit Riots or any other community riot to determine both the **causes and effects** of such an event. Present your findings in a report to the class and in a written report to your instructor. You could watch the PBS special *Zoot Suit Riots* for more information.

2. Camarillo notes several times in his essay the role of the "local press" in an incident. Consider the role of the media today, not just in newspapers and magazines, but television and Web sites as well. Do you feel they are presenting an unbiased report? For example, are both sides equally represented? Do the pictures in the articles and newscasts place one side in a bad light? Discuss your findings in an argumentative essay in which you take a position as to the truthfulness of reporting in the media.

The Stolen Party

Liliana Heker

Introductory Remarks: Short-story writer, novelist, journalist, and literary magazine editor, Liliana Heker is from Argentina. She wrote and published her first collection of short stories, *Those Who Beheld the Buming Bush*, while she was a teenager, and her other books followed, *Zonade Clivage* and *The Stolen Party and Other Stories*.

Pre-Reading Ideas: The idea of social class is a difficult one for children to understand, especially when children of different classes associate easily with one another in school and even in the home under certain conditions. However, when children socialize with children from outside their own social class, an outsider may discern insensitive attitudes and discrimination arising from children as well as from adults. The following story describes the initiation of a young girl into the social structures that are firmly held in her community. Can you think of times when you have seen behavior that discriminates against individuals on the basis of class? Does class just mean having money or is there more to being a member of a certain class? Class structure is clearly defined in many countries outside the United States; however, it also exists here, though there is more movement between classes. Think about and describe the social status as you see it in the communities in your hometown. Do you see it in any other places? Schools? Department stores? Hospitals? Churches? Write about what you discover.

Vocabulary: Looking up and understanding the following words prior to reading should prepare you for the author's message.

sneer	pompously	boisterous	rummaged

1   As soon as she arrived she went straight to the kitchen to see if the monkey was there. It was: what a relief! She wouldn't have liked to admit that her mother had been right. *Monkeys at a birthday?* Her mother had sneered. *Get away with you, believing any nonsense you're told!* She was cross, but not because of the monkey, the girl thought; it's just because of the party.

2   "I don't like you going," she told her. "It's a rich people's party."

3   "Rich people go to Heaven too," said the girl, who studied religion at school.

4   "Get away with Heaven," said the mother. "The problem with you, young lady, is that you like to fart higher than your ass."

5   The girl didn't approve of the way her mother spoke. She was barely nine, and one of the best in her class.

6   "I'm going because I've been invited," she said. "And I've been invited because Luciana is my friend. So there."

7   "Ah yes, your friend," her mother grumbled. She paused. "Listen, Rosaura," she said at last. "That one's not your friend. You know what you are to them? The maid's daughter, that's what."

8   Rosaura blinked hard: she wasn't going to cry. Then she yelled: "Shut up! You know nothing about being friends!"

9   Every afternoon she used to go to Luciana's house and they would both finish their homework while Rosaura's mother did the cleaning. They had their tea in the kitchen and they told each other secrets. Rosaura loved everything in the big house, and she also loved the people who lived there.

10   "I'm going because it will be the most lovely party in the whole world, Luciana told me it would. There will be a magician, and he will bring a monkey and everything."

11   The mother swung around to take a good look at her child, and pompously put her hands on her hips.

12   "Monkeys at a birthday party?" she said. "Get away with you, believing any nonsense you're told."

13   Rosaura was deeply offended. She thought it unfair of her mother to accuse other people of being liars simply because they were rich. Rosaura too wanted to be rich, of course. If one day she managed to live in a beautiful palace, would her mother stop loving her? She felt very sad. She wanted to go to that party more than anything else in the world.

14   "I'll die if I don't go," she whispered almost without moving her lips.

15   And she wasn't sure whether she had been heard, but on the morning of the party, she discovered that her mother had starched her Christmas dress. And in the afternoon, after washing her hair, her mother rinsed it in apple vinegar so that it would be nice and shiny. Before going out, Rosaura admired herself in the mirror, with her white dress and glossy hair, and thought she looked terribly pretty.

16   Señora Ines also seemed to notice. As soon as she saw her, she said:

17   "How lovely you look today, Rosaura."

18   Rosaura gave her starched skirt a slight toss with her hands and walked into the party with a firm step. She said hello to Luciana and asked about the monkey. Luciana put on a secretive look and whispered into Rosaura's ear: "He's in the kitchen. But don't tell anyone, because it's a surprise."

19   Rosaura wanted to make sure. Carefully she entered the kitchen and there she saw it: deep in thought, inside its cage. It looked so funny that the girl stood there for a while, watching it, and later, every so often, she would slip out of the party unseen and go and admire it. Rosaura was the only one allowed into the kitchen. Señora Ines had said: "You yes, but not the others, they're much too boisterous, they might break something." Rosaura had never

broken anything. She even managed the jug of orange juice, carrying it from the kitchen into the dining room. She held it carefully and didn't spill a single drop. And Señora Ines had said, "Are you sure you can manage a jug as big as that?" Of course she could manage. She wasn't a butterfingers, like the others. Like that blonde girl with a bow in her hair. As soon as she saw Rosaura, the girl with the bow had said:

20   "And you? Who are you?"

21   "I'm a friend of Luciana," said Rosaura.

22   "No," said the girl with the bow, "you are not a friend of Luciana because I'm her cousin and I know all her friends. And I don't know you."

23   "So what," said Rosaura. "I come here every afternoon with my mother and we do our homework together."

24   "You and your mother do homework together?" asked the girl, laughing.

25   "I and Luciana do our homework together," said Rosaura, very seriously.

26   The girl with the bow shrugged her shoulders.

27   "That's not being friends," she said. "Do you go to school together?"

28   "No."

29   "So where do you know her from?" said the girl, getting impatient.

30   Rosaura remembered her mother's words perfectly. She took a deep breath.

31   "I'm the daughter of the employee," she said.

32   Her mother had said very clearly: "If someone asks, you say you're the daughter of the employee; that's all." She also told her to add: "And proud of it." But Rosaura thought that never in her life would she dare say something of that sort.

33   "What employee?" said the girl with the bow. "Employee in a shop?"

34   "No," said Rosaura angrily. "My mother doesn't sell anything in a shop, so there."

35   "So how come she's an employee?" said the girl with a bow.

36   Just then Señora Ines arrived saying *shh shh*, and asked Rosaura if she wouldn't mind helping serve out the hotdogs, as she knew the house so much better than the others.

37   "See?" said Rosaura to the girl with the bow, and when no one was looking she kicked her in the shin.

38   Apart from the girl with the bow, all the others were delightful. The one she liked best was Luciana, with her golden birthday crown; and then the boys. Rosaura won the sack race, and nobody managed to catch her when they played tag. When they split into two teams to play charades, all the boys wanted her for their side. Rosaura felt she had never been so happy in all her life.

39   But the best was still to come. The best came after Luciana blew out the candles. First the cake. Señora Ines had asked her to help pass the cake around, and Rosaura had enjoyed the task immensely, because everyone called out to her, shouting "Me, me!" Rosaura remembered a story in which there was a queen who had the power of life or death over her subjects. She had always loved that, having the power of life or death. To Luciana and the

boys she gave the largest pieces, and to the girl with the bow she gave a slice so thin one could see through it.

40   After the cake came the magician, tall and bony, with a fine red cape. A true magician: he could untie handkerchiefs by blowing on them and make a chain with links that had no openings. He could guess what cards were pulled out from a pack, and the monkey was his assistant. He called the monkey "partner." "Let's see here, partner," he would say, "turn over a card." And, "Don't run away, partner: time to work now."

41   The final trick was wonderful. One of the children had to hold the monkey in his arms and the magician said he would make him disappear.

42   "What, the boy?" they all shouted.

43   "No, the monkey!" shouted back the magician.

44   Rosaura thought that this was truly the most amusing party in the whole world.

45   The magician asked a small fat boy to come and help, but the small fat boy got frightened almost at once and dropped the monkey on the floor. The magician picked him up carefully, whispered something in his ear, and the monkey nodded almost as if he understood.

46   "You mustn't be so unmanly, my friend," the magician said to the fat boy.

47   "What's unmanly?" said the fat boy.

48   The magician turned around as if to look for spies.

49   "A sissy," said the magician. "Go sit down."

50   Then he stared at all the faces, one by one. Rosaura felt her heart tremble.

51   "You, with the Spanish eyes," said the magician. And everyone saw that he was pointing to her.

52   She wasn't afraid. Neither holding the monkey, nor when the magician made him vanish; not even when, at the end, the magician flung his red cape over Rosaura's head and uttered a few magic words . . . and the monkey reappeared, chattering happily, in her arms. The children clapped furiously. And before Rosaura returned to her seat, the magician said:

53   "Thank you very much, my little countess."

54   She was so pleased with the compliment that a while later, when her mother came to fetch her, that was the first thing she told her.

55   "I helped the magician and he said to me, 'Thank you very much, my little countess.' "

56   It was strange because up to then Rosaura had thought that she was angry with her mother. All along Rosaura had imagined that she would say to her: "See that the monkey wasn't a lie?" But instead she was so thrilled that she told her mother all about the wonderful magician.

57   Her mother tapped her on the head and said: "So now we're a countess!"

58   But one could see that she was beaming.

59   And now they both stood in the entrance, because a moment ago Señora Ines, smiling, had said: "Please wait here a second."

60   Her mother suddenly seemed worried.

61   "What is it?" she asked Rosaura.

62   "What is what?" said Rosaura. "It's nothing; she just wants to get the presents for those who are leaving, see?"

63   She pointed at the fat boy and at a girl with pigtails who were also waiting there, next to their mothers. And she explained about the presents. She
knew, because she had been watching those who left before her. When one
of the girls was about to leave, Señora Ines would give her a bracelet. When a
boy left, Señora Ines gave him a yo-yo. Rosaura preferred the yo-yo because
it sparkled, but she didn't mention that to her mother. Her mother might have
said: "So why don't you ask for one, you blockhead?" That's what her mother
was like. Rosaura didn't feel like explaining that she'd be horribly ashamed to
be the odd one out. Instead she said:

64   "I was the best-behaved at the party."

65   And she said no more because Señora Ines came out into the hall with
two bags, one pink and one blue.

66   First she went up to the fat boy, gave him a yo-yo out of the blue bag,
and the fat boy left with his mother. Then she went up to the girl and gave
her a bracelet out of the pink bag, and the girl with the pigtails left as well.

67   Finally she came up to Rosaura and her mother. She had a big smile
on her face and Rosaura liked that. Señora Ines looked down at her, then
looked up at her mother, and then said something that made Rosaura
proud:

68   "What a marvelous daughter you have, Herminia."

69   For an instant, Rosaura thought that she'd give her two presents: the
bracelet and the yo-yo. Señora Ines bent down as if about to look for something. Rosaura also leaned forward, stretching out her arm. But she never
completed the movement.

70   Señora Ines didn't look in the pink bag. Nor did she look in the blue
bag. Instead she rummaged in her purse. In her hand appeared two bills.

71   "You really and truly earned this," she said handing them over. "Thank
you for all your help, my pet."

72   Rosaura felt her arms stiffen, stick close to her body, and then she noticed her mother's hand on her shoulder. Instinctively she pressed herself
against her mother's body. That was all. Except her eyes. Rosaura's eyes had a
cold, clear look that fixed itself on Señora Ines's face.

73   Señora Ines, motionless, stood there with her hand outstretched. As if
she didn't dare draw it back. As if the slightest change might shatter an infi-
nitely delicate balance.

➤ Follow-Up Questions

1. What is your opinion of the mother at the beginning of the story and at the end? Does
   it change and, if so, why?
2. How does Rosaura view her friend Luciana and her mother?
3. Review the events of the party and determine those occasions when Rosaura helped
   with the party. Why was she not given a parting gift?

➤ Short Writing Assignments

1. In a short essay, explain the significance of the money at the story's ending. Conclude
   your essay with your reason why the party was "stolen."

2. Is Luciana really Rosaura's friend? Defend your **position** in paragraph form. Consider the events in the whole story before you make your decision.

➤ Extended Writing Assignments

1. Part of maturing is to acquire a realistic view of society. Consider an embarrassing event in your childhood, when you were not aware of how you were being used or when you misunderstood what was happening. Compose a **personal narrative** in which you describe the event and the people involved, and your reactions when you discovered the truth about the person or occurrence.

2. Children have to learn many lessons in life, and the older they are, the more complicated the lesson. Determine three major lessons that children should learn in life so that they will not be taken advantage of as adults. Explain your ideas in an essay and conclude with a statement as to which of the three is the most important.

CONCLUSION

Judging people by appearances instead of getting to know them first can lead to misconceptions about what a person is really like. "Oh, she's Asian. I bet she's good in math." Stereotypes, even if they are complimentary, are unfair and can be destructive, and because they are, care should be taken to work against them. Sometimes it's simply a matter of calling a person's attention to comments that are biased and stereotypical. At other times, it becomes difficult when we have to confront a person who is a bigot. And the worst of times occurs when prejudice and hatred are so widespread that they lead to the extermination of individuals of certain ethnicities, a practice not ended with the Nazis but continuing, in, for example, the attempted ethnic cleansing in Bosnia. By acting as a role model for others and using language that is free of sexist, ageist, racist, and homophobic comments, we can begin to help improve life for others, but that is only a beginning.

➤ Further Writing Topics

Personal Narrative

Have you or other members of your ethnic group ever been the subject of a racist attack, verbal or physical? Describe what happened. What did you do? How did you feel? How did it end? What did you learn from the incident? Write a **personal narrative** recording your experience. What advice would you offer someone who might be in your position in the future?

Exposition

The Rodney King incident, the James Byrd, Jr., murder, and the Matthew Shepard beating and murder are events caused by racism or homophobia. The world has seen the effects of these forms of bias. Write an essay that discusses the **causes** of racism or homophobia.

Analysis

Liliana Heker, author of "The Stolen Party," describes an individual who is clearly a classist. Choose one of the many forms of prejudice and write a **process analysis** paper that develops each step in describing how to combat the form of prejudice you selected. Do not just list the steps. Fully explain each step and how to put it into practice.

Argumentation

The First Amendment to the Constitution guarantees citizens the right to freedom of speech in the United States. As a result, individuals are protected from prosecution even if they say things that are racist, sexist, classist, ageist, or homophobic. Many states have passed hate crime laws to protect individuals specifically targeted by alleged criminals for their race, ancestry, national origin, religion, disability, age, gender, or sexual orientation. However, the law cannot address activities that are under the protection of the First Amendment. Some people believe the hate crimes law should never have been passed while others believe it is necessary in fighting prejudice. Write an **argumentative** essay supporting your **position** on hate crime laws.

➤ Suggested Chapter Projects

1. The United States is perceived as a society without a class structure, yet many of the stories in this chapter deal with the idea of a class hierarchy. Review several of the stories in this chapter or consider your own understanding of American society and determine the characteristics which often separate people into a hierarchy, a class. Compose an essay in which you determine whether such a class structure exists in America and explain your reasons for such perceptions.

2. Investigate the many ways one becomes a citizen of the United States. A major source of information would be the federal Immigration and Naturalization Service (INS), but you should also consider other sources, such as interviews with immigrants and others who have acquired citizenship. Keep in mind that immigration is not the only way one becomes a citizen. When you have finished your investigation, compose an essay explaining your findings and conclude your essay with an evaluation of the most difficult process available for gaining American citizenship.

3. Often countries exclude potential immigrants from entering their borders for multiple reasons. **Research** these reasons which could include criminal activities and possible disease. Then prepare a report to the class explaining the major reasons for exclusion from the United States. Your presentation should include a brief handout for your audience and a detailed, written report for your instructor. Conclude your presentation and report with an **evaluation** of those reasons for exclusion that you feel are justified and those that are not.

CHAPTER 9

Cimetiere du Pere Lachaise, Paris
Source: Linda Daigle, Photographer

Finalities: Facing Illness, Age, and Death

The topics of aging and death are ones that many individuals prefer not to think about unless they are directly affected by them. Beginning as early as childhood through the death of a pet, children may experience loss and may or may not suffer effects from it. From a different perspective, the death of a grandparent is another loss that many children must face. Depending on the child's age and relationship with the deceased, he or she might accept the passing with relative ease or might grieve extensively. Usually death is a private event, shared with family members and close friends. However, when death occurs to someone in the public eye, in a violent manner, such as President John F. Kennedy or Princess Diana, an entire nation—as well as citizens of other countries—stops to mourn privately and publicly. Frequently we use a death as a marker in time to date events: "Oh, that happened before Grandpa died," or "I was there after John Kennedy, Jr.'s, death."

The works in this chapter are primarily poems and personal narratives that recount memories of the writer's experiences. Andrew Lam and Sharon Klander recount time they spent with their aging grandmothers; Fortuna Benudiz Ippoliti describes the cultural rituals surrounding the death of her grandmother; and Francisco Sierra, Jr., writes sensitively about a child's death. From a different perspective, Virgil Suarez describes his encounter with death when his father brings home turtles for dinner.

The topic of death can lead to powerful, moving pieces of writing, whether they arise from real events or from fictional representations. However, cultural practices and rituals at the death of individuals can be topics of interest also. Two issues not covered in this chapter are the issues of cremation and cryonics, or the freezing of the dead to preserve the body free of decay until time when medical technology can improve whatever conditions led to the death. Many individuals who are concerned with the environment are choosing to be cremated rather than buried so as not to take up space in the earth. Others are choosing to experience cryonics in the hopes of being brought back to life when medical technology is able to improve their quality of life. Investigate and gather opinions and information about either of these two controversial topics to use in an argumentative essay.

They Shut My Grandmother's Room Door

Andrew Lam

Introductory Remarks: An award-winning journalist, Andrew Lam immigrated to America from Vietnam and currently lives in San Francisco. He is the associate editor for the Pacific News Service, and his articles have appeared in *The Nation, Mother Jones,* and the *Washington Post.* Lam was one of three writers who edited *Once upon a Dream: The Vietnamese-American Experience.*

Pre-Reading Ideas: Sometimes, family members are unable to provide the kind of care and attention that an elder needs, regardless of how much they love that person, because the elder has become incapacitated or otherwise demanding. As a result, relatives find it necessary to shift the responsibility for the care of their elderly to individuals trained to meet their needs. This decision is frequently accompanied by feelings of guilt and remorse, as the family breaks cultural traditions. On the other hand, homes for senior citizens or retirement communities can offer their residents the companionship of peers and many activities a family setting might not provide. Yet the knowledge that death is near is inescapable, as even those who may be healthy pass on. In the following narrative, notice how the caretakers attempt to hide death from the residents and their visitors, and how the grandmother describes her home in her old country.

Vocabulary: Looking up and understanding the following words prior to reading should prepare you for the author's message. Other words will be defined in the margin.

Tet   filial   liquid nitrogen   monsoon

1   When someone dies in the convalescent home where my grandmother lives, the nurses rush to close all the patient's doors. Though as a policy death is not to be seen at the home, she can always tell when it visits. The series of doors being slammed shut reminds her of the firecrackers during Tet.

2   The nurses' efforts to shield death are more comical to my grandmother than reassuring. "Those old ladies die so often," she quips in Vietnamese, "every day's like new year."

3   Still, it is lonely to die in such a place. I imagine some wasted old body under a white sheet being carted silently through the empty corridor

on its way to the morgue. While in America a person may be born surrounded by loved ones, in old age one is often left to take the last leg of life's journey alone.

4 Perhaps that is why my grandmother talks now mainly of her hometown, Bac-Lieu: its river and green rich rice fields. Having lost everything during the war°, she can now offer me only her distant memories: life was not disjointed back home; one lived in a gentle rhythm with the land; people died in their homes surrounded by neighbors and relatives. And no one shut your door.

war: in this case, the Vietnam war

5 So it goes. The once gentle, connected world of the past is but the language of dreams. In this fast-paced society of disjointed lives, we are swept along and have little time left for spiritual comfort. Instead of relying on our neighbors and relatives, on the river and land, we deal with the language of materialism: overtime, escrow°, stress, down payment, credit cards, tax shelter. Instead of going to the temple to pray for good health we pay life and health insurance religiously.

escrow: third-party control of property

6 My grandmother's children and grandchildren share a certain pang of guilt. After a stroke which paralyzed her, we could no longer keep her at home. And although we visit her regularly, we are not living up to the filial piety° standard expected of us in the old country. My father silently grieves and my mother suffers from headaches. (Does she see herself in such a home in a decade or two?)

piety: devoutness

7 Once, a long time ago, living in Vietnam we used to stare death in the face. The war in many ways had heightened our sensibilities toward living and dying. I can still hear the wails of widows and grieving mothers. Though the fear of death and dying is a universal one, the Vietnamese did not hide from it. Instead we dwelt in its tragedy. Death pervaded our poems, novels, fairy tales, and songs.

8 But if agony and pain are part of Vietnamese culture, pleasure is at the center of America's culture. While Vietnamese holidays are based on death anniversaries, birthdays are celebrated here. American popular culture translates death with something like nauseating humor. People laugh and scream at blood-and-guts movies. The wealthy freeze° their dead relatives in liquid nitrogen. Cemeteries are places of big business, complete with colorful brochures. I hear there are even drive-by funerals, where you don't have to get out of your own car to pay your respects to the deceased.

freeze: a reference to cryonics

9 That America relies upon the pleasure principle and happy endings in its entertainments does not, however, assist us in evading suffering. The reality of the suffering of old age is apparent in the convalescent home. There is an old man, once an accomplished concert pianist, now rendered helpless by arthritis. Every morning he sits staring at the piano. One feeble woman who outlived her children keeps repeating, "My son will take me home." Then there are those mindless, bedridden bodies kept alive through a series of tubes and pulsating machines.

10 But despair is not newsworthy. Death itself must be embellished or satirized or deep-frozen in order to catch the public's attention.

11   Last week, on her eighty-second birthday, I went to see my grand-mother. She smiled her sweet sad smile.

12   "Where will you end up in your old age?" she asked me, her mind as sharp as ever.

13   The memories of monsoon rain and tropical sun and relatives and friends came to mind. Not here, not here, I wanted to tell her. But the soft moaning of a patient next door and the smell of alcohol wafting from the sterile corridor brought me back to reality.

14   "Anywhere is fine," I told her instead, trying to keep up with her courageous spirit. "All I am asking for is that they don't shut my door."

➤ Follow-Up Questions

1. Describe the conditions that Lam objects to in the convalescent home.
2. What aspects of his homeland does Lam most value in the essay?
3. Lam criticizes America because the elderly die alone, but he also notes that his family does not keep the grandmother at home. List what you consider reasons why Lam's family would place the grandmother in a convalescent home.

➤ Short Writing Assignments

1. Discuss in a group some of the assumptions about dying that Lam believes Americans hold. Then each group member is to write a paragraph explaining what he or she considers to be the two major ideas Americans believe about care of the dying. Conclude your paragraph with a statement of whether you agree or disagree with Lam in his **evaluation** of America, and why.
2. Was there ever a time, as Lam states, that was "once gentle" and "connected," or is he idealizing the past? In your essay, state your **position** and consider the actual realities of that past, such as medical treatment, sanitation, and conveniences.

➤ Extended Writing Assignments

1. Compose an essay in which you agree or disagree with Lam's statement that American is a land of "materialism." Give specific examples to support your **claim.**
2. Investigate the services offered by two or three nursing home facilities in your area. You should consider the services they provide, who qualifies for such care, and the costs involved. Then prepare an essay explaining your findings and concluding with an evaluation of the quality of care such facilities provide.

Karoline's Morning Bath

Sharon Klander

Introductory Remarks: Sharon Klander, award-winning poet and professor of creative writing, women's literature, and American literature, has published poetry in numerous literary journals and in two creative writing textbooks, along with essays on the creative process. Klander graduated from The

University of Texas with a BA in Journalism, from The University of Houston with an MA, and from Ohio University with a PhD in Creative Writing and American Literature. Klander writes often about personal experiences, viewing them in the contexts of time and place. Her first poetry collection is forthcoming.

Pre-Reading Ideas: Some of the most difficult moments that relatives of elderly family members experience occur when caring for those who have had a stroke or who suffer from Alzheimer's disease. These individuals are frequently left invalids because they are paralyzed. They may also have lost part of their memory and are unable to recognize even those whom they see daily. In the following poem, the narrator cares for her grandmother with gentleness and sensitivity, subtly revealing that the older woman has been in this condition for some time. Caring for seniors in these conditions can be difficult and frustrating; but observe how the narrator's tenderness and love move beyond the obstacles of reality by recalling a time when her grandmother had a different life.

Somehow she knows my name, calls it
with stroke-drawn mouth
as I pull a rag around
her neck, let the soap's iridescence
5 follow the scar penciled pink
between her breasts.
Whom God would mark He would also take.
In my dreams she walks,
cuts hyacinth for crystal
10 and blown magnolia to float.
With long-handled shears
she clips wisteria draped
like fabric on the line,
the climbing, green-collared roses.
15 What is love if not recognition.
Gently, I touch her feet with ointment,
seal the sores with gauze, lay clean,
flanneled plastic under.
I search her eyes for *Karoline* until the blue runs.

➤ Follow-Up Questions

1. What is the significance of opening the poem with an image of bathing someone who is ill?
2. What is the setting of the poem in lines 8 through 14? What is its significance when compared to the settings of the other lines in the poem?
3. Explain the meaning of the poem's last line, "I search her eyes for *Karoline* until the blue runs."

➤ Short Writing Assignments

1. Lines 8 through 14 give an idealized and imagistic view of what is often seen as a dominant natural setting for women, a beautiful garden. Consider what would be such an idealized and romantic setting for a man and then write a stanza of approximately seven lines as Klander does, describing your chosen setting.
2. Klander refers in line 7 to the phrase, *"Whom God would mark He would also take,"* emphasizing the phrase by italics. Speak to a religious leader to discover the meaning of this phrase and explain your findings in a short essay.

➤ Extended Writing Assignments

1. One of Klander's major points in the poem is made in line 15 when she states, "What is love if not recognition." Write an essay *explaining* what you see as Klander's meaning in the line and conclude your essay by stating whether you *agree or disagree* with this statement and why.
2. Klander refers to several flowers in her poem, such as "hyacinth" and "roses." In literary and social tradition, each flower represents an emotion or gesture. Hence, when someone sent a bouquet made up of different flowers, that person was also sending many silent messages. **Research** the meaning of the flowers in the poem plus any five others and explain your research in essay format, including a picture of each flower. Conclude your essay with an explanation of the messages Klander incorporates into her poem through the grandmother's garden.

Mama Sarah

Fortuna Benudiz Ippoliti

Introductory Remarks: Mother of two daughters whom she and her husband are raising in traditional Jewish custom, Fortuna Ippoliti has recently begun writing as a way to find her voice and to express her deepest feelings. She has passed on this love of writing to her daughters, who are also prolific. An immigrant who fled to the United States with her family from Morocco as a child, Ippoliti has lived in Los Angeles for most of her life. The closeness her family felt for her grandmother and other family members, which Ippoliti reveals in her essay is a reflection of that closeness she shares with her family today and the customs she is also passing on to her daughters.

Pre-Reading Ideas: The traditions surrounding aging and death vary among cultures. Here a young Moroccan Jewish woman describes the mourning rituals she was exposed to as a young girl, rituals quite different from those practiced by members of contemporary Anglo-American society. Yet regardless of how cultures display their respect for the deceased, the surviving friends and loved ones experience the loss and express their grief in their own personal way. In Chapter 1: Myths and Legends, Carlos Villacis describes the altars people construct to honor their deceased either in their homes or at the cemeteries on the Day of the Dead. Although some traditions have changed, Ippoliti believes that those she experienced taught her a great deal about herself and her community. Are the traditions surrounding death and burial among the "essential traditions"? Write a brief paragraph explaining your views.

1   The year was 1962, and I was an energetic, wiry young 10-year-old girl living in Los Angeles. Everything in my little universe was exciting and new. We were living in a new land, new city, and a new house. My parents, my sister, Sarah, and I had arrived from Morocco just six years earlier and everything in life for me was an adventure. Though my parents were struggling to acculturate themselves to this new land and new language, I just went about my life thinking everything was grand.

2   My maternal grandmother, Mama Sarah, was living with us as well. She had come from Morocco to the United States in 1957 to help my mother with the birth of my brother Solomon. Even though his arrival meant extra work for my sister and me, we somehow managed to escape the drudgery of washing and folding all his diapers thanks to Mama Sarah. She always came to our aid as my sister and I sat there staring at this mound of diapers waiting to be folded. And then Mama Sarah got sick, very sick, and had to go to the hospital.

3   My mother would take three to four buses every day to visit her at the hospital. In those days, children were rarely, if ever, allowed to enter adult wards. I was mildly curious but somewhat relieved that I couldn't go to visit her. After ten days, my mother told us that Mama Sarah was coming home from the hospital. My sister and I were so excited, as we missed her terribly (not to mention the fact that our diaper duty was wearing thin!). My mother and father came home to collect some clean clothes for Mama Sarah's homecoming when the telephone rang. It was the hospital. My mother's expression went from joy to confusion to anger. She kept repeating, "No, there must be some mistake, you must have her confused for someone else. . . . No, no, she is being discharged today . . . we're just on our way to pick her up, no, no, no." She then dropped the phone and fell to her knees and let out a wail.

4   Her death was so unexpected. How could this have happened? My mother blamed herself for not being with Mama Sarah when she died. My mother and father's agonizing screams of disbelief were too much for me. I remember running to the closet and holding my ears to block the terrible sounds coming from my parents. What was happening? Why couldn't someone explain to me what was happening? Of course, my parents were in too much shock and pain to know we even existed. Though I was unclear as to what was happening or how could it have possibly happened, I knew enough to know that my carefree existence was shattered.

5   In the Jewish faith, the deceased gets buried within twenty-four to forty-eight hours. During the period right after my grandmother's death, I remember my mother going through the motions of life trance-like, as if she were

sleepwalking. The Moroccan Jews are unlike the American Jews, who are primarily of Ashkenazi descent. As Moroccans, we are Sephardic, originating from Spain centuries ago. Consequently, we view life and death very differently from American Jews. Among Jews in general, grief and sorrow are powerfully expressed. Among the Moroccans, in particular, the belief in outward grieving is so vital that in Morocco, there were professional "wailers" or "grievers" who, through their loud shrieks, pulling their hair, and other displays of frenzy, were instrumental in assisting mourners who were too unable or in shock to begin the mourning process. This process creates an almost palpable rawness in the reality of death. The belief behind this overflow of pure unadulterated emotion is that the more quickly the wound of death is opened, the more quickly the healing can begin for the mourners.

6   On the day of her funeral, my sister, Sarah, my brother, Solomon, and I stayed home with an adult friend of my mother's. Once again, we were kept apart from the rituals of death and burial. Though now as an adult I can understand my mother's attempt at shielding her children from the sorrow expressed at my grandmother's funeral, I still wish I could have attended, if for no other reason than to say goodbye. We couldn't see her at the hospital or be a part of the mourners. After the funeral, everyone came to our house to eat and reminisce about Mama Sarah. When I saw my mother entering our house, hunched over like the elderly, I noticed that her black blouse was torn. In the Jewish religion, relatives of the deceased tear a piece of their garments, a custom completed at the beginning of the funeral service. I was once again frightened and hid in my favorite closet to gather my thoughts. After gathering up my nerve, I ventured out and sought out my mother. I so desperately wanted to console her, to stroke her, to tell her everything would be okay, but she was inconsolable.

7   For seven days, the rabbi, friends and family, and quorum of ten men (called a *minyan*) came to our house to pray and give comfort to my family. All the mirrors in our house were covered up completely with cloth and the cushions on our sofas were removed so my mother and her sisters could sit at a lower level than the guests. This period of time and mourning is called *shivah*. My poor mother was in a complete fog the entire week. To this day, I have never felt as completely and totally helpless as I did then. There was nothing my sister or I could do to "cheer" my mother up. In my child's way of thinking, I couldn't understand why my mother couldn't snap out of it. How long would this blanket of gloom continue? If Mama Sarah was with G-d now, why wasn't everyone happy for her instead of crying all the time?

8   I never did get answers to any of my questions, but it was then that I learned that the exciting and exhilarating adventure was over. As is customary among the more religious Jews, my mother was in mourning for one year. That meant no parties, no listening to music, or dancing. For one year, there was a dark pall that hung over our lives. Mama Sarah was such an integral part of each and everyone's lives, that no one was ever the same without her. Even after the year of official mourning ended, it took us many, many months to reenter the world of festivities and happiness.

9   For me, that year marked a turning point in my life. I learned at a tender age to appreciate the carefree times. On some level, I learned that life is indeed an adventure, but one with many twists and turns. The year of mourning also taught me about a sense of Jewish community. According to Jewish custom, the year of mourning is designed for the bereaved to gradually adjust to life. My family's friends gave us all great comfort and support during the more difficult times. Through their visits, I learned even more about Mama Sarah, my family, and Judaism.

10   My Mama Sarah probably taught me much more after she died than while she was still alive. I learned to cherish the joyful times in life and to let those you care for know now, while still alive, how much you love them. And for all that, I will always cherish you, Mama Sarah.

➤ Follow-Up Questions

1. Why does Ippoliti appreciate her grandmother's presence in her home?
2. How are the Moroccan Jews culturally different from the American Jews?
3. What are some of the particular customs of shivah that the Sephardic Jews follow?

➤ Short Writing Assignments

1. Write a paragraph or short essay that explains what you would consider the reasons for mourning the loss of a loved one for one year.
2. Ippoliti describes the Moroccan view of "outward grieving," which includes "professional" mourners as a way to help the "mourning process" for the deceased's family. Write a paragraph in which you take a **position** either favoring or opposing a public display of grief and explain your reasons.

➤ Extended Writing Assignments

1. Often children hide from the harsh realities of life. In Ippoliti's narrative, she hides in a closet. However, children have other ways to cover up or hide from a harsh truth. Research a major form of denial that children use to cover up their feelings. You may want to interview a person knowledgeable in psychology to help. Then prepare an essay that explains your findings.
2. Ippoliti mentions the Sephardic Jews in her essay. Research the various forms of Judaism that exist today and explain your findings in an **informative** essay using various **patterns of development**.

Jicotea Turtle

Virgil Suarez

Introductory Remarks: Virgil Suarez is a favorite in the classroom. Frequently asked to speak to creative writing students, Suarez travels around the country reading his works and helping graduate students improve their writing. In addition to teaching at Florida State University in Tallahassee, Suarez, a Cuban who moved to the United States in 1974, draws on his culture in his novels, *Latin Jazz* and *Havana Thursdays*. He has also edited two anthologies: *Iguana Dreams: New Latina Fiction*, and *Paper Dance: 54 Latino Poets*.

Pre-Reading Ideas: Being introduced to death can be a traumatic experience for a youngster, especially when death comes to a loved one, a parent, or a grandparent. Sometimes adults fail to understand that the death of a pet can also cause a great deal of sorrow for a child. But how does death affect a child when he or she is required to participate in the activity of killing animals that will be used in a meal? Suarez addresses the issue in his narrative describing his experiences with his father.

Vocabulary: Looking up and understanding the following words prior to reading should prepare you for the author's message. Other words will be defined in the margin.

yute	carapaces	*tortugitas*	machete	slaughter
Camilo Cienfuegos		**Che Guevara**	**José Martí**	**Karl Marx**
	Máximo Gómez	**Vladimir Lenin**		

1   They arrived in *yute* sacks. Their carapaces forming lumps as they pushed against the weaved strings of the brown sacks. Once my father put down the sack on the cemented patio of the house in Havana, I walked around the lumpy pile, intrigued. I was still at an age where guesswork led to endless questions. My father said he'd gotten lucky this time at La Cienega de Zapata, a pocket of the province of Las Villas. My father was from this swampy area of the island of Cuba.

2   *What is it?* I asked. *Jicoteas*, he said and smiled, then reached into his shirt pocket for a cigarette. This was the time when my father still smoked, even though he suffered from asthma. *Jico*—I began but my tongue stumbled over the word—*teaas? Tortuguitas, let me show you one.* He opened the mouth of the sack and reached into it the way a magician might into his hat to pull out a rabbit by the ears.

futile: useless

3   It appeared: a turtle. Startled, waving its claws? Feet? Legs? In the air as if making a futile° attempt at a swim/escape. *See?* my father asked. *Surely you've been shown pictures at school.* (At school we'd only been shown pictures of Camilo Cienfuegos, Che Guevara, José Martí, Karl Marx, Máximo Gómez, Vladimir Lenin, etc.)

4   *Give me a hand*, he said. At first I was reluctant, but then my father turned the sack upside down and let about thirty of these turtles free. *But they'll get away*, I told him. And again, he smiled, then blew smoke out of his nostrils.

5   *No, no, no*, he said. *See how they move? They are slow. They can't get away fast enough.*

6   Get away from what? I thought. Indeed, these *slowpo* creatures tried to make a path on the cemented patio—and I swear—making little scratch sounds with their nails against the surface.

7   My father crushed the cigarette under his shoe, reached to the sheath tied to the side of his right thigh, and pulled out his sharp machete. *This is what I want you to do, son,* he said and showed me.

8   He grabbed one of the turtles, stepped on it so that it couldn't move, then with his free hand he pulled and extended the neck of the turtle. *Like this, see?* He stretched. . . .

9   I looked, not catching on yet. Then to my surprise, he swung the machete downward so fast. There was a loud, crushing sound. There was a spark as the machete sliced through the turtle's neck and hit the hard concrete underneath.

plantain: a type of banana

10   The creature's neck lay on the floor like a piece of rotted plantain°. It was still twitching as I looked up at my father, who was saying, *It's that simple, you grab and pull and I chop.*

11   As reluctant as I was, I did as I was told. I grabbed every one of those thirty turtles' necks, pulled without looking into their eyes, and closed my eyes each of the thirty times the machete came down. Turtle, after turtle, after turtle. All thirty.

12   *After this you help me clean up, no,* my father was saying. *We need to remove the shells so that your mother can clean the meat and cook it.*

13   Yes, we're going to eat these turtles, these jicoteas (the sound of the word now comes naturally), and there was nothing I could say on behalf of the creatures I had helped my father slaughter.

14   And so the idea of death had been inflicted upon me quickly, almost painlessly, with the sacrifice of thirty jicoteas.

➤ Follow-Up Questions

1. Which descriptions in the story help create sympathy for the turtle? For the child?
2. What lesson(s) does the father teach the child? Consider the whole story in your answer.
3. What do the turtles represent to the family?

➤ Short Writing Assignments

1. Consider all the foods that you have eaten within the last week and make a list of all the animals that were killed so that you could eat.
2. **Research** the game laws in your state either for the hunting of a specific animal, such as a deer or wild hog, or for fishing in either fresh or saltwater. Your regulations can be for a county, state, or federal area. Write a short essay in which you explain the basic games laws.

➤ Extended Writing Assignments

1. For the most part, Americans enjoy prepackaged food and do not have to go through the difficulties that the child learns in the story. However, even such packaging and labeling must be regulated to avoid possible health hazards. Investigate various items

in a grocery story to see how they are packaged and labeled. If possible, interview the butcher in the meat and fish section, the personnel in the deli section, and the baker to see if there are any specific requirements for these departments as well. Then prepare a report that explains your findings.

2. In this story, killing and death are associated with the male figures of the father and son. Do you believe that such efforts are a strictly male province, or is such killing and feeding of the family a female domain as well? Write an **argumentative** paper in which you take a position on killing in relation to males and females; support your **claim** with specific **examples**.

Amanda Rose

Francisco Sierra, Jr.

Introductory Remarks: Born in San Antonio, Texas, Francisco Sierra, Jr., also lived in Los Angeles, California before finally settling down in San Antonio with his family. A former teacher and administrator in elementary, middle, and high school, Sierra graduated from San Antonio College, Texas A&M University, and Southwest Texas State University. Sierra began writing later than most poets, but once he found his voice and the belief that "I could write poetry," he became quite prolific. He has published several times in a number of volumes of *Lone Star* and is quietly writing about personal topics.

Pre-Reading Ideas: This poem shows the physical relationships that end prematurely when a baby dies. Francisco Sierra, Jr., attempts to capture in his poem the feelings one has at the loss of a child. Losing a loved one at any age can be difficult, but losing a baby is frequently more painful. Yet the thought that a connection remains even after the passing of the loved one seems to give emotional support to many people. Death frequently has a strong impact on people, especially when the one who dies was the central figure in a family or group of friends. How does death bring survivors closer together? How do relationships flourish or perish after the death of an individual? Read the following poem and determine the feelings of those who survive the death of a child.

palpitations:
heartbeats

How sweet the sound
Of a silent breath
Of heartfelt palpitations°
Within our hearts
5 A soul that created much happiness
Of infinity
For, somewhere beyond the stars
Our love in silent waves traverses
To our hearts
10 A silent breath of happiness.

➤ Follow-Up Questions

1. How do the terms "sound" versus "silent" coincide with the theme of death in this poem? Look at how many times each word occurs in the poem to determine which is more dominant.
2. What could the words "Our love" in line 8 mean?
3. What are the possible meanings for the phrase "somewhere beyond the stars" in line 7? Why leave the meaning vague?

➤ Short Writing Assignments

1. The poem gives the impression of death without ever stating that an actual death has occurred. In a short essay, **analyze** the poem for other words and phrases that could be seen as signifying death and their meanings. Conclude with a statement of why you think the poet does not directly mention death in the poem.
2. Often in daily conversations people discuss the death of someone without actually saying the words "died," "dead," or "death." Interview several persons who have had to deal with the death of a friend, family member, or loved one. Listen closely to their conversations and make an extended list of all the ways our daily language talks about death without ever mentioning it.

➤ Extended Writing Assignments

1. Research what an ancient culture, such as the Egyptians, thought of the afterlife and then research the views of the afterlife for a religion practiced today. Then write a **comparison-and-contrast** paper that explains how each viewed several main aspects of the afterlife.
2. Research the views of the afterlife for children in two or three of the major religions practiced today. In your investigations, consider such issues as the age at which the child is considered an adult, whether there is a special location in the afterlife for children, and whether they are subject to a separate form of reward and punishment than adults. Then present your findings in an informative essay format using several **patterns of development.**

CONCLUSION

Illness, aging, and death are three aspects of life we cannot avoid. Even though illness and death may precede aging, more people live longer lives today, due to advanced medical technology, drugs, and proper personal attention to diet and exercise than they did in the past. This, however, does not ease the mourner's emotional pain when that loved one dies. Even though the rituals of death are intended to help the survivors and show respect for the dead, each survivor must cope with the experience in his or her own way, as the authors in this chapter describe.

➤ Further Writing Topics

Personal Narrative

Losing a loved one, whether it is a well-loved pet, a relative, a close friend, or a public fig-ure, requires grief and mourning. That grief and mourning, however, can be private and personal as well as public. Sometimes writing about the deceased or about the incidents surrounding the illness and/or death of a loved one helps the writer cope with repressed or unresolved feelings. It can also be a tribute to that person, one the writer never voiced before. Write a **personal narrative** discussing the illness and/or death of a loved one.

Exposition

One of the most discussed and dreaded forms of illness that can precede death is Alzheimer's disease. Research and testing have been devoted to discovering more about this illness that attacks the brain. Many Internet sites offer help and information about this research (for example, the Alzheimer's Foundation has a Web site). Write a **research** paper that discusses the characteristics and stages of Alzheimer's disease and the meth-ods being used to treat the symptoms.

An alternative to writing about Alzheimer's disease is to investigate and write about a form of cancer, heart disease, or AIDS.

Analysis

Fortuna Ippoliti presents in her personal narrative a description of several of the rituals surrounding death. In "Mama Sarah," Ippoliti describes the personal process she went through during the ritual mourning period. **Analyze** the essay for the effect the ritual has or could have on those involved in the activities before and after burial.

Argumentative

Many individuals believe it is the responsibility of the relatives—children and/or grandchildren—to care for the elderly in their families as they become more and more un-able to care for themselves. Others, however, believe that their senior members are better served by being placed in a nursing home or in a retirement community so they can re-ceive the attention they need and the companionship of others their age. Take a position on this issue and write an **argumentative** essay trying to persuade your readers to be-lieve your **claims.**

➤ Suggested Chapter Projects

1. Create a group and find the names and addresses of cryonics laboratories in the United States and write to them or get information about them on Internet. Also **re-search** the science of cryonics and investigate the different uses for cryonics and the advances that have been made over the years. Also investigate the ethics and moral views individuals hold about the issue of being cryonically preserved with the hope of being brought back to life at a future date for an improved quality of life. What are the moral and ethical differences between using cryonics for that purpose and for pre-

serving parts of the anatomy for transplantation? Write a research paper that covers these issues. Present this as a panel discussion to your class, with each member of your group becoming the expert on a different part of the material you researched. For example, one student could be the cryonics expert, explaining what it is and how it works for body preservation and revival. Another student could explain the use of cryonics in organ preservation for transplants. One student could explain the ethics of cryonics, and one student could explain the moral views religious individuals of various denominations have concerning cryonics.

2. Using the same procedure as above, investigate, write about, and deliver a class presentation on the topic of cremation.

3. One of the political arguments in America surrounding the issue of death is the estate tax, which many survivors must pay. Research this political issue and prepare an argumentative essay that explains the issues involved in the estate tax and your **position** either in favor of or opposed to its continuance.

CHAPTER 10

The Traditional
Source: Fortuna Ippoletti

The Nouveau
Source: Anne Perrin, photographer

Confrontations: Controversial Issues in Society Today

There are frequently issues in society that people disagree about. If these concerns will affect the residents of communities, towns, or the nation, they are brought to a vote. For example, giving the vote to women, desegregation of public schools, abortion, and the presidency are topics that have generated opinions of support and dissent. By reading the newspaper and newsmagazines; watching television programs such as *Face the Nation, 60 Minutes, Politically Incorrect*; or by participating in community concerns, you can discover a variety of issues that provoke people's emotions and opinions. Not all problems are, however, of such a global nature. The timeliness of garbage pickup, the raising of rent without notice and without additional improvements, or the failure of the city to repair street problems in front of your home could be controversial points that you have to deal with.

This chapter provides discussion of four topics about which people disagree: cloning, same-sex marriage, the World Wide Web, and living wills. Although readers may not have any interest in some of these topics, taking the time to read the articles will help them understand the construction of an argument. The articles on cloning, same-sex marriage, and the Internet are argumentative essays, which take a position and discuss supporting as well as opposing views. However, an essay that opposes cloning has been omitted, leaving the student to supply one as an assigned writing. The last two articles, "Life, Death, and the Living Will" and "Hopes and Wishes" are personal narratives that provide scenarios based on the authors' experience with living wills. Even though they do not argue in the traditional sense of argumentation, they are works that provide specific supports for their positions.

Convincing others to believe what you believe requires skill and an understanding of your opposition's beliefs. In this kind of writing, knowing your audience is essential. For example, a gay rights activist/ professor always surprises her students when she tells them she watches *The 700 Club*. They are amazed that she would watch a conservative, homophobic program, until she explains that she needs to know her opposition's arguments so she can counter them. If a writer is not current on his or her topic, she or he may lose readers because of outdated arguments or because research has provided new data or information about the topic. If you are assigned an argumentative essay, choose a topic that you are interested in and that you can find current information about. If you are not interested in your topic, there is a good possibility that you will lose your reader and fail to write a convincing argument.

Second Thoughts on Cloning

Laurence H. Tribe

Introductory Remarks: A professor of constitutional law at Harvard, his alma mater, Laurence Tribe writes books for audiences involved in the legal profession as well as for the layperson. For example, Tribe produced *Constitutional Choices, On Reading the Constitution,* and *Abortion: the Clash of Absolutes* for the general public. The following piece was published in the op-ed section of the *New York Times* in 1997.

Pre-Reading Ideas: If you are at all interested in the controversial issue of cloning, you should enjoy this considered presentation of the issue. Tribe, a cautious proponent, uses an argumentative style that presents legitimate supports used by his opposition before he begins the presentation of his side. Look carefully at the persuasive evidence or both sides. In addition to finding other authors who voice different reasons to defend or reject cloning, you might want to research in further depth some of the issues Tribe points to so that you can discover whether the arguments do, indeed, contribute to the author's position.

Vocabulary: Looking up and understanding the following words prior to reading should prepare you for the author's message. Other words will be defined in the margin.

prohibition	theologians	perversion	replication
ethicists	generate	bioethics	gestational

1   Some years ago, long before human cloning became a near-term prospect, I was among those who urged that human cloning be assessed not simply in terms of concrete costs and benefits, but in terms of what the technology might do to the very meaning of human reproduction, child rearing, and individuality. I leaned toward prohibition as the safest course.

2   Today, with the prospect of a renewed push for sweeping prohibition rather than mere regulation, I am inclined to say, "Not so fast."

3   When scientists announced in February that they had created a clone of an adult sheep—a genetically identical copy named Dolly, created in the laboratory from a single cell of the "parent"—ethicists, theologians, and others passionately debated the pros and cons of trying to clone a human being.

solace: comfort

incremental: increase in a regular way

insemination: to introduce semen into the female

in vitro fertilization: fertilization outside the body

casual: not serious

prohibitionist: those who want to forbid by law

articulate: having good speaking skills

detractors: a person who negatively criticizes

embodiment: example

severing: cutting or stopping

apotheosis: the ultimate achievement

credence: belief

surrogate motherhood: substitute mother

ordained: ordered

criminalization: to make into a crime

inevitable: bound to happen

stigma: bad mark, mark of disgrace

plight: bad state

contraband: illegal goods

4   People spoke of the plight of infertile couples; the grief of someone who has lost a child whose biological "rebirth" might offer solace°; the prospect of using cloning to generate donors for tissues and organs; the possibility of creating genetically enhanced clones with a particular talent or resistance to some dread disease.

5   But others saw a nightmarish and decidedly unnatural perversion of human reproduction. California enacted a ban on human cloning, and the President's National Bioethics Advisory Commission recommended making the ban nationwide.

6   That initial debate has cooled, however, and many in the scientific field now seem to be wondering what all the fuss was about.

7   They are asking whether human cloning isn't just an incremental° step beyond what we are already doing with artificial insemination°, in vitro fertilization°, fertility enhancing drugs, and genetic manipulation. That casual° attitude is sure to give way before long to yet another wave of prohibitionist° outrage—a wave that I no longer feel comfortable riding.

8   I certainly don't subscribe to the view that whatever technology permits us to do we ought to do. Nor do I subscribe to the view that the Constitution necessarily guarantees every individual the right to reproduce through whatever means become technically possible.

9   Rather, my concern is that the very decision to use the law to condemn, and then outlaw, patterns of human reproduction—especially by invoking vague notions of what is "natural"—is at least as dangerous as the technologies such a decision might be used to control.

10   Human cloning has been condemned by some of its most articulate° detractors° as the ultimate embodiment° of the sexual revolution, severing° sex from the creation of babies and treating gender and sexuality as socially constructed.

11   But to ban cloning as the technological apotheosis° of what some see as culturally distressing trends may, in the end, lend credence° to strikingly similar objections to surrogate motherhood° or gay marriages and gay adoption.

12   Equally scary, when appeals to the natural, or to the divinely ordained°, lead to the criminalization° of some method for creating human babies, we must come to terms with the inevitable°: the prohibition will not be airtight.

13   Just as was true of bans on abortion and on sex outside of marriage, bans on human cloning are bound to be hard to enforce. And that, in turn, requires us to think in terms of a class of potential outcasts—people whose very existence society will have chosen to label as a misfortune and, in essence, to condemn.

14   One need only to think of the long struggle to overcome the stigma° of "illegitimacy" for the children of unmarried parents. How much worse might be the plight° of being judged morally incomplete by virtue of one's man-made origin?

15   There are some black markets (in narcotic drugs, for instance) that may be worth risking when the evils of legalization would be even worse. But when the contraband° we are talking of creating takes the form of human beings, the stakes become enormous.

grave: serious

caste: divisions in a society

marginalized: made unimportant

ironclad: unbreakable

intrinsically: by its very nature

entrenchment: defense

16   There are few evils as grave° as that of creating a caste° system, one in which an entire category of persons, while perhaps not labeled untouchable, is marginalized° as not fully human.

17   And even if one could enforce a ban on cloning, or at least insure that clones would not be a marginalized caste, the social costs of prohibition would still be high. For the arguments supporting an ironclad° prohibition of cloning are most likely to rest on, and reinforce, the notion that it is unnatural and intrinsically° wrong to sever the conventional links between heterosexual unions sanctified by tradition and the creation and upbringing of new life.

18   The entrenchment° of that notion cannot be a welcome thing for lesbians, gay men, and perhaps others with unconventional ways of linking erotic attachment, romantic commitment, genetic replication, gestational mothering, and the joys and responsibilities of child rearing.

19   And, from the perspective of the wider community, straight no less than gay, a society that bans acts of human creation for no better reason than their particular form defies nature and tradition is a society that risks cutting itself off from vital experimentation, thus losing a significant part of its capacity to grow. If human cloning is to be banned, then the reasons had better be far more compelling than any thus far advanced.

➤ Follow-Up Questions

1. What are the pro-cloning arguments that Tribe initially offers?
2. What problem does Tribe see with society's view of the illegal clone? What is an "illegal clone"?
3. What ultimately is Tribe's reason not to ban human cloning at this time?

➤ Short Writing Assignments

1. Tribe makes the analogy between the illegal drug market and cloning. Is this a valid and reasonable association or is it misleading? In a short essay, **compare and contrast** the issue of the illegal drug market and cloning and conclude your essay with your own **evaluation** of Tribe's analogy.
2. Would human cloning eventually create a "caste system" in society? Research the term "caste" and then compose an **argumentative** paragraph in which you elaborate your **position** to decide if such a system could result from cloning.

➤ Extended Writing Assignments

1. **Define** the term "natural" in both the traditional and contemporary sense of the word as it is applied to reproduction. Such a definition paper should give specific examples to explain your ideas.
2. Besides cloning, what is another of the major bioethical arguments being debated today? Your **research** should consider interviews with medical personnel and library sources. Then prepare an **informative** essay that explains the bioethical issue and the **pro and con arguments** surrounding it. You do not have to support one side or another; simply write in an **expository pattern.**

Let Gays Marry

Andrew Sullivan

Introductory Remarks: Andrew Sullivan is an outspoken writer who champions gay rights. Surprisingly to many people, although Sullivan is a self-disclosed gay, his politics are conservative, and he is a Roman Catholic. Sullivan is an editor at the magazine *New Republic* and author of *Virtually Normal: An Argument about Homosexuality*. He also writes essays for other magazines such as *Newsweek*.

Pre-Reading Ideas: The institution of marriage has undergone changes in its legal definition, and in an effort to protect it, Congress, during the Clinton presidency, passed the Defense of Marriage Act, which declared marriage to be legal between a male and female—in other words, between heterosexuals. The Act's passage came on the heels of various states' attempts, including Hawaii and Vermont, to pass laws legalizing marriage for same-sex couples. Despite the courts' and legislatures' attempts to prevent it, a few same-sex marriages have been legally performed because of a loophole in the law. Andrew Sullivan's article argues that same-sex marriage should be allowed and same-sex couples should be treated the same as heterosexual couples. Before you read this piece, make a list of prewriting ideas that give reasons for supporting same-sex marriage. When you finish, you may add reasons that Sullivan has discussed.

Vocabulary: Looking up and understanding the following words prior to reading should prepare you for the author's message. Other words will be defined in the margin.

> **lobby**   **civil**   **monogamy**   **subvert**   **polygamy**   **fidelity**

deem: judge

1 '**A** state cannot deem° a class of persons a stranger to its laws," declared the Supreme Court last week. It was a monumental statement. Gay men and lesbians, the conservative court said, are no longer strangers in America. They are citizens, entitled, like everyone else, to equal protection—no special rights, but simple equality.

2   For the first time in Supreme Court history, gay men and women were seen not as some powerful lobby trying to subvert America, but as the people we truly are—the sons and daughters of countless mothers and fathers, with all the weaknesses and strengths and hopes of everybody else. And what we seek is not some special place in America but merely to be a full and equal part of America, to give back to our society without being forced to lie or hide or live as second-class citizens.

3   That is why marriage is so central to our hopes. People ask us why we want the right to marry, but the answer is obvious. It's the same reason anyone wants the right to marry. At some point in our lives, some of us are lucky enough to meet the person we truly love. And we want to commit to that

person in front of our family and country for the rest of our lives. It's the most simple, the most natural, the most human instinct in the world. How could anyone seek to oppose that?

radical: extreme 4   Yes, at first blush, it seems like a radical° proposal, but, when you think about it some more, it's actually the opposite. Throughout American history, to be sure, marriage has been between a man and a woman, and in many ways our society is built upon that institution. But none of that need change in the slightest. After all, no one is seeking to take away anybody's rights to marry, and no one is seeking to force any church to change its doctrine in any way. Particular religious arguments against same-sex marriages are rightly debated within the churches and faiths themselves. That is not the issue here: there is a separation between church and state in this country. We are only asking that when the government gives out *civil* marriage licenses, those of us who are gay should be treated like anybody else.

5   Of course, some argue that marriage is *by definition* between a man and a woman. But for centuries, marriage was *by definition* a contract in which the wife was her husband's legal property, and we changed that. For centuries, marriage was *by definition* between two people of the same race. And we changed that. We changed these things because we recognized that human dignity is the same whether you are a man or a woman, black or white. And no one has any more of a choice to be gay than to be black or white or male or female.

6   Some say that marriage is only about raising children, but we let childless heterosexual couples be married (Bob and Elizabeth Dole, Pat and Shelley Buchanan, for instance). Why should gay couples be treated differently?

sanctioning: approving   Others fear that there is no logical difference between allowing same-sex marriage and sanctioning° polygamy and other horrors. But the issue of whether to sanction multiple spouses (gay or straight) is completely separate from whether, in the existing institution between two unrelated adults, the government should discriminate among its citizens.

7   This is, in fact, if only Bill Bennett could see it, a deeply conservative cause. It seeks to change no one else's rights or marriages in any way. It seeks merely to promote monogamy, fidelity and the disciplines of family life among people who have long been cast to the margins of society. And what could be a more conservative project than that? Why indeed would any conservative seek to oppose those very family values for gay people that he or she supports for everybody else? Except, of course, to make gay men and lesbians strangers in their own country, to forbid them ever to come home.

➤ Follow-Up Questions

1. What is Sullivan's response to the issue of why gays want to marry?
2. According to Sullivan, why does the moral argument not apply to the issue of gay marriages?
3. How does Sullivan propose to change the definition of marriage?

➤ Short Writing Assignments

1. Contact a gay/lesbian organization in your community or through the Internet to find out the latest problems and status regarding the issue of gay marriages. Then prepare a report that explains your findings. Conclude your essay with a statement of your own **position** on this issue.
2. **Interview** several gays and/or lesbians to find out their views on the idea of gay marriage. You may find that many may be opposed to such a process and favor another form of legal partnership. Explain your findings in a short essay.

➤ Extended Writing Assignments

1. **Research** the laws within your own state regarding the issue of gay/lesbian marriages and find out whether any pertinent bills are currently pending in the state legislature. Prepare a report explaining your findings.
2. Sullivan notes in his article that "no one has any more of a choice to be gay than to be black or white or male or female." Do you agree with this statement? Prepare an **argumentative** essay in which you elaborate your position, citing specific **examples** for support.

Leave Marriage Alone

William Bennett

Introductory Remarks: William Bennett first published this article in *Newsweek* (1996).

Pre-Reading Ideas: In opposition to Andrew Sullivan's article endorsing gay marriages, William Bennett provides arguments that support the maintenance of the status quo with regard to the illegality of same-sex marriages. Before you read this piece, make a list of prewriting ideas presenting as many reasons as you can in support of traditional marriage. After you have read the article, you may add the reasons Bennett gives to your list.

Vocabulary: Looking up and understanding the following words prior to reading should prepare you for the author's message. Other words will be defined in the margin.

proponents   **consensual**   **polygamous**

1   There are at least two key issues that divide proponents and opponents of same-sex marriage. The first is whether legally recognizing same-sex unions would strengthen or weaken the institution. The second has to do with the basic understanding of marriage itself.

2   The advocates of same-sex marriage say that they seek to strengthen and celebrate marriage. That may be what some intend. But I am certain that it will not be their reality. Consider: the legal union of same-sex couples

endorse:
approve

antithetical:
opposite

tenets: beliefs

obscure:
to conceal

consequential:
resulting

principled:
based on a code
of conduct

sexual
relativism:
sexual truths
that vary

forsaking:
giving up

component:
part

moralistic: rules
of right or wrong

arbitrary:
random

construct: idea

propagate:
reproduce

nurture:
to keep safe

sustain: to keep
going

crucial:
important

revered:
worshipped

would shatter the conventional definition of marriage, change the rules which govern behavior, endorse° practices which are completely antithetical° to the tenets° of all of the world's major religions, send conflicting signals about marriage and sexuality, particularly to the young, and obscure° marriage's enormously consequential° function—procreation and child rearing.

3   Broadening the definition of marriage to include same-sex unions would stretch it almost beyond recognition—and new attempts to expand the definition still further would surely follow. On what *principled*° ground can Andrew Sullivan exclude others who most desperately want what he wants, legal recognition and social acceptance? Why on earth would Sullivan exclude from marriage a bisexual who wants to marry two other people? After all, exclusion would be a denial of that person's sexuality. The same holds true of a father and daughter who want to marry. Or two sisters. Or men who want (consensual) polygamous arrangements. Sullivan may think some of these arrangements are unwise. But having employed sexual relativism° in his own defense, he has effectively lost the capacity to draw any lines and make moral distinctions.

4   Forsaking° all others is an essential component° of marriage. Obviously it is not always honored in practice. But it is the ideal to which we rightly aspire, and in most marriages the ideal is in fact the norm. Many advocates of same-sex marriage simply do not share this ideal; promiscuity among homosexual males is well known. Sullivan himself has written that gay male relationships are served by the "openness of the contract" and that homosexuals should resist allowing their "varied and complicated lives" to be flattened into a "single, moralistic° model." But that "single, moralistic model" has served society exceedingly well. The burden of proof ought to be on those who propose untested arrangements for our most important institution.

5   A second key difference I have with Sullivan goes to the very heart of marriage itself. I believe that marriage is not an arbitrary° construct° which can be redefined simply by those who lay claim to it. It is an honorable estate, instituted of God and built on moral, religious, sexual, and human realities. Marriage is based on a natural teleology, on the different, complementary nature of men and women—and how they refine, support, encourage, and complete one another. It is the institution through which we propagate°, nurture°, educate, and sustain° our species.

6   That we have to engage in this debate at all is an indication of how steep our moral slide has been. Worse, those who defend the traditional understanding of marriage are routinely referred to (though not to my knowledge by Sullivan) as "homophobes," "gay-bashers," "intolerant," and "bigoted." Can one defend an honorable 4,000-year-old tradition and not be called these names?

7   This is a large, tolerant, diverse country. In America people are free to do as they wish, within broad parameters. It is also a country in sore need of shoring up some of its most crucial° institutions: marriage and the family, schools, neighborhoods, communities. But marriage and family are the greatest of these. That is why they are elevated and revered°. We should keep them so.

➤ Follow-Up Questions

1. What are Bennett's opening oppositions to same-sex marriage?
2. How would same-sex marriage "stretch" the definition of marriage, according to Bennett? Is this linkage correct?
3. Despite the changes over time regarding the legality of marriage, such as age and race, Bennett states that it "is not an arbitrary construct which can be redefined simply by those who lay claim to it." What is his reasoning behind his statement?

➤ Short Writing Assignments

1. Bennett's **argument** cites the promiscuous behavior of gay men as a reason for not allowing them the legal right to marry. He bases this denial of legal rights on the idea that faithfulness "is an essential component of marriage." Write a short **argumentative** essay in which you consider Bennett's argument and either defend or argue against his position.
2. Bennett concludes with the statement that America is on a "moral slide," in terms of its values. Do you agree with his view of American morality? In a short essay, first **define** what a moral is, then assume an **argumentative position** and either defend or argue against Bennett's view of the country's moral state.

➤ Extended Writing Assignments

1. Form a **research** group to investigate the criticism that occurred when the marriage laws were being changed regarding interracial marriages. Take notes on the speeches and newspaper columns that discussed this issue, noting the **pro and con arguments** offered. After your investigation, **compare and contrast** those arguments with Bennett's arguments. Then prepare an oral presentation for class that explains your findings. Such a presentation should have a brief handout for your audience and a written report for your instructor.
2. Sullivan's article argues for same-sex marriage from a legal standpoint. Bennett argues from the viewpoint of ethics and morality. Which of these two viewpoints do you feel should control the argument? Elaborate your **position** in an argumentative essay.

Using the Web in the Classroom

Maria C. González

Introductory Remarks: A professor of English, Maria C. González has taught for many years. Her scholarship includes work on Mexican-American writers, feminist writers, Chicana lesbian writers, and queer theory. González is the author of *Contemporary Mexican-American Women Novelists: Toward a Feminist Identity*. She received her BA and MA degrees in English from Our Lady of the Lake University in San Antonio, Texas, and her PhD in English from Ohio State University. She currently teaches in the English Department at the University of Houston.

Pre-Reading Ideas: The World Wide Web has become an invaluable tool for some researchers. It provides immediate access to information, to library catalogues, to online journals, magazines, and books, and to services such as online bookstores. In the classroom, it has opened up students' knowledge to a variety of sources that they might otherwise not have known about. However, it does have its drawbacks. The following two articles describe the good and bad points about the World Wide Web and what it has to offer students. If you have used the Web for help in creating research papers, take some time before you read these essays to decide your feelings about the Web as opposed to traditional library research. Has the Web helped or frustrated you? Have your papers improved since you have had access to the Web? Do you have access to the Web when you need it? Jot down some prewriting notes taking a position on the value or drawbacks the Web offers.

Vocabulary: Looking up and understanding the following words prior to reading should prepare you for the author's message. Other words will be defined in the margin.

information retrieval   mediocre

1   The World Wide Web is here to stay, and teachers should not be afraid or dismissive° of new technologies. Our job as teachers in whatever scholarly field we are in is to learn how to use the Web as another tool in the classroom. Our students will use the Web whether we like it or not. As a teacher of writing, I have found that the Web can be a useful new technology in the classroom. All teachers need to do is learn how to harness the power of the Web as one of the more efficient information retrieval sites now available to us, in the same way we try to teach our students the use of the actual physical library. We as teachers are still responsible to our students to help them develop the critical thinking skills they need to differentiate° between good and mediocre sources, how to paraphrase and quote useful sources, and how to cite those sources appropriately. The Web can be as useful a research tool as the actual library is to scholars. Above all, we must remember that true scholars use all available resources in their research, including libraries, archives, and the World Wide Web.

2   Our students are in the early stages of becoming scholars. For many of them, learning to tell the difference between a good and useful source and one that is mediocre is part of their initial education. Using the World Wide Web, pulling a few examples off the Web, and walking a student through the many kinds of resources on the Web, represents one of the many ways to teach from the Web. A student needs to learn to navigate the Web in the same way she must learn to navigate the library. Just as there are useful information and reference desks at libraries, there are useful search engines on the Web. The critical thinking skill needed to navigate efficiently through the endless possibilities of information resources available requires specific concrete train-

dismissive: rejecting

differentiate: to distinguish

ing in the classroom. Too often teachers assume students know the difference between good sources and mediocre sources. Students must be taught and shown the difference. To the uninitiated, if the source discusses, in whatever form, the general topic, it must be acceptable. I argue that many of the complaints against students using the Web stem from our students' inability to tell the difference between a mediocre generalization° and a useful specific example. The difference is something that a teacher must consciously make clear to students. Giving a wide variety of examples between generalizations that say very little and specific information that can make an argument concrete provides the student with a clear difference between good and mediocre sources. These examples should include articles from mass culture, academic journals and books, as well as good and mediocre sites from the Web. By using a variety of examples, the student comes to understand that good information can and does come from a variety of sources.

generalization: an assertion that includes every thing or every person

3   Once a student has a myriad of resources available on a given topic, the next challenge is to be able to use those sources properly. To quote and paraphrase properly is a specific writing skill that our students must learn. The Web has been accused of causing the destruction of our students' writing skills. That our students commit the great crime of plagiarism more now than ever before because the Web has made it easier for them is another charge made against the Web. It is very difficult to substantiate such a claim as today's student is a far worse writer than the student of the past or that students commit plagiarism more today than in the past. What I can say is that students find it very difficult to incorporate outside sources smoothly into their essays. They unconsciously and sometimes consciously commit plagiarism. And yes, the Web does make it easier to download essays. There are, however, search engines available to capture such blatant acts of plagiarism. My job is to teach students how to paraphrase and quote appropriately and correctly from a variety of sources. This includes asking students to provide the original sources at different points in the writing process. Other instructors simply ask that all sources be included as part of the final product. The writing skills needed to incorporate outside sources in an essay should be taught throughout the student's academic career. This is a progressive skill not mastered in a single semester, in a single class. The Web provides an almost unlimited number of sources, but a student must learn how to paraphrase and quote those sources the same way she learns to use sources available in a traditional library.

4   Finally, after students have found appropriate outside sources, they must also cite those sources properly. The Web is no different from an academic journal or book in terms of having to be very clear as to where the researcher got the information she is using. Teachers do not accept half-identified books or articles. Why, then, do they accept partially identified sources from the Web? Manuals available in each field provide specific examples as to how to cite the new electronic technologies properly. We should ask students to be as responsible for knowing and using those rules as they are for knowing and using the traditional rules of citation in fields such as Psychology or English. If a student fails to cite the Web properly, the student is committing a case of

plagiarism. For many of our students, plagiarism can simply mean they are unaware of the proper way to cite a source. Because the Web is simply another source, another tool, our students must learn how to cite the Web just as they learn how to cite a book.

5   The World Wide Web is another useful tool in the arsenal of a scholar. It is not the answer to our writing challenges. It is not a monster that must be kept out of the classroom. It is another information resource available to teachers and students. We decide how to use it. But like all developments in education, we must also learn how to use it so it adds to our students' base of skills. The World Wide Web is a very efficient means of retrieving information, but it can never replace the more complex challenge of how to use that acquired information in one's writing. A teacher and a student must work together to make sure the student attains that much more difficult skill. The Web is just another useful information source available to students in our classrooms, and we as teachers must teach them how to use the Web appropriately.

➤ Follow-Up Questions

1. What are some of the teacher responsibilities that González lists?
2. What does González recognize as the specific complaints against the student's use of the Internet? How can these problems be overcome?
3. What are the pros and cons that González points out regarding effective use of the Internet in the student's writing?

➤ Short Writing Assignments

1. Choose a topic that can be researched on the Internet. Then, using the Internet, find three top-quality academic sources and three "mediocre" sources. Prepare a report that briefly **summarizes** the information for each source, notes its strengths and weaknesses, and cites the source in the format acceptable for your class.
2. Interview students to discover their views of the positive and negative points about using the Internet in the classroom and the often frustrating logistics associated with such use. Then, in a short essay, explain your findings.

➤ Extended Writing Assignments

1. The issue of plagiarism is one that is often on the minds of students and instructors alike. Often plagiarism occurs because the student is unaware of exactly how to document a source or has quoted incorrectly or has even forgotten to include it on his/her Bibliography or Works Cited page. **Research** the **definition** of plagiarism and the many ways it can occur in a paper. Then prepare a report explaining your findings, supporting them with specific **examples.**
2. The Internet contains a wide variety of sources of different types, such as an article from a journal which is different from a professional Web site that gives information. Each is documented differently. Refer to Appendix 3: MLA Documentation and Sample Paper to discover the ways to document each source. Search the Internet to find ten different types of sources. Then create a Works Cited page to record each of these sources.

How the Web Destroys the Quality
of Students' Research Papers

David Rothenberg

Pre-Reading Ideas: This is the second of the textbook's two articles about the World Wide Web. From the title, you should be able to determine David Rothenberg's position about the use of the Web for students' papers. The view of Web use as a shortcut to research is like the argument against *Cliff's Notes*. Both are tools that facilitate learning, and both are tools that have been abused. Whether you use the Web (or *Cliff's Notes*) or not, you should think about the values and the distractions that it causes before you take a side with either essay. Determine where you stand. Prewrite for a while before you read the essay and support the decision about where you stand. If either author sways you to his or her side, then be able to defend your change of position based on what you have read.

1   Sometimes I look forward to the end-of-semester rush, when students' final papers come streaming into my office and mailbox. I could have hundreds of pages of original thought to read and evaluate. Once in a while, it *is* truly exciting, and brilliant words are typed across a paper in response to a question I've asked the class to discuss.

2   But this past semester was different. I noticed a disturbing decline in both the quality of the writing and the originality of the thoughts expressed. What had happened since last fall? Did I ask worse questions? Were my students unusually lazy? No. My class had fallen victim to the latest easy way of writing a paper: doing their research on the World Wide Web.

3   It's easy to spot a research paper that is based primarily on information collected from the Web. First the bibliography cites no books, just articles or pointers to places in that virtual land somewhere off any map: *http://www.etc.* Then a strange preponderance° of material in the bibliography is curiously out of date. A lot of stuff on the Web that is advertised as timely is actually at least a few years old. (One student submitted a research paper last semester in which all of his sources were articles published between September and December 1995; that was probably the time span of the Web pages on which he found them.)

preponderance: a great amount

4   Another clue is the beautiful pictures and graphs that are inserted neatly into the body of the student's text. They look impressive, as though they were the result of careful work and analysis, but actually they often bear little relation to the precise subject of the paper. Cut and pasted from the vast realm of what's out there for the taking, they masquerade as original work.

5   Accompanying them are unattributed quotes (in which one can't tell who made the statement or in what context) and curiously detailed references to the kinds of things that are easy to find on the Web (pages and

pages of federal documents, corporate propaganda, or snippets of commentary by people whose credibility is difficult to assess). Sadly, one finds few references to careful, in-depth commentaries on the subject of the paper, the kind of analysis that requires a book, rather than an article, for its full development.

6   Don't get me wrong, I'm no neo-Luddite. I am as enchanted as anyone else by the potential of this new technology to provide instant information. But too much of what passes for information these days is simply *advertising* for information. Screen after screen shows you where you can find out more, how you can connect to this place or that. The acts of linking and networking and randomly jumping from here to there become as exciting or rewarding as actually finding anything of intellectual value.

algorithms:
ways to solve
a problem

query: question

7   Search engines, with their half-baked algorithms°, are closer to slot machines than to library catalogues. You throw your query° to the wind, and who knows what will come back to you? You may get 234,468 supposed references to whatever you want to know. Perhaps one in a thousand might actually help you. But it's easy to be sidetracked or frustrated as you try to go through those Web pages one by one. Unfortunately, they're not arranged in order of importance.

machinations: a
crafty plan

8   What I'm describing is the hunt-and-peck method of writing a paper. We all know that word processing makes many first drafts look far more polished than they are. If the paper doesn't reach the assigned five pages, readjust the margin, change the font size, and . . . *voilà!* Of course, those machinations° take up time that the student could have spent revising the paper. With programs to check one's spelling and grammar now standard features on most computers, one wonders why students make any mistakes at all. But errors are as prevalent as ever, no matter how crisp the typeface. Instead of becoming perfectionists, too many students have become slackers, preferring to let the machine do their work for them.

synthesize: to
bring parts
together

montage: a
composite of
several separate
elements

9   What the Web adds to the shortcuts made possible by word processing is to make research look too easy. You lose a query to the machine, wait a few minutes, and suddenly a lot of possible sources of information appear on your screen. Instead of books that you have to check out of the library, read carefully, understand, synthesize°, and then tactfully excerpt, these sources are quips, blips, pictures, and short summaries that may be downloaded magically to the dorm-room computer screen. Fabulous! How simple! The only problem is that a paper consisting of summaries of summaries is bound to be fragmented and superficial, and to demonstrate more of a random montage° than an ability to sustain an argument through ten to fifteen double-spaced pages.

10   Of course, you can't blame the students for ignoring books. When college libraries are diverting funds from books to computer technology that will be obsolete in two years at most, they send a clear message to students: Don't read, just connect. Surf. Download. Cut and paste. Originality becomes hard to separate from plagiarism as no author is cited on a Web page. Clearly, the words are up for grabs, and students much prefer the fabulous jumble to the hard work of stopping to think and make sense of what they've read.

repositories: storage places

11   Libraries used to be repositories° of words and ideas. Now they are seen as centers for the retrieval of information. Some of this information comes from other, bigger libraries, in the form of books that can take time to obtain through interlibrary loan. What happens to the many students (some things never change) who scramble to write a paper the night before it's due? The computer screen, the gateway to the world sitting right on their desks, promises instant access—but actually offers only a pale, two-dimensional version of a real library.

12   But it's also my fault. I take much of the blame for the decline in the quality of my student research in my class. I need to teach students how to read, to take time with language and ideas, to work through arguments, to synthesize disparate sources to come up with original thought. I need to help my students understand how to assess sources to determine their credibility, as well as to trust their own ideas more than snippets of thought that materialize on a screen. The placelessness of the Web leads to an

ethereal: airy, abstract

randomness: wandering

ethereal° randomness° of thought. Gone are the pathways of logic and passion, the sense of the progress of an argument. Chance holds sway, and it more often misses than hits. Judgment must be taught, as well as the methods of exploration.

wane: lessen

13   I'm seeing my students' attention spans wane° and their ability to reason for themselves decline. I wish that the university's computer system would crash for a day, so that I could encourage them to go outside, sit under a tree, and read a really good book—from start to finish. I'd like them to sit for a while and ponder what it means to live in a world where some things get easier and easier so rapidly that we can hardly keep track of how easy they're getting, while other tasks remain as hard as ever—such as doing research and writing a good paper that teaches the writer something in the process. Knowledge does not emerge in a vacuum, but we do need silence and space for

sustained: continued

sustained° thought. Next semester, I'm going to urge my students to turn off their glowing boxes and think, if only once in a while.

➤ Follow-Up Questions

1. What characteristics does Rothenberg state are usually in papers that used the Web for source material?
2. What problems does Rothenberg see with search engines?
3. What are the problems with spelling and grammar that Rothenberg links to the use of word processors for papers?

➤ Short Writing Assignments

1. Rothenberg notes that sometimes the academic reliability of a source is difficult to determine. **Research** what you would consider an academic topic on the Internet. Collect ten sources and then prepare a report that identifies the credentials of each source and a short statement for each in which you **evaluate** the reliability of that source.
2. Select an academic topic, do a search of that topic, and then start counting. Visit as many sites as possible to determine the number of sites your search engine pulled up for that topic and how relevant each site was. You do not have to visit or read each site,

but you do have to review the short **summary** given by the search engine when it lists the sites. Then prepare a report explaining your **process**/procedure; if you became frustrated and stopped before finishing, explain what problems led you to this action.

➤ Extended Writing Assignments

1. Choose an academic topic which is of a general nature, such as weapons of World War II or the history of the airplane. **Research** your library for five sources on your topic. Then research the Internet for the same topic. Write a report **comparing and contrasting** not only your efforts at research but the number of sources available through each, and the quality of the material available.

2. Interview the librarians in your school's library to discover how the function of the library has altered over the last five to ten years. Then prepare a report explaining your findings.

Life, Death, and the Living Will

Elizabeth Rodriguez Kessler

Introductory Remarks: Currently teaching a variety of literature courses at California State University at Northridge, Elizabeth Rodriguez Kessler moved to California from Houston, Texas, where she lived and taught English the majority of her life. She graduated from the University of Houston with her BA in English, from Sam Houston State University with her MA in English and her credential in mid-management for secondary education, and from University of Houston with her PhD in English. Kessler has taught high school English as well as English at Houston Community College, Sam Houston State University, and University of Houston. Kessler is currently working on several anthologies, including a collection of personal narratives from World War II veterans and their families and a collection of her own personal narratives and poetry.

Pre-Reading Ideas: This is the first of the textbook's two articles on creating living wills. Before you read either article, determine how you feel about creating a living will. Enter a paragraph or two into your journal discussing your position and reasons for feeling this way. Now, consider your ideas in relation to a person who is close to you who might one day be terminally ill and in suffering that no medication can alleviate and who has directed the doctor and/or family members how to care for him or her in extreme circumstances. Are your feelings the same when you personalize the issue as opposed to when you think about it as a concept?

1 Heart attack vs. Alzheimer's disease? Car accident vs. old age? The sudden vs. the drawn out? I would like to die in my bed, relatively unaware of a massive attack that destroys my heart or my brain in an instant, rather than

linger for days, months, or years, slowly losing my self-sufficiency, my mobility, and my dignity or remaining in a comatose state where I must be tended to indefinitely. Yet few of us are allowed to give people like me the opportunity to slip away peacefully, avoiding the horrors that a slow death perpetrates on the body as well as the infinite agonies it inflicts on the families of the loved one. A simple flip of a switch, pull of a plug, or disconnection from a machine takes moments and saves endless distress and pain. However, in most states, that simple act is considered murder, and concerned individuals are not given the choice to invoke euthanasia when it is clearly a procedure performed in the patient's best interest. To avoid this problem, many individuals have chosen to write a living will, a legal document constructed by an individual prior to going into surgery directing the doctor and/or relatives how to treat him or her if complications arise. Doing this removes the responsibility from the patient's relatives of deciding whether or not to allow the patient to receive heroic measures to save his or her life or whether to remove life-sustaining equipment from a patient in a coma. If the patient is in complete control of his or her mental capacities when making the will, the doctors and relatives are required to follow the patient's wishes. Although this can be a benefit to some, I believe that it is also a death sentence that robs a patient of valuable time needed to help him or her survive a coma.

angioplasty:
procedure to
unclog an artery

2   "He's just going in for an angioplasty°."

3   My mother's words still ring in my ears six years after my step-father entered St. Joseph's Hospital for a routine procedure. The night before the simple surgery, Floyd began having chest pain. Already in the cardiac unit, he was treated immediately for a mild heart attack, but it was not serious enough to cancel the next day's event. We were looking forward to a time after his clogged arteries were cleared so he could return to normal activity: playing golf, swimming daily at the local "Y," and teaching senior citizens how to swim. This seventy-five-year-old retiree was not an overweight "couch potato" who had nothing to do after working all his life. He was vital, active, and generally healthy. Unfortunately, his heart and arteries were not cooperating.

4   After going through the attempted angioplasty, Floyd was diagnosed as a candidate for a quadruple bypass. The procedure had not been sufficient to clear his blocked arteries. We were disappointed and concerned, but fear had not yet entered the picture. My mother had been a nurse for many years, and although she had left the profession and distanced herself from medicine, she still knew the danger signs and the medical language she heard. Stoicism, her old ally as a nurse, returned to her as the wife of a patient. Her strength spread to Floyd and to me, and we prepared mentally and emotionally for the next day's surgery.

5   When I arrived at the hospital the next morning, I discovered Floyd had had a more serious set of pains as they prepped him, and the doctors were delaying surgery until he was stabilized. Mother and I waited, sitting among other cardiac patients' families as they moved in and out of surgery, assembly-line fashion. Soon a doctor came to announce that Floyd had gone into surgery, and we settled in for the long wait. Mother flipped mindlessly through magazines while I concentrated on my newest intricate counted cross-stitch

piece: a Christmas angel. Anyone who does counted cross-stitch knows that absolute concentration is needed or stitches have to be ripped out and re-done. This was my form of therapy as hours passed. Lunch came and went. Mother and I walked the halls, shifted positions, called our offices, visited with a few friends, and generally avoided talking about the one important person in our lives who was in jeopardy.

6   By 6 o'clock, our endurance was spent, and we began annoying nurses or anyone who looked "official" for information. The news came: "He's being wheeled out of surgery now, and it was successful." We hugged, cried, and joined others in the waiting room who shared our news and congratulated us. We did not know, however, that the joy would be short-lived.

7   We walked into the Intensive Care Cardiac Unit to find Floyd connected to a respirator, a tube in his mouth, IV bags hanging from a metal pole drip-ping medication and other vital fluids into his body, a portable blood pressure machine next to the bed, a bag hanging at the side of his bed to collect and measure urine, and a nurse standing at the foot of the bed jotting notes on his chart. Mom stood beside him, rubbing his cold hand, transferring her warmth and strength to him, fully confident that within a couple of hours, we would accompany him to his room on the cardiac floor. We believed the nurse and we took hope from others who were being released after their anesthetic had worn off. We waited.

8   Can you imagine watching a strong, vital man of close to two hundred pounds and six feet tall deteriorate before your eyes? In only a couple of days, the tube resting on his lip created a wound. His skin became quite frag-ile when nutrients weren't being properly absorbed by his body. Weight loss occurred despite liquid diets of turkey and dressing and pot roast. Bed sores formed regardless of how many times the patient was turned or how many pillows nurses and aides placed between his knees, now bony, or between his hips and the sheets. And the involuntary fighting while he was in the coma resulted in having to strap him down, further irritating wrists and an-kles. By day seven, Floyd had not yet come out of the anesthetic; he had gone into a coma, brain damage was feared, and pneumonia complicated by his diabetes was creating stress on his heart. The ironic part was that his heart was the best functioning part of his body. "The surgery was successful, but the patient died": a little morbid humor at a time when everything else looked hopeless.

9   The doctors consulted with my mother at least twice daily if not more, as my mother and I were moved to a less-used waiting room and mother "held court." Sometimes we had crowds of visitors. Sometimes we had each other. My angel sustained us both as we saw small portions beginning to take shape. Finally the doctors announced that if they saw no improvement in the next twenty-four hours, the prognosis would be bleak. They hinted gently that Mom should consider removing him from the respirator, especially since Floyd had left a living will. It indicated that in the event of complications, he should not remain on life-support systems for more than a week if he were incapacitated. Mother, in her stoicism, listened and consulted with me. For the

first time in my life, I had to confront my own principles. I ran to my ivory tower sanctuary that protected me from reality, seeking answers from the rational world, but I lived in a human, emotional world apart from the sterility of my books. I flew to my brain for answers, but I looked into my soul. We had twenty-four hours to accept the decision.

10   The doctors reassured us that Floyd was in no pain, but they could not explain why he wouldn't wake up. We searched for little signs. He squeezed our hands. No, it's muscle spasms. He smiled. Gas. He moved his leg. Involuntary muscle movement. Time, which had moved at such a snail's pace for a week, now fled past us, speeding through eternity. As Saturday morning was moving to afternoon, I called home to tell my eighteen-year-old son and his father to come visit that evening. And Mother and I wrestled privately with the event we would have to witness Sunday morning.

11   Mother and I were already by Floyd's bedside when David and Jim arrived. David relied on us to know how to react. Although he knew his grandfather's condition, no one had told him the gravity of the situation. But David inherited the Stoicism gene from his grandmother. He kissed her, then me. Then the miracle occurred. He walked over to his grandfather, took his hand and said, as if it were a normal Sunday afternoon visit, "Hi, Grandpa. How're you doin'?" Suddenly the "involuntary spasm" was choreographed with a weak smile (gas), and an actual look of recognition in Floyd's eyes. We were stunned. We were silent. And then we were cautiously jubilant. We called the nurse, and even she could see a change in her patient's eyes. He was back. Recovery would take three months, but he would recover fully.

12   Because of Floyd's miracle recovery, I maintain my position that the creation of a living will in which a patient determines his own medical destiny is inappropriate. Floyd tried to relieve his as well as our unanticipated suffering in the event that it could not be reversed or halted. He chose to end it after what he believed to be a reasonable period. Doing so removes any possibility of a cure or of the patient's ability to fight back successfully. Had he not responded to David's greeting, we would have been legally required to comply with his directions. Fortunately, Floyd stopped his own decree. Today he is healthy, happy, and with us, having barely escaped a self-imposed, premature end.

➤ Follow-Up Questions

1. Why is it surprising to Kessler that Floyd would develop such a serious heart problem?
2. What change in Floyd's recovery prompted the doctors to consider removing the life support system from Floyd?
3. What is the "miracle" in the story?

➤ Short Writing Assignments

1. Choose either a heart attack or Alzheimer's disease and **research** the symptoms and effects of such a disease on the body. Prepare your findings in a short essay.

2. An **oxymoron** is the joining of two contradictory terms that are accepted as true. Consider the phrase "living will." Is this an oxymoron and, if so, how? Explain your **analysis** in essay form. Conclude your essay with a list and explanation of four other oxymorons you know.

➤ Extended Writing Assignments

1. Reread the story, but stop at the point just before David arrives. In essay format, explain whether you would have removed Floyd from life support or not and the reasons for your decision.
2. Consider the practices of mercy killing or euthanasia versus that of assisted suicide, such as practiced by Dr. Kevorkian, or an order in a living will. Choose two of the practices and write a **comparison- and-contrast** essay that considers the major factors relating to each. Conclude with your own **evaluation** of each practice as to its ethical merit.

Hopes and Wishes

Anne Perrin

Introductory Remarks: For biographical information, see Perrin's essay "Kids" in Chapter 2, Youth.

Pre-Reading Ideas: In the second of this textbook's two articles on living wills, Perrin provides the supporting argument for the writing of the will. Before you read either article, be sure you understand what a living will is and how you feel about writing one for yourself or recommending that a loved one write or not write one for himself/herself.

Vocabulary: Looking up and understanding the following words prior to reading should prepare you for the author's message. Other words will be defined in the margin.

terminally ill   incapacitated   CPR   Parkinson's disease

1   There weren't very many visitors that Thanksgiving evening when I went to visit my father at Northwest Memorial Hospital. Most of my immediate family had already visited my father that day, while I had stayed behind to clean up after the meal we had eaten. To tell the truth, trying to recall the exact *sequence°* of events during that stage of my father's illness is rather *fruitless°*. Anyone who has ever taken care of a terminally ill person knows that time and the normal events of the day or week just become a blur. The only references you end up with are the major shocks and the pathetic little victories. You start referring to time as "three days before surgery" or "two hours until his next medication." What I remember about that Thanksgiving evening is stepping out of that hospital elevator on my father's floor and hear-

sequence: order
fruitless: useless

ing a continuous bloodcurdling scream coming from a room way down the hall. At the time all I could do was hope my father was able to get some rest despite all the noise and to feel pity for the poor soul who was in such agony. As I got closer to my father's room, the screams got louder, and I remember that as I got further down the hall, I started getting upset that the nurses weren't helping that patient, whoever he was. When I got to door of my father's room, I realized that he was the poor soul. I can honestly tell you that knees do buckle. The surgery to remove the malignant brain tumor had left my father with an enormous number of staples in his head and in delirious pain, which no amount of medicine could alleviate. I spent the rest of the evening sitting in that room listening to my father's agony, hoping that the operation had bought him the year we had hoped for and firmly believing that for the time being, this was the worst it could get.

2   My father was a very practical man and no quitter. He had spent over forty years of his life as the chief engineer on ocean freighters°, mostly for the Sinclair and Arco oil companies, so he was realistic about the world. When the doctors discovered he had Parkinson's disease, the family grieved and thought that was about the worst that could happen. It is a horrible sight to see a man whose hobby was master carpentry deteriorate to the point that someone had to cut his food because his hands were shaking so badly. My parents, realizing the inevitable, sought the help of my older sister, Susan, who had worked as a legal secretary for a number of years, to arrange their affairs before my father got to the point of being incapacitated. When I heard that my parents both had written living wills, I was floored. I had taken CPR refresher courses just to be on the safe side if anything should happen to a family member, and here, when death loomed as a distant but inevitable fact, the idea of refusing to try anything to save a loved one was beyond me.

freighters: large ships that carry cargo

3   After one of his hospital visits for treatment of his Parkinson's, I told my mother to talk to the doctors because my father looked and moved worse than before. The end result was more doctor visits and tests during which time his motor skills diminished to the point that we had to tie him to a wheelchair to keep him from sliding out and tie his arms to the arms of the chair because they would fall and turn blue from poor circulation. The test results prompted a visit by my parents, one of my brothers, and me to a surgeon's office. Time became a blur for me starting with that visit. I remember my father was in his wheelchair, tied in, on my left, my mother in the chair to my right. I know the doctor was in a desk right in front of us, but his presence is only a shadow in my mind, formless and inconsequential to the moment. The image burned into my memory from that visit is the X-ray posted above the doctor's head showing a black spot in my father's brain, a malignant tumor the size of a small fried egg. To hear that my father had only two months to live without treatment was, up to that time, the worst I could imagine. The hope offered was in the form of surgery, radiation, and chemotherapy, which could buy my father a year. How does one make such a decision affecting a parent? Fortunately, my father's mental awareness, which was now gradually ebbing away by the hour, revived for a brief time, enough to understand the doctor and enough to give him one directive: "Do it!" Hope truly does spring eternal.

4   Even that Thanksgiving visit was not without a glimmer of possibility, of knowing that one could cheat Fate just a little longer. The surgeon had said the operation went fine, but a few days later the radiologist informed the family that there was no way he would even consider treating my father because of his Parkinson's disease and general condition. We were crushed. The end result of the operation was excruciating pain relieved somewhat by medication, whose side effect was a yeast infection in his mouth and throat which made it difficult for my father to eat. Instead of the last two months of his life gradually fading into a coma, my father's last months were spent mostly in pain and complications from medications. I never saw the surgeon after he came out of the operating room that day and said everything went well, and quite frankly, for my own peace of mind, I hope I never do. I'll let God deal with him.

5   On Christmas Day, 1993, my father slipped into a coma and would have died that day if my sister Susan had not insisted that an ambulance take him to a hospital where, among other things, she made the hospital aware of my father's living will. There family members were given the opportunity to say their final good-byes, and he was given the last rites. I volunteered to spend the nights there, keeping vigil while the rest of the family got some rest. Late in the evening of the second day, as I was falling asleep on the hospital cot, my father's breathing changed, and I knew what was happening. I don't remember how, but in the next second I was in the hall screaming for the nurse. She instructed me to run to the nurse's station to get a suction device to clear my father's throat, but it brought him no relief. She then informed me that he was going and asked me if I wanted him put on life support. I told her he had a living will, but she asked again what I wanted. There are some questions a person should not have to answer, decisions that go beyond the responsibilities of parent/child, beyond what one human being owes another. Here I was, the one with all those CPR refresher courses, the one who felt comfortable letting my older sister arrange for a living will, the one who had opposed the living will from the beginning, having to decide then and there whether to keep my father alive any longer. No time for legal or moral discussions, no time for family meetings or doctor consultation. How does one decide? What criteria do you use, what standard? How are you supposed to live with these decisions? When it mattered the most, the only priority, the only criteria I had was my father's own wishes. "No, let him go" was all I told her. He passed away a few minutes later.

6   There is a particular character in Shakespeare's *King Lear* whom I often think of. His name is Edgar, and he spends part of his time in the play saying that each tragic event is the "worst" in his life. What he learns in the play is that no matter how bad things appear, they can always get worse. I won't say my decision that night was the worst I'll ever make; I do not wish to tempt my Fates. What I will say is that my father made the decision a comfortable one

for me by letting me know his wishes. His living will was his last gift to me. Thank you, Papa. Sweet dreams.

➤ Follow-Up Questions

1. What are the specific conditions which Perrin's father suffered from in the story?
2. What is the initial difference between her parents' views of a living will and Perrin's? Does Perrin change her attitude in the story?
3. Perrin describes her father as "no quitter," and as someone who makes a living will. How can you reconcile these two descriptions?

➤ Short Writing Assignments

1. Explain what you see as the significance of the title, "Hopes and Wishes," in relation to the story.
2. In the narrative, Perrin states that "There are some questions a person should not have to answer, decisions that go beyond the responsibilities of parent/child, beyond what one human being owes another." Determine what one of those questions could be and explain both the question and the possible effects of having to deal with such an issue.

➤ Extended Writing Assignments

1. Research the legal requirements of a living will in your state. Include in your investigations not only what rights and wishes such documents can protect, but also the forms and documents needed, and how such a living will is put into effect. Then prepare a report that explains your findings.
2. Consider what would be the pros and cons of having a living will. Your **research** may include Internet and library sources regarding such a document and possibly interviews with individuals who either have such a document in place or are in the process of having one made. Then determine your **position** on such a document and prepare an argumentative essay in which you support your decision.

CONCLUSION

This chapter has presented opposing viewpoints on several controversial issues that are of current interest because they have recently been introduced to society, such as the extensive research on cloning and the increased use of the Web, and issues that are of traditional concern, such as living wills and same-sex marriages. In addition, controversial issues and topics have been introduced at the end of each chapter in this text. As you can see from the articles in this chapter, argumentation may take the traditional essay form or it can be presented through exemplification in a personal narrative as Kessler and Perrin wrote. Writers also use Letters to the Editor to express their opinions. Regardless of the mode, the purpose remains to convince your reader to believe your position.

➤ Further Writing Topics

There are plenty of current articles and essays on the following topics which will provide information you can use to write a well-developed argumentative essay:

Capital punishment	Zero tolerance policy in schools
Violence on television	Sex education in high schools
Pornography	Cheating in schools
Abortion: the morning-after pill	Legalizing marijuana
HMOs	Prayer in public schools
Assisted suicide	New forms of contraception
Day care for infants and toddlers	Single-sex schools
Requiring entrance exams for universities	Affirmative action

➤ Suggested Chapter Projects

1. One of the more controversial issues related to capital punishment is whether to execute those individuals who have been found guilty of a capital crime but who are considered mentally incapable of comprehending their crime or punishment. Research the discussions that have occurred within the last ten years on this topic to gain a perspective on the major issues involved and to determine whether such points have changed over time. Then explain both sides of the argument in a report and conclude with your own evaluation of whether to execute the mentally incapacitated. Write this as an argumentative essay in which you use a delayed thesis, one that announces your position in an inductive argument.

2. Many school districts in the United States have invested large amounts of money in equipping schools with computers. Investigate a school district in your area or possibly your college to discover the pros and cons of such an investment. Such research should consider not only the initial cost of the equipment and software, but also the "hidden costs" of subscribing to online indexes, warranties on equipment, maintenance agreements, and upgrades to accommodate new technologies. Then prepare an argumentative essay in which you decide whether such costs are of real benefit to the school or whether such monies could be better spent on books, better teacher salaries, or other school improvements.

3. The launch of the space shuttle, once considered a momentous event, is now regarded by the general public as an ordinary part of life. However, the nature of such missions is never fully disclosed to the general public in news broadcasts. Research the launch of at least one shuttle mission, noting who was in the space craft and their fields of study, how long the shuttle was in space, and what projects were reported on the news broadcasts, as an example on which to base your discussion. Then prepare an argumentative report in which you either favor or oppose the full disclosure of activities and research done on a shuttle mission.

PART THREE

Expanding Your Reading and Writing Skills

Reading and Writing about Nonfiction

Nonfiction literature is at a disadvantage: it is defined by what it isn't rather than by what it is. It is literature that does not rely on the conventions of fiction to develop it. Thus, there are normally no characters and no plot development. Instead, nonfiction prose relies on rhetorical conventions, those used in persuasion, and on any of the patterns of development mentioned in the sections "The Paragraph" and "Writing the Essay" (see Part I). Now that you know how to write nonfiction prose and have read examples of nonfiction prose, you will be able to analyze it and write *about* it.

THE INFORMATIVE ESSAY

First, we will begin with the informative essay. If you consider what you have learned about writing it, you will discover that experienced writers do the same things you are expected to do so they can communicate with their audience. They also use the same patterns of development you learned about in Part I. Below is a brief review of what each pattern does. If you need to review how each is constructed, you should refer to the individual examples in the section "The Paragraph" in Part I. If you need to review how they are incorporated into an essay, you should review "The Cat's Meow" in the section, "Writing the Essay." You might also review the paragraphs you wrote earlier that are examples of the patterns listed.

PATTERNS OF DEVELOPMENT

Narration—telling a story or relating an event

Exemplification—developing through examples

Cause and effect—showing how one event caused the consequences of another   *continued*

PATTERNS OF DEVELOPMENT CONTINUED

Process—explaining how to do something or showing how something is done

Division and classification—breaking a subject down into its parts and classifying them according to certain categories

Description—explaining the physical characteristics of a subject

Comparison-and-Contrast—showing the similarities and differences of two or more subjects

Expository—presenting information or explaining an idea

Definition—explaining a term through denotation and connotation

To write a critical analysis of nonfiction prose, a writer must first be a good critical reader. The "Steps for Successful Reading" in the section "The Reading Process" (Part I) are good preliminary steps. They help the reader understand the passage or the longer work. To analyze, however, goes beyond the understanding level and relies on critical reading skills. Because the assignment is to analyze an informative passage, you should follow these steps and answer all questions.

- **Consider the title.** What clues does the title give you to the work? Does it raise your curiosity?
- **What is the purpose of the article?** Is it written to entertain? To reflect about emotions, attitudes, beliefs, agendas? To inform? Or to persuade? Just as essays incorporate different patterns of development, informative essays frequently incorporate other purposes. Look at Fortuna Benudiz Ippoliti's essay, "Mama Sarah," on death in Chapter 9, Finalities. She combines personal narrative, which is reflective, with the expository pattern, which is informative.
- **What is the thesis of the article?** Is it stated or implied? If it is stated, underline or highlight it, identifying it as the thesis. Look for the topic sentences. If it is a long passage, one idea or topic might be developed within several paragraphs. Does each topic sentence support the thesis or the subtopic? Identify each topic sentence. Basically, you are looking for the literal meaning of the work: what is the author trying to say?
- **What is your personal response to the article after your first reading?** Did you like it? Dislike it? Enjoy it? Express your immediate response by stating what the article said to you.

- **What patterns of development does the author use to support her thesis?** Return to the section "Writing the Essay" in Part I and reread the paragraph labeled "To Inform." That paragraph discusses the eight patterns of development Carol Tarvis uses in her twelve-paragraph essay, "How Friendship Was 'Feminized.'" The essay you analyze might not incorporate as many patterns as the Tarvis essay, but you should be reading with an analytical eye to discover the patterns the author used. Highlight and identify passages that supply examples of the patterns.

- **Are there any specialized terms that are specifically related to the article?** If you do not know the definition of every word in the essay or cannot determine its meaning through context, look them up and write the appropriate definitions in the margin. Can you rely on denotation alone, or does the author use words connotatively?

- Is there an observable organizational plan to the article? It might be developed
  - chronologically, in time sequence;

  - through spatial description of a location—top to bottom, north to south, etc.;

  - in a listing sequence, going from least to most important or most to least;

  - through classification by providing categories, divisions, branches;

  - through a process; or

  - by moving from general to specific or specific to general.

- **Does the author employ a specific tone in the piece?** Is it angry, comic, critical, intimate, sad? Highlight the words you believe display the tone. Reread "The Cat's Meow" and determine what its tones.

- **How does the author emphasize important points?** Look for repetition of key words and phrases. Italicizing and capitalizing words, incorporating quotations for support, and exaggeration are also ways to emphasize.

STEPS FOR ANALYZING A READING

Consider the title.

Identify the purpose of the article.

Identify the thesis.

Determine your response to the article after the first reading.

Identify the patterns of development used to support the thesis.

continued

> ## STEPS FOR ANALYZING A READING CONTINUED
>
> Identify and define any specialized terms in the article.
>
> Determine the organizational plan of the article.
>
> Determine the tone.
>
> Look for the important points the author emphasizes.

➤ Short Reading/Writing Assignment

To practice critical reading skills, read Dixon's essay, "Landscapes of Home: Thoughts on Urban Nature?" and answer the above questions as you read. In some cases you will be highlighting, in others you will be making marginal notes, and in others you will be actually writing answers on a sheet of paper.

THE ARGUMENTATIVE ESSAY

Analysis of argument begins with the same steps and questions as analysis of the informative essay, so the steps will continue with the specialized questions for analysis of argumentation following.

- **Did the author distinguish between fact and opinion?** Is the author being objective through the use of fact, or subjective through the use of opinion (as exemplified by value-laden words). Look at the following examples.
  - **Fact**—In 1969 the first astronaut, an American, walked on the moon.
  - **Opinion with value-laden words**—The most important moment in aerospace achievements was the significant step made by the first American to walk on the moon in 1969.
- **Did the author combine fact and opinions in the same sentence?** If you find any facts, opinions, or value-laden words, highlight and identify them. See the example that follows.
  - **Fact and opinion**—Coming home from the hospital after the birth of her first child, Cathy believed she was the luckiest woman in the world.
- **Does the author use persuasive terminology or methods to convince her readers?** She might use a biased approach, privileging her prejudices or political or religious agendas. The author can do this through tone, word choice, deliberate omission of other points of view and or by including quotations from recognizable authorities who support her position.

- **Does the author use logical fallacies or appeals to emotion, morals, aesthetics, or values?** Review the list of logical fallacies discussed "The Argumentative Essay, Presenting Evidence" in Part I. Highlight and identify any examples of appeals and/or fallacies you find.
- **Does the author present relevant evidence?** To be relevant, it should be timely, current, and written by specialists in the field.
- **Does the author manipulate facts, quotations, or statistics?** Both of the following statements say the same thing about a given town. But if the author is trying to encourage the government to give the town federal money to help those without homes, which sentence is more persuasive?
  - Nearly 5% of the population lost their homes in the recent flood.
  - Almost 200,000 people are homeless after the recent flood.

STEPS FOR ANALYZING ARGUMENTATIVE ESSAYS

Identify the facts and opinions the author uses.

Identify examples of facts and opinions used in the same sentences.

Identify examples of persuasive terminology and methods the author uses.

Identify any logical fallacies or appeals to emotions, morals, aesthetics, and values.

Identify the evidence.

Determine if the evidence is relevant.

Examine facts, quotations, and statistics for any signs of manipulation.

Writing Analysis: The Thesis

Although writing literary analysis is similar to writing rhetorical analysis, the two forms of analysis have their own section in the appendices. The following discussion applies to writing rhetorical analysis of nonfiction prose.

Now that you have read the article by Terrell Dixon and you have answered all the appropriate questions, you have completed your prewriting stage. Using the information you have gathered from the questions, you must develop your thesis by first determining what the author's thesis, or controlling idea, is. Yours will be stated in terms of the author's purpose. For example, if you worked with Dixon's essay, you would want to begin with the author as subject and assert his purpose in the essay, which you have discovered by identifying his stated or implied thesis.

Acceptable analytical thesis: Terrell Dixon describes the gradual loss of urban nature and offers suggestions about how to protect what is left in his article "Landscapes of Home: Thoughts on Urban Nature."

Unacceptable analytical thesis: Urban renewal is the reason for the loss of urban nature, and, according to Terrell Dixon's essay "Landscapes of Home: Thoughts on Urban Nature," should be stopped.

Although the second example is an assertion that could be inferred from Dixon's article, it does not state the purpose of his essay. Each thesis is good, but the first is an example of one written for an analysis of the work, whereas the second is an example of one that a student might use when incorporating Dixon's essay along with others, to support and develop an expository essay. A key to writing analysis of a prose nonfiction work is to keep the author in the subject position.

➤ Short Writing Assignment

Using Laurence Tribe's article, "Second Thoughts on Cloning," write an analytical thesis based on his argument.

Writing Analysis: The Essay

Once you have written your thesis, writing an analytical essay follows the same basic rules as those you have already used to write other essays. This kind of essay is informative whether it is an analysis of an informative work or an argumentative one. Use the following points as a review and guide to set up and write your analytical essay about a prose nonfiction piece.

- **Always identify the title and author of the work you will analyze.** This usually comes in your thesis and always comes in your introduction.
- **After the thesis, refer to the author by last name only.** Some students want to use a title, such as Mr., Ms., Dr., or they want to refer to the author by the first name. Because the paper is usually formal, the appropriate strategy is *to refer consistently* to the author by last name only. An exception: If you use two authors with the same last name, refer to each by first and last name, using first name only if repetition of the full name becomes cumbersome in the sentence. For example:
  Cumbersome: In her 1850 Preface to *Wuthering Heights*, Charlotte Brontë acknowledges that the "moorish and wild" aspect of nature in the novel is a "natural" (xxxiv) result of Emily Brontë's familiarity with the surroundings she used as the novel's setting. Charlotte Brontë reflects that had Emily Brontë's "lot been cast in a town, her writings . . . would have possessed another character" (xxxiv).
  Better: In her 1850 Preface to *Wuthering Heights*, Charlotte Brontë acknowledges that the "moorish and wild" aspect of nature in the novel is a "natural" (xxxiv) result of Emily Brontë's familiarity with the sur-

roundings she used as the novel's setting. Charlotte reflects that had Emily's "lot been cast in a town, her writings . . . would have possessed another character" (xxxiv).

Explanation: Even though a writer should not normally refer to the author(s) by first name, to repeat "Brontë" in the second sentence, after the identity has already been determined, is to be unduly repetitive. In such a case, using a first name is acceptable.

- **Provide background information in the introduction.** This introduction will probably fit the rectangle pattern better than the triangle. If the essay is on a specialized topic, a definition paragraph is appropriate. If you want to let the reader know more about the work, a short summary of two or three sentences is appropriate. Avoid the temptation to retell the story of the essay or argue with the author.
- **Use present tense.**
- **Use third person.** Because you are analyzing a given work, avoid reference to "I" (for example, "I believe" or "I think"). Your focus is on the author and the work, not on yourself. Do not say, "I think Dixon offers. . . . " Rather, say, "Dixon offers" or "Tribe argues. . . . " The last two beginnings offer definite approaches to the work, giving the impression that you know and understand the author's purpose. The first sounds tentative and uncertain.
- **Develop and support your points.** When you offer the points of your analysis, you should develop them enough to acquaint your reader with the ideas; then you may use quotations to support your point. Do not simply make an assertion of your point and support it with a quotation. Develop your point from your interpretation of what your author says and support it from the text with a quotation. Provide a follow-up sentence. Explain the relationship of the quotation to the preceding information because your audience might not see the connection that you are making. Remember also that quotations are used to support and advance your analysis, not to repeat it.
- **Use documentation for each quotation.** See Appendix 3: MLA Documentation and Sample Paper for a discussion about plagiarism.
- **Do not argue with the author.** Although you might mentally disagree with him or her, it is not your purpose to counter the arguments or prove the author wrong.
- **Choose an informative title.** Just as you look at the title of a published essay for an idea about the substance of the work you are reading, your audience also wants an indication of what your paper will be about.
- **Include a Works Cited page.** Possible exceptions: Sometimes if you use a single work or write your paper in class, your instructor will not require a Works Cited page. Follow her directions. Use the following paper as a model of a summary analysis of a nonfiction essay.

WRITING ANALYSIS

Identify the title and the author of the work you will analyze.

Refer to the author by last name only unless it will create confusion.

Provide background information in the introduction.

Use present tense.

Use third person.

Develop and support your points.

Use documentation for each quotation.

Do not argue with the author.

Choose an informative title.

Include a Works Cited page.

➤ Extended Writing Assignment

Using Laurence Tribe's essay, "Second Thoughts on Cloning," write an analytical essay explaining his thesis and how he develops his claims.

SAMPLE ANALYTICAL ESSAY

Li 1

Sandra Li

Professor Lynn Baker

English 155

25 November 2001

Private vs. Public Sex

Although the contemporary generation did not invent
sex, their public display of sexual behavior appears to
announce their discovery of it and their presentation
of it to the world. The humorous part is that today's
youth is acting almost the same way youth from the last

few generations acted. Are you old enough to remember the Hippies of the 1960s? "Make love not war" was their motto. However, the public display of affection or sexuality beyond a quick kiss or handholding is frequently not approved by those who believe sex is sacred and private. S. I. Hayakawa, in his article, "Sex Is Not a Spectator Sport," argues that intimate sexuality between two people is a private, beautiful activity when participated in privately, but it becomes obscene and pornographic when exposed to public view and as a public act in movies should be censored.

Hayakawa initiates his discussion of sexuality by distinguishing between participants and observers. Agreeing that sexual behavior between two loving adults enhances a relationship, he further explains the importance of sexual intercourse: "a rich relationship is reaffirmed and made richer by their lovemaking" (1165). This comment establishes Hayakawa's credibility as an individual who supports sexual behavior rather than one who censors it. In fact, he firmly asserts that "sexual behavior is not itself obscene" (1165). This declaration solidifies his position as an individual who is not attempting to censor what a loving couple does in the privacy of their bedroom.

On the other hand, Hayakawa takes a stand on the issue of obscenity and pornography. With regard to the act of lovemaking, Hayakawa moves to the observer, whom he believes defines obscenity: "Obscenity is particularly the evaluation of the outside observer" (1165). Much like the cliché, beauty is in the eye of the beholder, so, too, for Hayakawa is obscenity. As an observer who watches the activity from the outside, he or she is incapable of experiencing the beauty and intimacy shared by the couple. For the observer, the act becomes mechanical and appeals to the hormones rather than to the emotions. Its display in venues such as "a nightclub act or on stage, [in] arts such as painting, photography or movies" (1165) is objectionable because the activity is "seen from the outside, from a spectator's point of view" (1165). Thus to be a spectator is to substitute the beauty that is involved in the activity for the titillation gained from the observation.

Hayakawa does, however, admit that not all sexuality is performed out of love for one's partner. He lists deviant activities that couples engage in for various reasons and denounces them as well. When an observer views these acts, however, the participants "are all 'doing the same thing' ": having sex (1165). As a result, this "same thing" becomes important only for "the mechanics of sex" and "ignore[s] altogether its human significance" (1166). This departure from the human reverts to instinctual activity that lacks the passion driven by love.

Thus, Hayakawa ends with his assertion that while the ACLU can defend pornographic movies, he will not support their right to be shown. By citing specific "hard-core" (1166) movie titles after discussing the prurient interest observers take in watching sexual activity, Hayakawa writes a strong article for the issue of censorship.

Work Cited

Hayakawa, S. I. "Sex Is Not a Spectator's Sport." *The Norton Reader*. 9th ed. Eds. Linda Peterson, John C. Brereton, and Joan E. Hartman. New York:

Norton, 1996. 1164–66.

A P P E N D I X 2

Research

In addition to writing primary source essays, in which you must include quotations, you must also write research papers. When students complete research, they expand their paper with information that comes from a variety of secondary sources and that they must formally cite and document. If you are required to do some research for this paper, you should remember that when you are in the library or by your computer, there is a wealth of information that you can access, if you give yourself an adequate amount of time. Sometimes students fail to get all the information they need when they find the appropriate sources. In other words, in their haste to find the material, they make a copy of the article, chapter, or pages, or they take notes, but they forget to copy the required bibliographical information, thus requiring another trip to the library or to the Web. Another problem can be the failure to find the needed material in the library stacks. Other problems can and do occur. If you are a student who has not been required to do much research in the past, the following discussion should be a helpful guide as you begin, conduct, and complete the research process.

TO BEGIN

First, begin your research early. What does that mean? Find out what the due date is for your paper and begin working a little at a time—immediately. To wait until the last minute will result in many problems, which we will discuss here. Also be sure that you know exactly what the topic is that you are to research. Are you looking for biographical information? Does your instructor want you to concentrate on a particular theme rather than on biography? Will you be completing literary research or will you be writing a paper on a nonliterary topic? If you are unsure about what you are to research, ask your instructor.

If you have a computer and access to the Internet, you will be able, in many cases, to access your institution's library online catalogue, as well as other resources that can direct you to information you need. You may begin your research from the comfort of your own home whenever you have a moment, instead of feeling that all your research must be done at the library. A good rule to remember is: Ask your instructor if you can use articles that are on the Internet. Your instructor may say no; if so, don't be discouraged. There are many more places to look, and in many cases, the sources may be more useful.

If your instructor says you may use the Internet for your articles, be sure to find out what information you need to copy for your Bibliography or your Works Cited page. Many times the bibliographical information is printed at the top of the page or at the end of the article. Many instructors require different formats, so it is important to find out what format you will be using to write this paper. Ask your instructor, if he or she has not yet told you. You may be using MLA or APA, the two most popular formats for students. Ask your instructor what information your bibliography must contain, or consult Appendix 3: MLA Documentation and Sample Paper. Be sure to take this text with you when you go to the library and have it at hand when you are working at the computer.

LIBRARY RESEARCH

Whether you are using your own computer or one in the library, you have several options. You may look in the online catalogue and choose books that are in the library stacks; magazines that are in the stacks, or, if they are recent, in the periodical room; or the MLA Bibliography or other bibliographies for listings of journal articles. If you are writing a literary research paper, the MLA Bibliography provides excellent journal sources, but if you are completing nonliterary research, the *Readers' Guide to Periodical Literature* is one of the first references you should consult. Remember that magazine and journal articles are not the same. Magazine articles are written for wide circulation. Journal articles are usually academic, published in journals that are devoted to a particular area (English, medicine, history, and so forth) and are highly specialized. They usually do not come out weekly or monthly, and their authors write to a highly select audience. Although journal articles usually save students who have waited until the last minute when all the books are checked out, journal articles are not always foolproof. The library might not subscribe to the journal that carries the article you need. A less scrupulous student might have torn the article out of the journal instead of making a copy of it. Or the article might be written in theoretical language that is difficult to understand and will take more time to read with comprehension. If you begin your research relatively early, you might try the Interlibrary Loan (ILL) service in your library. Given enough time, the librarians there can order what you need from another library. On the other hand, many journals and other resources have become part of electronic collections, providing material ready for researchers to download.

Once you have found entries in your library catalogue, whether they are books, magazine articles, or journals, be sure to copy the call number of the source accurately. Go to the location where you will find the material you want. Before you leave the place you found the material, be sure that all the pages you need are there, and skim the material to see if you can actually use it. It becomes frustrating to find that you pulled books with missing material, or that the article had a great title but the material is not what you need. You might want to look at other books near the one you pulled, to see if your topic might be covered in those books also. Check the index of the books for your topic, and you might find information that you were not expecting. Another excellent source that students frequently do not think to consult is the Bibliography or Works Cited that is in the book that you have found on your subject. The author of the book or article had to do her research also and had to list the sources. Something your author used might be helpful to you.

If you decide that you want to take notes instead of checking out the books, you can do this in several ways.

- **Take organized notes.** Keep specific topics on different note cards or on different pieces of paper so that your information won't overlap. This will be handy when you organize the paper into an outline form and discover how many cards you have made about each topic.
- **Include the bibliographical information on each card.** You will have the information you need when you begin to write your paper. It is frustrating to discover that you have forgotten needed information and will have to make another trip to the library. It becomes even more frustrating when you discover that the material you used has since been checked out by another student. Don't forget to copy down the page numbers where you got your information.
- **Take notes in a consistent method.** Always quote the information instead of paraphrasing it so that you will always know that the information on your note cards/paper is quoted and not paraphrased or summarized. That way, when you begin writing your paper, you will know that the information needs to have quotations marks around it when you transfer it to your paper.

On the card below, you will see that the student has included all the necessary bibliographical information, copied the information in quotation marks, and provided the page number of the material—176. The student has also noted the topic on this card. You may place the topic and the page numbers wherever it is convenient for you. Notice that the student has used brackets, [ ], around the name "Emily." That is because the source only used Dickinson's last name, and the student inserted the information that was not provided. You are allowed to do that as long as you indicate, by using square brackets, that this is your information—not information provided by the source.

```
Style/Prose
Higgins, David J.M. "Emily Dickinson's Prose." Emily Dick-
    inson: A Collection of Critical Essays. Ed. Richard B.
    Sewell. Englewood Cliffs, NJ: Spectrum-Prentice-Hall,
    1963. 162-77.
176 "Other oddities of the [Emily] Dickinson prose style
    includes archaisms and localisms."
176 "Emily's capitalization of words within the sentence
    may be called archaic, but it is not a problem of
    style. . . . "
```

- **Bring change or a copy card.** If you don't want to check out the books, or if they cannot be checked out, be sure you have a pocketful of change or a copy card, which can be bought at most libraries. Copy the pages you need, plus the title and copyright pages. If you are using a journal, copy the table of contents for the journal issue that your article is in. Usually, bound journals contain the three or four issues published in a given year, in one volume. You want to get the bibliographical information for the specific issue that your article is in. If you can't find the information, ask the librarian or your instructor for help.

- **Underline or highlight needed information on the copies.** Do not do this in the book itself. If you choose to copy the material, you can take the information home and complete the research there.

- **Complete a working bibliography of all sources you have.** It is *working* rather than *final* because you may find that you will add more sources and/or delete those that are repetitive or unnecessary. If you are using downloaded information, consult Appendix 3: MLA Documentation and Sample Paper to see how to incorporate such sources into a Works Cited page. If you use an online journal or magazine article, its bibliographical format is slightly different from the print version.

INTERNET RESEARCH

With the need for immediate access to information, technology has provided researchers with tools that can get them material almost instantly. As a student researcher, you, too, have that capability at your fingertips. The key is knowing how to use the Internet, the Web, and search engines. To find information that might help you in writing your paper, you can follow these steps.

- To use the Internet for research, you first need a search engine that is geared to the kind of information you need. Search engines such as Alta-Vista and Yahoo, two of several popular engines, connect to the full Web; there are other search engines that address specific needs. To access the engine, type in its address. For example, Yahoo's address is *www.yahoo.com*.

- Once your search engine appears on your screen, you may enter the subject you want to research in the search box. If you are going to write a persuasive essay in opposition to Laurence Tribe's essay, "Second Thoughts on Cloning," you could enter the term *cloning* in the search box.

- After waiting a moment, you will find that Yahoo completed the search and found four categories and sixty-six sites for information. If you are interested in the category "Human Cloning," five sites appear on the first page, but more are listed on subsequent pages. At the bottom of the first page of results, a button appears labeled Next 20 Matches .

Much like a library catalogue that offers references, Yahoo offers Web sites and information you may download and use with the proper documentation. Just as with the library resources, you must determine the quality and appropriateness of the material you have found. Ask yourself the following questions:

- Is it timely? While there may be historical information that won't change, is there current information that provides up-to-date material about the latest discoveries and processes?
- Is it written by someone in the field, or is it another student's research paper? Are the credentials of the author given?
- Was it published in a reputable publication?
- Does it have a particular religious or political slant? Does it give a balanced discussion with various points of view?
- Does it fit your needs?

If you want to access specific magazines or newspapers for articles, you can do that also. In the search box of your engine, type the name of the periodical you want, for example, *Time* magazine. You will get a screen that displays *Time*. Click on it, and a screen displaying the cover of Time.com will appear. Adjacent to it is another search box, in which you may type "cloning" and enter. At the time of this writing, 130 matches were noted. If you click on the first entry, "Newsfile: The Genetics Revolution," you will find a variety of sources written from different perspectives. Once you have searched and retrieved all the information you need, you may begin organizing your material. (See "Steps in Completing Research," on the next page.)

ORGANIZATION

Now that you have finished reading the material you have gathered, you are ready to begin organizing it so you can start writing. Although you did not necessarily have a clearly defined thesis in mind when you started, you now need to set up a tentative one based on the material you have and on the directions your instructor provides. Although your instructor may determine the actual style and structure of the required assignment, you should rely on the foundations established in your previous readings to help you determine your approach. For example, to maintain unity and to give direction to your work, you need to use a thesis, transition words and/or sentences, and topic sentences.

With your thesis in mind, it is a good idea to construct an outline. Some instructors require a formal outline, an informal outline, or no outline at all. Even if your instructor does not want one, it is a good idea to construct one so that you will see the direction that you want to take with your paper. Using the note cards or notes on paper that you have taken, you can begin to build your outline by using the topic you recorded on the notes to determine what will be included

STEPS IN COMPLETING RESEARCH

Start early.

Know your subject.

Ask your instructor about using articles on the Internet.

Refer to Appendix 3: MLA Documentation and Sample Paper to find out what information you need to get for your sources.

At your computer, access the menu to the library catalogue's listing of books, magazines, and journals.

Copy the call numbers accurately.

Go to the location where your books are shelved.

Make sure the information you need is in the source you pulled.

Look at the books on the same shelf to see if they might have information you need. Check the index for your topic.

Check the Bibliography or Works Cited pages of your resource.

Copy all bibliographical information, especially the page numbers of your information.

Use the Internet to access information.

Take notes in a consistent and organized manner.

Copy the information as well as the title and copyright pages and electronic information required by MLA.

Underline or highlight information on the copies.

Make a working bibliography.

in your paper. You will then organize the notes so that all the notes on a single topic are together. By putting them together in outline form—whether formally or informally—you will begin to see how much information you have and how much information you might still need. If you need more material, you might have to return to the library or to the Internet for more sources. If you do, be sure to add the sources to your bibliography immediately.

ORGANIZING YOUR MATERIAL

Determine a tentative thesis.

Organize the notes by topic.

Create a formal or informal working outline.

Determine whether you need more sources.

Add or eliminate material as you see necessary.

PLAGIARISM

Now that you have found your information and taken your notes in the form of quotations, documentation is essential. Failure to document correctly or to enclose words copied from the text in quotation marks could result in your being charged with plagiarism even if your mistake was accidental. Care should be taken whenever you quote or paraphrase. Plagiarism is a serious charge, and it could possibly result in disastrous consequences, especially if it is extensive and proven. To be safe and to avoid a possibly embarrassing or legal problem, take the time to use quotations and to document. The only exception to this rule is information that is common knowledge, material that most people already know, or information that is found repeated in numerous sources. For example, if you would like to know an accurate date about Christopher Columbus's sailing for the New World, you would look in a variety of resources. The most popular date will be 1492. You were taught that in your history classes with the other students, and that is a piece of cultural knowledge that most students in America have learned. This is common knowledge and found in many resources; therefore, the place you found it in does not need to be documented.

Most cases of plagiarism come not from words consciously copied directly from a source but from faulty paraphrasing. For example, let's say that a student is doing research about using the Internet for research. He has found an article written by Maria González, "Using the Web in the Classroom," that has information regarding his topic. The following is part of one paragraph from that article, found on page 296 of this textbook:

> Using the World Wide Web, pulling a few examples off the Web, and walking a student through the **many kinds of resources on the Web** represents one of the many ways to teach from the Web. **A student needs to learn to navigate the Web in the same way she must learn to navigate the library.** Just as there are useful information and reference desks at libraries, there are

useful search engines on the Web. The critical thinking skill needed **to navigate efficiently** through the endless possibilities of information resources available requires specific concrete training in the classroom. Too often teachers assume students know the difference between good sources and mediocre sources. Students must be taught and shown the difference. To the uninitiated, if the source discusses, in whatever form, the general topic, it must be acceptable. I argue that many of the complaints against students using the Web stem from our students' inability to tell the difference between **a mediocre generalization and a useful specific example.** The difference is something that a teacher must consciously make clear to students. Giving a wide variety of examples between generalizations that say very little and specific information that can make an argument concrete provides the student with a clear difference between good and mediocre sources.

In an attempt to incorporate information from this source, the student writer began writing his paragraph with the following sentences:

> [1]The contemporary student now has the advantage of electronic research when searching for information. [2]This new source allows a student **to navigate efficiently** through the **many kinds of resources on the Web** including **mediocre generalizations and useful examples** which he might not have considered or had available to him in the past.

Look at the bold words in the original passage and in the student's passage. While this example shows that he has used quotations from the original in his own sentences, he still copied directly without using quotation marks and without giving credit at the end of the information to the source from which it came. Now look at the next example:

> [1]The contemporary student now has the advantage of electronic research when searching for information. [2]This new source allows a student **to navigate efficiently** through the **many kinds of resources on the Web** including **generalizations and useful examples** which he might not have considered or had available to him in the past (296-97).

Even though he placed the page number in parenthesis after the information, as the above example shows, blatant copying of information directly from the text without the use of quotation marks still makes this passage an example of plagiarism. In the next example, plagiarism occurs again.

> [1]The contemporary student now has the advantage of electronic research when searching for information. [2]This new source allows a student to maneuver through the all types of material on the Internet, both of a general nature and those applicable to his topic, which he might not have considered or had available to him in the past.

While there is little direct use of words or phrases from the original source, the writer copied the idea that the original source introduced. The material is **plagiarized** if credit is not given because it allows the reader to believe that the student wrote this idea which in fact was found in the original passage.

PLAGIARISM

It is plagiarism if

words copied from a source do not have quotation marks around them;

words copied from a source are not in quotation marks and are not followed by documentation;

words have been paraphrased incorrectly; or

ideas have been used without giving credit to the author.

Many students question the problem that English instructors find inherent in plagiarism and wonder why such an issue is made about it. Remember that because words and thoughts are our personal form of expression and sometimes our way of life, to use another person's words and/or thoughts without giving credit to the creator of those words and thoughts and to take credit for them yourself, is to steal. The purpose of the copyright laws is to give protection to the writer, the originator of the thoughts and words, and to ensure that if anyone attempts to claim those words and thoughts as his or her own, that person will be prosecuted. While it is frequently difficult to prove, plagiarism is a crime and is subject to legal recourse. If you are unsure about whether you have plagiarized or not, ask your instructor for help. The best rule of thumb is to be sensible and honest about your writing.

TO AVOID PLAGIARISM

Quote accurately.

Paraphrase correctly.

Use quotation marks appropriately.

Use documentation after each quotation.

continued

TO AVOID PLAGIARISM Continued

Use documentation to give recognition to the author who supplied your ideas.

Also provide a bibliography or a Works Cited page.

Plagiarism is the theft of intellectual property, and it is punishable by law if it is done extensively. The student who commits plagiarism is also subject to the rules and regulations governing plagiarism of his or her institution of higher learning.

THE FIRST DRAFT

You are now at the point when you need to set aside a block of time that you can devote to writing your first draft. Some students fail to notice the word before draft: *first*. Although you might have only one more draft, you must take the time to write a copy that will be edited and revised so that you can submit the best product possible.

When you have the time set, arrange your notes so that they follow the organization established in your working outline. Follow the pattern you have set up based on your thesis, but do not worry about the details of spelling, punctuation, and final wording yet. The important issue is to begin writing and to develop the ideas that you are working with. You will be able to take care of the flaws in the editing and revising process. You may find that you cannot complete your entire paper in one sitting; this is normal, considering a student's hectic schedule. If you can complete one major heading during your first sitting, you will have accomplished a great deal. Be sure to set realistic goals for your writing, rather than saying that you will write the entire paper at once.

The organization of your paper should follow the outline, so that one major point on the outline will correspond to several paragraphs, which are themselves composed of the topics in your notes. You may find that you will condense some material and combine some topics that are similar, rather than writing short undeveloped paragraphs. On the other hand, you may find that you have a good deal of information on a particular topic that needs to be eliminated because it will overwhelm your presentation, or that needs to be divided into separate paragraphs because it is essential to the development of your idea. In either case, don't worry about the changes. That is a normal step.

If you have not yet written your introduction or conclusion, you should do that after you have finished your paper. It was more important to develop the major ideas in your work than to work on the beginning and ending, which possibly would have needed to change as you developed your paper. Now you need to introduce your reader to the topic. As in most writing, you want to capture your reader's attention, but you must remember that this is a formal paper, and your **tone** and **diction** must maintain that formality. Your introduction is also the place where your thesis will be stated. Be sure to ask your instructor whether he or she prefers to read the thesis at the beginning, middle, or end of the introduction.

Your conclusion is important also, because you do not want to stop writing and fail to draw your ideas together for your reader. Because you are now the "expert" on this topic, your voice is quite important in the conclusion. You must let your reader know what you want him to understand from what you have written. At this point, you may add your informed opinion about the topic, the work, the material, or the direction you took. You may want to end with a significant quotation that adds importance to the paper. Regardless of your ending, you do not want to leave your reader with questions, misunderstandings, or a feeling that there should be more to come. Nor do you want to introduce new material that must be explained and developed. And you especially do not want to conclude with a declaration about something that is totally irrelevant to the topic you have written about.

FORMAT

Although many students find formatting difficult and tedious, there are reasons for it. Your instructor will tell you which format you are to use. Many English Departments rely on the latest edition of the *MLA Handbook for Writers of Research Papers*, but other formats are equally useful, and different formats are required by different departments. Any acknowledged format simply standardizes the formula for presenting bibliographical information, enabling the reader familiar with the style to identify the components of each entry. While it is not necessary to be precise in your draft with your formatting, it will be easier when you begin editing to make sure that you have your documentation in place for all your quotations. Appendix 3: MLA Documentation and Sample Paper provides you with guidelines, examples, and explanations for formatting the most common types of research sources (such as books, periodicals, CD-ROMs, and others).

STEPS FOR DRAFTING YOUR RESEARCH PAPER

Set aside a block of time to work.

Have your outline and notes before you.

Follow the organizational pattern in your outline, and establish it in your thesis.

continued

STEPS FOR DRAFTING YOUR RESEARCH PAPER Continued

Begin writing, completing one major division of the outline at a time.

Determine if you need to eliminate or add information to each point.

Add the introduction and conclusion.

Add the Works Cited page.

EDITING AND REVISING

When you have completed your first draft, you will want to put it away for a while. Most instructors and authors of writing handbooks make this recommendation even though they know that in reality many students wait until the night before the paper is due to write it, sometimes completing only two drafts or maybe one. The consequences arising from this practice can be numerous and unpleasant. The advantages of starting early are much more pleasing. By separating yourself from your work for at least a day, you can return to it with a fresh mind, able to see flaws in sentence construction and grammar that you might have missed earlier.

Sometimes you might "fall in love" with your own work, feeling that it is part of yourself and thereby making it difficult to detect problems with logic and/or development. In this case, you should take it to a peer editor, one who will be honest rather than kind. Choose a person who has some knowledge about writing and about your topic, possibly a fellow classmate, who can offer constructive criticism. Or, consult your institution's writing or tutoring lab. Even though most tutors are instructed to help and not to edit, you can get some good direction and suggestions from them. If they help you correct any errors at all or smooth out rough syntax, those are problems your instructor will not find and hold you accountable for. You might also consult with your instructor. Most are not only willing but eager to make an appointment with a conscientious student who is interested in doing her best in the class. After all, who is better qualified to help than the one who made the assignment and gives the grade? Sometimes the instructor has provided written directions or a grading profile which will be used in marking your paper. Be sure to follow these guidelines carefully, for they are the voice of your instructor when you are away from class. Finally, be sure to read your essay one more time before you submit it. You'll be surprised that regardless of the number of times you have revised and edited it, there is usually one typographical error that you missed or that your Spell-Check did not catch because the word was spelled correctly but was the wrong word. Remember Julian's error with "close" and "clothes."

For your convenience, the following checklist should help you as you prepare to edit and revise your first draft. Be honest with yourself as you use it.

Remember that any guide is only as good as the person using it. Since it is intended to help you improve your paper, you want to be objective and distant. Be the reader of the paper rather than the writer. Put yourself in the audience's position and read it from someone else's perspective. If you are still too close to your subject, ask someone else to read it with the checklist beside her. Again, be sure that the reader is honest rather than kind. If you follow the directions for editing and revising, your final draft should be much better than your first.

The key to writing a good paper is to give yourself plenty of time to create, write, and revise. The reality of the situation is that because of other responsibilities, you may find yourself pressured to complete the assignment at the last minute. If that is the case, you should attempt to use your Spell-Check for minimal editing of spelling errors, and you should always proofread your paper at least once before you submit it. In that final check, do not forget to look for proper documentation and the format that your instructor required. The better the appearance of the paper, the better the first impression will be. While that might not make a difference in your grade, you at least have a subtle advantage over the student who submits a paper pockmarked by correction fluid or marred with numerous handwritten corrections. Taking pride in your essay begins with an early start and ends with submitting a spotless, punctual product to your instructor. (See below for Checklist for Editing and Revising the First Draft.)

CHECKLIST FOR EDITING AND REVISING THE FIRST DRAFT

There is a section in your paper for each major division on your outline.

Each section is fully developed; several paragraphs are devoted to the topic.

Each section has quoted and paraphrased material to support your ideas.

Each quotation is followed by parenthetical documentation.

Each set of ideas that you develop is documented to give credit to the author of those ideas.

The author of the work you used is cited in the sentence introducing the quotation or in the parenthetical documentation.

You rely more on your own wording than on quoting.

Each quotation is blended within your own sentences rather than set apart independently.

continued

CHECKLIST FOR EDITING AND REVISING THE FIRST DRAFT
CONTINUED

Each paragraph flows smoothly from one to the next by the use of transitional words, phrases, and/or sentences.

You use Spell-Check or your dictionary to ensure proper spelling.

You proofread your work to catch any misspellings or wrong words that Spell-Check did not catch.

Your formatting is accurate.

Your paragraphs support and develop your thesis.

You bring closure to your paper.

You include your Works Cited page.

A P P E N D I X   3

MLA Documentation
and Sample Paper

USE OF MODERN LANGUAGE ASSOCIATION (MLA) FORMAT FOR DOCUMENTATION

The following are examples of the more common types of sources a writer encounters when doing research. Often a student is unable to determine the exact type of source she is using. When in doubt, always consult with either your instructor or the librarian. For more extensive examples and explanations, consult the *MLA Handbook for Writers of Research Papers*, 5th edition. Always double-space each citation.

➤ Examples: A Book

1. By One Author:

Kirkpatrick, Robin. <u>English and Italian Literature from Dante to Shakespeare: A Study of Source, Analogue and Divergence</u>. New York: Longman, 1995.

2. Two or More Works by the Same Author:

Limón, Graciela. <u>The Memories of Ana Calderón</u>. Houston: Arte Público, 1994.

---. <u>Song of the Hummingbird</u>. Houston: Arte Público, 1996.

Note: To avoid repeating the author's name for additional works, the three hyphens are used in subsequent citations. Also, note that the writer is responsible for using the correct spelling for an author's name. In this example, the writer is responsible for accenting the "ó" in "Limón." If your computer does not have this capability, you are responsible for writing in such marks by hand.

3. By Two Authors:

Tyack, David, and Elisabeth Hansot. <u>Learning Together: A History of Coeducation in American Schools</u>. New Haven: Yale UP, 1990.

Note: The letters "UP" are used as the abbreviated form of "University Press."

4. By Three Authors:

Belzer, Richard, Larry Charles, and Rick Newman. <u>How to Be a Stand-Up Comic</u>. New York: Villard, 1988.

Note: The full name of the publisher as it appears on the title page is "Villard Books." However, in many instances, the MLA format allows the publisher's name to be shortened as long as the pertinent information is kept so that the publisher can be identified. In this instance, the word "Books" is not needed to identify the publisher; hence, only the word "Villard" appears in the citation. Consult the *MLA Handbook* for additional directions on abbreviating a publisher's name.

5. By Four or More Authors:

Chapman, Graham, et al. <u>The Complete Monty Python's Flying Circus: All the Words</u>. Vol. 1. New York: Pantheon-Random, 1989.

Note: When a text has four or more authors or editors, indicate the first name on the list and refer to all other authors or editors by the term *et al.* In this example, the work has six authors: Graham Chapman, John Cleese, Terry Gilliam, Eric Idle, Terry Jones, and Michael Palin.

6. By a Corporate Author:

International Union of Biochemistry. Nomenclature Committee. <u>Enzyme Nomenclature 1984</u>. Orlando: Academic, 1984.

7. By an Anonymous Author:

<u>The Sourcebook of Medical Science</u>. New York: Torstar, 1986.

Note: When a book has no author mentioned, nothing is written in the author's place, such as "anonymous" or "unknown." The title of the book begins the citation; however, if the title begins with the article "A," "An," or "The," the citation appears in alphabetical order according to the word that follows the article, in this case "Sourcebook."

8. With One Editor:

Barish, Jonas A., ed. <u>Ben Jonson: A Collection of Critical Essays</u>. Englewood Cliffs, NJ: Prentice, 1963.

9. With Two Editors:

Renov, Michael, and Erika Suderburg, eds. <u>Resolutions: Contemporary Video Practices</u>. Minneapolis: U of Minnesota P, 1996.

Note: Notice that in identifying the publisher of this work the word "University" is abbreviated to "U" and the word "Press" is abbreviated to "P."

10. With an Author and an Editor:

Plath, Sylvia. <u>The Collected Poems</u>. Ed. Ted Hughes. New
York: Perennial Library-Harper, 1981.

11. With a Publisher's Imprint:

Thorburn, David, and Howard Eiland, eds. <u>John Updike: A
Collection of Critical Essays</u>. Englewood Cliffs, NJ:
Spectrum-Prentice, 1979.

Note: An imprint is another name that a publisher uses; such information is found on the title page of the work. In writing a citation, use the imprint first, followed by a hyphen and the name of the publisher.

12. An Anthology or Compilation:

Gilbert, Sandra M., and Susan Gubar, eds. <u>The Norton
Anthology of Literature by Women: The Traditions in
English</u>. 2nd ed. New York: Norton, 1985.

13. A Work in an Anthology:

Herrera-Sobek, María. "The Treacherous Woman Archetype, A
Structuring Agent in the Corrido." <u>Aztlán: Chicano
Culture and Folklore: An Anthology</u>. Ed. José "Pepe"
Villarino and Arturo Ramírez. New York: Primis Custom-
McGraw, 1997. 127-39.

Note: Be careful to cite the pages for the article or work from start to finish, including any pictures, graphs, maps, notes, etc. Note: "Ed." is used as plural here.

14. A Cross-Reference from an Anthology:

Bucknall, Barbara J., ed. <u>Critical Essays on Marcel Proust</u>.
Boston: Hall, 1987.

Johnson, J. Theodore, Jr. "Proust and Painting." Bucknall
162-80.

Rivers, J. E. "Proust and the Aesthetic of Suffering."
Bucknall 118-33.

Note: Often one collection will contain several useful articles for research. When two or more articles from the same anthology are cited in an essay, the documentation on the Works Cited is in the form of a cross-reference. Note the abbreviated citation form for Johnson and for Rivers which directs the reader to Bucknall's text. The citation for the anthology apears first only because Bucknall is first alphabetically.

15. An Untitled Introduction, Foreword, Preface, or Afterword:

Portales, Marco. Introduction. <u>Crowding Out Latinos: Mexican
Americans in the Public Consciousness</u>. By Portales.
Philadelphia: Temple UP, 2000. 1-17.

Note: The phrase "By Portales" indicates to the reader that Marco Portales wrote not only the introduction but the text itself. Untitled introductions, forewords, prefaces, and afterwords are not enclosed in quotation marks.

16. A Titled Introduction, Foreword, Preface, or Afterword:

Gentry, Marshall Bruce. "Tracks to the Oven of Redemption."
    Introduction. <u>Flannery O'Connor's Religion of the
    Grotesque</u>. By Gentry. Jackson, MS: UP of Mississippi,
    1986. 3-20.

Note: If the introduction is titled, the title—but not the word Introduction—is placed in quotation marks.

17. A Multivolume Work:

Bell, Whitfield J., Jr. <u>Patriot-Improvers: Biographical
    Sketches of Members of the American Philosophical
    Society</u>. 2 vols. Philadelphia: American Philosophical
    Soc., 1999.

Note: When you use information from more than one volume in a multivolume work, you cite the complete number of volumes on the Works Cited page. Individual volumes used are cited within the essay by volume and page numbers, for example (Bell 2: 4-8). Also, as stated previously, some terms may be shortened when identifying the publisher; in this instance, the word "Society" has been shortened to "Soc." when identifying the publisher.

18. Subsequent Editions of a Work:

Blum, Richard A. <u>Television Writing: From Concept to
    Contract</u>. Rev. ed. Boston: Focal-Butterworth, 1984.
Thoreau, Henry D. Walden <u>and</u> Resistance to Civil Government:
    <u>Authoritative Texts, Thoreau's Journal, Reviews, and
    Essays in Criticism</u>. Ed. William Rossi. 2nd ed. New
    York: Norton, 1992.

Note: See section 25. "A Title within a Title" for an explanation of how to underline the title of Thoreau's text.

19. Part of a Series:

Grange, J. M., A. Fox, and N. L. Morgan, eds. <u>Immunological
    Techniques in Microbiology</u>. Soc. for Applied
    Bacteriology Technical Ser. 24. Boston: Blackwell
    Scientific, 1987.

20. Signed Work in a Reference Text:

Swanson, Alan. "Ferlin, Nils." <u>Encyclopedia of World
    Literature in the 20th Century</u>. Ed. Leonard S. Klein.
    Rev. ed. 4 vols. New York: Ungar, 1982.

Note: Reference works that are well known may be cited in a shorter format, which identifies the author [if known], title of the article, title of the reference work, edition, and publication year. For example, based on the above, the citation would be: Swanson, Alan. "Ferlin, Nils." <u>Encyclopedia of World Literature in the 20th Century</u>. Rev. ed., 1982.

21. Unsigned Work in a Reference Text:

"Kipling, Rudyard." <u>The Concise Encyclopedia of Modern World
      Literature</u>. Ed. Geoffrey Grigson. New York: Hawthorn,
      1963.

22. A Government Publication:

United States. Office of the Federal Register: National
      Archives and Records Administration. <u>The United States
      Government Manual 1998/1999</u>. Washington: GPO, 1998.
United States. Cong. House. Committee on Energy and
      Commerce. <u>Hearings before the Subcommittee on Health
      and the Environment: AIDS Issues (Part 1)</u>. 101st Cong.,
      1st sess. Washington: GPO. 1989.

Note: The publisher's name, "Government Printing Office," is abbreviated to "GPO."

23. Published Conference Proceedings:

Farberow, Norman L., ed. <u>Proceedings: Fourth International
      Conference for Suicide Prevention</u>. International
      Association for Suicide Prevention. 18–21 Oct. 1967.
      Los Angeles: Suicide Prevention Center, 1968.
<u>Proceedings of the 2nd Annual International Conference on
      the Emerging Literature of the Southwest Culture</u>. 13–15
      Sept. 1996. El Paso, TX: U of Texas P at El Paso, 1996.

24. A Translation:

Sagan, Françoise. <u>The Heart-Keeper</u>. Trans. Robert Westhoff.
      New York: Dutton, 1968.

Note: The identification of the individual who translated the work is noted by the term
"Trans." followed by the individual's name.

25. A Title within a Title:

Bloom, Harold. <u>Herman Melville's</u> Billy Budd, <u>"Benito
      Cereno," "Bartleby the Scrivener," and Other Tales</u>. New
      York: Chelsea, 1987.

Note: The above example is the method more acceptable to MLA. When the title of a work
usually underlined, such as the novel <u>Billy Budd</u>, appears *within* the title of another work
that requires underlining, such a text is not underlined. In the example above, <u>Billy Budd</u>
is normally underlined, but because Harold Bloom's book requires its own underlining,
one does not double-underline <u>Billy Budd</u>. Instead, the underlining for <u>Billy Budd</u> is removed. For other formats, see the *MLA Handbook*. See Section 18 also—Thoreau.

26. Published before 1900:

Dunbar, Paul Laurence. <u>The Uncalled</u>. New York, 1898.

27. A Published Dissertation:

Kurth, Rosaly Torna. <u>Susan Fenimore Cooper: A Study of Her
      Life and Works</u>. Diss. Fordham U, 1974. Ann Arbor: UMI,
      1974. 7419668.

Note: While the information required for a published dissertation is similar to that of a book, one may indicate additional information. In the above example, the ending number "7419668" is the University Microfilms International catalog number for Kurth's text.

28. An Unpublished Dissertation:

Rodriguez Kessler, Elizabeth. "Language, Nature, Gender, and
    Sexuality: Theoretical Approaches to Chicana and
    Chicano Literature." Diss. U of Houston, 1998.

➤ Examples: Articles in Periodicals

29. Signed Article from a Daily Newspaper:

Recer, Paul. "Panel: 3 Allergy Drugs Need No Prescription."
    Houston Chronicle 12 May 2001, *** ed.: A1, A18.

Note: Attention should be paid to how each newspaper indicates its editions. For example, the *Houston Chronicle* uses a "*" system, whereas the edition examples used in this Appendix for the *Los Angeles Times* are indicated by a title, the "Valley ed." Also be aware that some editions have special designations, such as "final" or "late," and such designations should be noted in the citation. See the entry 35. "An Editorial" for another example.

30. Unsigned Article from a Daily Newspaper:

"U.S. Removes Curbs on Sale to Iraq." Los Angeles Times
    2 June 2001, Valley ed.: A6.

31. Article from a Monthly or Bimonthly Magazine:

Zimmerman, Eilene. "Suffer the Children." San Diego Magazine
    July 2000: 62+.

Note: When the published pages of an article do not run continuously, note the first page of the article followed by a "+" sign. In this example, Zimmerman's article was on pages 62-64 and 186-87. Instead of noting all these pages, the indication "62+" is used.

32. Article from a Weekly or Biweekly Magazine:

Nordland, Rod. "Sarajevo's New Boom in Babies." Newsweek
    3 Jan. 1994: 60-61.

33. Article in a Journal with Continuous Pagination:

Sullivan, Patricia A., and Lynn H. Turner. "The Zoe Baird
    Spectacle: Silences, Sins, and Status." Western Journal
    of Communication 63 (Fall 1999): 413-32.

Note: "Continuous pagination" means that the periodical does not start the first page of each issue with the number one within a given year. For example, if the first issue of a journal for 1998 *ended* on page 84, the second issue would *start* with page 85. When continuous pagination occurs, the writer does not have to cite the number of the issue, only the volume number. In this example, the writer only has to cite volume "63" of the journal.

34. Article in a Journal without Continuous Pagination:

Stone, Gerald. "Measurement of Excellence in Newspaper
    Writing Courses." Journalism Educator 44.4 (Winter
    1990): 4-19.

Note: The issue number follows the volume number with a period separating the two numbers. Do not use the abbreviation "Vol." or "No." before the numbers. In this example, to show volume 44 and number 4, simply indicate "44.4" before the date.

35. An Editorial:

Balzar, John. "The Law of Average-ness." Editorial. <u>Los Angeles Times</u> 10 June 2001, Valley final ed.: M5.

36. A Review:

O'Connell, Daniel C. "Some Intentions Regarding Speaking." Rev. of <u>Speaking: From Intention to Articulation</u>, by W. J. M. Levelt. <u>Journal of Psycholinguistic Research</u> 21.1 (1992): 59-65.

MacAdam, Alfred. "Lost in Translation." Rev. of <u>Flight of the Swan</u>, by Rosario Ferré. <u>Los Angeles Times Book Review</u> 10 June 2001, Valley final ed.: 6.

37. Article Whose Title Contains a Quotation or the Title from Another Work:

Schleifer, Ronald. "'What Is This Thing Called Love?': Cole Porter and the Rhythms of Desire." <u>Criticism</u> 41.1 (Winter 1999): 7-23.

➤ Examples: Electronic Sources: CD-ROM

38. A Nonperiodical Publication:

<u>Encyclopedia of Science</u>. CD-ROM. Vers. 2.0 for Windows and Macintosh. New York: Dorling Kindersley Multimedia, 1997.

➤ Examples: Electronic Sources: Internet and the Web

39. A Professional Site:

@sle Online. 8 June 2001. Association for the Study of Literature and Environment. 11 June 2001 <http://www.asle.umn.edu/>.

Note: The first date cited, 8 June 2001, is the date the Web site was constructed or possibly revised. The second date, 11 June 2001, is the date the writer acquired the information and preceded the URL. The construction date is sometimes not given.

40. A Book:

Birkland, Thomas A. <u>After Disaster</u>. Washington, DC: Georgetown UP, 1997. 8 June 2001 <http://www. netlibrary.com?academic...Y.ASP?EV=888183&ID= 21644&advquery=>.

Note: The address for a Web site is termed the Uniform Resource Locator (URL). If the URL is too long to fit on one line, it may be broken up, but only after a slash mark. In this example, the only slashes occur near the beginning of the URL. See the next entry for a further example. Be careful not to add any marks, such as dashes, to the URL.

41. A Poem:

Rossetti, Christina Georgina. "A Birthday." Find a Poem.
    <u>Poem Finder</u>. 8 June 2001 <http://www.poemfinder.com/
    poem.cfm…=592851&CFTOKEN=51305409&id=445798>.

42. Government Information:

United States. U.S. Census Bureau. "Race, Hispanic or
    Latino, and Age: 2000: Geographic Area: Harris County,
    Texas." <u>Census 2000 Redistricting Date (Public Law 94-
    171) Summary File</u>. 2000. 7 June 2001
    <http://factfinder.census.gov/bf/_1…PL_U_QTPL_geo_id=0
    5000US48201.html>.

43. Signed Article in Reference Database:

Szathmary, Arthur. "Bergson, Henri (1859-1941)." <u>Americana
    Online</u>. 2001. Encyclopedia Americana. 8 June 2001
    <http://ea.grolier.com/cgi-bin/buildpage?artbaseid=0044310>.

44. Unsigned Article in Reference Database:

"Modernism." <u>Americana Online</u>. 2001. Encyclopedia Americana.
    8 June 2001 <http://ea.grolier.com/cgi-bin/build-
    page?artbaseid=0273610-00>.

45. Signed Article in a Journal:

Baker, Jennifer Jordan. "Benjamin Franklin's <u>Autobiography</u>
    and the Credibility of Personality." <u>Early American
    Literature</u> 35.3 (2000): 14 pp. 8 June 2001
    <http://muse.jhu.edu/journals/early_american_literature/
    v035/35.3baker.html>.

46. A Review:

Lombardo, Daniel. "<u>The Emily Dickinson Handbook</u>." Rev. of
    <u>The Emily Dickinson Handbook</u>, ed. Gudrun Grabher,
    Roland Hagenbuchle, and Cristanne Miller. <u>The Emily
    Dickinson Journal</u> 9.1 (2000): 3 pp. 8 June 2001
    <http://muse.jhu.edu/journals/emily_dickinson_journal/
    v009/9.1lombardo.html>.

Note: When citing information from a periodical, try to provide as much information as
possible regarding the publication information normally given. Also note that when the
page numbers are known, they are given as the total number. In this example, there are
three pages, "3 pp." in the article. Some articles are referenced by paragraphs and cited
using the term "pars."

47. Article in a Newspaper:

Seib, Gerald F. "Oliver Leads a Drive For Fuel Standards On
    SUVs in U.S." <u>Asian Wall Street Journal</u> 7 June 2001.
    8 June 2001 <http://proquest.umi.com/
    pqdweb?TS+…3&Sid=1&1dx=2&Deli=1&RQT=309&Dtp=1>.

48. Article in a Magazine:

Muliwa Kituku, Vincent. "Know Your Roots: Black Kids-White
    Parents." <u>Biracial Child</u> 30 Sept. 2000. 8 June 2001
    <http://www.softlineweb.com/softlin...2bh5.49.softTemplate.
    w&softtpl-toc>.

➤ Examples: Other Types of Sources

49. A Performance:

<u>She Stoops to Conquer or The Mistakes of a Night</u>. By Oliver
    Goldsmith. Dir. Stuart Vaughn. Perf. Patricia
    Falkenhain and Albert Quinton. Phoenix Theater.
    Phoenix. 3 Jan. 1961.

Note: The term "Perf." indicates the major performers or stars of the production.

50. A Recording:

Manilow, Barry. "This One's For You." <u>Barry Manilow Live</u>.
    LP. Arista, 1977.

Note: If your source is not a compact disc, you must identify the type of recording you are
citing. In this example, the material cited is a long-playing record, identified by "LP" in the
citation. Other sources include "Audiocassette" and "Audiotape."

51. Art Works:

Example A

Ingres, Jean-Augusti-Dominique. <u>Princesse de Broglie</u>.
    Robert Lehman Collection. Metropolitan Museum of Art,
    New York.

Example B

Raguenet, Jean-Baptiste. <u>Ile de la Cité</u>. J. Paul Getty
    Museum, Los Angeles.

Note: In Example A, the writer is able to determine which collection the painting is part of
in the museum and noted such in the citation.

52. A Film:

<u>Pleasantville</u>. Dir. Gary Ross. Perf. Tobey Maguire, Jeff
    Daniels, Joan Allen, William H. Macy, J. T. Walsh, and
    Reese Witherspoon. New Line Home Video, 1999.

53. A Cartoon:

Unger, Jim. "Herman." Cartoon. <u>Los Angeles Times</u> 3 June
    2001, Valley final ed.: 4.

54. An Advertisement:

Citizen. Advertisement. <u>Time</u> 19 Feb. 2001:4.

55. A Map or Chart:

<u>The Thomas Guide 2001: Los Angeles and Orange Counties:
    Street Guide and Directory</u>. Map. Irvine, CA: Thomas
    Bros. Maps-Rand, 2000.

56. Published Letter:

Whittier, John Greenleaf. "To Thomas Wentworth Higginson."
    Letter 554 of <u>The Letters of John Greenleaf Whittier</u>.
    Ed. John B. Pickard. Vol. 2. Cambridge: Belknap-Harvard
    UP, 1975. 119-20.

57. Interview:

Anaya, Rudolfo. "An Interview with Rudolfo Anaya." By
    Ishmael Reed. <u>Conversations with Rudolfo Anaya</u>. Ed.
    Bruce Dick and Silvio Sirias. Jackson: UP of
    Mississippi, 1998. 1-10.
Castillo, Ana. "An Interview with Ana Castillo." By Bryce
    Milligan. <u>South Central Review</u> 16.1 (Spring 1999):
    19-29.
González, Maria. Personal interview. 4 May 2001.
---. Telephone interview. 8 June 2001.

DOCUMENTATION WITHIN THE ESSAY

As researchers, two very important functions you are required to perform are
to keep a clear record of your sources and to document those sources you
used both in your essay and in your Works Cited page. Otherwise you risk
plagiarizing someone else's work and jeopardizing your own scholarship. Although the Works Cited page provides your readers with detailed information
regarding the sources you have used in your paper, the list of sources does
not state exactly what part of each source was used nor does the list identify
where in your paper you used the information. To identify exactly where in
your paper you are citing a source and the exact information you use, you
need what is termed *parenthetical documentation*, which very briefly identifies the source and pages placing them in parentheses, within your essay.
Such documentation is the reader's key to coordinating information cited in
the essay with the list of information on the Works Cited page. The following
are some of the more common forms of parenthetical documentation and
brief comments on specific points you should know. Take a few minutes to
familiarize yourself with some of the details required in the citations. The
main feature a writer should always be aware of is that the citation in the essay is the key to finding the source on the Works Cited page. For further examples and explanations, please see the *MLA Handbook for Writers of Research Papers*, 5th edition.

➤ Examples: If the Author Is Known

1. One Author

One important part of Native American mythology is the
character of "Hlahi or doctor, the sorcerer" (Curtin 52).

Note: Because the author's name *is not mentioned* in the sentence, the writer is required to identify the source by using the author's last name within the parenthesis. The number following the author's name is the page from which the information is cited. Notice that no "p." or "page" is placed before the number. Notice also that the period for the sentence comes after the documentation. A reader would look for the name "Curtin" on the Works Cited page for more detailed information on the source; in this case, Curtin wrote a book.

```
As Curtin notes, one important part of Native American
mythology is the character of "Hlahi or doctor, the
sorcerer" (52).
```

Note: In this example, the writer identified the author *within* the sentence. Therefore, the only information that needs to be written in the parentheses is the page number for the information cited.

2. Multiple Works by an Author

Example A

```
Charlotte Brontë's novel, Jane Eyre, shows this trend to
establish what her own character Jane termed a "happy"
marriage with Edward Rochester at the end (447).
```

Note: This example and the one following are taken from the essay in this Appendix (see below). Not only are two different Brontës cited in the essay, Charlotte and Emily, but two works by Charlotte Brontë are used in the essay, as well. Here are some basic rules to follow to help solve this situation.

1. Since the essay is mainly about Emily Brontë's <u>Wuthering Heights</u>, the writer only has to show her last name once, the first time the novel is cited. Such a citation would appear as (E. Brontë 3). The "E." is used to alert the reader that he/she should refer to "Emily" Brontë on the Works Cited page. All other references to the primary source, <u>Wuthering Heights</u>, are indicated simply by the page number in parentheses.
2. To indicate Charlotte Brontë's two works, the writer must designate the usual information regarding author and page number but also designate which of the two works is being quoted. Such a distinction should indicate Charlotte's name, the specific text quoted, and the page number(s): for example, (C. Brontë, <u>Jane</u> 447). To avoid such an extended citation, the writer of the sample paper wisely chose to include both the author and the work within the sentence; that way, the only information that needs to be cited is the page number of the quotation, (447).

Example B

```
Charlotte Brontë acknowledges that the "moorish and wild"
aspect of nature in Wuthering Heights is a "natural"
(Preface xxxiv) result of Emily Brontë's familiarity with
the surroundings Emily used as the novel's setting.
```

Note: Example B shows that Charlotte Brontë's Preface is being cited in the same essay in which her novel, <u>Jane Eyre</u>, is used. In this example, because the sentence clearly shows that Charlotte Brontë is the author of the information quoted, only the Preface and the page quoted are cited.

3. Two Authors

Recent investigations regarding the disposal of America's trash show that roughly "10 percent is incinerated" and that "80 percent [. . .] is sent to old-fashioned dumps and landfills" (Grossman and Shulman 464).

Note: Only the last name of both authors is included, in the same order they appear in, in the source. Because the Works Cited page is alphabetized, one would look for "Grossman" on the Works Cited page to find out that the two authors wrote an article in an anthology.

4. Citing a Source Quoted within a Source

According to Doug Wilson, America views dumps as "'a large compost pile'" (qtd. in Grossman and Shulman 465).

Note: In this example, the information cited is from a source which is itself quoted within another source. Grossman and Shulman quoted Doug Wilson in their essay. To show the reader that Grossman and Shulman are quoting someone else in their work, the writer must indicate that Wilson was quoted; you do this by writing "qtd. in" in the parentheses, before the author's name(s).

5. Corporate Author

Example A

Many Americans do not know that "[h]ydropower is really a form of solar energy" and often overlook the economic benefits it can bring to their community's energy problems (World Resources Inst. 77).

Example B

According to the World Resources Institute, many Americans do not know that "[h]ydropower is really a form of solar energy" and often overlook the economic benefits it can bring to their community's energy problems (77).

Note: This is an example of a corporate author; in this case, the World Resources Institute compiled an almanac. To avoid such a lengthy documentation, the preferred way to handle the information is to place the name of the author within the sentence and to cite only the page number [Example B]. However, either way is correct. Notice also that the word "Institute" is abbreviated to "Inst." See the *MLA Handbook* for further forms of abbreviation that are acceptable.

➤ Examples: Poetry

6. Poem

Example A

Maxine Kumin references one form of religion when she notes in her poem "In the Park," "You have forty-nine days between / death and rebirth if you're a Buddhist" (1-2).

Note: The information in parenthesis is not the page number on which the poem is found, but the line numbers of the poem cited. Because the number of lines quoted is three or fewer, the lines are not set off by indention. The "/" is used to separate the two lines quoted. Notice also that there is a space before and after the slash.

Example B

> You have forty-nine days between
> death and rebirth if you're a Buddhist.
> Even the smallest soul could swim
> The English Channel in that time (1-4)

Note: In Example B, the number of lines quoted is more than three. In this case, the lines are indented ten spaces or one inch from the left margin. If the lines in the source are indented somewhat you should try, as best as you can, to reproduce the spacing used in the original text. Do not use "l." or "ll." to indicate that these are line numbers.

➤ Examples: Other Types of Sources

7. Introduction, Foreword, Preface, and Afterword

Margaret Fuller's <u>Summer on the Lakes, in 1843</u> is viewed by critics as "the product of [Fuller's] journey through [. . .] the far western frontier in mid-nineteenth century America" (Smith vii).

Note: The documentation directs the reader to Smith's entry on the Works Cited page; there the reader will find that Smith's work is the Preface to Fuller's text. Notice also that the numbering of the page is as found in the text. Some works use small Roman numerals, such as Smith's Preface, which is on page vii, whereas other texts use Arabic numbers, such as the number "7." As a researcher, you are responsible for using whichever numbering system the book uses to identify an introduction, foreword, preface, or afterword. Notice also that the quotation has been shortened, and the missing part of the quotation is indicated by an ellipsis surrounded by brackets, shown in the above example as "[. . .]." Often when an ellipsis comes at the end of a line, the computer will divide the ellipsis into two parts. When this occurs, it becomes the writer's responsibility to see that the bracketed ellipsis is kept intact.

8. Interview

Because of the recent flooding along the coastal regions of Texas, the mosquito problem "is an increasing threat to the population" (González).

Note: In this instance, the writer is required to give the name of the source. But, because an interview has no page or paragraph numbers, only the name is cited. If the writer uses both a personal and a telephone interview, a distinction must be made by including the word "Personal" or "Telephone" after the interviewee's name. For example (González Telephone).

9. Unknown Author

One theme which appears in ancient literature involves the idea that "whatever is natural to anyone can hardly be discontinued" ("Legend" 1).

Note: When there is no author or an author is unknown, the writer cites the work using the first major word in the title. In this example, the quotation comes from "The Legend of the Jackal and the Color Blue." Notice that the article "The" is not considered in identifying the title of the work.

10. A Sacred Text

One of the quotations frequently used in a Christian ceremony notes that "In the beginning God created the heaven and the earth" (<u>The Holy Bible</u>, Gen. 1.1).

Note: The title of a sacred writing is underlined when a specific edition is cited. In this example, <u>The Holy Bible Containing the Old and New Testaments and the Apocrypha</u> is cited, but instead of page numbers, the book, chapter, and verse are identified. However, a general reference to a sacred scripture, such as the Bible or Koran, is not underlined. The titles of biblical chapters are abbreviated; consult the *MLA Handbook* for acceptable abbreviations. The chapter is cited first, followed by the verse number. In this example, "1.1" refers to chapter 1, verse 1. If more than one verse is cited, then the beginning and ending verse numbers are separated by a hyphen, for example, Gen. 1.1-4. The <u>Holy Bible Containing the Old and New Testaments and the Apocrypha</u> would be cited on the Works Cited page like any other book that is published.

SAMPLE LITERARY RESEARCH PAPER

The following sample paper should be used as a guide for MLA format for page number placement, quotations, documentation, Note page, and Works Cited page.

Toy 1

Ronald Toy

Professor Lynn Baker

English 155H

26 November 2001

Images of City and Country in <u>Wuthering Heights</u>

   Emily Brontë's novel <u>Wuthering Heights</u> (1847) has long been associated with the Romantic writer, William Blake, and with certain elements of mysticism. Certainly, the implied appearance of Catherine's ghost in the novel supports this claim.[1] But, such a view of the novel fails to consider the "historical narrative" (Helsinger 17) of rural England during the novel's time span, a change in the countryside's attitudes that moved from the Romantic preference for what Michael Waters terms the "wild and extreme [of] Nature" (153) to the later Victorian desire for the refined "garden" (154) and "home" (238). In <u>Wuthering Heights</u>, what Brontë does is to combine the Romantic use of nature as an influence on the individual with the Victorian desire for the domestic life of home and the family represented by the setting of Thrushcross Grange at the novel's end. Brontë illustrates this blend of the Romantic and Victorian views of rural England in the novel through its main urban character,

Toy 2

Lockwood, and how his own desires move from the wild to the refined. Thus, by investigating not only how Lockwood relates to nature, but the novel's physical settings, and the eventual movement of the novel's characters at its end, one can conclude that Brontë' s <u>Wuthering Heights</u> is a literary work which blends characteristics of both the Romantic and the Victorian movements.

In terms of the novel's Romantic characteristics, Lockwood sees physical nature as a psychological anchor in life and as a refuge from the chaos of urban life. He seeks the seclusion of the English countryside for his retreat which he describes as "a beautiful country" (E. Brontë 3) away from London's urban life. However, Lockwood does not totally embrace nature as the Romantics favored. Instead, he exhibits an attitude toward nature that was common in Victorian times. Simply put, he sees nature "as merely something 'out there' " (Waters 154). Furthermore, Lockwood's wish for "[a] perfect misanthropist's Heaven" (3) away from the London crowds is fulfilled when he meets the novel's true misanthrope, Heathcliff, who compares himself to his dogs. Despite his shock at the brutal nature of Heathcliff's "savage[ry]" (12), Lockwood

Toy 3

himself mimics Heathcliff's own violence when Lockwood attempts to "to box [Hareton's] ears" (14). But, during a trip on the moors in which he gets lost, Lockwood soon realizes that he is in need of a "guide" (12) indicating he is not able to exist independently in the wild.

Brontë further illustrates both Romantic and Victorian attitudes towards nature through the novel's main plot which moves from the Heights, rustic physical setting to that of refinement and domesticity at Thrushcross Grange. When Lockwood is finally able to leave the Heights, he does not refuse Heathcliff's unsolicited offer to act as his guide, fully recognizing how difficult it is for him to find his way alone on the moors. Used to man-made objects of the city, Lockwood is only able to recognize and to describe those altered structures which man has made on the moors, markers such as "upright stones" covered with "lime" to make them easier to see "in the dark" (31). Lockwood's ability to maneuver on his own the four miles from the entrance of the Grange park area to the manor itself indicates the true level of assimilation to nature which Lockwood achieves. He prefers the more refined or controlled concept of nature, represented by the

Toy 4

stones and his ability to trespass only the Grange park area alone. While he may want "to restore the animal heat" in him at the Grange, he nevertheless describes himself as "a kitten" (32) and indicates to Mrs. Dean his preference of the Grange over the "inferior" (34) Heights. Thrushcross Grange exhibits elements every bit as violent as the Heights: when Heathcliff and Catherine secretly visit the Grange, they see that Isabella and Edgar have almost pulled their pet dog in two. However, as Richard Benvenuto notes, the Grange does offer a counterbalance to those violent element through the "social law and convention" (91) represented by its "library" (91). Brontë never attempts to move Lockwood to a permanent residence within nature, but only to expose him to its influential qualities.

Brontë uses the final scenes of the novel to illustrate a progression to the social aspects of domesticity and refinement which Lockwood now exemplifies and which the Victorians privilege. The first indication that the Heights has been transformed occurs when Lockwood tests the gate to the Heights which had been locked to him before; the handle now "yield[s]" (304) to his grip. Such a social "improvement" (304), as Lockwood terms

Toy 5

it, is matched by Cathy's and Hareton's restructuring of Joseph's garden to include "wall flowers" and "homely fruit trees" (304), to replace Joseph's "currant and gooseberry bushes" (314). More important to the concept of refinement in relation to the garden is the "importation of plants from the Grange" (314), thus equating the refined "garden" (Waters 154) or redesigned alterations by man with domestic, social progression which the Victorians favored. Finally, instead of remaining at the Heights, Cathy and Hareton relocate to the Grange and establish their family within its refinement.

In her 1850 Preface to <u>Wuthering Heights</u>, Charlotte Brontë acknowledges that the "moorish and wild" aspect of nature in the novel is a "natural" (xxxiv) result of Emily Brontë's familiarity with the surroundings she used as the novel's setting. Charlotte reflects that had Emily's "lot been cast in a town, her writings [. . .] would have possessed another character" (xxxiv). It is this difference in "character" (C. Brontë xxxiv) which separates the Romantics from the Victorians; a difference in location produces a difference in perspective. Charlotte Brontë's novel, <u>Jane Eyre</u> shows this trend to establish

Toy 6

what her own character Jane termed a "happy" marriage with Edward Rochester at the end (447). Brontë does not use nature as a source of "divinity or immanent power" (150) normally associated with the Romantics, but she does see nature, in the novel, as a teaching tool as did similar Romantic writers. She also goes further and uses man's control of nature as a social marker for the Victorian domesticity developing during her era. The increasingly industrial society of England in the early 1800s and the parallel shift to the urban would gradually contribute to the end of the "cottage" (Ford 31) way of life for rural England. Emily Brontë's moors allowed her to fashion a novel which could look back on the "wild workshop" (C. Brontë, Preface xxxvii) of rural England, thus preserving a glimpse of a vanishing lifestyle, while looking forward to the more socialized view of home and the city. Such a point of reference is a rare occurrence for a writer to develop and one which Emily Brontë fully embraced.

Toy 7

Note

[1]To simplify further references to the two Catherines in the novel, Catherine Linton will be referred to as "Catherine," and Catherine Earnshaw will be referred to as "Cathy."

Toy 8

Works Cited

Benvenuto, Richard. Emily Brontë. Boston: Twayne, 1982.

Brontë, Charlotte. Jane Eyre. Penguin/Godfrey Cave ed. Penguin Popular Classics. New York: Penguin, 1994.

Brontë, Emily. Wuthering Heights. Ed. Pauline Nestor. New York: Penguin, 1995.

Helsinger, Elizabeth K. Rural Scenes and National Representation: Britain, 1815-1850. Princeton: Princeton UP, 1997.

Nestor, Pauline, ed. "Editor's Preface to the New [1850] Edition of Wathering Heights." Wathering Heights. By Emily Brontë. New York: Penguin, 1995. xxxiii–xxxvii.

Waters, Michael. The Garden in Victorian Literature. Cambridge: Scolar, 1988.

Glossary of Literary and Composition Terms

Abstract: An abstract idea that is not concrete. It is usually explained by examples. Love, patriotism, and joy are examples of abstract ideas.

Analyze: To analyze a topic is to break it down into smaller pieces so that you may get a better look at it and understand it. There are various ways to go about this. For example, if you are told to write a paper about an essay you have read, you must look at different aspects of the essay. You might want to talk about logical fallacies. Or you might like to discuss the impact of the time period on the essay, if it is a work that discusses a particular historical period, such as the Civil War, the Roaring Twenties, and so forth. As you can see, you can analyze the essay for aspects.

Argument: A pattern of development used, often in an argumentative essay, to change the way readers think, using rhetorical strategies and the opposition's views.

Argumentative essay: See **Argument.**

Assertion: A declarative statement or claim made in support of an argumentative topic.

Brainstorming: A **prewriting strategy** used to generate ideas. It may be done on a general topic, for example, pets; or it may be done on a specific topic, for example, *La Llorona.*

Collaborative Brainstorming: A prewriting strategy completed in a group and used to generate ideas.

Cause and effect: A pattern of development that shows how one event caused the consequences of another.

Character: A fictional character or persona in a story.

Chronological development: The sequence of events in a story arranged in the order in which they happened.

Claim: An assertion that supports an argument. The central claim of an argumentative paper is the thesis. A counterclaim is an assertion that challenges the thesis.

Cliché: A frequently used or overused phrase or clause.

Clustering: Also called webbing or mapping. A prewriting activity used to generate ideas through free association about the central topic and about the ideas generated from the central topic.

Coherence: Connections between ideas in a paragraph or essay created through transitions.

Collaborative brainstorming: A prewriting strategy completed in small groups or with the class.

Comparison-and-contrast: A pattern of development in which the writer describes the similarities or differences between two subjects.

Comparison paragraph: A paragraph that is developed by showing the similarity of two or more ideas or objects.

Concluding sentence: The final sentence of a paragraph or essay, which brings closure to the passage.

Conclusion: The final paragraph(s) in a work. The conclusion usually begins with a restated thesis sentence and can be developed through the use of summary, drawing conclusions from previously stated information, or giving personal opinion. It brings closure to the essay.

Concrete: A thought or word referring to something material, for example, cat, table, or book.

Connotation: Connotation refers to defining a word by the meanings the word suggests.

Contrast: To contrast means to point out differences between two or more objects.

Contrast paragraph: A paragraph that is developed by showing the differences between two or more ideas or objects.

Deductive Reasoning: Reasoning that moves from a general claim, to a specific claim, to a conclusion. This is also called a syllogism. For example:

Major Premise: All fathers are men.

Minor Premise: Bill Clinton is a father.

Conclusion: Bill Clinton is a man.

Definition: A definition explains a term through denotation and/or connotation.

Denotation: Denotation refers to the definition found in the dictionary.

Describe/Description: Description is a pattern of development for an informative essay. A descriptive piece of writing communicates to readers how something looks, smells, sounds, tastes, and/or feels. This can be accomplished through the use of adjectives: "The young blond child walked beside her tall, brunette sister." Or it can be done through the use of other patterns of development, such as exemplification, comparison-and-contrast, and so forth.

Details: Forms of information, such as facts, statistics, descriptions, and so forth, used to support or develop ideas.

Division and Classification: A pattern of development that divides a broad idea into smaller parts and organizes many small parts into categories.

Draft: The complete text of a work is a draft. A draft goes through various stages, beginning with the first or rough draft and proceeding through revision until it arrives at the final draft.

Evaluate: To determine the quality of a given item. Students are sometimes asked to evaluate the quality of secondary sources they might use in a paper. At other times they are asked to evaluate the quality of another student's paper or their own, based on given criteria or standards. They are asked to determine to what extent the work meets standards of usefulness or meets given standards.

Example: illustrations, patterns or models of subject being explained or discussed

Exemplification: A pattern of development that uses examples to expand the topic.

Expository writing: a pattern of development that presents information to the reader, usually a report. This is also called explanatory writing, because it explains an idea or gives information.

Expressive writing: One of the purposes of writing is to express the author's emotions. This is usually done in **personal narratives, journal** entries, and in personal **letters.**

Fallacy: Logic that is incorrect or flawed and that can manipulate the reader by appealing to fear, prejudice, and other emotions.

Figurative language: Language used in creative writing that makes

comparisons (metaphors, similes, personification), exaggerates (hyperbole), and uses other figures of speech to create an interesting or different approach to a topic/subject.

Final draft: See **Draft.**

First draft: See **Draft.**

Focused Brainstorming: A prewriting strategy that generates ideas on a specific topic.

Focused Freewriting: Whereas freewriting can be done over a general topic from which the writer can move to a specific topic, focused freewriting is completed to generate ideas about a specific topic.

Folklore: A tale or story that relies on customs, rituals, superstitions, and other elements of a region or ethnic group.

Formal outline: see **Outline.**

Freewriting: A prewriting activity used to generate ideas by requiring the writer to write nonstop for five to ten minutes to generate ideas about a topic.

Generalization: A conclusion that is arrived at without sufficient evidence (hasty generalization) or one that includes everything or everyone in its assertion, allowing for no exceptions (sweeping generalization). For example: Everyone should eat three meals a day.

Hyperbole: Exaggeration.

Image: A concrete picture painted in a reader's mind through the use of figurative language.

Inductive reasoning: A method of reasoning and argument that moves from specific ideas to a specific conclusion. Inductive reasoning can lead only to probable conclusions.

Inference: A conclusion made from known facts.

Informal outline: See **Outline.**

Informative: An informative paper is one that provides information to the reader. Several patterns of development can be used in writing an informative essay, such as narration, description, exemplification, process analysis, cause and effect, comparison-and-contrast, division and classification, or definition. Rather than limit a piece to one pattern of development, authors frequently use several patterns.

Informative essay: See **Informative.**

Irony: A figure of speech in which the intended meaning is the opposite of the literal meaning of the written words.

Journal: Many writers keep personal writing in journals. These are collections of thoughts, ideas, questions, opinions, conclusions you have drawn, and other pieces of writing that might express your emotions and private beliefs. Journals help the writer think through problems or release anger, frustration, or other possibly destructive feelings in a positive, nonviolent way. The material that you collect in your journal can sometimes provide you with ideas for a larger paper or for stories that you might want to write later. Some instructors require that you keep a journal in which you record your responses to reading selections for class discussion. Doing this will

help you understand the text better and allow you to jot down notes or questions about the assignment that you might not understand at the time and forget before you return to class. Most journals are written in an informal manner because they are usually private and shared only with those you choose to share them with or with an instructor as an assignment.

Journalistic questions: A prewriting activity used to generate ideas by asking the questions who? what? when? where? why? and how? about a topic.

Legend: An account of the adventures of a historical personality, whether real or imaginary. Legends are distinguished from **myths** in that legends have less of the supernatural.

Letter: Correspondence in either formal or informal format.

List/Listing: A prewriting activity that enumerates items of importance about a topic. The resulting list is a series of words and or phrases can be used to generate other ideas.

Mapping: See **Clustering.**

Metaphor: A figure of speech that compares two unlike subjects without using the words "like" or "as."

Modes: Also called patterns of development. Methods used by writers to develop their paragraphs or essay. The modes are: expository, comparison-and-contrast, narration, exemplification, cause and effect, process, division and classification, description, argument, and definition.

Myth: A story that usually describes the interactions among human beings, animals, and gods. Myths are usually anonymous and based on folk beliefs.

Narration: A type of composition used to inform, instruct, entertain, or interest its readers.

Narrative: A narrative tells a story and is usually organized chronologically; however, it may be organized differently.

Objective: Impersonal way of discussing an issue; without feeling or emotion.

Outline: An outline can be formal or informal. A formal outline is a structural view of a paper's development, using Roman numerals and Arabic numbers, upper-and lowercase letters, and so forth, to divide the paper into major divisions sub-divisions, sub-sub-divisions, and so forth. An informal outline is not so detailed. Either form, however, presents the writer with the basic elements of the paper so she can write it in a systematic way. All outlines are subject to change.

Oxymoron: A figure of speech that links two contradictory terms, such as jumbo shrimp or freezer burn.

Paraphrase: A restatement of an idea or passage in the writers own words to expand or clarify an idea.

Patterns of development: See **Mode.**

Peer analysis: An activity in which members of a student's class read and evaluate each other's writing based on given criteria.

Peer editor: A fellow student who contributes to peer analysis.

Personal narrative: Personal narratives are works that tell a story. The story may be about the author of the story and may use first-person pronouns (I, me, we, us) to indicate that the author is telling the story about himself or herself. In this case, it becomes a first-person **narration.** Usually, but not always, a narration is told in chronological order. Sometimes a narrative relates a lesson the author learned as a result of the episode he or she experienced. Readers must be careful, however, to distinguish a short story or novel, which is fiction, from a first-person narrative. Some short stories or novels are told using first-person point of view, but that does not mean that the protagonist is the voice of the author.

Personification: A figure of speech that gives animals, ideas, abstractions, and inanimate objects human form, character, or sensibilities. They can take on human personalities, intelligence, and emotion. We frequently personify deities.

Persuasion: In writing, persuasion is one of the purposes of communication. A persuasive essay not only attempts to convince a reader to change his mind but also to act in a specific way. For example, the reader should not only believe that a candidate is the best person for an office, he should vote for the candidate and actively campaign for her.

Persuasive essay: See **Persuasion.**

Plot: The element of fiction that describes the events of a story and their relationship to each other.

Position: an opinion or stand on a particular topic

Prewriting strategies: Many writers prewrite before they begin to write their essay or other assignment. To do this, the writer realizes that in order to discover what he or she has to say, the ideas must be jotted down. This may be done informally so that you can find associations between words that are related to your topic. Prewriting strategies include brainstorming, freewriting, clustering, outlining, answering journalistic questions (who? what? when? where? how? why?), or exploring more in-depth questions about your topic. Some writers may use several strategies. Not every writer necessarily completes prewriting strategies. Others are able to think about the topic they want to write about while they drive home from classes or relax. The prewriting strategy that you choose must suit your needs and help you arrive at a clear vision of your topic; otherwise it won't work.

Primary source: In literary analysis, the poem, short story, play, or essay a writer will discuss.

Process analysis: Sometimes known as a "how-to" essay, a process analysis gives directions for completing an activity or describes a procedure. This is a **mode,** or pattern of development.

Proposition: In argumentative essay writing, a proposition is another word for thesis.

Purpose of communication/writing: Usually there are four purposes: to entertain, to express, to inform, and to persuade.

Reader response journal entry: A journal response to an assigned reading. This may be written, based on the directions of the instructor, in personal response to a writing. Usually, responses discuss if you agreed or disagreed with the article and why; if you liked or disliked the article and why; if you can associate with the events in the article and how; if you can identify with any of the characters/people in the article and how; if you learned anything from the article; if you would recommend this article to a friend and why; and/or what your response to the author might be if you had a chance to talk to him or her. Your instructor might ask you to summarize the assignment, but generally response is preferred over summary.

Reflective: Looking back and examining one's feelings, attitudes, ideas, and so forth, in light of present situations.

Research: To use research in the writing of a paper indicates the need to find information from the library, Internet, interviews, and so forth to explain a topic.

Satire: A literary way to criticize an existing thought or institution by suggesting humorous ways to improve it.

Secondary source: In literary analysis, an article, book, or other published work that interprets primary source material.

Simile: A figure of speech that compares two unlike subjects using the words "like," "as," "than," or "resembles."

Stereotype: A sweeping generalization that makes assumptions about all members of a race, religion, gender, nationality, age, or other feature.

Style: The language, attitude, creativity, and mood an author uses as he or she writes.

Subjective: Writing that uses a personal, expressive, emotional response, as opposed to **objective,** which is impersonal, analytical, and lacking feeling.

Summary: A brief restatement of a longer work, in student's own words. An instructor may ask you to summarize a piece in a journal entry, for example.

Symbol: Symbolism is the use of one object, a symbol, to represent another object or concept. For example, if a driver arrives at an intersection at which there is an object hanging from wires in the middle of the street, he or she looks at it to see the color of the light that is burning. If the driver sees red, he or she knows to stop. If the light is green, the driver knows to proceed. If the light is yellow, the driver knows to proceed with caution or to prepare to stop. The lights are not the command themselves but represent a command. Thus, the lights have symbolic meaning. The lights are symbols.

Synonym: A word that means the same thing as another word and can sometimes be used interchangeably.

Thesis: The controlling idea of an essay, usually stated in one or two sentences.

Tone: The attitude the writer has toward the subject of the written work. The tone usually depends on the purpose of communication.

Topic sentence: The controlling idea of a paragraph, usually stated in one sentence.

Transitions: Words, phrases, or sentences that provide connections between different thoughts and ideas to ensure coherence of a work.

Unity: The concept that a piece of writing has an organizing or controlling idea, which draws the parts of the writing into a whole.

Webbing: See **Clustering.**

Credits

Index